Crisis in Print

CRISIS IN PRINT

Desegregation and the Press
in Tennessee

HUGH DAVIS GRAHAM

Vanderbilt University Press

To Jennings Perry
and Hugh Baskin Patterson
—Southern newspapermen
whom success did not spoil.

Acknowledgments

To the Woodrow Wilson National Fellowship Foundation I owe my greatest thanks, for not only did their Dissertation Year Award enable me to accomplish most of the research upon which this study is based, but their initial fellowship, awarded in 1960 while I was a fledgling newspaper reporter with the Nashville *Tennessean,* enabled me to begin my graduate studies at Stanford University. While pursuing my doctorate there, no professor was more generous with his time and advice—of the former he had so little, yet of both he gave so much—than David M. Potter, Coe Professor of American History and a close student of Southern history. To David Potter, my patient teacher and friend, I owe my warmest thanks. Also generous with their time and advice at Stanford were professors Otis Pease of the Department of History (now at the University of Washington) and Richard Fagen of the Departments of Communication and Political Science.

During the entire summer of 1963 and on several subsequent occasions while traveling in my native South I was able to explore thoroughly the primary sources in Tennessee. Had it not been for the willing and patient help offered me by Jim Leeson, Reed Sarratt, Bob Campbell and the fine staff of the Southern Education Reporting Service, and by the equally helpful staff of the Tennessee State Library and Archives, I would surely have been unable to complete my research with such expedition and in such pleasant company.

I am also indebted to Professor Dewey Grantham of Vanderbilt

University for his persistent encouragement, to the sympathetic support of Robert McBride and Sam Smith of the Tennessee Historical Society, to my close colleagues Bud and Glenda Bartley and H. Glynn Thomas, who provided ideological support, to my brother and fellow historian Otis for his always keen analytical insight and to his wife Ann for typing the original manuscript. Robert P. Emmitt, Associate Editor of Vanderbilt University Press, has made a substantial contribution to the book's clarity and style. I have profited from interviews with Harold Bradley, professor of political science at Vanderbilt and member of the Tennessee Legislature; Jennings Perry, former editor of the *Tennessean;* John Seigenthaler, editor of the *Tennessean*; and from correspondence with James Stahlman, publisher of the Nashville *Banner*. A grant from San Jose State College enabled me to pursue my research beyond the dissertation and to purchase valuable resource material.

A less direct contribution, but perhaps in the long run the most substantial one, was made by my parents, in whose loving nurture I became a Tennessean. My final and most personal acknowledgment is to the patience and devotion of my wife Ann, whose marriage to a professor and historian wittingly endowed her with the professional paraphernalia of five-by-eight cards, microfilm, and typewriter—a burden she carries with splendid grace.

HUGH DAVIS GRAHAM

The Johns Hopkins University
September 1967

Contents

CRISIS IN PRINT

Introduction

IT is currently fashionable to introduce one's book by first explaining what it is *not* all about. At the risk of overworking this useful device, I propose to resort to it also, for although this inquiry is addressed to the controversial field of Southern race relations, I have attempted to approach an old problem in a new way.

First, then, this is not primarily a history of desegregation in Tennessee. Although the narrative traces to a considerable extent the destruction of at least the legal basis of Tennessee's historical biracial system, the focus is less on the events themselves than on a particular response to them. Nor is this merely a catalogue of old newspaper editorials on desegregation, written by Southern editors in hopes that they might influence public opinion and thereby the events of that crucial decade that followed the epochal Brown decision of 1954. Rather, this is an investigation prompted by a specific question—how did the Tennessee press respond editorially to the initial decade of desegregation?—not *primarily* because of any wide interest in this question (although I am convinced that such a story in itself would interest quite a few), but because the four essential elements involved in this question were selected for the larger and more ambitious purpose of further illuminating the dark shadows surrounding the role of race in Southern society. Why, then, were these four elements—desegregation, newspaper editorials, a mid-twentieth century decade, and the state of Tennessee—chosen?

The first of these, the question of desegregation, has these past few years prompted a profusion of books and articles in which students of Southern society and history have revealed that, however their philosophical convictions might differ, they share the implicit assumption that Southern society and history are simply inexplicable without central reference to the role of the Negro. The student of Southern history will discover early from a perusal of this literature that a fundamental cleavage exists in the ranks of those who seek to interpret the region's fascinating past. Because the great themes of Southern history—Negro slavery, the Civil War and Reconstruction, Jim Crow, the Lost Cause, and the one-party system, to mention only a few—are so hypercharged with moral and political implications, it has been difficult for students of the region's history to avoid the emotional response of taking sides. History has always been used consciously or unconsciously as a political tool, and historians of the South provide abundant examples of this unhappy tendency. Conservative historians have tended to emphasize the predominance of strict constructionist sentiment, class distinctions, and biracialism in the Southern legacy and to suggest, at least by implication, their approval of these traditions. Liberal historians have been prone to see the equalitarian and agrarian radical heritage of Jefferson through Populism as the primary one and to censure diversions from that legacy as unfortunate aberrations from the true progressive Southern heritage.

A fine opportunity for this philosophical polarity to manifest itself was presented when the conservative Ulrich B. Phillips, dean of Southern historians early in this century, wrote in 1928 an essay entitled "The Central Theme of Southern History." In it, Phillips found at the core of distinctive Southernism a fixed purpose on the part of whites that the South "shall remain a white man's country." Many liberal historians have since felt compelled to take sharp issue with what struck them as such a gloomy and pessimistic notion. And yet, as David Potter has suggested, it is ironical for liberals, concerned as they are with the "sick South," to reject a formula which explains the chronic nature of the illness.[1] In sharing a humanitarian concern over the human con-

1. See David M. Potter's discussion of this tendency in "The Enigma of the South," *Yale Review* (Autumn 1961), pp. 142–151.

sequences of this malady, I must nevertheless confess that, although a native Southerner, I feel no acute discomfort or sense of philosophical betrayal in largely agreeing with Phillips. It is my conviction that a determination to preserve biracialism has been, if not the *only* key to Southern cohesiveness, at least so central a motive in Southern white society that any threat to disturb the biracial system would evoke a more fundamentally revealing response than any other issue the social and intellectual historian might choose.

My choice of the press is based in part on the proposition that the standard focus on Southern *political* institutions has generally produced a somewhat distorted image that has tended to emphasize the region's most ultraconservative sentiments. This political distortion is generally ascribed by political scientists to a legacy of malapportionment and disfranchisement. The abiding refusal of Southern (although by no means exclusively Southern) legislatures to adjust their districts to account for changes in population has fastened an increasingly anachronistic pattern of rural control upon these legislatures; growing urban populations have consequently suffered a relative decline in political influence. The historic disfranchisement of Negroes—and not a few poor whites—has combined with malapportionment to distort further Southern political reflections. One unfortunate consequence of this reality is that the nation has been led to picture the South largely in terms of stereotyped if colorful biography—whether it be of Jim Crow as the legislatures have created and nurtured him, of the demagogic Tillmans, Vardamans, Talmadges and Bilboes, or of their latter-day exemplars, the Thurmonds and the Wallaces.

My own conviction that this monolithic picture enjoys a wide currency in contemporary America has been personally reinforced by the frequency with which the mere classroom mention of a Southern state will elicit a ripple of mirth from California college students, whose understanding of the American South reminds us that prejudice is a two-way street. It is depressing to the student of recent Southern history that the image so much of the nation—and surely, after the charade of 1957, much of the world—seems to hold of Little Rock is a kind of Rorschach of a racist Governor Faubus responding obediently to his monolithic constituency of white mobs snarling at terrified black chil-

dren. It is with no apology for the deplorable mobs that I nevertheless assert how different, and surely more accurate, would that national impression be were there only more awareness of the considerable
social diversity that Little Rock contained in 1957, and even a casual
familiarity with the city's highly competitive newspapers would have
reflected both the existence of that diversity and, indeed, one of the
causes of it. To the degree, then, that the prime function of history is
less to censure than to understand the past, a more profitable approach
to understanding the South might be to direct our attention to a nonpoliti-
cal Southern institution whose greater display of variety might more
realistically reflect the diversity of Southern society.

The reader may feel prompted at this juncture to object that trying
to get at central attitudes in Southern society by turning to the press
implies the assumption that press opinion accurately reflects public
opinion—or forms it. I am well aware of the enormous complexities involved in the formation of social attitudes and of the difficulty of
distinguishing cause from effect in this hen-and-egg relationship. But,
to the extent that a kind of slow and self-adjusting balancing mechanism seems inherent in this reciprocal relationship, constantly adjusting
press and public opinion to one another, it is assumed that the resulting
rough congruence of the attitudes of the press and of the public
makes such a study as this profitable.

Even if one has no quarrel with that broad assumption, can it not
be more specifically objected that by substituting the press for politics as
a primary institutional focus, one has merely rejected the conservative
bias of white upper class- and rural-dominated Southern politics only to
embrace the widely recognized conservative bias of most newspaper
publishers and editors? "Like their colleagues everywhere," observed
Harry Ashmore, "Southern publishers are prone to stand in the bar of
the country club and assume that they are listening to the voice of the
people." [2] But if the cliché is valid that the nation's press is generally
more conservative than the body politic, it is also true that a Harry
Ashmore or a Ralph McGill could not long survive, much less prosper,

2. Harry S. Ashmore, *An Epitaph for Dixie* (New York: W. W. Norton &
Co., Inc., 1957), p. 164.

in constituencies whose sentiments were fully expressed in the 1950s by Governor Faubus or the Georgia legislature. Still, we know that press and public opinion cannot simply be equated, and to the degree that a differential does exist between them, it is worthwhile to attempt to measure, even in a necessarily imprecise fashion, the dimensions of this differential.

In directing my attention to the large metropolitan dailies and their lesser cousins, I have confined my scrutiny to one primary source: the editorial. But editorials, it may be objected, are notoriously unreliable sources. They are, indeed, unreliable sources for the determination of overt events, which are best reconstructed from the testimony of eye-witnesses. But they are excellent sources, in intellectual and social history, for the reconstruction of attitudes and opinions. For the student of opinion, of course, the opinion that prevailed is important, whether it was sagacious and reflective of a widely informed mind or nonsensical and irresponsible.[3]

It might be further objected, and rightly, that editorials are but a small part of a newspaper, the bulk of which is composed of news stories which, by their balance and play, are heavily instrumental in forming opinion. I would concede this, but I would also observe that much useful work has already been done in this area.[4] This body of

---

3. Since the editorial must be analyzed against a background of the event upon which it reflects, some trustworthy source must be found to tell of such events. For the student of the Southern response to the crisis over desegregation, an excellent secondary source is available in *Southern School News* (hereafter abbreviated as *SSN*). Widely acclaimed for its objectivity, *SSN* was the monthly report of the Southern Education Reporting Service (hereafter abbreviated as SERS), a Ford Foundation project established in 1954 to monitor the process of desegregation in Southern schools. In June 1965, SERS ceased publishing *SSN* and replaced it with the *Southern Education Report;* published every two months, *SER* focuses more broadly on the substance of Southern education, and especially on the problems of educating the poor, and correspondingly less on the process of racial desegregation than did its predecessor.

4. Roy E. Carter, Jr., director of the Research Division of the University of Minnesota School of Journalism and formerly professor of journalism at the University of North Carolina, is author of two relatively recent articles based on research in the field of news coverage in newspapers of racial relations. In "Segregation and the News: A Regional Content Study," *Journalism Quarterly*

research generally supports the conclusion that although Southern newspapers varied considerably during the initial decade of desegregation, their treatment of racial news was decidedly more balanced than were their editorials about it. My concentration on the latter is designed to supplement, not to contradict, knowledge produced by the former approach.

Another relevant objection that must be dealt with here is the familiar contention that readers of editorials constitute only a small, coterie audience which merely seeks reaffirmation of its own prejudices. Communications research has affirmed that their number is indeed relatively small (more contemporary Americans, we are told, read the sports pages than any other section of their newspaper). But, while reducing our estimate of the number of such information seekers, recent research in communications has at the same time considerably enhanced the reputation of these individuals for efficacy in molding public opinion.[5] The picture that emerges from this research is one of the

---

(Winter 1957), pp. 3–18, Carter reported a study of a sample of newspapers from Southern states. His analysis revealed that, contrary to what one might have expected, the news content of those newspapers was about evenly divided in its support for and opposition to segregation. In "Racial Identification Effects upon the News Story Writer," *Journalism Quarterly* (Summer 1959), pp. 284–290, Carter concluded: "There is some evidence to the effect that the general performance of the Southern press is improving. . . . Recent studies of the Southern press treatment of the segregation issue indicate that newspapers are doing a reasonably responsible job, over-all." In a more recent study of racial stories in the news, Walter Spearman, professor of journalism at the University of North Carolina, concluded: "Southern newspapers generally are doing a conscientious job of reporting racial news. They are conforming more closely to the accepted standards of good journalism than the atmosphere of the times or the charges of their critics would indicate." See "Racial Stories in the News," *Racial Crisis and the Press* (Atlanta, The Southern Regional Council, 1960).

5. See Elihu Katz, "The Two-Step Flow of Communications: An Up-to-Date Report on an Hypothesis," *Public Opinion Quarterly* (Spring 1957), pp. 61–79. Katz reports that postwar research had led students of public opinion to discard the old one-step flow or communicator-to-audience notion of mass communications and to adopt instead a multi-step-flow theory which emphasizes the interceding role of the local opinion leader as a kind of entrepreneur of public opinion. "The image of the audience as a mass of disconnected individuals hooked up to the media but not to each other," Katz noted, could not be reconciled with the idea of a two-step flow of communications implying, as it did, networks

great mass of citizens taking their cues on public issues not directly from the mass media but from a network of local "opinion leaders" who tend to follow the media closely. These opinion leaders thereby function as the catalytic agents in the formative process of public opinion; the late V. O. Key, Jr., whose study of Southern politics remains the classic in the field, referred to them as "the influentials" and the "political activists." [6] The opinion leader thus emerges as a conduit, however devious, through which editorial writers may eventually reach large numbers of sports- and comic-loving citizens and voters who normally disdain to read such exhortatory prose. Sylvan Meyer, editor of the Gainesville, Georgia, *Daily Times* and recipient in 1957 of Sigma Delta Chi's Distinguished Service Award for editorial writing, has celebrated intuitively this trickle-down phenomenon that the communications researchers have been trying scientifically to trace:

It has been said that editorial pages no longer mold public opinion. Don't believe that. Opinion molders read editorials and consciously or unconsciously adopt phrases therefrom and find their thinking either modified or directed, or at least provoked, thereby. Logical argument doesn't convert the disbeliever overnight, but it wears him down over the long haul. If nothing else, it forces him to argue the issues as defined in the editorials he reads.[7]

In sum, while communications research has elevated the role of *psycho-logic* at the expense of Meyer's faith in the efficacy of old-fashioned logic, it seems to have ratified his professional confidence in the importance of newspaper editorials in forming public opinion.

We customarily speak of newspapers as having editorial voices, but these are of course the voices of men. The editorial stance of most newspapers is determined by a variety of circumstances. In small newspapers, the publisher-editor usually runs a one-man show, and

---

of interconnected individuals through which mass communications are channeled." This number of the quarterly also contains excellent summary articles on 20 years of public opinion research by Harold Lasswell, Elmo Roper, and George Gallup.

6. A good summary of communications research in this area is available in chapters fourteen and fifteen of Key's *Public Opinion and American Democracy* (New York: Alfred Knopf, 1961).

7. Sylvan Meyer, "The Press and the Schools," *Racial Crisis and the Press* (Atlanta: The Southern Regional Council, 1960), p. 36.

we know whose prose we are reading and whose thoughts are trying to persuade us. But the larger newspapers are likely to employ a battery of editorial specialists who enjoy varying degrees of freedom from their publisher. Since editorials, unlike political columns, are customarily printed without by-lines, there is no easy way to link the editorial to the man, other than to go behind the editorial "we" and do an inside story on the anatomy of the newspaper—as, for instance, Meyer Berger has done in *The Story of the New York Times, 1851–1951*.[8] Such studies are useful and make interesting reading, but the nature and broad scope of my task precluded such an approach. Consequently, I have not attempted to go behind the editorials, other than to sketch in my first chapter the character of the publishers or editors of the major dailies in Tennessee who clearly have set their newspapers' editorial tone.

Both the press and the biracial system have a long history in the South, and their relationship could of course be studied profitably at almost any point in Southern history. In *Freedom of Thought in the Old South*, Clement Eaton has shown us how the antislavery crusade generated in the ante-bellum South such intense proslavery counter-pressure that dissenting editors were driven either into conformity, silence, prison, or their graves.[9] Eaton thereby taught us much about the ante-bellum Southern press, but he revealed even more about a society so united in its provocation that it hounded its editors into a monolithic orthodoxy. My choice of the decade following the Brown decision of 1954 as a temporal context is premised upon the somewhat self-evident assumption that it represents a period in which the attention of Southerners of all callings and persuasions were so riveted on the compelling question of biracialism's fate that the massive airing of views this issue provoked would reveal a great deal about Southern society. The decade began with the Brown doctrine that separate education was "inherent-

8. (New York: Simon and Schuster, 1951). See also Edwin Emery, *The Press and America* (Englewood Cliffs, N.J.: Prentice-Hall, Inc., 1962), pp. 745–759.

9. See especially "The Freedom of the Press in the Upper South," chapter seven of the Harper Torchbook edition (1964). Eaton's study was originally published by Duke University Press (1940).

ly unequal," and it closed with the passage in 1964 of the most comprehensive civil rights act since Reconstruction.[10] The year 1964 marked no terminus for the process of desegregation, as we know only too well. But it was within these years—the years of what C. Vann Woodward has called the "Second Reconstruction" [11]—that the pattern of the South's response to desegregation emerged, and it is to this response that we turn for insight.

This study, then, ultimatey seeks to offer a few generalizations about the role played by the Southern press in relation to Southern white society and its commitment, however deep, to biracialism. But history, as an inductive discipline, must approach any broad generalizations it might modestly suggest from the particular end of the con-

10. It is revealing to observe that Negro students of desegregation, understandably concerned that proper attention be called to the essentially Negro origins and direction of "the Movement," have tended to date its beginning not from the judicial edict of nine white men but from the first day of December, 1955, when Mrs. Rosa Parks boarded the Cleveland Avenue bus in Montgomery, Alabama, and refused to let a white man have her seat. A typical example of this tendency is Louis E. Lomax's *The Negro Revolt* (New York: Harper & Row, 1962). Lomax managed to avoid any mention at all of *Brown* v. *Board of Education* in his book, and he lists neither the Brown decision nor the Supreme Court in his appendix. He disposes of the school desegregation decision curtly and somewhat oddly by observing that *"as of* [emphasis added] May 17, 1954, 'separate but equal' was the law of the land; however, 'separate but equal' was, and still is, the practice and the reality" (p. 78 of the Signet paperback edition). In contradistinction to Lomax, Anthony Lewis, Supreme Court reporter for the New York *Times* during most of the decade, asserts in his *Portrait of a Decade: The Second Revolution* (New York: Random House, 1964) that "revolutions require a spark, a catalyst. For the revolution in American race relations this was the School Segregation case, decided by the Supreme Court on May 17, 1954." (p. 4.)

11. "From the First Reconstruction to the Second," *Harper's,* April, 1965, 123–127. To be sure, one might have selected with equal profit the period of the Dred Scott decision. The selection of a recent historical context is not prima facie evidence that the historian has succumbed to what the colonial historian Carl Bridenbaugh has decried as "the cult of the contemporary"; rather, it represents a purposeful attempt to enjoy the important advantage of having at one's disposal a greater quantity of evidence with which to establish one's case. See generally Bridenbaugh's denunciation of what he calls "The Great Mutation" in his presidential address to the American Historical Association in *The American Historical Review,* LXVII, No. 2, 315–331.

tiuum of human events. Had the researcher unlimited time and funds, he might seek a wide variety of source material in all Southern states—as Key was able to do in producing his encyclopedic *Southern Politics*.[12] If pressed by limited time and resources, as most of us are, he might seek a defensible shortcut by sampling narrowly but intensively from an area that is possessed of sufficient geographic and demographic variety that, while claiming to speak with authority only of its citizens, he might modestly suggest that this variety licenses a certain amount of cautious generalization away from the sampled area toward other Southern regions where conditions are roughly similar. It was in response to these theoretical considerations that I chose the state of Tennessee.

The quality of southernism is as much a function of a state of mind as of geography, and on both counts Tennessee clearly qualifies as a Southern state. It was a slave state in 1860, a member of the Confederacy during the Civil War, the birthplace of the Ku Klux Klan, and in May of 1954 its laws required separation of the races in public and private schools. While Tennessee was and remains pervasively Southern in tone, however, it lies largely outside the monolithic orbit of the Deep South, and consequently a greater diversity of opinion can be expected than that, for instance, which Howard Quint discovered in his study, *Profile in Black and White: A Frank Portrait of South Carolina*.[13] Further, not only does Tennessee present the variety that obtains in a so-called border state along the north-south axis, it also presents a perhaps unparalleled geographic and demographic variety along the east-west axis.

Tennessee is a parallelogram approximately 100 miles wide and 450 miles long. This narrow ribbon of real estate stretches from the 6,000-foot Appalachian peaks in the east to the Mississippi River, flowing less than 200 feet above sea level. That this extensive spread encompasses a watershed is the only element of geographic logic inherent in

12. Published in 1950 by Alfred A. Knopf, this modern classic is desperately in need of updating. The late Professor Key was assisted by Alexander Heard, now chancellor of Vanderbilt University.

13. Washington, D. C., Public Affairs Press, 1958.

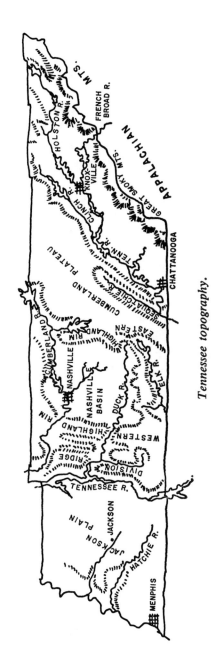

Tennessee topography.

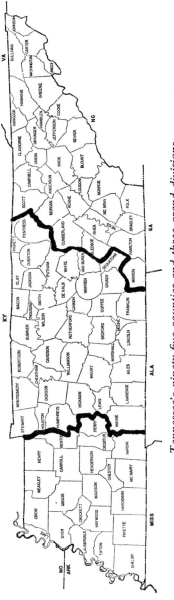

Tennessee's ninety-five counties and three grand divisions.

13

the state's boundaries, for the long northern and southern boundaries are but lines of longitude arbitrarily projected westward to the Mississippi by North Carolinian statesmen during the years of the American Revolution. These East Coast colonials thereby did great violence to the principle of geographical integrity, for they fastened under the future yoke of one state government three distinct areas with few features in common, other than that all three border on the river from which the state takes its name. The Tennessee River, in fact, neatly trisects the state in its nomadic search for the Mississippi. The three areas thus defined have traditionally been referred to in the lexicon of state politics and administration as "grand divisions," and they are represented in the state flag by three large stars.

The eastern grand division is composed of three subordinate areas: the Appalachian Mountain region, the eastern valley of the Tennessee River, and the eastern portion of the Cumberland Plateau. In the extreme east, the Great Smoky and Unaka mountains form a narrow border adjacent to North Carolina. The soil of these mountains is sandy, rock-filled, and largely infertile; more than four fifths of this area is forested. This is the legendary region of the long rifle and the demijohn; like most romantic legends, this one grows with the telling, enabling these "quaint" mountain folk and their Cherokee neighbors to supplement what is often a marginal existence by peddling trinkets to the tourists who annually flock to the cool and beautiful mountains with the coming of hot weather.

The eastern valley of the Tennessee River, so long ravaged by fickle nature and the rapacity of myopic men, has witnessed a heartening resurgence since the 1930s, when the Tennessee Valley Authority boldly attempted to harness both ravishers. Perhaps the ultimate tribute to the success of this unprecedented and, ironically, unrepeated experiment in regional planning is that even the most ultraconservative politicians in Republican East Tennessee have learned to pay glowing public homage to the virtues of this monument to federal intervention. TVA's abundant and cheap electric power prompted the federal government during the Second World War to build its atomic diffusion plant at Oak Ridge, near Knoxville. Since that war, Tennessee's traditionally Southern offering of readily exploitable resources, cheap labor, weak unions, sympathetic police, and generous tax benefits has combined with the appeal of TVA to lure a considerable amount of industry into the once destitute valley.

East Tennessee has been the most populous of the three grand divisions, for the valley is dominated, not by one city as are the other grand divisions, but by two: Knoxville and Chattanooga. Situated near the confluence of the Holston and the French Broad rivers, Knoxville's greater metropolitan area encompasses most of the citizens of Knox County, which in 1950 boasted a population of 233,000. Knoxville is blessed with a riparian location of great natural beauty, yet it has managed over the years to mask successfully much of that beauty with uninspiring architecture and industrial blight. Students at the main campus of the University of Tennessee there sardonically boasted in the fifties that Knoxville could add to its list of superlatives the unassailable fact that it was the largest metropolitan area in the United States—and perhaps in the world—that remained legally dry by repeated popular referenda. Sixty-eight miles southwest of Knoxville lies tiny Dayton, seat of Rhea County and William Jennings Bryan University, internationally famous for hosting the Scopes trial of 1925, and symbolically bearing further testimony to the devotion of so many Tennesseans to the canons of Protestant fundamentalism.

Whereas Knoxville presides over the source of the Tennessee River at mid-valley, Chattanooga presides over its exit southward into Alabama. Chattanooga is the seat of Hamilton County, which in 1950 was populated by 208,000 Tennesseans. In the popular mythology of state politics, Chattanooga has been known as a city of the very rich and the very poor. Because it has enjoyed the mixed blessings of considerable industry, Chattanooga's white proletariat has been the target of militant union and antiunion activity (the state passed an open-shop law in 1947). Chattanooga has been the principal city servicing nearby Georgia and Alabama (for statistical purposes, the Bureau of the Census considers contiguous Walker County, Georgia, an integral part of the Chattanooga Greater Metropolitan Area,) and more than 20 percent of Hamilton County's population was Negro in 1950. Slightly less

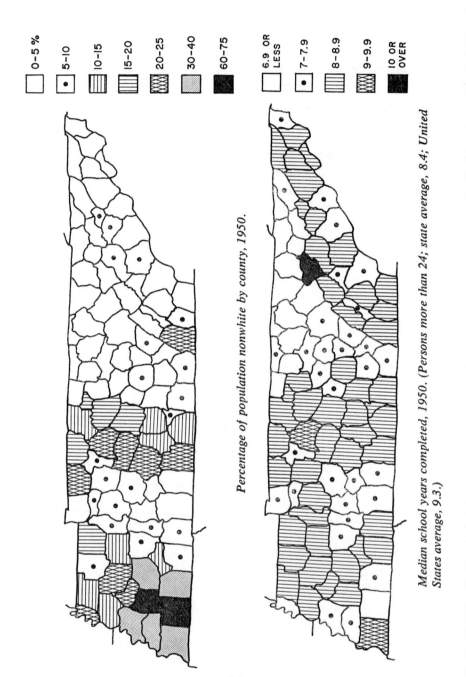

0–5 %	6.9 OR LESS
5–10	7–7.9
10–15	8–8.9
15–20	9–9.9
20–25	10 OR OVER
30–40	
60–75	

Percentage of population nonwhite by county, 1950.

Median school years completed, 1950. (Persons more than 24; state average, 8.4; United States average, 9.3.)

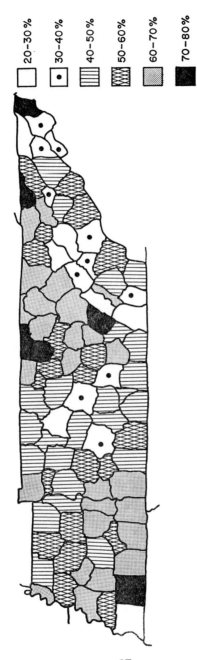

Median family income: percentage less than $3,000 annually, 1959 (state average, 38.3 percent).

17

than 10 percent of Knoxville's population was Negro. The census of 1960 found only 16.6 percent of Tennessee's Negroes living in East Tennessee, most of them in and near Chattanooga, and five eastern counties reported no Negroes at all.

The Cumberland Plateau divides East and Middle Tennessee, a portion of the plateau falling into each grand division. Only one tenth of this hilly area was farmed in the fifties, and with the exception of some sandstone, limestone, and gravel quarrying, this region throve or declined according to the health of the bituminous coal market. Because in the fifties the Cumberland miners were confronted not only with a chronically depressed coal market but also with a union growing increasingly indifferent to their plight, their morale as well as their physical well-being had deteriorated tragically.[14] For many Tennesseans, life in the Cumberland hills was hard and unrewarding. The young people tended to flee from the moribund little towns, and the new freeways ironically threatened to accelerate the region's isolation and decay.

The middle grand division is composed of the fertile Nashville Basin and the Highland Rim which neatly circumscribes it. The soil of this basin, agriculturally the most productive in Tennessee, has a limestone base equivalent to that of the Bluegrass region of Kentucky. Although less fertile, the low hills of the Highland Rim are suitable for small farms and livestock grazing, and much of the state's dark-fired tobacco has been grown in them.

Middle Tennessee is dominated by Nashville, the state capital, which straddles the Cumberland River in Davidson County (population in 1950: 322,000). Nashville has been an old and proud city, proud of its old families and their "old money," and proud also of the new industrialization and its pump-priming influx of new, often non-Southern families and "new money." The abundance of institutions of learning—

14. See Nat Caldwell and Gene S. Graham, "The Strange Romance between John L. Lewis and Cyrus Eaton," *Harper's* (December 1961) pp. 25–32. This article was written while Caldwell was a reporter and Graham an editorial writer for the Nashville *Tennessean*. A perceptive recent portrait of the depressed Kentucky Cumberlands is Henry Caudill, *Night Comes to the Cumberlands: A Biography of a Depressed Area* (Boston: Atlantic-Little-Brown, 1963).

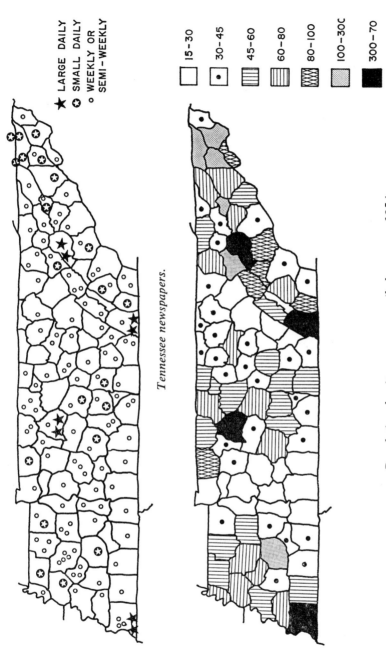

LARGE DAILY
SMALL DAILY
WEEKLY OR
SEMI-WEEKLY

Tennessee newspapers.

15-30
30-45
45-60
60-80
80-100
100-30C
300-70

Population density per square mile by county, 1954.

19

nine colleges and three universities, the most notable among them being Vanderbilt and Fisk Universities and Peabody College—long ago prompted enthusiastic local citizens to style their city the "Athens of the South" (to emphasize the point, city fathers in 1896 celebrated the state centennial by erecting, to the eternal astonishment of visitors, an anomalous replica of the Parthenon).

Once again crossing the Tennessee River, as it returns from Alabama and flows northward toward the Ohio, one enters the flat, cotton country of the western grand division. The rich, alluvial bottom land has a fertile soil of black silt loam, and it has made West Tennessee comparable in economy and geography to the Yazoo Basin of northern Mississippi. Here, the white leadership of rural Fayette County, bordering on Mississippi, faced the stern prospect that the 70 percent of its population that was Negro and had traditionally acquiesced in its disfranchisement might be encouraged by the desegregation crisis to assert its claim to full citizenship. The white minority of Haywood County, directly to the north of Fayette and 60 percent Negro, faced the same grim prospect.

A popular Southern chestnut has it that Mississippi has only two real cities: Memphis and New Orleans. The former was in 1950 a sprawling metropolis of 400,000 and the only real metropolitan center for a tri-state area of remarkable geographic and demographic homogeneity. Within a one-hundred-mile radius of Memphis, eighteen counties counted more Negro than white inhabitants (two in Tennessee, four in Arkansas, and the remaining twelve in Mississippi). Hundreds of thousands of Arkansans, Mississippians, and Tennesseans looked to Memphis (Shelby County) as their commercial and cultural mecca, and "Big Shelby" served them well by retaining the essential flavor of an overgrown river port that catered to their needs and in turn commanded their pocketbooks and their admiration. The awareness that Memphis served such a giant rural constituency has been so pervasive among city leaders that major institutions of Memphis have catered to this constituency's tastes and needs. Visitors are apt to be struck by the anomalously rural tone pervading the atmosphere of such a large and bustling city.

Throughout most of the twentieth century, Memphis had learned to acquiesce, and not without a certain muted pride, in the boss rule of a benevolent despot, Edward Hull Crump.[15] The Crump machine was accused by its hapless opponents of every dark tactic of bossism *except* venal corruption. For almost half a century, Crump administered his neat, orderly, and largely middle-class fief with an efficiency and apparent probity that prompted even many of his early detractors to rationalize that, had municipal democracy been unshakled —which it was not—Memphis could hardly have hired a finer city manager. If 1954 symbolically rang in a new era, it also ironically tolled the knell for an old one, for it was in October of that year that the controversial old man, full of years and service, fell into a coma and died. Because he had jealously run a one-man, authoritarian machine which had groomed no heir apparent, his demise created a power vacuum in the city's leadership structure that further weakened the foundations of the old order as the crisis over desegregation broke.

Tennessee's poet laureate, John Trotwood Moore, has described the state flag in the customary iambics as

> Three Stars upon a sky of blue
> A snow-white circle 'round
> Three Grand Divisions strong and true
> By kinship's circle bound.
> And one is East, and one is West,
> And one is Middle ground.

Kinship's circle, unfortunately, has proven over the years to be something of a frail bound, for political instincts deposited by a conspiracy of geography and history have kept Tennessee's three grand divisions

15. See William D. Miller, *Mr. Crump of Memphis* (Baton Rouge: Louisiana State University Press, 1964). Most of the literature which formed the national image of the colorful "Red Snapper" was written in a climate of opinion dominated by the Depression and the Second World War. As a consequence, "Boss" Crump's authoritarian rule and his vested interest in a restricted franchise looked ominously familiar to a democracy at war with fascism. Miller has attempted, with some justification, to refurbish Crump's tattered reputation by emphasizing his credentials as a Progressive and his loyalty to Roosevelt. Crump was probably his own worst enemy in this regard, for his penchant for ascerbic public denunciation of his detractors readily lent itself to ridicule.

in uneasy harness.[16] Because the rugged hills and valleys of East Tennessee were inhospitable to a plantation economy, the area's Jacksonian yeomanry had little use for slavery and rallied during the Civil War to the Union and the party of Lincoln—where they have since largely remained. Conversely, the cotton economy and plantation mentality of West Tennessee inspired its whites to fight tenaciously for the Confederacy, the Lost Cause, white supremacy and states' rights, and to rally to the Dixiecrats when the Democracy betrayed their trust in 1948. Almost 60 percent of the state's Negroes lived in West Tennessee, and two-thirds of these, or roughly 210,000, lived in Shelby County. Sandwiched between the two sharply contrasting grand divisions is Middle Tennessee, which, with one quarter of the state's Negroes, has generally inclined toward a cohesive moderation and Democratic loyalty. As the swing division, it has at times enjoyed the rewards that accrue to the courted in power-balance politics. But the generally progressive inclination of Middle Tennessee voters has been periodically frustrated as conservative western Democrats and likeminded eastern Republicans have joined from time to time in swapping votes for patronage to insure that control of the statehouse remained in safely conservative Bourbon hands. Crump was especially well-equipped to deliver on such arrangements with Memphis' large and well-disciplined bloc of votes. Like the Byrd machine of Virginia, Crump's organization benefitted mightily from that familiar accumulation of disfranchising devices (the poll tax, intimidation of rural Negroes, arcane registration requirements, and the powerful inertia of apathy) which, at least until mid-century, had kept the Tennessee electorate small and "pure."

16. Key's chapter on Tennessee, "Tennessee: The Civil War and Mr. Crump," 58–82, essentially stops with the election of Kefauver and Browning in 1948, when Crump's control of the state was broken. A useful recent textbook on Tennessee government has been produced by Lee Seifert Greene and Robert Sterling Avery, *Government in Tennessee* (Knoxville: University of Tennessee Press, 1962). While Greene and Avery have minimized interpretation, Norman L. Parks has perceptively analysed post-Crump political trends in "Tennessee Politics Since Kefauver and Reece: A 'Generalist' View," *Journal of Politics*, XXVIII, 144–168.

Thus, at the onset of the crisis over desegregation, Tennessee was still operating politically, not as a viable two-party system, or even as a typical Southern one-party system, but rather as two one-party systems coexisting symbiotically, and the historic Southern amalgam of biracialism—which of course translated into reality as white supremacy—and its supportive paraphernalia of malapportionment, disfranchisement, and an archaic constitution unreformed since 1870 still held sway. But it was also at this critical juncture in Southern history that the irresistable thrust of urban industrialism that had so transformed national politics since the Depression was bringing belatedly to the South what Southern historian C. Vann Woodward has called the "Bulldozer Revolution." [17] The emergence of these forces coincided with the crisis over desegregation, and together they threatened to destroy the old order and to create, in the South, a society more in tune with the rest of the nation.

There are many Souths and many a genre of Southerner. Tennessee has probably been better endowed with all of the major varieties than has any other Southern state, with the possible exception of North Carolina. Whether rural or urban Tennessean, Negro or Caucasian, Republican or Democrat, liberal or conservative—from the Bourbon aristocrat to the poor-white sharecropper, from the militant young Negro at Fisk to the broken old Uncle Tom of Fayette County—the crisis over desegregation intimately touched the lives of many of them and impinged upon the minds of them all. Whatever unknowing mischief our colonial statesmen unwittingly created for future Tennessee politicians and administrators, they rendered historians in search of a sample a noble service. It is almost as if a giant coring machine had ground into the Great Smoky Mountains and had emerged almost 500 miles westward on the banks of the Mississippi River, thereby laying bare the region's variegated stratifications for all to survey.

Access to such variety within a Southern state is vital to such a study as this. Whereas, in South Carolina, Professor Quint saw in the response of the press to desegregation a trend toward a monolithic

---

17. *The Burden of Southern History* (New York: Vintage Press, 1961), p. 6.

atmosphere of segregationist defiance that would brook no major exception, the response of Tennessee's press was one of considerable diversity. To be sure, most of Tennessee's Southern white publishers and editors were unhappy with the prospect of change from the segregationist status quo. Several, in fact, hurled defiance in the teeth of the nine old men on the high bench with a vigor that lived up to the finest traditions of Southern bombast. But even the most loudly advertised indignation of the segregationist editors could not camouflage the fact that a substantial number of important dailies throughout the state urged honest efforts at compliance with what they regarded as the law of the land. Quint found some editorial diversity in the ranks of the four South Carolina newspapers he selected as representative samples, but its importance to him seemed chiefly to lie in the melancholy fact of its subsequent erosion under the steadily intensifying pressures of the segregationists. Disentient South Carolina newspapers, for Quint, were exceptions that proved the rule.

In his more standard monograph, *Virginia's Massive Resistance,* Benjamin Muse[18] found somewhat more editorial diversity extant in the Old Dominion. But by far the preponderant balance of Virginia's major newspapers supported the abortive effort at massive resistance. Muse devoted but five pages to a consideration of the editorial stance of a dozen Virginia newspapers, plus three in Washington, D.C.; the remaining 172 pages are devoted ably enough to the straight narrative.

My investigation, then, seeks to add to our knowledge in two principal ways. First, although the literature on Southern journalism and the race issue is liberally sprinkled with references to the editorial stances and roles played by important newspapers, there exists to my knowledge no truly comprehensive survey of *all* of any one state's newspapers in regard to this vital issue. While Quint examined four South Carolina newspapers rather intensively and Muse cursorily reviewed for us the editorial positions of a dozen Virginia newspapers

18. Bloomington: Indiana University Press, 1961. A former Virginia State Senator turned popular historian, Muse was commissioned by the Southern Regional Council to survey the initial decade of desegregation. See his *Ten Years of Prelude* (New York: The Viking Press, 1964).

(this is not to imply criticism of the efforts of Quint and Muse as insufficient, for what they were trying to do differs from the aims of this inquiry, and the questions they were asking directed their research along other lines), I examined in the course of my investigations more than 150 Tennessee newspapers, from the largest daily to the meanest bi-monthly.[19] Their response to desegregation reads like the fever chart of a malaria patient, the major nuances of which soon become almost predictable to the attendant's practiced eye.[20] Court decisions seem to prefer Mondays, frequently in May; school openings fall in early September and, occasionally, after Christmas. But the long vigil can never truly be relaxed, for although kneel-ins come on Sundays, sit-ins occur at any time, and lynchings and church bombings are possessed of their own terrible and unfathomable inner logic, thereby defying effective anticipation.

The final task is the analytic one. Once the performance of the press in Tennessee during these years of crisis has been descriptively reviewed, a critical assessment of that performance is in order. The descriptive task is of course a necessary prior condition to any analytical effort, yet the historian, like a good reporter, should remain constantly aware that his values affect all of his perceptions. For the psychologists have taught us that inherent in the process of perception is the ten-

19. Two fortunate although unrelated circumstances conspired to enable me to digest this much material. First, the State Library and Archives, located in Nashville, has microfilmed every newspaper ever published in the state that could be located; its files are remarkably complete and its staff eager to help. Second, the SERS clipping file was also handily available in Nashville. Although SERS clipping policies were often arbitrary, the editorial morgue on the eight Tennessee dailies is full enough to constitute a valuable and appreciated shortcut, and the files on the two Nashville dailies are complete. In a curious and perhaps revealing omission, no printed or microfilm record of the state's several Negro newspapers was available in the Tennessee State Library. Further, the official reference edition of the *Tennessee Blue Book (1957–1958)* lists 28 dailies and 125 weeklies, none of them Negro.

20. This phenomenon proved to be a further valuable shortcut in regard to sampling. I was able to record every relevant editorial that appeared in the two Nashville dailies between May 1954 and November 1964 and to construct from this source an editorial frequency chart, the peaks of which directed my search through the microfilm library.

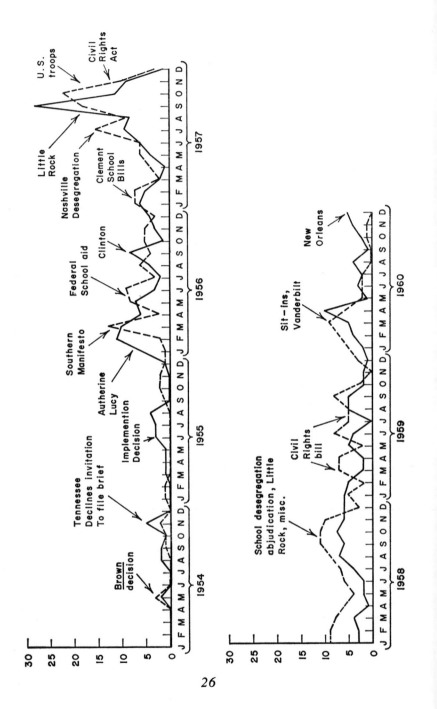

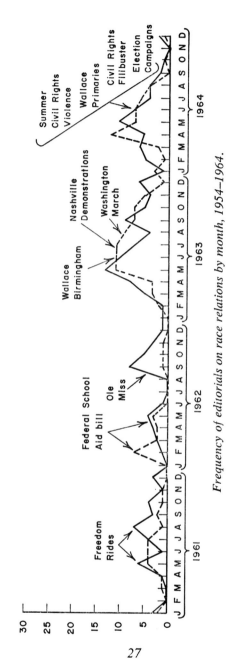

Frequency of editorials on race relations by month, 1954–1964.

Nashville Banner – – – – – – –   **Nashville** Tennessean ——————

30   25   20   15   10   5   0

JFMAMJJASOND JFMAMJJASOND JFMAMJJASOND JFMAMJJASOND JFMAMJJASOND

1961   1962   1963   1964

Freedom Rides

Federal School Aid bill

Ole Miss

Wallace Birmingham

Nashville Demonstrations

Washington March

Summer Civil Rights Violence

Wallace Primaries

Civil Rights Filibuster

Election Campaigns

dency of subjective bias to distort objective perception and to trans-
late that distortion, whether purposefully or unknowingly, into description.[21] Too much of the literature on Southern racial relations has been
casualty to this tendency. The historian, then, stands well admonished
that if he is going to editorialize on the editorials, he should at least
respectfully heed the canons of good journalism and take care to confine his editorials to his own editorial pages. The temptation is strong
to pause during the narrative and poke fun at the folksy provincialism
of the county weekly, or to pick a fight with an editorial eminence and
then bushwhack him by leveling, from the timeless seclusion of the
professor's study, the fire of devastating logic and unhurried research
upon an editorial prompted, perhaps, by angry dissent and written
necessarily in haste to meet the omnipresent deadline. Whether my
final analysis be deemed valuable, it is my prior hope that the narrative that follows be judged fair.

21. Our vain pride in the supremacy of human rationality has suffered still
another devastating blow at the hands of the psychologists. Laymen unfamiliar
with psychological jargon should find Leon Festinger's report on the theory of
"Cognitive Dissonance" both fascinating and highly readable. *Scientific American,*
October 1962, 207:27, 93–8+.

1

Brown v. *Board of Education*

ON 10 December 1953, the Supreme Court of the United States completed three days of hearings in the case of *Brown, et al.* v. *Board of Education of Topeka, et al.* Oliver Brown, a Negro, had sued Topeka's Board of Education to allow his daughter to attend a nearby white elementary school, rather than a distant Negro school.[1] Since that date, newsmen had crowded for twenty-three successive Mondays into the ornate marble chamber in Washington where the justices heard their cases and read their decisions—there only to discover that the explosive case challenging the practice of separating races in the schools was yet to be decided.[2]

On May 17, the third Monday in the month, tensions increased as a full cast looked down from the platform (Justice Robert H. Jackson, recovering from a heart attack, had left the hospital bed only that morning). The court had hinted at the importance of the occasion by failing to provide newsmen with the customary copies of the decision printed and distributed in advance of its oral delivery. At 12:52 p.m., Chief Justice Earl Warren began reading the opinion in the case of

1. It is ironical that the case that reopened the wounds of the Civil War and the Reconstruction originated in Kansas, a state, that, although never a part of the Confederacy, saw the first real shooting and bloodshed of the final conflict over slavery.

2. This account of the rendering of the decision ending segregation in public schools is distilled from Albert P. Blaustein and Clarence Clyde Ferguson, Jr., *Desegregation and the Law* (New York: Random House, 1954).

*Brow*n v. *Board of Education.* By 1:20 p.m. he concluded for a unanimous court

that in the field of public education the doctrince of "separate but equal" has no place. Separate educational facilities are inherently unequal. Therefore, we hold that the plaintiffs and others similarly situated for whom the actions had been brought are, by reason of the segregation complained of, deprived of the equal protection of the laws guaranteed by the Fourteenth Amendment.[3]

That fateful Monday was to be recorded in many Southern lexicons as "Black Monday." [4] But not in all.

The electric news that the Supreme Court had unanimously struck down racial segregation in the public schools was immediately relayed by the wire services to teletypes in city rooms all across the nation and, indeed, around the world. In Tennessee, as elsewhere, the afternoon dailies had time to rearrange their front pages in preparation for the bold streamer headlines and wire stories. Only one, however, had time to compose an editorial to comment on the momentous decision. Thus, with this single exception, it transpired that the morning dailies—though scooped of the news—got first crack at editorializing on it on Tuesday morning.

On that Tuesday in 1954, there was published in each of the state's four large cities both a morning and an evening daily, each of which enjoyed unchallenged hegemony over its half of the working day. This convenient, quasi-monopolistic arrangement had evolved not through any dark conspiratorial design but more as a kind of evolutionary reward for the eight fittest survivors of the lean depression years and the constant erosion of rising costs.[5] These eight big dailies, whose com-

---

3. *Brown* v. *Board of Education,* 347 U. S. 483, 74 Sup. Ct. 686, 98 L. Ed. 873 (1954).

4. Congressman John Bell Williams of Mississippi is credited with having first referred to "Black Monday" in a speech delivered on the floor of the House of Representatives in 1954. Mississippi Circuit Judge Tom P. Brady subsequently borrowed the term as title for his book which truculently denounced the Brown decision.

5. Nashville's two dailies provide a fine example of this mutually beneficial arrangement. In 1938, both the older *Banner* and the struggling *Tennessean* were plagued by hard times and aging printing plants. In order to ease the financial

bined weekday circulations in 1954 reached almost two thirds of a million, were the journalistic patriarchs of Tennessee and much of the mid-South, and as such they set the pace and the tone for the area's many lesser journalistic voices.

Four of the eight were published in the populous eastern grand division. In Knoxville, the morning *Journal* editorially represented the more conservative sentiments of Tennessee Republicanism. The *Journal's* 56-year-old editor, Guy Lincoln Smith, was a native Tennessean who had long been regarded as a Republican king-maker. Editor of the *Journal* since 1937, Smith was in 1954 chairman of the Republican state executive committee, member of the Republican national committee, and quadrennial delegate to the Republican national convention. He had successfully managed the Republican state campaign that threw Tennessee's eleven electoral votes to Eisenhower in 1952 (Tennessee had gone Republican only twice, for Harding and Hoover, since Reconstruction), and he was to repeat this notable achievement in 1956. Smith was allied with Brazilia Carrol Reece, Congressman from Tennessee's First District and also Republican national committeeman, in representing the conservative wing of the national Republican party. The *Journal's* editorial page commonly displayed the preachments of such conservative columnists as Westbrook Pegler, David Lawrence, George Sokolsky, and Fulton Lewis, Jr. Editorial cartoons frequently emphasized labor racketeering and the internal menace of the international Communist conspiracy. A prominent American flag was emblazoned on the masthead, sheltering beneath it a call to duty from the Grand Old Party's patron saint, and under Lincoln's words appeared

---

strain, both newspapers agreed to combine their physical resources and form the Newspaper Printing Corporation. Subsequently, one modern web perfecting press printed both newspapers, and a centralized office jointly handled advertising. In exchange for the *Tennessean's* agreement to withdraw its weak-sister evening edition, the *Banner* agreed not to compete with the *Tennessean* on Sunday mornings. This new co-operative arrangement proved immensely profitable to both dailies. Although they agreed to share the same printing plant and advertising offices, the editorial offices of the *Tennessean* and the *Banner* remained physically separated by several yards, and philosophically and politically they remained poles apart.

the Bible verse for the day. Inside, the evangelist Billy Graham frequently called the flock to repentance and salvation.

Given the conservative credentials of the *Journal,* and given the low opinion of most conservatives for the sociological jurisprudence of the "Warren court," it may have come as some surprise to many readers of the *Journal* that its editorial response to the Brown decision was an endorsement utterly without qualification. "No citizen," the *Journal* asserted, "fitted by character and intelligence to sit as a Justice of the Supreme Court, and sworn to uphold the Constitution of the United States, could have decided this question other than the way it was decided." As if that were not abundantly clear, the *Journal* added that "no person who understood the meaning of language could read the Fourteenth Amendment and conclude that school segregation was other than in direct violation of what it means."

One hundred miles to the South, Chattanooga's morning daily, the *Times,* voiced the sanguine, gradualist view that, given sufficient time, the South could learn to live with the decision. At first glance, the Chattanooga *Times* bears a striking resemblance in format and tone to the New York *Times.* That resemblance is no mere coincidence, for the *Times* of Chattanooga is indeed the father of the New York *Times.* Adolph Ochs, famous former publisher of the New York *Times,* bought the feeble Chattanooga *Times* in 1878 for a downpayment of only $250.[6] At the time of this purchase, Ochs was not yet twenty-one, and the circulation of the *Times* was at such low ebb that young Ochs had in effect paid one dollar per subscriber. The story of Ochs's success in Chattanooga, of his purchase of the New York *Times* in 1896 and of his subsequent triumphs is related elsewhere.[7]

6. Edwin Emery, *The Press in America,* 483–489. All references to newspaper numbers, political affiliations, and circulations are based upon information contained in R. Bruce Jones, ed., *Directory of Newspapers and Periodicals* (Philadelphia: N. W. Ayer & Sons, Inc., 1954), pp. 927–940, and William F. McAllister, ed., *Directory of Newspapers and Periodicals* (Philadelphia: N. W. Ayer & Sons, Inc., 1960), pp. 956–972.

7. Gerald W. Johnson, *An Honorable Titan* (New York: Harper Brothers, 1946), and Meyer Berger, *The Story of the New York Times: 1851–1951, op. cit.* Both *Times'* listed their political affiliations as "Independent Democratic." The

In 1954, the Chattanooga *Times* was still senior member of the Ochs family of newspapers, and its associate editor, 31-year-old Martin Shelby Ochs (a native Chattanoogan who was to become editor in 1958), had recently returned from a European apprenticeship as foreign correspondent for the New York *Times*. In Chattanooga, as in New York, banner headlines were reserved for occasions of extraordinary significance, and international news occupied more space than was usual in Southern newspapers. The editorials were generally progressive by Southern standards and gave the appearance of having been written with cool detachment and reserve.

Although highly industrialized, Chattanooga has managed to retain a good deal of the raw, buccaneering flavor that characterized its early history as a booming, almost frontier railroad terminus. As a result, the magesterial *Times* seemed almost out of place in unsophisticated Chattanooga, and some of the newspaper's less discerning detractors had long been known to malign its indigenous character with dark allegations that it was an organ of the international Jewish conspiracy. One might guess that the *Times* was keenly sensitive to this type of innuendo, for it carefully prefaced its editorial on the Brown decision

---

circulation of the Chattanooga *Times* in 1954 was 57,000 and its unchallenged Sunday edition reached 87,000.

In a state wherein election to political office has been predominantly determined in the Democratic primary, newspapers with Democratic or independent-Democratic affiliations outnumbered Republican or independent-Republican newspapers 62 to 11. Not surprisingly, their locations accorded with regional political consensus. In 1954, the Democratic party claimed 19 dailies and 49 weeklies, most of them located in the western and middle grand divisions. Their total daily circulation was 446,000, plus 96,000 weekly. Surprisingly, only a few hard-core Republican newspapers publicly championed the Grand Old Party in the eastern grand division. Republican-affiliated newspapers reached only 94,000 readers daily, and only 17,000 weekly.

A majority of Tennessee's newspapers affiliated with neither political party, but rather listed themselves as independent or nonpartisan. These 80 newspapers—twelve dailies and 68 weeklies—were spread fairly evenly throughout the state. Although there were numerous exceptions, most of the party-affiliated newspapers were established in the nineteenth century, when the tradition of a highly partisan press was still strong. Conversely, most nonpartisan newspapers were established in the twentieth century, when the concept of independence and objectivity was commanding increasing allegiance from the press.

by reviewing the legitimacy of its credentials as a Southern institution. "The Chattanooga *Times*," it took pains to affirm, "is a newspaper of Southern sympathies." Although frequently a quiet champion of progressive reform, the *Times,* like Justice Frankfurter, was conservative enough to prefer political channels to judicial ones, and on this occasion it confessed editorially that it would "have hoped that the South would have continued to do these things [progress towards equality of opportunity for all races] for itself." In keeping with its pride in its Southern identity, the *Times* insisted that

With all its so-called mercurial temperament on these racial questions, the South has in fact a deeper sympathy for the Negro race than any other section of this country. While working this thing out peacefully, we believe the South will, according to its habit, seek to be fair to the Negro.

In regard to the school desegregation decision itself, the only affirmative gesture the *Times* was willing to offer was to the effect that the South would at least no longer have to spend an extra four billion dollars a year duplicating school systems. The editorial concluded that, while hoping that the forthcoming decree to implement the court's new policy would be "suitably delayed," the *Times* hoped that it would indeed be final.

Nashville's morning daily, the *Tennessean,* enjoyed the largest circulation in the state. This wide readership combined with a location in the capital to give the *Tennessean*'s editorial voice probably a unique measure of influence in Tennessee. But this impressive pre-eminence was of relatively recent origin, for the *Tennessean* had been, during the first quarter of the century, little more than the personal organ of the flamboyant Colonel Luke Lea,[8] the stormy petrel of Tennessee politics during this period. The ambitious Lea had cajoled the legislature into

8. Jennings Perry, co-editor with John Nye of the *Tennessean* while it was in receivership during the mid-thirties, has written a lively, colorful, and decidedly partisan account of the *Tennessean's* arduous climb from the disrepair in which Luke Lea had left it to the pinnacle of crusading reform agianst Boss Crump and the poll tax during the forties. In his warm biography of Crump, William Miller dismissed Perry's book, *Democracy Begins at Home* (Philadelphia: J.B. Lippincott, 1944), as a "carelessly assembled work of pompous verbosity." See Miller, *Mr. Crump,* 298. Crump himself was even less generous, as Miller

electing him to the United States Senate in 1911, only to be ousted by the voters in 1917 in favor of K. D. McKellar, Tennessee's first popularly elected senator. Disappointed in office, Lea left for France and achieved enduring fame—or infamy—by leading a band of Tennesseans in a madcap and abortive attempt to kidnap the Kaiser. Lea's speculative fortunes crashed with Wall Street in 1929, and when called to account for his financial delinquencies by the state of North Carolina, he left the *Tennessean*'s reputation sordidly damaged and its plant in receivership to the Middle Tennessee Federal District Court.

In 1937, the *Tennessean* was bought by an aggressive New Dealer, Silliman Evans. A native of Texas, Evans had been nurtured in the newspaper business there under the tutelage of Amon Carter, celebrated publisher of the Fort Worth *Star-Telegram*. First a political reporter in Austin and later in Washington, Evans developed a taste for politics and an affinity for the Democratic variety practiced by John Nance Garner, Jesse Jones, and Tom Connally. Prior to his purchase of the *Tennessean,* Evans had been chairman of the board of Maryland Casualty Company and fourth assistant to Postmaster General James Farley. But Evans wanted to return to the newspaper business, and he wanted to create a Southern voice in support of the policies

---

fairly observed, and he was notoriously adept at his own patented brand of acid diatribe:

"Rat Jennings Perry is full of trickery, has a taste for low intrigue, and is mortgaged to the devil. . . . He wrote a book, *Democracy Begins at Home,* filled with lies, sent it free of charge to the legislators. He will not sell enough copies to get back the cost of the cover. . . . The insipid ass, the moron. . . . He is the perfect example of the type of man who travels from cradle to the grave without having been aroused from the state of invincible ignorance. Only a low filthy scroundrel, pervert, degenerate, would write lies for profit." (Quoted in Miller, *op. cit.* pp. 298–299)

If Crump's pronounced weakness for public malediction has led to the obscuring of the many positive contributions that Miller credits to his account, neither should the somewhat florid style of Perry's book detract from the fundamental fact that Perry's courageous career bears living witness to a strain of character that, though easily obscured by the highly visible legacy of racial prejudice, is nevertheless deeply ingrained in the Southern temper. His abiding devotion to democratic principles and his sympathy for the poor of whatever race translated not only into words but also into a long life of active reform.

of the Democracy of Franklin D. Roosevelt. The *Tennessean* was, after 1937, the only major daily in Tennessee that listed its political affiliation simply as Democratic, and it was in 1940 the only one of eight to support the third-term candidacy of Roosevelt. The professional staff of the *Tennessean,* under the leadership of John Nye and Jennings Perry, had taken full advantage of the respite granted them by the receivership to rebuild the reputation of the fallen daily by adhering to the canons of good journalism and by pursuing a path of governmental reform. Under Evans, the *Tennessean* continued in this tradition.[9]

9. Some of the problems involved in going behind the editorial are suggested by the differing character of the *Tennessean's* publishers and, in turn, their relationships with the editors they employed. In 1948, Silliman Evans recalled the highly regarded Coleman Harwell from the editorial staff of the New York *World Telegram* to edit the *Tennessean.* A native of Nashville, Harwell had joined the *Tennessean* in 1927 as a reporter and had worked his way up to managing editor by 1931, when he left for New York. New Dealers both, Evans and Harwell were congenial journalists, and the *Tennessean* spoke with unapologetically liberal convictions. But Evans died in 1955, and his namesake son inherited an editorial staff and posture with which he was not in full accord. By early 1960 the abrasive relationship had driven Harwell into exile to Cookeville, Tennessee, where he at last enjoyed the independence of publishing his own weeklies, the *Herald* and the *Citizen.* Young Evans replaced Harwell with Edward D. Ball, formerly head of Nashville's Associated Press bureau and a business-minded man whose more conservative politics and demeanor considerably muted the *Tennessean's* reformist tone—a noticeable modification that prompted *Time* magazine to observe disapprovingly (and with its customary editorial hyperbole) that "as the segregation issue shook the South, the *Tennessean's* editorials were models of cautious vapidity." "Fighting *Tennessean,*" *Time,* 80:73, 14 September 1962. Ball had been loath to support Senator Kennedy in 1960 until Senator Johnson accepted the vice-presidential nomination. But Silliman Evans, Jr., died in 1961, and control of the *Tennessean* passed to 30-year-old Amon Carter Evans, who promptly replaced Ball with John Seigenthaler, a brilliant 32-year-old former *Tennessean* city editor and Nieman Fellow who had joined the staff of Attorney General Robert Kennedy. Seigenthaler shared with the Kennedys a commitment to "tough-minded liberalism" (his work on behalf of the Justice Department had earned for him a cracked skull in racially disturbed Alabama), and under his leadership the *Tennessean* quickly regained its old, strident form. Some saw in Seigenthaler a latter-day Democratic model of the political kingmaker that the Republican *Journal's* Guy Smith had been.

The *Tennessean,* like the Chattanooga *Times,* avoided on that Tuesday morning any outright endorsement of the Brown decision. But, also like the *Times,* the *Tennessean* suggested that the South could and indeed should learn to live with it. Without directly approving or disapproving, the *Tennessean* stated flatly that desegregation of public schools was now "the law of the land." The court had "with sympathetic wisdom" allowed for a gradual adjustment, and the South would surely muster its better elements to solve this problem—as it "has met and overcome other problems rooted in a departed past." "And in so doing," the *Tennessean* candidly concluded, Southerners will "be paying new honor to the principle of democracy they so readily profess but, on occasion, so reluctantly practice."

Down in Memphis, the *Commercial Appeal* was the only morning daily in the Scripps-Howard chain. In 1954, its 200,000 weekday and 250,000 Sunday circulation topped that of any other Tennessee newspaper, although much of this circulation was in Arkansas and Mississippi. As its title suggests, the *Commercial Appeal* had been founded by a group of Memphis entrepreneurs whose devotion to the principle of laissez faire led them to look askance at Crump's early progressive attacks on the high-handed utilities companies. Its colorful "old-school" Southern editor, Charles Patrick Joseph Mooney, had earned for the paper a crusading reputation and, in 1923, a Pulitzer award for public service. Mooney, who had displayed a particular dislike for Crump, died in 1936—the year of the Scripps-Howard purchase—and since that time the conservatism of the paper's format has been reflected in its editorial columns.

Because of its large tri-state circulation, the *Commercial Appeal* has been sensitive to the need to tread lightly on the political eggs of three states. Its editor, Frank Ahlgren, was born and educated in the Midwest. But he had studied law and had worked as a reporter in Memphis during the twenties, and in 1937 he was called from Edward Scripps's old Cleveland *Press* to edit the chain's new acquisition in Memphis. By 1954, Ahlgren was a profoundly conservative gentleman of fifty-one who held many assumptions in common with the white leadership of his Black Belt constituency. Later in the fifties he was to manifest great interest in the neoracist anthropology publicized by Carleton Putnam.[10]

The *Commercial Appeal* had long been restive about the Supreme Court's nibbling encroachments on its original doctrine, enunciated in 1896 in the case of *Plessy* v. *Ferguson*,[11] approving separate-but-equal facilities. During the early summer of 1950, the Supreme Court had further qualified, without overturning, the doctrine of separate-but-equal facilities by ordering the state of Texas to admit a Negro to its school of law,[12] by ordering the state of Oklahoma to desist from providing special segregated arrangements for a Negro admitted to its school of law,[13] and by striking down requirements for segregated facilities in the dining cars of railroads engaged in interstate commerce.[14] In an editorial prompted by these decisions, the *Commercial Appeal*

10. See Carleton Putnam, *Race and Reason: A Yankee View* (Washington, D.C.: Public Affairs Press, 1961), p 5. Putnam, former chairman of the board of Chicago and Southern (now Delta) Airlines, and a biographer of Theodore Roosevelt, rallied around him in the late fifties a well-financed group of ultra-conservatives who entertained the conspiratorial view that modern equalitarian philosophy had subverted not only politics but science as well. This group was convinced that although abundant scientific evidence existed to prove the Negro's genetic inferiority (see especially Audrey M. Shuey, *The Testing of Negro Intelligence*, Lynchburg, Virginia: J. P. Bell, 1958, and Nathaniel Weyl, *The American Negro*, Washington, D.C.: Public Affairs Press, 1960) this scientific truth had been purposefully obscured by a conspiracy of leftist-leaning social scientists who had allowed their philosophical convictions to pervert their science. According to Putnam, the primary culprit had been "modern equalitarian anthropology," which had sacrificed genetics at the altar of environmentalism. The chief subversive had been Franz Boaz, the "father of equalitarian anthropology in America," who during his long tenure at Columbia University so successfully indoctrinated a stream of disciples—especially Melville Herskovits, Clyde Kluckhohn, and Ashley Montagu—that the Supreme Court was led in 1954 to cite the consensus of modern anthropology, and especially the Swedish socialist, Gunnar Myrdal's *The American Dilemma*, as conclusive evidence that the nine justices' conviction that school segregation was an unconstitutional evil was "amply supported by modern authority."

11. 163 U.S. 537, 16 S. Ct. 1138, 41 L. Ed. 256.

12. *Sweatt* v. *Painter*, 339 U.S. 629, 70 Sup. Ct. 848, 94 L. Ed. 1114.

13. *McLaurin* v. *Board of Regents*, 339 U.S. 637, 70 Sup. Ct. 851, 94 L. Ed. 1149.

14. *Henderson* v. *United States*, 339 U.S. 816, 70 Sup. Ct. 843, 94 L. Ed. 1302.

in 1950 had pointed out to its readers with relief that "the Court did not bar segregation as such in wholesale terms." [15] The editorial had emphasized, moreover, that "the South itself has long since realized that opportunities for Negroes in education must be expanded and improved. On the one hand this was a matter of equity and on the other of enlightened self-interest." But the *Commercial Appeal* had objected to the rulings of 1950 as "clearly another invasion of States' Rights and a blow at the principle of state sovereignty." The editorial had closed with the prescient admonition that the "most grave aspect of the rulings lies in their inference and assumption that the doctrine of States' Rights can be thus abridged and that customs and practices alien and undesirable to the people of any given section can be imposed upon them."

When on Monday, the 17th day of May, 1954, the Supreme Court confirmed the *Commercial Appeal*'s early and fearful premonitions, its editors nevertheless responded the following morning by urging readers to "approach this issue with calmness, reason, and a genuine spirit of co-operation." The editorial even specifically applauded the Memphis and Shelby County school administrators for having affirmed "that local authorities would abide by" the decision. The editorial concluded:

Whether for good or bad, the Supreme Court has ruled segregation unconstitutional, and it has been traditional for the American people to respect the dignity of the law.

The main thing now is for the American people to face this thing squarely, as an *accomplished fact* [emphasis added], and work out our destiny for the general good and the great glory of our nation.

When the Scripps-Howard chain purchased the *Commercial Appeal* in 1936, Memphis joined the growing ranks of American cities with a monopoly press. In 1906, the old Scripps-McRae League had founded the Memphis *Press,* which became a Scripps-Howard newspaper in 1922 when Roy Howard, head of United Press, merged his empire with the newspaper chain that Robert Paine Scripps had inherited from his father. In 1926, the *Press* absorbed the faltering *News-Scimitar* to become the Memphis *Press-Scimitar.* The Memphis newspaper monopoly

15. 7 June 1950.

remained largely a technicality, however, for the frequency with which the *Press-Scimitar* took issue with the editorial assertions of the *Commercial Appeal* was prima facie evidence in support of the chain's claim that considerable editorial autonomy remained in the hands of the local editors.

When Frank Ahlgren began his long tenure on the *Commercial Appeal,* he declined to continue C. P. J. Mooney's crusade against Crump, and so the mantle fell by default on the shoulders of a most willing recipient, Edward J. Meeman, who had been editor of the evening *Press-Scimitar* since 1931. A native of Indiana, Meeman had worked his way up to managing editor of the Evansville *Press,* which he left in 1921 to help found the Knoxville *News.* While editing the *News*—and, after 1926, the Scripps-Howard *News-Sentinel*—Meeman had displayed the idealistic devotion to progressive democratic self-government and the taste for crusading that was to bring him into headlong collision with the hypersensitive Crump. Given Crump's habit of responding to criticism with a purple pen, his quarter century-long battle with Meeman and the *Press-Scimitar* early took on all the overtones of a vendetta.[16] But Meeman's bête noir was dying in May of 1954, and Meeman's lifelong devotion to freedom and democracy was to be sternly challenged as the Supreme Court thrust an issue of great divisive potential into Memphis' civic arena.

Meeman's *Press-Scimitar* responded to the Brown decision with a

---

16. Crump had been fond of inserting full-page ads in the *Press-Scimitar* to denounce his political enemies—frequently by applying to them such derogatory appelations as "Judas Iscariot," or by metaphorically ascribing to them the undesirable traits of certain animals. On one celebrated occasion this colorful tactic boomeranged. When Crump in 1948 called Representative Estes Kefauver a pet coon who always had his hand in the drawer, Kefauver donned a coonskin cap, honorable badge of the pioneer, and boldly and successfully barnstormed for election to the Senate in Crump's home barony of Shelby County. Kefauver, who despite his ostensibly flamboyant campaign style was essentially a man of considerable reserve, spent the rest of his political life trying to take the ludicrous cap off. See Key, *Southern Politics,* 58–59. "Rat Meeman" joined Crump's despised category of rodents, in company with Jennings Perry, Silliman Evans, and the *Tennessean's* knowledgeable if somewhat heavy-handed political writer, Joe Hatcher.

plea for time and patience from the courts, but its editorial advised its readers flatly that the decision "was not unexpected and it will have to be accepted." Meeman echoed the *Commercial Appeal*'s applause of the statement of Milton Bowers, president of the school board, that Memphis schools would "abide by the law of the land." But the *Press-Scimitar* went further, calling approving attention to the degree to which the decision would improve the American image abroad: "Our preachments on democracy and dignity and equal opportunity of man will ring truer to Asia's fermenting millions when they learn that here in America equality was not graded by complexion." It was, perhaps, a backdoor method of confessing approval, but those words were to be read throughout the flat delta of the Mississippi and Yazoo basin, and within that context they were boldly affirmative ones.

The senior daily in Nashville was the evening *Banner,* established in 1876 and published by the prominent Stahlman family since 1885. The virulent rivalry between the *Banner* and the *Tennessean* dated from the early years of the century, when all the guile of Colonel Luke Lea could not master the iron determination of Major Edward Bushrod Stahlman. (During the First World War, Lea had even tried to have the German-born Stahlman interned as an enemy alien—a bizarre circulation-building scheme foiled by the intercession of Senator K. D. McKellar.)[17] Ralph McGill, who was a cub political reporter for the *Banner* during those turbulent years of old-fashioned personal journalism, has recalled the remarkable Major Stahlman with an admixture of warmth and awe:

In all those years the paper mirrored not so much the news as it did his personality and convictions. Always on the attack, he gloated in victory and never asked quarter or whined in defeat. Politics was his passion, but he was always an independent, never affiliated with party or faction, but fierce in his support of a candidate. He was ruthless and merciless in his opposition. Both affection for him and distaste of him were intense.[18]

In 1954, the Major's 61-year-old grandson, James Geddes Stahlman, proudly piloted the *Banner* full in the family tradition. A native

17. *The South and the Southerner* (Boston: Atlantic–Little, Brown, 1959), p. 91.
18. *Ibid.,* 90.

of Nashville, he had been appointed trustee to Vanderbilt University, his local alma mater. The editorial voice of the *Banner* had long been popularly regarded as the voice of Nashville's business community, and while Stahlman accurately and honestly reflected the conservative convictions of Nashville's businessmen, he stubbornly and successfully over the years refused to be owned by them.

The *Banner* in 1954 reached upwards of 90,000 mid-Southerners a day, and few could have long remained unaware of its publisher's firm political convictions. Stahlman felt an intellectual affinity for columnist David Lawrence and his confrères on the political right, and the *Banner* not infrequently ran front-page editorials denouncing unequivocally some encroachment on the sacred corpus of states' rights. The *Banner's* talented editorial cartoonist, Jack Knox, pilloried Stahlman's antagonists with an acid pen that was quick to link the NAACP–ADA–Left syndrome with the carpetbag—traditional symbol of Yankee exploitation—and with crass, unconstitutional opportunism in general. Probably no editorial cartoonist was reprinted in so many Southern newspapers as was Knox.

A former editor of the *Tennessean* has reflected the liberal view of the *Banner* by contemptuously referring to it as "spiritually the Southern edition of the Chicago *Tribune*."[19] Such critics of the *Banner* often made much of the "Prussian mentality" of the Stahlmans—a kind of *ad hominem* slur that prompted the highly sensitive James Stahlman to set the record straight by pointing with pride to the family's historic devotion to freedom:

The Stahlman family emigrated from Germany in the ninettenth century. The family had been residents of the duchy of Mecklenburg-Strelitz, one of the truly democratic duchys of what later became a part of the German Confederation.

My great-grandfather and great-grandmother were freedom-loving people, firm in their Lutheran faith and hostile to every restraint upon the democractic processes. By reason of the Revolution of 1848 and the subsequent restrictive constitutional measures in 1851 and '52, they brought their young brood to the United States, in order to enjoy the freedom which this country provided. They detested anything with a Prussian label.[20]

19. Jennings Perry, Nashville, letter, 30 January 1964, to the author.
20. James G. Stahlman, Nashville, letter, 1 July 1966, to the author.

Stahlman was also sensitive to the charge that his patriotism was of the excessive, flag-waving variety so frequently embraced by immigrant groups in an effort to prove to the older American stock that they truly belonged:

> My grandfather, the late Major E. B. Stahlman, was the oldest of the brood. His father died shortly after landing in America, and my grandfather became almost the total support of his mother and other minor children. In appreciation of the freedom which they had found here, they named my great-uncle George W. Stahlman, the first of the Stahlman name born in the United States, for the Father or our Country.
>
> That heritage, along with that from the Geddeses, the Claibornes, the Smiths, the Forts and the Burnhams, accounts for my love of this country and for all its fundamental institutions—sometimes characterized by my critics as superpatriotism or worse.[21]

Whatever Stahlman's critics thought of his "superpatriotism," that same unashamed devotion to the heritage of freedom engendered by America's "fundamental institutions" had earned for the *Banner*'s publisher the accolades of numerous conservative and patriotic organizations. In 1956, he received the American Award of the Americas Foundation, and in 1961 the Freedoms Foundation awarded him its Washington Medal.

The *Banner* was the only evening daily in Tennessee able to respond with an editorial on the day the desegregation decision was issued. In recognition of the extraordinary occasion, Stahlman inserted the editorial on the first page, as he was often wont to do (and, in keeping with the rules, he labeled his front page editorial as such). The title of the editorial suggested its content in calling for "A Time for Calm Appraisal." [22] Acknowledging the Brown decision as the most momentous one rendered since the "War Between the States," the editorial expressed the hope that both sides of the long controversy would foreswear "demagogic appeals." It called for a "reasoned and cautious treatment of the case presented to reconcile both the national interest and States' Rights on the Constitution, which is the firm foundation of both."

21. *Ibid.*
22. 17 May 1954, Editor of the *Banner* was G.H. Armistead, Sr.

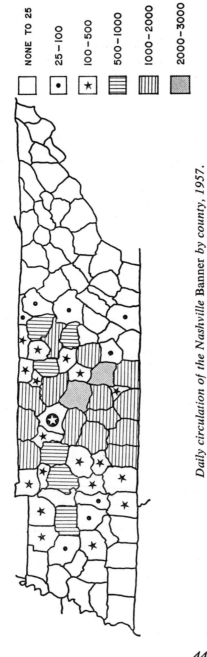

NONE TO 25

25 – 100

100 – 500

500 – 1000

1000 – 2000

2000 – 3000

3000 – 5000

5000 – 8000

DAVIDSON COUNTY:

BANNER: 59, III
TENNESSEAN: 94, 618

Daily circulation of the Nashville Banner *by county, 1957.*

Daily circulation of the Nashville Tennessean *by county, 1957.*

Banner:		Tennessean:	Daily	Sunday
Tenn.	102,850	Tenn.	118,595	194,335
Ala.	468	Ala.	855	2,022
Ky.	1,117	Ky.	2,097	6,352
Misc.	418	Misc.	572	899
total	104,871	total	122,157	203,690

Note: Circulation figures were derived from the official audit reports of the Audit Bureau of Circulations, Chicago, Illinois, for the Nashville *Banner* and the Nashville *Tennessean* for twelve months ending 30 September 1957. Courtesy of the Newspaper Printing Corporation, Nashville, Tennessee.

On the following day, the *Banner*'s editors composed a more lengthy editorial and deposited it on the editorial page. Many of the same themes prevailed: a calm and reasoned appraisal was in order, the court had wisely allowed time before ordering implementation, it was no time for demagogic appeals. It added on Tuesday, however, that the Eisenhower administration, which it supported, should not be blamed by angry segregationists for the decision, since Eisenhower had appointed only one of the nine justices to the bench. It revealingly reminded readers that "the controversy was accelerated by the 'New Deal' and 'Fair Deal,' whose treatment of the South was that of contempt, and which injected antagonism where antagonism had not existed." [23] Emphasizing that the "highest judicial authority in the land" had wisely left undecided the vital particulars of accommodation to its ruling, the *Banner* concluded that the case would not be closed "until a line of approach is found satisfactory both to the states and to the Federal Government." In suggesting that state and federal policies on the issue must coincide, the *Banner* did not yet suggest whose views should prevail should they collide.

Competing with the *Times* in Chattanooga was the evening *News–Free Press*. Its 53-year-old publisher, Roy McDonald, was a native of Graysville, Tennessee, and a successful Chattanooga businessman who first published the *Free Press,* an evening daily which he had built up from a humble beginning as an advertising throwaway. In 1941, McDonald bought out his evening competition, the Chattanooga *News,* and by 1954 his *News–Free Press* reached 59,000 readers in Tennessee, Georgia, and Alabama. McDonald saw political issues through the eyes of an aggressive entrepreneur of the classical laissez-faire persuasion; his ultra-conservative convictions were argued from the head, but by their intensity they hinted at visceral origins, and it seemed to be difficult for him to keep these opinions off the front page. McDonald's granite resolve to defend strict construction of the Constitution against the repeated assaults from what he conceived to be an opportunistic and fuzzy-minded left led him to wage political warfare with few holds

23. 18 May 1954.

barred.[24] One Tennessee politician of a liberal persuasion has privately confessed his conviction that endorsement by the uninhibited and heavy-handed *News–Free Press* was probably of greater value, politically, than the reserved approval of the aloof and stately Chattanooga *Times*.[25]

McDonald's old *Free Press* had lambasted the New Deal since its inception. When he devoured the *News* in 1941, he thereby doubled the number of eyes to which he might display his editorial appeals. Pre-eminent among these was a frequently repeated appeal to Southerners to desist from blind loyalty to a Democratic party whose national policies had been actively eroding values and institutions which conservative Southerners so long had cherished. Ever the stern realist, McDonald saw the desegregation decision strictly in terms of *realpolitik*. "The Negroes of the United States," began his editorial that Tuesday in May, "won the epochal victory . . . by exercising judgment in voting which was superior to that shown by the white people of the South for the past two decades." The lengthy editorial was entitled "Result of Blind Party Loyalty," and in it the *News–Free Press* treated its readers to a neat and largely accurate little lesson in political history—not without strong overtones of I-told-you-so. It all began with "the War Between the States and the brutal Reconstruction era which followed it." From that dismal time up to that of the New Deal, Southerners had reacted to the injustices imposed upon them by voting solidly Democratic; Negroes had supported the Republican party in gratitude for their liberation. When the "New Deal revolution" lured the Negro bloc vote into the Democratic party, however, the Southern white people blindly continued to support a party whose policies were largely repugnant to them. Thus these myopic Southerners,

24. During the gubernatorial campaign of 1958—a three-way race, fought primarily over segregation—Mayor Orgill of Memphis, a moderate, foolishly attempted to convince the intractable McDonald of the reasonableness of the moderate position. McDonald grilled the hapless mayor mercilessly, tape-recorded the interview, and by quoting selectively was able to stain Orgill successfully with the mark of an integrationist. (This was reported to the author by one of Orgill's distressed lieutenants.)

25. Fred Patterson Graham, member of the Orgill-for-Governor campaign committee, Nashville, personal interview with the author during that campaign.

"though they did not realize it, voted for two decades for the decision handed down by the Supreme Court yesterday." As for the court, it "was invading the legislative field when it handed down the antisegregation ruling." Although the *News–Free Press* of course "favors the just treatment of the Negroes, it regrets this ruling by our liberal-packed Supreme Court and thinks it deplorably unwise." As for the future, undoubtedly several states would seek "to devise means of evading the new Supreme Court law." The South and the nation will watch these efforts with much interest, the editorial concluded, "and many," the *News–Free Press* added, clearly implying self-inclusion, "will watch them with applause."

McDonald would find scant editorial applause for attempts at "evading the new Supreme Court's law" in Knoxville, however. While Guy Smith's Republican *Journal* shared McDonald's conservative politics, it held no strong brief for segregation and was certainly not about to participate in defiance of a Republican administration. The *Journal*'s competition, the evening *News-Sentinel,* was edited by 55-year-old Lloye Miller, an independent-minded native of Illinois who had worked as Ed Meeman's managing editor on the old Knoxville *News*. While Miller did not share Meeman's flair for crusading, he did share with Meeman a reformer's political convictions, and the two Scripps-Howard dailies occasionally printed identical editorials in expression of these mutual sentiments. Listing its political predilection as "Independent," the *News-Sentinel* circulated 105,000 copies a day in 1954—a circulation exceeding that of the *Journal* by more than 20,000, both on weekdays and on Sundays.

The Supreme Court found in Knoxville a wellspring of affirmation that Tuesday, for the *News-Sentinel* joined the morning *Journal* in affirming that the desegregation ruling "was a just and wise decision." Pointing to the success of desegregation north of the Mason-Dixon line generally, and to the surprising ease with which desegregation was accomplished in the armed forces after 1948, the *News-Sentinel* expressed confidence not only that, "given time, our Southern states will find a way to live with the Supreme Court's decision," but also that the ruling "in time will be so recognized [as just and wise] in our opinion even by those who are now troubled and shocked."

Thus it was that on the day following the delivery of the Brown decision, powerful voices in all four of Tennessee's major cities urged, with varying degrees of enthusiasm, compliance with the new ruling. Some, to be sure, hinted at misgivings, and one frankly invited defiance. But such was the variety of views advanced by the major editorial voices of the state that readers could respectably adhere to any of them without fear of isolation.

A few voices lesser than the large metropolitan dailies endorsed, at least by implication, the Brown decision. In the town of Bristol, which sits astride the border of Virginia and Tennessee high in the northwestern corner of the state, the daily *Herald-Courier* said in its editorial on Tuesday that "we believe it was right morally and legally." [26] The editorial was careful to point out that only 7.1 percent of Bristol's population and only 2 percent of Sullivan County's was Negro. It further listed the similarly small percentages of Negroes that resided in eight nearby counties.

In nearby Rogersville, county seat of adjacent Hawkins County, the weekly *Review* called the decision banning segregation in public schools "an historic pronouncement . . . in tune with the logic of events." [27] "The nine eminent jurists," the *Review* added, "have proven themselves jurists able to adapt the amazingly adaptable instrument, the

26. Competing for general readership with the eight large dailies in 1954 were twenty small dailies, none with a weekday circulation exceeding twenty thousand. These small daily newspapers were supported by towns of from ten to thirty thousand inhabitants, and they differed from the large dailies more in size than in content. The primary role they were attempting to fulfill—to inform their readers daily of local, national, and international news—was essentially that of the large dailies, although they relied more on wire services, syndicated material, and boilerplate than did their larger and more affluent counterparts. West and Middle Tennessee each supported in 1954 only four of these small dailies, while populous East Tennessee boasted twelve. Of the twenty-eight dailies in Tennessee, twenty-one were published evenings and only seven mornings. Because these morning dailies were usually those of the largest circulation, the smaller dailies tended to prefer to compete with the evening big-city dailies of usually more limited circulations (compare the circulation patterns of the morning *Tennessean* and the evening *Banner* on pages 44 and 45. In the life of a small city, it was easier to maintain a staff that worked by day to issue an afternoon paper than one which worked by night to issue a morning paper.

27. 3 June 1954.

Constitution, to meet the challenge that the United States, as a leader of democracies, must make an unequivocal declaration consistent with its own principles." Only 4 percent of Hawkins County was Negro.

The population of Henderson County, in West Tennessee, was 90 percent white. In the county seat of Lexington, the weekly *Progress* argued that the ruling should not have been much of a surprise because "by any and all standards we live by—those of our Constitution, the teachings of Christianity, and even those leading to the settlement of our country—Segregation was doomed." [28]

Although several major newspapers and a few lesser ones either explicitly or implicitly endorsed the Brown decision, the great majority of Tennessee newspapers neither endorsed nor denounced it. Only a few newspapers opposed it from the start. Whereas the seven white newspapers in Tennessee that did explicitly comment favorably on the decision circulated among 379,931 Southerners, the eight that manifested immediate hostility reached only 75,303.

By far the largest newspaper to take exception immediately to the new ruling was Roy McDonald's Chattanooga *News–Free Press*. In voicing dissent, the *News–Free Press* had raised almost all of the objections eventually to emerge as the pattern of the conservative attack upon the new doctrine. The Brown decision to them represented judicial legislation and, as such, a usurpation of the legislative function. Thus it was an unconstitutional invasion of states' rights as well as of the prerogatives of Congress. Further, the decision was a politically inspired one, born of a Supreme Court whose nine justices grossly misconstrued the basic constitutional function of their high office. Finally, the Brown decision represented that dangerous tendency toward social tinkering which seemed inherent in the make-up of political liberals. Here the conservative dissenters echoed Lord Falkland's timeless admonition that when it was not necessary to change, it was necessary not to change. It was a theme that readily lent itself to considerable elaboration. Anxious Tennessee editors who shared the convictions of Roy McDonald were to prove more than equal to that task.

28. 21 May 1954.

Seven county weeklies—only one of which, surprisingly, was published in racially sensitive West Tennessee—joined the *News–Free Press* in denouncing the decision (although the combined circulations of those seven weeklies totalled only 16,357). In West Tennessee, the weekly Trenton *Herald-Register* accused the Supreme Court of "Chasing a Will 'o the Wisp." Its editorial asserted that "inequality is inherent in educational opportunity." Since the court had inflicted "this unfortunate decision upon an unwilling people . . . apparently . . . with the intent of *securing absolute* [emphasis added] equality of educational opportunity," it followed that the goal was unattainable. The *Herald-Register* further criticized the court for setting its hearing on arguments for implementation on October 12 (the hearing was actually set for October 17), "which is expected by the court to last only one day!" Just where the *Herald-Register* got this last astonishing piece of misinformation remains a mystery.

Four county weeklies in Middle Tennessee took issue with the Supreme Court. In Columbia, a town of 10,000 situated in the southern portion of the Nashville Basin, the Maury (county) *Democrat* argued that the federal government had no jurisdiction over schools that it did not in large part finance.[29] The *Democrat* counseled a cautious wait-and-see policy until the nature and extent of the changes became clear. And if the changes were distasteful to the local majority, a reappraisal of the concept of public education might be in order. "At one time we had an excellent system of private schools," the *Democrat* reminded its readers. "This is a system the state and counties can well consider if necessary."

The Roberston County *Times* likened the decision metaphorically to the advice given by a doctor to a patient complaining of a cold to take a hot bath, then sit before an open window with a fan blowing on his back. " 'But Doc,' protested the patient, 'that would give me pneumonia!' 'For that,' the doctor sagely replied, 'we know what to do.' "[30] The *Times* then briefly rehearsed the history of Southern beneficence to the Negro, who had been brought by Southern

29. 20 May 1954.
30. 21 May 1954.

whites from a state of semisavagery to achieve gains "nothing short of phenominal [sic]." Further, it would be unnatural for races to lose their identity. For "if, in the general scheme of nature, the distinct lines were not intended, all men would be the same and blue birds would mate with cardinals."

In the unlikely event that any of its readers remained unconvinced by this teleological argument, the *Times* added the clinching *argumentum ad hominem* by referring to the movement in support of desegregation as "politically-inspired and Communist-fanned." The editorial concluded with a revealing hint at the *Times'* notion of why Negroes should and did exist within the confines of their peculiar culture:

if the justices who acted unanimously on this . . . think segregation is oppressive, let them look at what the *completely* free [emphasis added] Negro has done to himself in Chicago's South Side or Detroit's Near East Side. They're comparable to Nashville's Black Bottom and they're that way because the Negroes themselves *want* it that way.

The other two weeklies in Middle Tennessee that immediately opposed the decision were relatively more temperate in their remarks. The Manchester *Times* contented itself with observing that the Fourteenth Amendment, upon which the decision was based, was itself unconstitutional due to the irregular and coercive circumstances of its ratification.[31] In Pulaski—birthplace of the Ku Klux Klan—the *Citizen* advanced the familiar argument that no change could be anticipated because Negroes in Giles County preferred segregation and the friendliness and mutual affection that has traditionally existed "between the two tribes" as a product of the biracial system.[32] The *Citizen* accounted for the motives of those Negro "damn-fools" who sought desegregation by attributing them to jealously of the Southern Negro. "We would believe," explained the *Citizen,* "that those responsible for this act of injustice to their own race are in the majority those smartalecs who have been denied the many privileges enjoyed by the Southern Negro and have used this method to gain personal revenge." The editorial concluded with an ominous warning that dire consequences might ensue if the Negro bit the hand that would feed him.

31. 20 May 1954.
32. 21 May 1954.

In East Tennessee, two small weeklies published in counties border-ing on Alabama and Georgia complained of the decision. South Pitts-burg, in Marion County, was a community of fewer than 3,000, cling-ing to the western bank of the Tennessee River at Guntersville Lake. Alabama began only five miles to the south, and Georgia lay only ten miles to the southeast. There Roy Woodfin, editor of the South Pitts-burg *Hustler,* admitted that people naturally look to the daily press in an hour such as this, but he felt that no member of the newspaper profession should sulk in his tent.[33] The decision hit the *Hustler,* he said, pretty much as it hit Governor Talmadge, "who has long fought for white supremacy in the great state of Georgia." After urging Georgians to revise their constitution in order that Talmadge might run for re-election, Woodfin urged the "good Negro citizenship, such as we have here in South Pittsburg," to heed the admonition of Booker T. Washing-ton—"the greatest leader-friend of the colored race who ever lived":

Here is what he said with hand lifted in mid-air with outstretched fingers: "Let us remember this, that things social and educational in this nation of ours are just as separable as the fingers on your hand, racially speaking." He said with hands closed, "but, when it comes to matters of industry and development, that's another matter and they are just as compact as the hand itself."

Woodfin had taken certain broad liberties with Washington's remarks. What Washington had said at the Atlanta Cotton Exposition in 1895 was this: "In all things that are *purely* social [emphasis added] we can be as separate as the fingers, yet one as the hand in all things essential to mutual progress." [34]

Twenty-two miles east of tiny South Pittsburg, the Hamilton County *Herald* registered a greater sense of outrage than any newspaper in Tennessee. Published in Chattanooga, the forty-two-year-old weekly *Herald* nevertheless could muster only 2,124 of the faithful as sub-scribers. The weekly *Herald* had traditionally thundered its editorial dogmas from the front page. A tabloid-sized sheet six columns in width, the *Herald* frequently devoted four of those six columns on the front page to editorial comment. On May 28, 1954, the *Herald* charged

33. 19 May 1954.
34. 20 May 1954.

that the Supreme Court had written a dreary sequel to *Gone with the Wind*. For, just as the Civil War "brought an end to the charming plantation life of the old south," the Supreme Court by its "hateful decision" had "forever severed [the] kindly friendliness and sincere cooperation" that traditionally had prevailed between Southern whites and Negroes. The *Herald* truculently insisted that all but one of the justices had been appointed by Presidents Roosevelt and Truman to further their socialistic designs against the Republic. And the exception, Chief Justice Earl Warren, was a misfit who sat on the bench as a standing affront to the American bar. Further, the decision was dictated by an "alien philosophy—the result of the Communistic influence aimed at overthrowing the United States." Finally, the *Herald* added the assertion that kindly white Southerners had "rescued" the savages from northern and eastern slave traders and had "civilized them, educated them, built up in them a sense of the dignity of man, and gave them Christianity." And for this the South was to be rewarded by coercive desegregation, the latest form of New Deal–Fair Deal vengeance.

To be sure, Tennessee's county weeklies and semiweeklies were, for the most part, an unsophisticated lot. But, unlike the metropolitan dailies, they properly viewed as their chief function the dissemination of purely local news and community gossip.[35] Thomas D. Clark, a contemporary historian of the South, has said of the typical Tennessee weekly of the forties:

The material which the Tennessee weekly presented readers on its ready-print pages was frequently miscellaneous, always non-controversial, sometimes useful, and generally readable. This type of material had to be of an "evergreen" nature, which meant it was about as timely one month as another. There were stories on farming methods, care of livestock and children, the International Sunday School lesson, biographical sketches of famous men and women, travelogues, stories of how everything under the

35. Weekly newspapers flourished in Tennessee early in the century, as they did throughout the nation. The state was surfeited with a remarkable total of 238 of them in 1910; but—reflecting a national trend—they had declined by 1937 to 157 and were further reduced by 1948 to 123. At about this time, the descent stabilized into a plateau, for in 1954 there were 121 weeklies in Tennessee, and by 1960, p. 129.

sun was made, cooking recipes, modes of living of foreign peoples, and political editorials from "safe" Southern daily paper editors.[36]

and of their editors:

In many instances a college education was a drawback rather than an asset. . . . A nose for homey human interest stories was often worth more than a bachelor of arts degree *summa cum laude*.[37]

In the fifties, Tennessee weeklies continued on the whole to follow this proven formula, although most of those editors who commented on the desegregation crisis—and they were a decided minority—wrote their own editorials, and rather infrequently reprinted editorials from the big dailies—"safe" or otherwise. Customarily publishing on Thursday or Friday, a typical weekly might circulate 2,000 copies within the county. Especially if it enjoyed a county monopoly, as did 42 of Tennessee's 121 weeklies in 1954, it would include separate columns reporting, for instance, on the "Week's Happenings in Moscow" (this column, which commonly appeared in the Fayette *Falcon*, carried news not of the Soviet Union but of a small town in Fayette County), in order to appeal to readers living in outlying towns and villages. Frequently, a separate column reported on "News Among the Colored People"—never "Negroes." Rare was the weekly that did not include at least one Bible verse for the day, accompanied by the omnipresent Bible lesson and prayer. Patriotic allegiance was often cultivated by including such gleanings from the almanac as "This Week in American History"—invariably an antiquarian pot pourri of historical miscellany which, like one piece of a puzzle, was largely meaningless in its isolation.

During the mid-fifties, two syndicated columns appeared in a great many of the Tennessee weeklies. One was North Callahan's "This Is New York," a folksy, human-interest account of the fascinating sins and startling accomplishments that obtained in the Big City up north. The second feature was a column written by George S. Benson, presi-

36. *The Tennessee Country Editor* (Nashville: The East Tennessee Historical Society's Publications, 1949), No. 21.
37. *Ibid.*

dent of Harding College in Searcy, Arkansas. A talented promoter, Benson had put his tiny Baptist school solidly on the map by skillfully marketing an amalgam of fundamentalist evangelism, political arch-conservatism, and militant anticommunism. In 1957, Benson was touring Sweden, reporting back to his credulous rural constituency on the abundant evils of socialism.

Weekly editors as a rule editorialized infrequently and were more often content to let the likes of H. V. Kaltenborn edit the news. When prompted to editorialize, however, they were seldom inclined to temporize or to trifle with nuances or subtleties. In personal columns more often than not adorned by a folksy, vernacular sobriquet—such as "As I Was Thinkin," or "Just Knockin' Around"—the publisher-editor might remind his fellow countians that the March of Dimes, Fire Prevention Week, the Boy Scouts, Robert E. Lee's birthday, local civic clubs, the county Red Cross chapter, TVA, 4-H clubs, and National Newspaper Week were good things and deserving of community support. Reckless driving, grass fires, rabies, labor racketeers, Communists, outside agitators, and population loss were bad things and should be curbed. The latter evil—population decline—was particularly distressing to civic-minded county editors.

Because of the general decline of agriculture, most weeklies vigorously supported local attempts to lure in industries of the shirt-factory variety to add needed payrolls. These editors ceaselessly prompted citizens to vote yes on bond issues for this purpose, often urged workers to vote no on labor union elections, and cautioned all county residents to avoid the crowded big city and patronize the local merchants who advertised in their pages.

A few county weeklies were fortunate enough to have their horizons broadened by an editor who had spent his apprenticeship on a metropolitan daily. As a case in point, several reporters trained by the Nashville *Tennessean* eventually migrated to the hinterlands to have a go at running their own newspapers. James Charlet left the *Tennessean* for the nearby Clarksville *Leaf-Chronicle,* where he lent to that daily and the three weeklies it also published a progressive editorial stance that made itself felt throughout the northwestern corner of Middle

Tennessee and nearby Kentucky. Sam Neal moved to the Carthage *Courier* in Smith County, Gilbert Yarbrough to the Hickman County *Times,* and H. V. Wells left to publish the Clinton *Courier,* where he was to prove his mettle amidst the racial violence of 1956. Finally, the distinguished Coleman Harwell quit his high metropolitan desk on the *Tennessean* to publish two weeklies in Putnam County, high in the Cumberland Plateau.[38]

But most weekly editors sprang from local stock and started a county newspaper because they felt their community deserved and needed one (and felt also that they could make a living at it), or struggled to sustain a weekly that their forebears had started for the same reasons. And if the product of these years of inward focus was more often than not a parochial, even ethnocentric little journal that sophisticated metropolitans might scorn, it was also true that this was what the readers desired. Publishing and editing a county weekly was often a grim and uncertain enterprise in an era of rural decline. If a publisher could manage to hang on, he might reflect with justifiable pride that he had managed to preserve a time-honored institution that served to bolster his community's identity and its pride, to promote its best interests, and occasionally even to prick its conscience.

Whether the emotional diatribe of the angry Hamilton County *Herald* was likely to prick anyone's conscience or not, its arresting prose should not obscure the fact that of the 151 white newspapers herein surveyed, only a handful resorted to such malediction in May of 1954. In fact, only thirty-two of Tennessee's 151 newspapers were prompted by the Brown decision to editorialize at all on the subject. Predictably, among the thirty-two were all eight of the big dailies and most of the twenty small ones. As the crisis over desegregation gathered momentum, more and more newspapers began to editorialize about it. By September 1957, when Little Rock dominated the

38. The most able emigres from the *Tennessean* left the state to pursue their careers in mass communications: David Halberstam, Tom Wicker, Hedrick Smith and Fred Graham all were tapped by the New York *Times,* and Wallace Westfeldt moved to CBS. Most eminent of the *Banner's* emigres is Ralph McGill, publisher of the Atlanta *Constitution* and *Journal.*

headlines, fifty-five of Tennessee's white newspapers commented editorially on that explosive and dramatic episode. Feelings were running so strongly by then that several of the smaller weeklies felt prompted to break a tradition of editorial silence in order to voice their concern.

In 1954, the great majority of Tennessee's newspapers that did comment editorially on the Brown decision did so in a fashion that encouraged a calm and responsible—if stoic—acceptance of the new doctrine. These editorials shared several assumptions about the decision; their common elements created an editorial pattern that predominated throughout the state.

Six newspapers, four of them major dailies, insisted that the decision was no surprise.[39] Of these six, the Nashville *Tennessean* was joined by another five dailies in suggesting further that desegregation was inevitable.[40] The *Tennessean* in Nashville and the evening dailies in Knoxville and Memphis all noted with pride that with only a few exceptions the decision had been generally well received throughout the South. Five dailies accounted in part for this phenomenon by noting that school desegregation was not altogether new to the South. In a somewhat lengthy editorial, the Chattanooga *Times* cited a field study conducted in 1953 of seventeen of the twenty-two racially integrated Southern colleges and universities. Professor Guy B. Johnson of the University of North Carolina, who had directed the study, was quoted in the *Times* as emphasizing that the transition had been on the whole a peaceful one.

Several newspapers whose editors were explicitly opposed to the decision nevertheless joined in cautioning against any rash reactions or extremism. Even in Fayette County, where seven in ten were Negro, the Fayette *Falcon*, by cautioning the authorities to "make haste slowly," explicitly urged that the time should be used to "seek solutions which would allow the change to take effect without undue

39. The Nashville *Tennessean* and *Banner*, the Memphis *Commercial Appeal*, and *Press-Scimitar*, the Clarksville *Leaf-Chronicle*, and the Maury *Democrat*.
40. The Knoxville *Journal*, the Columbia *Daily Herald*, the Cleveland *Daily Banner*, the Kingsport *News*, and the Bristol *Herald-Courier*.

haste." [41] Of all the state's newspapers, only two published in Chattanooga—the daily *News–Free Press* and the weekly Hamilton County *Herald*—had forthrightly encouraged defiance.

Sixteen editors admitted that, like it or not, the Constitution was what the Supreme Court said it was, and consequently desegregation was now the law of the land. While admitting this, however, all emphasized the need for gradualism, and several chided the National Association for the Advancement of Colored People for demanding what appeared to them as instant integration. Dailies in all four metropolises and three county weeklies comforted fearful readers by assuring them that no immediate action would be taken. The Nashville *Tennessean* noted that even Thurgood Marshall, leading attorney for the NAACP, had confessed that desegregation might take as long as five years. This was close to the estimate of the Columbia *Daily Herald*. But the Robertson County *Times* thought fifty years would be a conservative estimate. To the Hamilton County *Herald,* never was too soon.

The four dailies of the old progressive coalition that had battled the Crump machine and the poll tax (the Memphis *Press-Scimitar,* the Nashville *Tennessean,* The Knoxville *News-Sentinel* and the Chattanooga *Times*) jointly urged local leaders to begin at once at least to plan for desegregation in the schools in order that they might control events and not be controlled by them. Even the conservative Memphis *Commercial Appeal* called for "a genuine spirit of co-operation."

Finally, two small dailies and three weeklies sanguinely asserted that desegregation would probably not present their local communities with great problems. Their reasons for expressing this optimistic outlook differed interestingly. The Bristol *Virginia-Tennessean,* entitling its editorial "Court Ruling Should Be No Problem Here," reminded its readers that, because they lived in the "Upland South" where few Negroes resided, desegregation should present no real problem.[42] And, deep in the Black Belt, the Fayette *Falcon* reasoned that few problems should be anticipated in Fayette County because Negro and white teachers were paid according to the same scale, and because both Negro and

41. 30 May 1954.
42. 18 May 1954.

white schools were so crowded that "few of them can take more pupils until they are enlarged." [43] Only the Chattanooga *Times* predicted with grim realism that "Chattanooga will face great difficulties in readjusting its school system." [44]

Tennesseans had been going to racially separate schools since the time of Reconstruction. A segregated system of schools, private as well as public, was the only system they had ever known. To the white majority, at least, segregation was a proven solution to a vexing problem and it was taken for granted. When the Supreme Court declared that time-honored system to be unconstitutional, the shock was severe. Even if the larger newspapers had anticipated the decision, it is doubtful that the average reader did. None of the newspapers had adequately prepared its readers for the impact of Monday, the 17th of May. But if this was a sin of omission, it was to the credit of the profession of journalism in Tennessee that the great majority of newspapers reacted to the Brown decision with a high sense of responsibility that was strong enough to override, at least for the moment, the personal feelings of a few publishers and editors who strongly preferred segregation. Because the relationship between public opinion and press opinion is a reciprocal one, it is impossible to assess accurately the impact upon public opinion of the moderate response to the Brown decision displayed by so much of Tennessee's press (whether that moderation was expressed overtly, or simply by refraining from excited commentary.) Yet, so sudden and unexpected

43. The *Falcon* was correct in its observation that Negro and white teachers were paid according to the same scale in Tennessee. In fact, the average salary of Tennessee's 3,725 Negro teachers was slightly *higher* than that received by their 20,827 white colleagues in 1954, although both salary scales were deplorably low by national standards. Negroes received more primarily because, on the average, they had received more higher education than had white teachers. Even so, Negro teachers in 1954–1955 averaged a meager $2,933 per year and white teachers averaged $136 less. See Edward D. Ball and Patrick McCauley (eds.), *Southern Schools: Progress and Problems* (Nashville: Benson Printing Co., 1959), prepared by staff members and associates of SERS.

44. The Chattanooga *Times*, 18 May 1954. In subsequent chapters, footnotes citing the eight major dailies in the four major cities will omit reference to the city, as, the *Commercial Appeal*, the *Times*, etc.

was the Brown decision that the press was able to speak first, before latent public opinion had time to crystalize. To that degree, it would be difficult to deny that the moderating impact of the press response upon public opinion was a substantial one. That high sense of responsibility displayed by most of the press was to be severely tested in the crucible of events during the critical years that lay just ahead.

2

Two Cheers for Segregation

IF the press of Tennessee had responded to the decision to desegregate the schools with, in the main, acquiescent moderation, how would the politicians react? Their intuitive assessments of public opinion were born of years of experience in sounding out opinion while on the hustings; their reactions would constitute a revealing barometer to gauge the sentiments of their constituents on this new and volatile issue.

In late May of 1954, the Tennessee political scene was being warmed by both gubernatorial and senatorial races. The Democratic primaries were scheduled for August 5. Frank Goad Clement, the popular incumbent governor, had engineered some months earlier a revision of the state's constitution—the first since 1870—which extended the term of the governor from two to four years, but prohibited governors elected after the adoption of the new provision from succeeding themselves. Consequently, in the spring of 1954, Clement was running for his and the state's first four-year gubernatorial term. Should he win, he would be the last governor of Tennessee to enjoy six consecutive years of control of state patronage through which to strengthen his political base. Clement's ambitions for national office were known to be keen. He was believed to be particularly interested in being the vice-presidential nominee on the Democratic ticket for 1956. For Clement, the stakes of the election of 1954 were high indeed.

Shortly after the Brown decision was handed down, Clement set the tone of official comment when he said:

> I must point out it is a decision handed down by a judicial body which we, the American people, under our Constitution and law recognize as supreme in matters of interpreting the law of the land. . . . Inasmuch as no final decree has been entered, and in view of the fact that the court has invited participation by the states in further deliberation, no change is anticipated in our school system in the near future.[1]

On June 5, the governor reasserted his essentially moderate posture in the opening address of his campaign at Lebanon. The Hamilton County *Herald* stuck consistently to its guns and denounced Clement's admonition to be calm as "sissy, vapid, and pusillanomous [sic]." But the balance of the press either commended the governor's stance or remained silent.

Clement's principal opponent in the race was former Governor Gordon Browning. The *Tennessean* had long championed Browning, not without good cause, as a reform governor who had perennially broken lances with the powerful machine of Boss Crump.[2] Browning, once a hard captain of artillery, had grown corpulent over the years. He was running a poor second to the young and attractive Clement. Late in the race, Browning seized upon the issue of desegregation with the apparent intention of bolstering his faltering campaign by marshalling popular prejudices against the incumbent's moderate stand. On July 31, only five days before the primary, Browning promised that there would be

> no mixing of the races in the public schools of this state while I am governor . . . and I shall use the full influence and power of my office as governor to keep separate schools for white children and equally good but separate schools for Negro children.

Browning's new stance was in direct conflict with the moderate position traditionally assumed by the *Tennessean*. But the daily did not on

1. Quoted in *SSN*, 3 September 1954, 14. Correspondents submitting reports on Tennessee to the Southern Education Reporting Service were James Elliott and Wallace Westfeldt, staff writers for the *Banner* and the *Tennessean*, respectively.
2. See Key, *Southern Politics*, pp. 58–75; and Perry, *Democracy, passim*.

this occasion jettison Browing; by the first of August, too much political blood had been spilled to switch sides. And the *Tennessean* had come to look upon Clement as little more than an unprincipled and hypocrital opportunist—albeit a politically adroit one. Meanwhile, the *Banner* stuck by Clement, thereby producing the anomalous picture of the *Tennessean* supporting a segregationist and the *Banner* a moderate.

A third candidate, Criminal Court Judge Raulston Schoolfield of Chattanooga, entered the lists late but with a fixed purpose. Schoolfield campaigned solely on the basis of maintaining segregation in the state's public schools. He labeled the Brown decision as "arbitrary and oppressive . . . and unlawful," and counseled "legal steps to avoid and circumvent that opinion." [3]

When the votes were officially counted, Clement had polled more than twice the combined votes of his opponents. His 481,808 votes constituted a landslide over Browning's 195,156, and dwarfed Schoolfield's inconsequential 29,866.[4]

In the senatorial primary, Estes Kefauver was seeking re-election to a second term. Kefauver had been elevated from the House to the Senate in 1948 by taking advantage of one of Crump's rare political blunders. Crump had allowed his support to be split between two candidates, and Kefauver had won with a mere plurality.[5] In 1954, Kefauver sought his first endorsement by the majority as senator against Congressman Pat Sutton. Sutton had also been elected to the Congress in 1948, and he had been twice re-elected to represent Middle Tennessee's sixth district. Campaigning in a helicopter, Sutton called himself a Jeffersonian Democrat who believed that "the federal government should take a back seat to states' rights," [6] he flatly opposed the Brown decision. Sutton's sentiments appealed to the strict constructionist convictions of the *Banner,* and in endorsing Sutton the *Banner* continued its consistent policy of opposing Kefauver.

The incumbent senator was a tall, large-boned Democrat from Mon

3. Quoted in *SSN, op. cit.*
4. *Tennessee Blue Book,* 1956, pp. 375–376.
5. Key, *op. cit.,* pp. 58–59.
6. Quoted in *SSN, op. cit.*

roe County in East Tennessee. His political convictions represented a curious admixture of a native populism polished with the liberal veneer provided by the Yale Law School. These convictions, firmly held, were to plague Kefauver throughout his political life, but never enough to cause his defeat. Once, in the early fifties when the liberal Senator Hubert Humphrey of Minnesota had attempted to absolve the Democratic party of Republican charges of treason by passing a bill designed to outlaw the Communist party, Kefauver had been the *only* senator in the Congress to vote no.

In order to avoid excessively offending conservative or segregationist-minded voters, Kefauver avoided taking a firm stand on the issue of school desegregation. In 1954, he steadfastly maintained that the question of the desegregation of public schools was not properly an issue in the senatorial race.[7] He argued that the only action the Senate could take in this regard was to resolve that an amendment be made to the Constitution making segregation in public schools mandatory. But since thirty-one of the forty-eight states had statutes prohibiting segregation, it was obvious to him that the amendment would not pass. Consequently, its passage would not be attempted. "Desegregation is a local question," he concluded, "to be decided on a local level by people of both races."

This position neatly if somewhat disingenuously avoided the issue and successfully kept the senator out of political hot water—and that was all he needed to do. Sutton lost badly, 186,363 votes to 440,497.[8] Simultaneously, Sutton lost his seat in the House to Ross Bass, former postmaster of Pulaski and a man of mildly liberal inclinations that were destined to grow. Sutton subsequently was unable to defeat Bass, and he disappeared from the political scene.

By the sixth of August, when the primary votes were counted, it was clear that strident appeals to segregationist sentiment were not nearly powerful enough to overcome the customary advantages of incumbency and personal attractiveness. It would be two more years before presidential and congressional elections would once again heat

7. *Ibid.*
8. *Tennessee Blue Book*, 1956, p. 376.

up Tennessee's political atmosphere. By that time, several dramatic confrontations would have riveted the public eye on the hypersensitive question of desegregation.

The completion of the Democratic primary election in August of 1954 had signaled a temporary cease-fire in politics (in Tennessee, the November general elections were then largely a ceremonial formality in years in which no presidential contest was involved). Because the seventy-ninth biennial session of the General Assembly was not to meet until January of the following year, a sort of political and emotional relapse set in.

This respite from hortatory public clamor lasted about five months. It was broken only by the restless staccato of the *Tennessean,* first needling Governor Clement to announce that Tennessee would accept the Supreme Court's invitation to file a brief before the hearings on implementation,[9] then chastising him repeatedly for failing to do so.[10]

Throughout the summer, political observers had assumed that Clement's moderate posture implied that he would submit a brief advancing Tennessee's position. On August 18, a news story which received statewide attention reported that the Tennessee brief would propose a plan for desegregation beginning in the first grade and advancing annually with the promotion of that initially integrated class until the process was completed.[11] Newspaper accounts attributed these recommendations to Attorney General Roy Beeler. The following day, Beeler temporized and labeled the stories as "premature." Clement's administration thereafter remained curiously silent on the issue, and sources close to the governor explained that his official policy was going to be one of "watchful waiting."

Soon it became clear that no brief from Tennessee was in the offing. Political pundits guessed that Clement's inaction was motivated by two principal fears.[12] First, if suggestions were submitted, the administration thereby would place itself on record, and would consequently run the

9. 15 August 1954.
10. 5 October, 18 and 20 November 1954.
11. *SSN,* 1 October 1954, 13.
12. *Ibid.*

risk of alienating a large bloc of legislators whose support was essential to Clement's school program. Second, the possibility existed that, by filing a brief, Tennessee might place itself under the direct jurisdiction of the court sooner than if it stayed out of the case.

On August 15, the *Tennessean* strongly urged Clement's administration to submit a brief to the Supreme Court. The editorial argued that Tennessee would benefit from the exchange of information and ideas between states sharing her problem. Tennessee should not forfeit this chance to have a hand in the shaping of her future educational institutions and policies. Nothing was said for or against desegregation. On September 1, the *Banner* urged approximately the same course of action upon a governor whose candidacy it had supported. But the official silence continued.

A few days later, 716,000 children entered traditionally segregated public schools throughout Tennessee.[13] In Nashville, approximately fifty Negroes enrolled in two formerly all-white parochial schools operated by the Roman Catholic church. There were no untoward incidents. Five Negroes had applied for admission to Memphis State College, but the State Board of Education denied their request, citing the clause in the state constitution requiring segregated schools. Negroes had been attending the graduate school of the University of Tennessee at Knoxville since 1952. In 1953, the Episcopal Church–affiliated University of the South at Sewanee had admitted a Negro to its seminary for the summer session. As bi-racial school systems throughout the South opened their doors that September under the shadow of the Brown decision, school superintendents and members of boards of education from eleven Southern states met in Atlanta to discuss their new predicament.[14] But Tennessee sent no official representatives. On September 8, the *Tennessean* expressed alarm that Tennessee was not participating with her sister Southern states. By November 18, it strongly criticized Clement in a long editorial entitled "Tennessee Just Drifts." Two days later, it reiterated its displeasure.

Throughout this running monologue, most of Tennessee's news-

13. *SSN,* 3 September 1954, 14.
14. As reported in the *Tennessean,* 8 September 1954.

papers remained strangely silent. By echoing Clement's policy of silent watchful waiting, they seemingly endorsed it. But political realities were destined to force the governor's hand, for in January of 1955, the Seventy-ninth General Assembly convened. At the top of the legislature's agenda was Clement's record-breaking bill providing for an appropriation for schools of 200 million dollars for the biennium 1955–1957.[15]

As early as December 10, 1954, State Senator–elect Charles A. Stainback had elicited statewide attention with a public announcement that he intended to introduce into the legislature a bill designed to perpetuate segregation in Tennessee's public schools. Stainback was sent to the capitol by the voters of Fayette and Haywood counties. His home town was Somerville, Fayette County seat, and some two-thirds of his senatorial constituency were Negroes, although *not one* of them was registered to vote in Haywood County in 1954.[16]

15. *SSN,* 6 January 1955, 16. Clement knew that Tennessee could ill afford to have the school appropriations bill fall casualty to a floor fight over desegregation. During the school year 1954–1955, Tennessee's expenditure per pupil in average daily attendance was a dismal $197.38—an expenditure exceeding only that of Alabama, Arkansas, and Mississippi. The Southern regional average was $271.77, and this regional average was boosted by the inclusion of such relatively affluent border states as Delaware, Maryland, and Missouri. The national average was $356.09. See Ball and McCauley (eds.), *Southern Schools,* pp. 106–107. In partial exoneration, it must be added that of *all* the states in 1950, only nine surpassed Tennessee's 3.3 percent of total income spent on schools. In that same year, the 11 formerly Confederate states—those with generally the lowest per capita incomes—spent an average of 3.2 percent of their incomes on schools, whereas the remaining states spent on education an average of only 3.1 percent of their generally much higher total incomes. See Harry Ashmore, *The Negro and the Schools* (Chapel Hill: University of North Carolina Press, 1954), pp. 144–145. It is a testimony to the more recent importance attached to education in Tennessee that expenditures for education accounted for 45.6 cents of each tax dollar spent during the 1961–1963 biennium. See Green and Avery, *Government in Tennessee,* 182. Critics have charged, not without some truth, that this figure is also testimony to the slight regard with which Tennessee in particular and Southern states in general have viewed other areas of social responsibility—such as welfare, unemployment compensation, public health, and the penal system—that have attracted such a large portion of the budgets of many non-Southern states.

16. *SSN,* June 1960, p. 7.

Stainback spurned the notion of abolishing the public schools as unnecessary. He proposed instead to invoke the police power of the state

to preserve the peace, protect the health and morals, to improve the educational opportunities of all the pupils of all the public schools in the state and insure the peace, health, contentment, happiness and general tranquility of all the people of the state. . . .[17]

His proposal did not mention the legally vulnerable words white or Negro or segregation or race. Its control mechanism was contained in the broad provision stating that local school boards

shall take into consideration the educational needs and welfare of the child involved, the welfare and best interests of all the pupils attending the school . . . an*d other* [italics added] factors which the board of education may consider pertinent.[18]

Stainback noted with candor that "if the bill, incidentally, should preserve segregation in the schools, it will be the most beneficial bill ever passed by the Tennessee legislature." [19] The proposal was signed by seven other senators—all from Middle and West Tennessee, and all Democrats.

Senate Bill No. 62—the Stainback bill—was reported out of the senate committee on education on February 22 with the recommendation that it be passed by the senate in plenary session.[20] Stainback, a member of the committee, was joined by five other Democratic senators in voting for the bill; the lone dissenter was a Republican senator from Knoxville.

When the committee on education recommended that the Stainback bill be enacted, the bill was automatically referred to the calendar committee, which was to determine when the bill would be considered by the senate. By February 28, when the calendar committee met in closed executive session to consider the Stainback bill, it was known that Governor Clement's powerful forces in the legislature were not in favor of the bill.[21] On the evening of the twenty-eighth, the calendar commit-

17. Charles A. Stainback, Quoted in *SSN*, 3 February 1955, p. 16.
18. *SSN*, 6 January 1955, p. 14.
19. *SSN*, 3 February 1955, p. 16.
20. *SSN*, 3 March 1955, p. 15.
21. *SSN*, 7 April 1955, p. 16.

tee voted "by an overwhelming voice vote" to table the bill. On the following day, March 1, the angry Stainback attempted on the senate floor to force his bill from the calendar committee. The vote on his motion was fifteen to thirteen in his favor. But a majority of the 33-man senate, or seventeen votes, was needed.

Frustrated in his attempt to pass a general bill to preserve statewide segregation, Stainback shortly thereafter introduced two "local bills"—one each for Fayette and Haywood counties. A local bill was one that applied only to a county or city represented by the author. By tradition, local bills were automatically approved by both houses of the legislature and seldom vetoed by the governor. Of the few local bills that had been vetoed in the past, the great majority had been subsequently reinstated by legislatures understandably displeased by gubernatorial trespass on their traditional prerogative. In public hearings held by the senate committee on education, Fayette County Court Judge H. M. Ray had confidently declared in support of Stainback's local bills that both Negroes and whites in his county were satisfied with separate school systems.[22] He also warned that his county court had vowed not to vote any appropriations for desegregated schools. Stainback's local bills were passed by the senate, as were similar bills for Tipton and Sumner counties. But it was known that Governor Clement did not smile upon them.

The governor's forces in fact had been actively working to pass the bill for general education without amendments designed to cut off funds for desegregated schools. On March 2, the senate rejected by a voice vote Stainback's eleventh-hour attempt to append a segregationist

22. *SSN,* 3 March 1955. 15. In the anachronistic structure of county government in Tennessee, the judge was an elected official who presided over the county court of quarter sessions. As such, he was the nearest equivalent to a chief executive, but his powers were generally severely limited, forcing him to rely for authority upon whatever prestige he might possess as a high-status local politician, or upon his personal persuasive powers and knowledge of parliamentary procedure. His court generally consisted of a cumbersome body of elected officials that might include, variously, a sheriff, trustee, registrar, county court clerk and circuit court clerk, county superintendent of schools, tax assessor, and a phalanx of justices or magistrates representing the county's civil districts. See *Government in Tennessee, op. cit.,* pp. 325–44.

amendment to the bill for education. The bill was then passed by a vote of 29 to 3.

Would Clement veto the local segregation bills? There was strong evidence that he would. On March 14, Knoxville *News-Sentinel,* in an editorial written by Loye Miller, urged veto of the Stainback bills, saying:

> If the Stainback bills become law, we will have counties of our state operating school systems side by side—one under a situation where the police power of the state is involved, the others without such legislation.
>
> It would be inconsistent if not absurd to have a local law applicable to one side of a county line and an entirely different and perhaps contradictory law on the other side of that county line.

Miller was a close personal friend and strong supporter of Governor Clement. On the same day, a political columnist for the pro-Clement *Banner* also predicted that Clement would veto.

The *Banner* was right. On the evening of March 14, Clement vetoed all four of the local bills. The governor condemned the local bills unequivocally as representing "an attempt to circumvent the efficacy of the recent opinion handed down by the Supreme Court of the United States banning segregation in public schools," [23] and he warned that the bills if enacted would "foment racial hatred and disorder where none exists." The next day, Stainback pleaded with the senate for half an hour to override the governor's veto. When a vote was taken on the local bill for Fayette County, thirteen favored it and nine opposed. But seventeen votes were needed to override.

Editorial reaction to Clement's veto was generally favorable. In an editorial entitled "Logical and Sound," the Chattanooga *Times* on March 16 declared that the governor's message advocated the "patience and sound reasoning which represent the majority opinion of the people of the state. . . ." In Nashville, the two normally warring dailies joined hands to endorse Clement's veto. The *Banner* followed the custom of introducing its editorials rather elaborately by suggesting their message with both a title and a subtitle. Its one-two punch on this occasion

23. Frank G. Clement, as quoted in *SSN,* 7 April 1955, p. 16.

read: "A Time for Calm Appraisal: This Veto Should Stand." [24] The *Tennessean* was equally forthright in confessing that, for once, it was capable of agreeing with both Clement and the *Banner*.[25]

Clement had by his leadership demonstrated that a Southern governor—or at least a governor of the upper south—need not bow to segregationist demands in his legislature as the ineluctable price of political survival. The question was academic whether his veto was motivated purely by self-interested political ambitions, as the editorial staff of the *Tennessean* privately believed, or by a devotion to "statesmanlike consideration [and] prayerful thought," [26] as the governor himself described them. He had stemmed, for the moment, the segregationist tide and had thereby increased his national stature as a statesman of the Southern moderate variety while apparently not suffering serious political damage in Tennessee.

On the last day of May, 1955—a little more than one year after the Supreme Court ruled on the Brown case—the court decreed, somewhat enigmatically, that desegregation of the public schools should proceed "with all deliberate speed." The court directed the federal district courts to implement desegregation by determining that local officials make a "prompt and reasonable start." In order to ease the burden of decision thus dropped into the lap of the lower courts, the Supreme Court further directed that, in view of the paucity of useful precedent, the district courts might "properly take into account local problems."

The immediate reaction of the press to the implementing decision ranged in Tennessee from the silence of the majority to what may generally be described as an audible sigh of relief. Of the eight major dailies, five remained silent on the issue on the first day of June. No editorial on the new decree emananted from Nashville or Chattanooga, but both dailies in Knoxville expressed their pleasure with the new ruling. The *Journal* felt that the decision was "dictated by common

24. 15 March 1955.
25. "Premature and Unsound," 16 March 1955.
26. Frank G. Clement, as quoted in "Excerpts from Veto Message," *SSN,* 7 April 1955, p. 16.

sense and sound statesmanship." In a somewhat lengthy editorial entitled "Reasonable—and Right," the *News-Sentinel* emphasized that,
while the implied grant of additional time should be welcomed in the
South, it did not imply a lessening of the responsibility to act. Southern
states should "use that time for finding solutions, not for seeking
ways to defeat the high purposes and simple justice which led to this
decision." Only ten percent of the population of Knox County was Negro. But in Shelby County, where the percentage nonwhite approached
forty, Ed Meeman's *Press-Scimitar* on June 1 boldly echoed the theme
that the welcomed grant of additional time should be used not to evade
but "To Work Out Desegregation."

Yet, while the implementing decision did indeed seem to endorse
gradualism and grant additional time, it in one sense brought desegregation one big step closer to Knox and Shelby counties. For in two

Knox in the Banner

separate instances, Tennessee Negroes had already filed suit to attend
the state's white public schools. In Knoxville, five Negro students of
high-school age had petitioned the federal district court of Judge Robert L. Taylor in 1951 to attend their neighborhood high school in nearby Clinton.[27] The practice had been for eleven Clinton Negroes of high-
school age to ride a bus eighteen miles into Knoxville to attend a
Negro high school there. (In the light of later developments in the
desegregation crisis, it was ironical that the Negroes were first to object
to the principle of long-distance bussing and to demand their right
to attend neighborhood schools.) Judge Taylor had denied their plea,
citing the state constitution as his legal authority. Shortly after the

Summer School

Knox in the Banner

27. *SSN,* 6 July 1955, p. 9.

Brown decision, however, the United States Circuit Court of Appeals remanded the case back to Taylor and directed him to rule in accordance with the new decree. Taylor refused to do so until the implementing policy was decreed. During the summer of 1955, Judge Taylor accordingly reconsidered the case.

On May 26, 1955, five Negroes of college age had brought suit against the state in the federal district court at Memphis to attend Memphis State College.[28] Chief defendant in the suit was Dr. Quill E. Cope, state commissioner of education and chairman of the state board of education. In response to the suit, Cope met with the board and, on June 15, ended thirteen months of official silence by approving a two-part gradual plan for desegregation. First, Tennessee's six state-supported colleges would desegregate in five years by beginning the following September only at the graduate level, then working downward yearly. Second, Cope placed responsibility for desegregating public elementary and secondary schools squarely on the shoulders of local school officials.

Officials of the state branch of the NAACP voiced their displeasure with the new gradual plan. The five Negro students in Memphis continued their suit in the court of Federal District Judge Marion S. Boyd, who set October 17 for hearing the suit. But the major dailies, with the prominent exception of Roy MacDonald's *News–Free Press,* were favorably disposed toward the gradual approach. The *Tennessean* approved of the board's gradual approach as sensible and in good faith, but it urged the board to implement its plan in September, and not delay one additional year by waiting for Judge Boyd to rule in October.[29] The *Commercial Appeal* praised the board's "sincere gesture as both revolutionary and courageous," while roundly damning the NAACP for condemning the gradual approach.[30]

On October 18, Judge Boyd ruled unconstitutional Tennessee's constitutional provision that "no school . . . shall allow white and negro

28. *Ibid.*
29. 17 June 1955.
30. The *Commercial Appeal,* 17 June 1955. The tactic of damning the NAACP was to become a favorite means of balancing a moderate statement on the racial issue, or of simply calling attention to a newspaper's Southern credentials.

[*sic*] children to be received as scholars together in the same schools." [31] But he simultaneously denied the five Memphis Negroes their plea for immediate admission and granted approval to the board's gradual approach. To this, the *Banner,* the *Journal* and the *Times* all expressed their pleasure.[32] In Chattanooga, the *Times* was also pleased that the Chattanooga School Board had vowed eventually—but not the coming September—to desegregate that city's public schools. But the *News–Free Press* firmly asserted its regrets that the board had "so readily accepted the unconstitutional order of the Supreme Court." [33] The *News–Free Press* thought it preferable

for this community to await further rulings by lower courts and further action by those more strongly resisting, so our decisions might have the advantage of following the experience of others.

When school doors opened in Tennessee in September of 1955, no Negroes attended state schools—below the graduate level—with whites. Roman Catholic parochial schools in Nashville had survived a year of desegregation without serious disruption. Finally, the public schools in Oak Ridge desegregated in September of 1955 with only minor protest.[34] But Oak Ridge was under federal jurisdiction, and its schools—not technically a part of the state system of schools—were ordered to desegregate by the federal government in Washington. Newspapers in Tennessee took little more than judicial notice of that event. On September 21, Judge Taylor granted additional time to the officials of Anderson County's school system to prepare a plan for desegregating the county's only high school. That high school was located in Clinton— a peaceful little town of fewer than 4,000 residents who had little premonition of the turmoil that was in store for them. There was little

31. Article XI, Section 12, Tennessee Constitution of 1954, *Tennessee Blue Book, 1957–58,* 282. The year 1954 was an ironical one for the Tennessee Constitutional Convention to reaffirm such language.
32. The *Banner,* 18 October 1955; the *Journal,* 7 November 1955; the *Times,* 19 October 1955.
33. Quoted from *SSN,* August 1955, p. 16. Beginning with the edition of August 1955, *SSN* ceased citing the day of publication.
34. See *SSN,* October 1955, p 12.

doubt that Judge Taylor would order the desegregation to take place in September of 1956.

The year that transpired between the issuance of the exceedingly controversial Brown decision and the implementing decree was generally characterized by a curious, quiet lull. It was similar in some ways to the period of the so-called "phony war" in Hitler's Europe; war had been declared, but no major battles were being fought. With the exception of the legislative in-fighting over the Stainback bill, the issue of desegregation seemed almost moot. But when procedures for implementing desegregation had been decreed, prospects for genuine desegregation seemed more and more imminent. Beginning in the summer of 1955, a negative reaction began to set in. Some of the important dailies began to reflect in their editorials these increasing pressures against desegregation. A few—but, it is important to note, not all— eventually began to reflect the rising tide of Southern resentment, and to some degree thereby to sanction it.

While the *News–Free Press* had proven immediately hostile to any notions of altering the biracial system, the *Commercial Appeal* and the *Banner* had responded initially to the Brown decision with a cautious, perhaps even grudging, moderation. Yet Frank Ahlgren and "Jimmy" Stahlman shared to a considerable extent Roy MacDonald's convictions about states' rights—if not his exceptionally robust style. Their steadily increasing concern over what they deemed to be the darker side of desegregation began to be reflected more and more openly in their editorial pages. They had not really been happy with the Supreme Court since Justice Roberts's mercurial reversal of 1937—the famous "switch in time" that "saved nine" and paved the way for the court's acceptance of most of the New Deal. Now was their chance to let the public know just how unhappy they were with the modern trend toward sociological jurisprudence.

On the eve of the 4th of July, 1955, the *Commercial Appeal* initiated what was to become standard tactic on the part of the segregationist-minded press: it pointed the accusing finger of hypocrisy toward the difficulties desegregation had produced in schools of the District of Columbia. To the *Commercial Appeal,* the implications were clear enough to be summarized in the title of the editorial: "Integration Haste Unwise." On September 22, the *Commercial Appeal* once again registered its displeasure with the NAACP. The Mound Bayou, Mississippi, chapter of the NAACP had complained that agents of the FBI investigating infractions of federal law in the South were lacking in diligence and zeal, and the national headquarters of the NAACP had demanded an investigation. The *Commercial Appeal* responded to this impertinence by suggesting on September 27 that the inquiry be made a two-way affair:

Let's find out the source of all its income. Let's bring out all the facts of its financing and the backgrounds of some of its agitating friends. Let's find out, above all to what extent Red infiltrators have penetrated the NAACP.

On November 7, the Supreme Court affirmed that its ruling of 1954 against racial segregation applied also to public parks, beaches, swimming pools, and golf courses. For the *Banner,* this was too far and too fast. After first urging Tennesseans to ponder the wisdom contained in the forty-first verse of the twenty-sixth chapter of the Gospel according to Saint Matthew—to the effect that the spirit was willing but the flesh was weak—the *Banner* got on with its editorial by announcing that "This Time the High Court Has Gone Too Far." [35] The *Banner's* editorial cartoonist, Jack Knox, illustrated the theme by picturing the heedless federal juggernaut as smashing through recklessly into the proper jurisdictions of cities and states. The editorial argued from the strict constructionist premise that neither the Constitution nor any Congress or legislature had granted federal jurisdiction over state- and municipally-owned recreational facilities (Tennessee maintained fifteen state parks for whites and two for Negroes). This argument was bolstered by the practical observation that, while schools desegregated by mature students would be under the constant supervision of trained adults, the beneficently restraining hand of these adults and the controlled environment of the classroom would not be present in recreational facilities.

35. 8 November 1955.

The next day, November 9, the *Commercial Appeal* accused the court of entertaining the "preposterous" assumption that social acceptance can be forced by legal fiat. On the first day of December, Memphis' morning newspaper devoted a lengthy editorial to the argument that the Supreme Court, pressed by an impetuous NAACP, had repudiated the doctrine of gradualism and thereby alienated many Southern white sympathizers. Two days later it endorsed the proposal of Senator James Eastland of Mississippi that the South should take the offensive and actively advertise to a maliciously propagandized nation the merits of a social system of which it should be proud. The editorial concluded by striking a passing blow at a "capricious . . . Supreme Court which, in submitting to the cries of pressure groups and agitators, has moved from the field of constitutional law into that of theoretical sociology." Two weeks later, the *Commercial Appeal* de-

Too Far and Too Fast!

Knox in the Banner

clared that the NAACP presumed to speak for the vast majority of Negroes which it did not in fact represent.[36] "Sooner or later," the daily was confident, the Negro majority would "recognize the damage being done and put the meddlers in their place." To the *Banner,* the tactics of the NAACP were "arrogant, intemperate, irritating." [37]

The coincidence of four events during the early months of 1956 served to further the polarization of Tennesseans' attitudes toward desegregation. First, on the 4th of January, Judge Taylor directed officials of the public schools in Anderson County to desegregate the high school at Clinton "no later than" the next fall.[38] Thus, those Tennesseans of strong segregationist convictions were faced with the prospect of standing by helplessly as the state's precedent for the desegregation of its public schools was set in Clinton later that year. Since Governor Clement had successfully thwarted the Stainback bills, Tennessee was left with no laws specifically designed to defend segregated schools. Further, the legislature was no longer in session; it was not scheduled to convene again until January of 1957.

The second event occurred when ardent segregationists decided to march on Nashville and demand that Clement summon a special session of the legislature. On January 23, two groups of segregationists, representing two recently organized, *ad hoc* committees to maintain segregation, converged on the state house.[39] One, the Pro-Southerners, drove in a motorcade from Memphis. The other, originating in Chattanooga, styled itself the Tennessee Society to Maintain Segregation. Both motorcades were liberally decked out in American and Confederate flags and sported placards emblazoned with such slogans as "Segregation or War" and "God, the Original Segregationist." Clement heard the groups' spokesmen demand that a special legislative session be called to consider (1) ordering a constitutional convention to abolish public schools; (2) providing for the use of state funds in private grants of tuition; and (3) earmarking Negro tax money for Negro schools and white tax money for white schools.

36. 17 December 1955.
37. 24 January 1956.
38. *SSN,* February 1956, p. 9.
39. *Ibid.,* p. 8.

Clement heard them out, then courteously rebuffed their demands and criticized their heavy-handed pressure tactics. He further accused the group of being the NAACP's greatest ally in fighting for immediate integration. Like Kefauver, the governor avoided taking a stand on the issue of desegregation per se by insisting that it was a local issue and as such did not require action by the state.

The following day, January 24, the *Banner* joined the *Tennessean* in commending Clement's action. But, while the *Tennessean* concentrated its alliterative editorial censure on the "race rabble rousers," the *Banner* digressed into yet another diatribe against the NAACP. Both the *Banner* and the *Commercial Appeal* were increasingly directing their editorial firepower against the NAACP. During 1956, the *Banner* devoted nine editorials and the *Commercial Appeal* four to assaulting that symbol of Negro protest and aspirations. Both dailies had been quick to denounce racial violence, and they deplored the heavy-handed tactics of such unsophisticated groups as the Ku Klux Klan, whose unlawful protests and unimpressive personnel only served to blemish further that cause they were defending. But the two conservative dailies, while publicly castigating the Klan, nonetheless shared with it an affection for the biracial culture it sought to defend. Thus they were quick to welcome the formation of a new organization led for the most part by respectable citizens and designed to defend Southern culture through legal means only by invoking the doctrine of states' rights.

Such a new group, the Tennessee Federation for Constitutional Government, incorporated in Tennessee on 30 June 1955.[40] It was an affiliate of a loose regional federation formed earlier that year through meetings held in Atlanta and Jackson, Mississippi. President of the Tennessee chapter was Donald Davidson, Professor of English at Vanderbilt University and one of the twelve fugitive agrarians who had contributed to the volume *I'll Take My Stand* in 1930. The purpose of the group was twofold. First and most immediately, it was to organize conservative and respected Southerners to wage strictly legal warfare against desegregation. Second, it aspired in the long run to publicize the doctrines of strict construction under the banner of states'

40. Hereafter referred to as the Federation. See Muse, *Ten Years of Prelude*, pp. 95–99.

rights.[41] When Jack Kershaw, a spokesman for the federation and one of its more erratic promoters,[42] suggested in February that Nashville abandon its parks and that Tennessee abandon the public schools rather than desegregate them, the *Tennessean* reacted with a stinging, scornful editorial entitled "This Way Lies Madness." [43]

A third event—or rather, series of events—that furthered the polarization of attitudes in Tennessee was the outbreak of racial violence that accompanied the court-ordered admission of a Negro coed to the state university of neighboring Alabama. On February 1, twenty-six-year-old Autherine Lucy registered at the 125-year-old campus at Tuscaloosa. On Friday, February 3, she attended her first classes and encountered little more than quiet curiosity.[44] But by Saturday night, the unhappy confluence of high emotional tension on the part of some students, alcohol, the presence of numerous agitating nonstudents, and the conspicuous absence of police conspired to produce a mob. The following Monday, the uncontrolled mob seriously threatened Miss Lucy's life. The ensuing violence was severe, an angry and distraught Miss Lucy accused university officials of conspiring in it, and the trustees of the university voted to suspend her.

Dailies in Chattanooga, Nashville, and Memphis all decried the resort to mob rule. All agreed that a lesson was to be learned from Alabama's unhappy experience, but they differed significantly on what that lesson should be. The *Times* and the *Tennessean* emphasized that the issue

41. See *SSN,* August 1955, 1, pp. 16–17; and "Serious and Far-Reaching," The *Commercial Appeal,* 27 January 1956.

42. While the *Banner* publically welcomed and supported the efforts of the Federation, Stahlman was aware that the group contained an irresponsible element—what the press had come to call the "lunatic fringe" of such activist citizens' lobbies—and it would be unfair to imply that the *Banner's* embrace of the Federation was *carte blanche.* Stahlman has insisted in a letter to the author that "while The Banner was in sympathy with some of the positions of the Tennessee Federation of Constitutional Government, we never subscribed to some of the extreme positions of Mr. Davidson, and we positively neither wanted nor had any part of Jack Kershaw," 1 July 1966.

43. 29 February 1956.

44. For a detailed account, see *SSN,* March 1956, 6–7; and Muse, *op. cit.,* pp. 53–54.

was no longer one of segregation versus desegregation. They contended, rather, that it was one of law and order versus the anarchy of the mob.[45] The *Tennessean* was critical of the NAACP's choice of Miss Lucy on the grounds that her age, her tendency to over-dress, her Cadillac escort, and her generally haughty demeanor were ill-suited to achieve successful integration. It further criticized her apparently unfounded charges that university officials had "conspired" in the mob violence. But it nevertheless defended her right to attend, and it charged that the trustees had capitulated to anarchy. Tom Little, the *Tennessean*'s Pulitzer Prize–winning editorial cartoonist, equipped Mr. Mob Rule in Alabama with hood and bullwhip.

'I Am the Law'

Tom Little in the Tennessean

45. The *Times*, 2 March 1956; the *Tennessean*, 12 February 1956.

In an editorial entitled "No Klan—No Carpetbaggers," the *Banner* strongly disapproved of the mob, but it reserved most of its fire for the carpetbag mentality that creates havoc in its zeal to achieve major social gains immediately.[46] The long editorial concluded with a few kind words for the Virginia interpositionists and a few not-so-kind for the NAACP. The *Banner* once again elaborated on the latter theme on March 2 by addressing sixty-three editorial lines to the iniquities of its familiar nemesis, the NAACP. Knox's editorial cartoon in the *Banner* faithfully echoed the editorial thesis (Knox's carpetbagger always seemed to bear a striking and, one might guess, not wholly fortuitous resemblance to Senator Estes Kefauver).

The *Commercial Appeal* was alarmed by the mobs. It called editorially for the organization in Memphis of a committee of moderates who would work to preserve mutual trust among the races and attempt to weed out any threat of racial strife or violence.[47] (State Senator Stainback shortly thereafter told a segregationist rally in Memphis that the policies of both Memphis dailies were dictated by the carpetbag sentiments of their Northern owners.)[48]

Symptomatic of the growing Southern resentment toward desegregation was the reactivation of the old Jeffersonian doctrine of interposition. The doctrine held that a state could "interpose" its sovereign veto against the federal government if the latter trespassed on areas in which the states were granted exclusive jurisdiction by the Constitution.[49] The term "interposition," then, was essentially a euphemism for nullification. The governors of South Carolina, Georgia, and Virginia were talking loudly of interposition, and the editors of the *News–Free Press,* the *Banner,* and the *Commercial Appeal* told their readers that the doctrine was valid and merited a test. The *Banner* pointed out in February and again in March that such illustrious forebears as Jefferson, Madison, and Calhoun had understood the Constitution in this

46. 10 February 1956.
47. *SSN,* March 1956, p. 15.
48. *Ibid.*
49. See "Legal Expert Explains Interposition Doctrine," *SSN,* March 1956, pp. 1–2.

way (understandably, there was no mention of Tennessee's own Andrew Jackson, who as President had taken a dim view of South Carolina's attempt at nullification.) The *Banner* even went to the trouble on March 2 of unearthing and reprinting a letter the aging Jefferson had written in 1823 to Associate Justice William Johnson—one of Jefferson's own appointees to the bench—outlining the strict constructionist understanding of the Constitution. But the *Tennessean* was quick to point out that interposition represented no more than a completely ineffective protest against desegregation. Even the admittedly segregationist attorney general of Tennessee, George McCanless (Beeler had died the previous year), confessed that interposition was "a vague governmental doctrine with no judicial recognition." [50]

The *Commercial Appeal,* however, was so interested in the possi-

Troubles Travel in Pairs

Knox in the Banner

50. Quoted in the *Tennessean,* 31 January 1956.

bilities of interposing state sovereignty against desegregation that it ran a special article on it in its huge Sunday edition of January 28. The article was a report on an extensive survey that James Ewing, the daily's capitol reporter, had made to sound out the sentiments of politicians and other opinion leaders in all ninety-five counties of Tennessee. Ewing concluded that the vast majority of Tennesseans were quietly but strongly resisting desegregation. Even in the five counties in East Tennessee that contained no Negroes, Ewing had found abundant segregationist sentiment. Further, he reported, outside the big cities Negroes were satisfied with separate facilities which in Tennessee *were* usually equal. Finally, Ewing observed that the doctrine of interposition was rapidly gaining attention, particularly in West Tennessee.

Three days later, on January 31, the *Commercial Appeal* called attention to the survey in a position-paper type of editorial entitled "Tennessee and Integration." The big daily went further than merely to endorse and explain the theory of interposition. It suggested how the theory might be applied:

> Interposition is, in effect, an appeal to the court of last resort—the states. Under the Virginia plan, an amendment would be proposed to the Constitution declaring that the Supreme Court has the authority to order desegregation in the state, a kind of reverse-English approach that would become effective only if three-fourths of the states ratified it. Only thirteen opposing votes would be required to defeat it.

But the *Tennessean* on the same day pointed out the obvious fallacy that this method entailed: the Constitution would still be left as it was when the Supreme Court ordered desegregation. Nevertheless, Frank Ahlgren's enthusiasm was undampened.

This backdoor or "reverse-English" method of overturning the Brown decision was consistent with the finest traditions of Southern ingenuity in matters pertaining to Constitutional construction. But the initiating steps would have to be taken in the Congress. Thus it would be useful if some method could be devised whereby Southern congressmen who were unhappy about desegregation and who subscribed to the doctrine of states' rights could, through some dramatic public gesture, stand and be counted to impress the nation—and themselves—with their numbers and power. Such a gesture would exert extreme pressure on Southern legislators who were guilty of foot-dragging on the racial question to conform to the accepted code. The device designed to accomplish this rallying of the troops was not long in forthcoming. On March 12, Southern congressmen introduced into both houses of the Congress a document, ultimately to be signed by 101 Southern congressmen, entitled "Declaration of Constitutional Principles." The debate over interposition had thus culminated in the signing of the so-called Southern Manifesto—the fourth event to further the polarization of attitudes toward desegregation in Tennessee during the early months of 1956.

The *Banner* and the *Commercial Appeal* were immensely proud of this "mild and temperate document," [51] outlining as it did the high principles of states' rights. And Roy MacDonald's *News–Free Press* was predictably delighted. The *Banner* carefully and emphatically insisted that its quarrel with the Supreme Court was not merely that of a disgruntled segregationist. The *Banner*'s habit of couching its defense of segregation in the rhetoric of states' rights was a familiar phenomenon in Southern journalism. When the drift away from accepting the Brown decision set in, it took the form, not of a straightforward defense of segregation per se, but of the identification of segregation with other principles, such as states' rights, which could be better defended. The *Banner* did openly embrace segregationist assumptions, to be sure, but it insisted that the fundamental issue at stake was ultimately less concerned with the segregation of races than with the segregation of the three branches of government. The issue, to Stahlman's *Banner,* was not simply one of bad social thinking. It was one of trespass.

Eight of Tennessee's eleven congressmen signed the document. The *Banner* registered faint surprise that Senator Albert Gore—who was up for re-election in two years—had failed to sign. It was further disappointed that Nashville's able and senior representative, Democratic Whip of the House J. Percy Priest, had also failed to sign. But it was

51. Both editorials were published on 13 March 1956. Alley's cartoon shows only ninety-seven signers. Four more signed soon after March 13, to total 101.

not in the least startled that Senator Estes Kefauver—an active candidate for the Democratic presidential nomination—had refused to go
along. The *Banner*'s Knox joined the *Commercial Appeal*'s Cal Alley in
picturing the manifesto as a philosophical statement of high political
principle, noble in purpose, which opportunistic northern liberals might
denigrate but could never really comprehend.

In Nashville, the *Tennessean* took the manifesto and its signers
soundly to task.[52] Its editors bluntly pointed out that the manifesto, de-

Handed Down From Higher Up

Alley in the Commercial Appeal

52. 13 March 1956.

spite its impressive pretensions, amounted to "nothing more than a collective protest" against the Brown decision. It was constitutionally binding on no one. The editorial reminded enthusiastic supporters of the manifesto that the only meaningful defensive action that segregationists could take would be to pass a constitutional amendment specifically guaranteeing to the states the right to operate racially separate schools. And the chances of getting the necessary thirty-six states to ratify such an amendment, the *Tennessean* noted, were slim indeed. In his editorial cartoon, Tom Little depicted the manifesto as generating great heat but little light. On March 14, the *Tennessean* explicitly commended three of Tennessee's nine congressmen who had refused to be pressured into signing the manifesto—three whose candidacies it had supported—as "Three Above Expediency."

By the early summer of 1956, official policy in Tennessee continued to follow the path of moderation, while in Virginia to the north and in Georgia to the south, talk of massive resistance to desegregation and of defiantly abolishing public schools had carried the day. Unlike many of her sister Southern states, Tennessee had passed no new

"And On The Other Side

Knox in the Banner

All Heat and No Light

Tom Little in the Tennessean

laws designed to circumvent desegregation. Her governor continued to stand his ground on a policy of moderation. Finally, powerful voices within the press continued to maintain a posture of gradualistic acquiescence to the Supreme Court's revolutionary decree. The social and political climate in Tennessee seemed to be different—not totally committed to maintaining segregation whatever the costs.

But other powerful voices within the press were hedging on their initial stoic acceptance of the implications of the Brown decision. Not yet willing to assault frontally the very notion of desegregation, these newspapers increased attacks on the supporters of desegregation—the NAACP and northern liberals—and priase for the defenders of a theory of constitutional construction on which segregation was based. There had, moreover, been no actual desegregation of public schools in the state system since that memorable Monday in May of 1954. When such desegregation did finally occur, it would be catalytic. The supreme test still lay ahead. For early in September, five Negroes were scheduled by court order to enter a previously all-white high school at Clinton.

3

The Crucible at Clinton

FACED with the prospect of imminent desegregation at Clinton, Tennessee's newly organized and highly vocal segregationist groups spent the summer of 1956 generating a rising chorus of dissent. While most of the drumfire was directed at the allegedly usurpacious Supreme Court, much of it was reserved for Governor Clement and Senator Kefauver. Both were loudly accused by the segregationists of being lured by the siren song of national political ambition into betraying the segregationist sentiments of their Southern constituencies. Clement was to make the keynote speech to the Democratic national convention that summer, and Kefauver was to emerge from that convention as the party's vice-presidential nominee. Both men were well aware of the high premium placed in Democratic circles on Southern moderates who, as vice-presidential nominees, could woo the Southern vote while not alienating Northern liberals.

In July, the Federation sponsored a speech by Senator J. Strom Thurmond, Democrat from South Carolina. Thurmond, who had been the presidential candidate of the Dixiecrats in 1948, was enthusiastically introduced in Nashville by none other than James G. Stahlman.[1] Later in July, the Federation joined three Memphis-based segregationist groups—We the People, Citizens Council of Shelby County, and Pro-

1. *SSN.* July 1956, 7. The *Banner* energetically advertised Thurmond's appearance and praised him editorially as a "distinguished statesman" and a "great soldier." The *Banner*, 17 June 1956.

Southerners—in sponsoring a speech by Senator James Eastland, Democrat from Mississippi.[2] Speaking in Memphis, Eastland impugned the motives and attacked the performance of the Supreme Court by denouncing those recent "procommunistic" decisions that had "woven a web of protection around the Communist party." [3]

During July, some 308 candidates for the state legislature intensified their campaigns as the Democratic primary, scheduled for August 2, drew near. Despite the efforts of the segregationist groups, however, the question of desegregation largely failed to materialize as a hotly contended issue in the campaign. That almost all candidates affirmed their preference for segregation accounted in part for this phenomenon. But few, on the other hand, were willing at this time to stand, like Horatius at the bridge, in bold defiance of court-ordered desegregation. This relative torpor disturbed the Federation, which consequently mailed a questionnaire to all of the candidates, demanding of them a firm stand on the issue. Only 100 candidates, or fewer than one third, bothered to return the questionnaire. Further, one fifth of those willing to respond disagreed with the tactics proposed by the Federation. Still, enough vociferously segregationist legislators were elected, especially from the counties surrounding Memphis and Chattanooga, to insure that the Clement administration would be presented with a number of segregationist bills when the General Assembly reconvened in January of the following year. With Tennessee and Southern eyes increasingly focusing on the issue of desegregation, legislators would be under considerable pressure to vote for such bills. The degree to which the press supported these bills would be vitally important.

Late in August the Federation made a last-ditch attempt to prevent desegregation in Clinton by legal means. On Monday, August 20, fifteen Negroes had registered at Clinton High School. Two days later, the Federation filed a suit in Anderson County Chancery Court seeking to enjoin the principal of the high school from admitting the Ne-

2. The bromide had long circulated among newsmen that the two southernmost points in the United States were Key West, Florida, and "Jimbo" Eastland.
3. *SSN,* August 1956, p. 13.

groes.[4] On the 27th, Chancellor Joe M. Carden dismissed the suit as being without merit, and the Federation immediately appealed to the state supreme court.[5] But its eleventh-hour appeal had run into the twelfth; the orderly process of desegregation continued unhindered at Clinton, and there was every reason to believe that the town had stoically accepted the change.

But on Saturday afternoon, the 25th, a tall, somewhat austere looking young man of twenty-six appeared in Clinton. He identified himself as Frederick John Kasper, executive secretary of the Seaboard White Citizens Council.[6] A native of New Jersey, Kasper operated out of Washington, D.C., where he had worked in a bookstore. Saturday and Sunday Kasper conducted a door-to-door campaign, asking parents whether they wanted their children to go to school with "niggers" and urging them to picket the school in protest against desegregation. Sunday afternoon, a group of the town's leading citizens—including Mayor W. E. Lewallen and H. V. Wells, Jr., editor and publisher of the weekly Clinton *Courier-News*—met with Kasper and asked him not to stir up trouble. They assured him that they also preferred segregation and that they had fought desegregation for five years. But now, they said, they had no legal alternative but to obey the court's order and they intended to do so. According to Wells, Kasper replied that under common law, people were superior to the courts, and if enough of them opposed a rule, they could change it.[7] But he reportedly assured the delegation that whatever he did would be peaceable.

That evening, Kasper called a mass meeting in front of the Anderson County court house. But only about fifty people heard him urge that the school be picketed and boycotted. Late that evening, the assistant district attorney swore out a warrant charging Kasper with

4. Suit was filed on August 22, 1956, and was heard and dismissed on August 27, 1956. *SSN,* September 1956, p. 3.

5. By pressing its legal action, the Federation ironically caused the state supreme court to strike down, considerably earlier than it ordinarily might have done, the clause in the state constitution requiring segregation in the schools. The court so ruled on 5 October 1956.

6. *SSN,* September 1956, p. 3.

7. H. V. Wells, Jr. as quoted in *SSN,* September 1956, p. 5.

vagrancy and inciting a riot. Kasper was promptly jailed in lieu of $5,000 bond. The *Tennessean* took judicial notice of Kasper's jailing and approvingly if prematurely hailed his "Mission [as] Unaccomplished." [8]

When school opened Monday morning, fewer than a dozen teenagers were present to picket the high school. They displayed crudely painted cardboard signs denouncing the presence of the Negroes. One grinning, crew-cut youth carried a sign calling for a "Strike Against Intergration [*sic*] of Clinton Hi." But when twelve of the fifteen Negro enrollees showed up for classes and entered the school, three of the picketing students put down their signs and dutifully entered the school also. The day passed quietly and without major incident.

On Tuesday, Kasper was freed from jail on the grounds that evidence in support of the charges against him was lacking. He promptly went to the school, accompanied by about two dozen adults, and demanded that the principal, D. J. Brittain, Jr., either "run the Negroes off or resign." The forty-one-year-old principal said he would resign only if 51 percent of the parents of school children wanted him to. That evening approximately 500 people attended yet another mass meeting held at the courthouse, where Kasper handed out pamphlets explaining his intention to form a White Citizens Council in Clinton, and invited all to join him in marching on Clinton high school the next morning.

Early Wednesday, the 29th, Kasper appeared at the school accompanied by about twenty-five teenagers and seventy-five adults. The restive crowd was emboldened by the strength of its numbers, and it soon grew ugly. About half of the crowd chased down and beat a Negro boy, and three Negro students had to be rescued and escorted into the school by members of the football team. Inside the school building the students met in assembly without the presence of teachers and voted 614 to 0 that Brittain should keep his job (attendance had dropped by about fifty to sixty students that day). When asked to poll their parents on the same question, they returned the next day with a tally of 447 to 6 in favor of retaining the principal.

8. 29 August 1956.

Wednesday evening, Kasper again held a mass meeting in front of the old brick court house. This time Kasper's hard core of acolytes was augmented by about a thousand curious onlookers. Kasper's speech was briefly interrupted when a United States marshal presented him with a warrant temporarily restraining him from hindering or impeding desegregation at the school. The restraining order had been issued at the request of apprehensive local officials by Federal District Judge Robert Taylor of Knoxville. After hearing the restraining order read, Kasper continued to exhort the crowd. The next morning, the *Tennessean* expressed approval of Judge Taylor's order and pleasure in the students' vote of confidence in Brittain.

Thursday was the publication day of Clinton's weekly newspaper, the *Courier-News*. On this Thursday, the 30th of August, editor Wells earnestly beseeched his four thousand subscribers to take serious thought about the future of their normally quiet little community. Wells began his editorial by affirming that he and the great majority of his neighbors preferred segregation:

We have never heard anyone in Clinton say he wanted integration of students in the schools, but we have heard a great many of the people say: "We believe in the law. We will obey the ruling of the Court. We have no other lawful choice." 9

Wells was convinced that the majority felt as he did because 803 students had showed up for desegregated classes on that first day of school.

in spite of the picket lines, in spite of the rain and in spite of all the trouble that had been brought on the community by a man who has absolutely no interest in the community, no faith in our government and no belief in the orderly processes of law—by his own admission.

The editor reminded his readers that he had "personally urged the county court to carry on the fight *to maintain segregation,* and we appeared before the board of education and made the *same plea* there." But, "now that the Supreme Court has spoken, we believe in obeying the law." Wells identified Kasper by name, labeled him as a smart trouble-

9. "As We See It." the Clinton *Courier-News,* 30 August 1956.

maker who had nothing to lose, and presciently warned that "when he leaves, the scars on the community will mark his passing."

But Wells knew his readers well enough to know that, like most Americans, they would harken less attentively to general caveats than to specific ones which touched upon their sensitive pocketbooks:

The trouble this man Kasper is creating will serve only two purposes—to line his pockets with membership fees he will collect and turn this community upside down—bringing us headlines throughout the country, headlines that will make it practically impossible to interest new *industries* to come and locate here, that will drive away people who might want to come here and build homes.

And as for the omnipresent allegation that desegregation served the cause of the Communists:

This country of ours was founded on the Constitution—and Kasper would have you throw away the Constitution. He calls others Communists, but he is using the very same tactics they use, and the end result of his efforts—should they be successful—would be mob rule, and that is just what the Communists would like, too.

Wells then closed his editorial with a final supporting argument which was in fact something of a *non sequitur:* "This is a democracy—if 803 students and their parents are willing to accept the ruling of the court and attend school, then the majority certainly has ruled and that should be the final decision." Kasper had earlier enunciated to Wells his theory that under democratic common law, local majorities could properly nullify a court order. But Wells' concluding inconsistency had perhaps gone largely unnoticed by readers of the *Courier*; they knew that Wells had addressed himself forthrightly to both their highest instincts and to their purse strings.

But on the same Thursday that the *Courier* was published, an angry crowd of 200 hurled tomatoes, stones, and billingsgate at the young Negroes as they left school. Local police arrested three whites, but Clinton's six-man force was experiencing increasing difficulties in controlling the growing mobs.

On Friday the 31st, the *Banner* strongly implied that integrationists and segregationists were equally to blame for the violence in Clinton. In an editorial once again entitled "No Klan—No Carpetbaggers," the

Banner fired its first broadside against that special bête noir, the Carpet-bag element.

Anyone who had been pressing for compulsory integration—the impatient, can't-wait element who construed the Supreme Court ruling as the privilege to light a fuse—had better pull up short and think a bit.

And as for the Klan element:

Morever, anyone who believes the time is ripe to out-Klan the Imperial Kleagle and lead a mob to storm a school, had better hie himself back to where he came from. The people are in no mood to IMPORT talent either pro or con to settle a quarrel in which they are sovereign parties of the first part.

That done, the *Banner* hinted at its assessment of the balance of blame by returning again to chastise the carpetbaggers—whom, in this case, it failed to identify by name:

Unquestionably the Carpetbag element has sought to use that Clinton situation, too. Its handiwork always is disruptive when allowed to get away with such intrusion—for it is contemptuous of Southern standards and the right of jurisdiction at the local and state level.

In Knoxville that same day, Judge Taylor convicted Kasper in absentia of contempt of court and promptly sentenced him to one year's imprisonment in a federal penitentiary. The incendiary Kasper was thereby removed as a catalytic agent from Clinton's explosive environment. But he had done his work well. As Friday ended the month and introduced the long Labor Day weekend, tensions had been generated that for three long days could not be vented upon Negroes commuting to the high school, and as a consequence the volatile situation was ripe for exploitation.

Friday evening, Asa (Ace) Carter arrived from Birmingham. Carter, president of the North Alabama White Citizens Council, stepped into a vacuum of leadership vacated by Kasper, and delivered a fiery segregationist appeal at the courthouse to a crowd estimated at 1,000.[10] Carter left town immediately after completing his speech, but

10. *SSN*, October 1956, p. 15. See generally Anthony Lewis, *Portrait of a Decade*, pp. 36–43; and Margaret Anderson's marvelously sensitive *The Children of the South* (New York: Farrar, Straus and Giroux, 1966).

the restless and youthful crowd stayed on. Soon, traffic grew increasingly congested on U. S. Highway 25—a major north-south artery that becomes Clinton's Main street within the city limits. Cars containing Negroes were singled out as appropriate vehicles upon which the mob could vent its spleen. Automobiles containing terrified Negroes were tilted, windows and windshields were smashed and tires slashed as Clinton's village constabulary stood by helplessly.

On Saturday morning, September 1, the *News–Free Press* expressed profound misgivings about Judge Taylor's stiff and summary sentence of Kasper. The *News–Free Press* harbored no fondness for Kasper's type, and it strongly disapproved of the violence at Clinton. But Roy MacDonald's daily expressed fear that justice had suffered with Kasper.

Kasper has not been shown to have been directly connected with any overt act in violation of the law. What violence has occurred has taken place in his absence. Those individuals who have committed illegal acts are the ones who deserve stiff sentences. But it appears Kasper has been seized upon because he was "available" to serve as an example and a convenient target of the court's indignation.

It was, then, a matter of protecting civil liberties:

If the unconstitutional encroachment of the Federal judiciary upon the Constitution-protected rights of the states is to be followed by judicial action to deny freedom of speech to those who dissent, we have indeed come to dangerous times.
When such far-reaching precedent is set, where will the line be drawn between what we may say and what we may not? If such rulings become accepted, they might well be applied to all who are critical and not only to agitators like Kasper.

The *News–Free Press* thought Clinton a fine example of ugly excesses "by the mob on one side and the Federal judiciary on the other"—an ugly situation that was bound to "recur in other communities that refuse to face the issue in time." And how might the issue be faced? Perhaps, the editorial suggested, by the "replacement of public schools with private ones." The editorial closed with an ominous note: "Clinton is not far from Chattanooga in miles—or in time."

That same morning, Mayor Lewallen, the board of aldermen, and Sheriff Glad Woodward appealed in desperation directly to Governor

Clement for state assistance. At 5:45 p.m., Clement responded by announcing that 100 state highway patrolmen were being sent to Clinton, and that they were to be relieved the next day by troops of the National Guard. In announcing his decision, Clement said he could not "sit back as governor and allow a lawless element to take over a town and county in Tennessee." [11] He was careful to deny any intention "to promote integration or segregation," and he further emphasized that every one of the fifty telegrams appealing for aid from Anderson County had come not from Negroes but from whites.

That evening, all the state's major segregationist groups hurried to take advantage of the news spotlight newly focused on Clinton. The Federation and four other groups co-sponsored a rally in the square.[12] Billed as the principal speaker was Judge Raulston Schoolfield, the ardent segregationist from Chattanooga. Restlessly awaiting Schoolfield's appearance, the expectant crowd of approximately 2,000 grew increasingly excited. The Clinton police, aided by a hastily recruited but heavily armed home guard, resorted to the use of tear gas grenades in a desperate attempt to buy time until the state troopers arrived. When the motorcade of state troopers finally rolled noisily into town, order was quickly restored. And when Schoolfield inexplicably failed to materialize, the disappointed crowd was dispersed.

On Sunday morning, September 2, the *Tennessean* applauded Clement's move to send state troopers and the guard into Clinton as consistent with his avowed state policy of supporting local school boards. The editorial even hinted that state assistance had been belated. In Memphis, the Sunday edition of the *Commercial Appeal* also carried an editorial approving of the governor's action, while at the same time asserting that "had the state taken proper action in time matters would not have reached the stage where they are a disgrace to Tennessee and a challenge to its sovereign authority." But the *Commercial Appeal* could not resist adding an *obiter dictum*: "that

11. Quoted in the *News Free–Press,* 1 September 1956.
12. Co-sponsoring the rally with the Federation were the Tennessee Society to Maintain Segregation, the States' Rights Council of Tennessee, the Pro-Southerners, and the White Citizens Councils.

the situation resulted from efforts to impose upon the people of Clinton the Supreme Court's sociological school decision is now beside the point."

Later that morning, seven big M-41 tanks and three armored personnel carriers rumbled into Clinton. The heavy armor led a contingent of 633 battle-equipped national guardsmen under the command of State Adjutant General Joe W. Henry.[13] Newspapers around the world carried an arresting wirephoto of a bemused Clintonian staring incredulously at a 50-ton army tank which in turn was squatting anomalously in a maple-shaded lane. Gazing down from atop the tank, an equally bemused tank crew appeared similarly perplexed as to just what the appropriate target for their ninety-millimeter cannon might be. That evening, General Henry's troops fixed bayonets and dispersed a crowd that had gathered again in the square. The next day, September 3, Henry issued orders prohibiting outdoor assemblies within Clinton, outdoor public speaking, parking or assembling in the courthouse square after 6 p.m., and the use of public address systems out of doors. Henry also dispatched an expeditionary force of two tanks and seventy-one troops to quell racial violence that had spread to the nearby mining community of Oliver Springs.

That afternoon the *Banner,* which did not publish on Sundays, editorially approved of Clement's decision to send troops. Simultaneously, the *Times* in Chattanooga applauded the governor's action and condemned Kasper's appeal as "sheer white supremacy." Kasper could find no friends in the press, and Clement could find few critics.

When the high school reopened Monday morning, all twelve Negroes attended, but only 257 of the 803 white students showed up. Principal Brittain claimed that a campaign of intimidation was being waged in the county to keep the students out of school. But county officials remained firm, and attendance steadily rose. By September 11, the last detachment of the national guard had left Clinton, and by the 15th Brittain reported that his school was once again operating on a normal basis.

13. *SSN,* October 1956, p. 15.

As the crisis eased, Tennessee editors reflected back upon the hectic events of the preceeding days and searched for a meaning to them and a moral to be derived from them. Their reflections produced an unusual consensus. In Clinton, editor Wells indulged himself and, by proxy, his community in an essay in soul-searching.[14] Like almost all Tennessee editors who commented on the anomalous violence that had occurred in a traditionally peaceful, even sleepy little mill town like Clinton, Wells condemned the hypocrisy of decrying outside agitators only if one disagreed with their motives. "While shouting about the principles of 'states' rights'," Wells complained, "they were denying us the right to run our own community! While yelling about the 'Communist threat', some of them were using the very tactics the communists use."

In Memphis, the *Press-Scimitar* also read "The Lesson at Clinton" to be that Southerners should understand that not all "outside agitators" were Carpetbaggers.[15] The *Press-Scimitar* called for "moderate leaders of both races [to] get busy now in all the other communities of Tennessee and the South and see to it that their towns and cities are prepared against the rash and ruthless actions that have upset Clinton." Even the *Commercial Appeal*—despite its normal tendency to equate outside agitators with Carpetbaggers—carried an editorial cartoon by Cal Alley picturing law and order giving the boot to the imported segregationist agitators in Clinton. Both dailies in Knoxville, and the *Times* in Chattanooga, also admonished against Southern hypocrisy and strife at Clinton. A small daily in Henry county, located in the northeast corner of west Tennessee and bordering on the Tennessee river and Kentucky, supported the decisions of both Governor Clement and Kentucky's Governor Chandler to respond to pleas of local officials by sending in their respective national guards.[16] The Paris *Post-Intelligencer* was responding to criticism that had been directed at the two governors by local segregationists. The editorial pointed

14. The Clinton *Courier-News,* 6 September 1956. Wells was subsequently awarded three national citations for courageous journalism.

15. 4 September 1956.

16. The Paris *Post-Intelligencer,* 13 September 1956. In Kentucky, the violence occurred at the small towns of Clay and Sturgis.

out, incorrectly, that "the Supreme Court has ruled all school students have a right to attend the school of their choice, or the one in their district." But the *Post-Intelligencer* applauded the use of the national guards in preventing outside integration and those too eager to enforce it."

Of all Tennessee newspapers, the *Tennessean* was the most vociferous in broadcasting the vital lessons learned so painfully at Clinton. During the critical period, editors of the *Tennessean* wrote ten editorials commenting directly on the incidents at Clinton. Other newspapers had been content merely to point out that outside agitators can

Get to the Seat of It

Alley in the Commercial Appeal

Clinton, Tennessee—An unruly group, fired to unrest by an Alabama White Citizens' Council leader, stops a car of Negroes in the main street. The driver sped his car away before the group could enter it.

Clinton, Tennessee—A boy on a bicycle gets a look at a National Guard tank in front of Clinton High School.

White pupils and a mother look on as Negro parents escort children to a newly integrated school.

Clinton, Tennessee—Fired to an outburst of unruliness by White Citizens' Council leader Asa Carter, a group of youths rock the automobile of Michigan Negro tourists who happened through town, going south. The driver finally sped away.

Memphis—Police Lieutenant C. F. Hill, gesturing with his thumb, orders Negro demonstrators to leave the main public library in Memphis. When they refused, forty-one were arrested, including reporters and photographers for two Memphis Negro newspapers.

Clinton, Tennessee—Guard tanks rumble slowly past the Anderson County courthouse that has been cleared of spectators and take up positions in the event of another outbreak.

work both sides of the street. But the *Tennessean* went them one better. Its editorials broadened the ranks of segregationist agitators to include "white-collar race baiters"; it painted with the same brush Kasper's irregulars and Professor Davidson's elite. On the 5th of September, the *Tennessean* extracted from a news story about the violence at Clinton a quotation of remarks reportedly made by a millworker there, and based its editorial on the quotation. The millworker was reported to have said:

It's not only outsiders like this guy Kasper from up there in Washington that causes our troubles; its those guys from other parts of Tennessee and the South. They outa stay the hell out of here.

The *Tennessean* addressed its editorial specifically to the Federation, and entitled it, bluntly, "Stay the Hell Out." First, the editorial pointed out, the august title appropriated by the segregationist organization—the Tennessee Federation for Constitutional Government—was an ironical misnomer because the political philosophy embraced by the group was in fact tantamount to anarchy. In brazenly calling for defiance of the Supreme Court, the organization was in fact subverting the principles of law and order to which its title so impressively alluded. Furthermore, the Federation had hurriedly dispatched to Clinton from Nashville its vice-president as an official spokesman to preach its message of defiance to the volatile crowd gathered around the courthouse there. Yet this spokesman, the sometime artist and realtor Karl (Jack) Kershaw, "was so brazen as to preface his harangue in Clinton Saturday night with the absurd statement that he had intruded upon that community 'to help you maintain peace.'" In huckstering the "fatuous line" that compulsory segregation had not been—and in effect, could not be—outlawed in Tennessee by the nation's highest tribunal, the Federation was perpetrating a "cruel hoax that can only add confusion at a time when enlightenment is needed." It was in fact astonishing, mused the *Tennessean*, that the Federation's legal advisers seemed actually to believe their own propaganda. The language employed by the Supreme Court in striking down compulsory racial segregation in the schools had been abundantly clear. Subsequently, first Federal District Judge Marion Boyd in Memphis, then Chancellor William J. Wade in Nashville, and most recently Chief Justice A. B. Neil of the supreme court of Tennessee had specifically told the Federation that their repeated attempts to block desegregation legally were wholly without merit. The final absurdity had followed the latter verdict. Counsel for the Federation had solemnly pronounced that he was going to appeal his reversal to the Supreme Court of the United States! Were the vainglorious efforts of the Federation not so dangerous, they would be comic. "The finest service the great legal minds" of the Federation could perform, in fact,

would be to quit giving so much unsolicited advice and start taking a little for a change.

And none is more appropriate, where Clinton is concerned, than the invitation to "stay the hell out"!

Ten days later, Kasper spoke to a segregationist rally held in Birmingham, urban citadel of segregation.[17] In a widely reported diatribe, Kasper proudly styled himself a "rabble-rouser," and appealed for "all the rabble-rousers we can get."[18] "We want trouble and we want it everywhere we can get it," he shouted. "A collapse of law and order is at hand! Our legal fight is finished." The purpose of his White Citizens Councils, Kasper forthrightly asserted, was "seizing local control of local affairs—and I mean seizing it." He then announced his intention of returning to Tennessee in one week to "organize Tennessee county by county."

In reporting Kasper's remarks and threat, the *Tennessean* was careful in an acerbic editorial to link Kasper, the "incendiary interloper" from Washington, inevitably with his ideological bedfellows in Tennessee. The latter were, the editorial explained, "home-grown bigots" of the white-collar variety who had confessedly "pinch hit" for Kasper after he was jailed in Clinton. The editorial specifically identified the Federation and two lesser segregationist organizations as prime examples of this home-grown bigotry. The Federation, stung by the *Tennessean*'s constant ridicule and frustrated by its series of legal reversals,

17. Kasper was out of jail on bond pending his appeal of Judge Taylor's sentence of one year's imprisonment for contempt of court.
18. As reported in the *Tennessean,* 16 September 1956.

turned in desperation to the federal district court in Nashville. It asked Federal District Judge William E. Miller to declare unconstitutional the Fourteenth Amendment to the Constitution.[19] Sims Crownover, an attorney for the Federation, argued that the court should take cognizance of the irregular fashion in which the amendment had been ratified ninety-one years previously and consequently declare the amendment to be null and void. Judge Miller politely declined to do so. He said that he did not doubt Crownover's sincerity nor deny the validity of the historical evidence Crownover had marshalled in support of his claim. But Miller also observed that much good had resulted from the amendment, regardless of the manner in which it was ratified. Furthermore, he noted that the Supreme Court had held in *Coleman* v. *Miller* that the manner of ratification was a political question and as such was not justiciable.

The sad plight of the Federation was in many ways typical of the fate of white-collar segregationist organizations in Tennessee. In Mississippi, Hodding Carter had referred scornfully to such groups as "uptown klans." But Carter's *Delta Democrat–Times* was a lonely if courageous voice that was largely ineffectual beyond the immediate vicinity of Greenville. Newspaper consensus in Mississippi strongly supported the segregationist movement, and Mississippi's White Citizens Councils not only prospered as respectable and powerful private organizations, but their goals and methods were granted official blessing and public finance in the form of a State Sovereignty Commission. In Tennessee, a governor ambitious for national office avoided the embrace of such groups as that of a tar baby, and the courts turned deaf ears to their desperate pleas. And—no less important—in Tennessee, major journalistic voices held them up in public ridicule and insisted that they could not advance their defiant cause and still remain respectable. The *Banner* had warmly welcomed the Federation to the lists and had watched with distress as the segregationist lobby had abortively tilted with the judges. Frustrated by the coolness of the judges and constantly stung by the *Tennessean*'s biting sarcasm and slashing satire,

19. *SSN,* November 1956, p. 6.

the Federation was never able to achieve that vital degree of respectability that was the key to the success of the White Citizens Councils in Mississippi.

The passions stirred by Kasper and his new recruits in Clinton did not die easily. On November 17, a jury composed of citizens of Anderson County acquitted Kasper of state charges of sedition and inciting to riot.[20] Despite a warning from the judge, the verdict was greeted by a loud cheer from approximately 200 partisans who had jammed the courtroom. In a rambling, contumacious defense of his actions, Kasper had spoken for half an hour about Negroes, the "Communistic Supreme Court," "the dirty press," and "the Jew-led National Association for the Advancement of Colored People." Several hundred people, mostly poorly educated farmers and millhands, had come to regard the tall, brooding Kasper with intense devotion.

Kasper's acquittal was greeted as a rallying cry by his temporarily dispirited devotees. Shortly thereafter, 107 students from Clinton, Lake City, and Norris high schools formed Tennessee White Youth, a sort of white citizens council for teenagers. The girls wore white turtle-neck sweaters emblazoned with the stars and bars. At Clinton High School, a hard core of these ardently segregationist students, estimated by teachers to range from forty to fifty, began a systematic campaign of harassment against the Negro students.[21] Rocks and eggs were thrown at the Negroes, ink was spilled in their lockers, malicious trippings became frequent in the halls and on the stairs, and epithets and vile insults were hurled at the hapless young Negroes. In addition, the window of Mayor Lewallen's furniture store was surreptitiously smashed, and a private detective was employed by Kasper's group to investigate the high school's asthenic, balding and bespectacled, but determined principal.

The Negroes withstood one week of this intimidation, then they refused in a body to return to school unless their safety were guaranteed,

20. *SSN,* December 1956, p. 5. No Negroes sat on the jury.
21. *Ibid.* See also Wilma Dykeman and James Stokely, *Neither Black nor White* (New York: Rhinehart & Co., Inc. 1957) pp. 350–356; and Anderson, *op. cit.*

and two of the twelve Negroes vowed never to return to Clinton High School. But the school board responded that it could not make such a guarantee, and the resulting stalemate implied victory for Kasper's newly chartered Clinton White Citizens Council and its teenage affiliate. Thus emboldened by its heady success, the council fielded a slate of candidates to test its strength at the polls in the municipal elections scheduled for December 4.

In response to this new outburst of harassment, the *News-Sentinel* in nearby Knoxville drearily catalogued "More Woe at Clinton." [22] Its editorial criticized county officials, and especially members of the school board, for being evasive and failing to back up the courageous Brittain. "What started out last August as a noble experiment," complained the Knoxville daily, "has become a sorrier mess than ever." Loye Miller additionally registered his displeasure at reports that his friend Frank Clement was leaning in a "prosegregation" direction. On the same day, November 29, the *Tennessean* rhetorically asked, "Is This 'A Way of Life'?" If so, the *Tennessean* replied, it was not worth preserving.

On Monday, December 3, the Reverend Paul W. Turner, minister of Clinton's largest Baptist church, persuaded the Negroes to agree to return to school on the condition that he would escort them.[23] The next morning, the white, thirty-three-year-old minister walked up Foley Hill—the area Clintonians referred to as their "niggertown"—and escorted six Negro boys and girls down the hill toward the high school. Turner was soon joined by the mayor's son and an accountant from nearby Oak Ridge, and together the three white adults led the Negro students past the familiar gauntlet of jeering whites and into the school. On his way home, the young preacher was waylaid by a gang of angry white men and one woman and battered bloodily to the sidewalk. News of this event startled and electrified Clinton. Brittain had that morning warned the student body that further incidents would result in expulsion (one youth tested the principal's resolve by shoving

22. 29 November 1956. Within half a year, Brittain was awarded and accepted a fellowship to pursue his doctorate in education in New York.

23. Dykeman and Stokeley, *op. cit.*, pp. 352–354. See also a special report in *SSN*, January 1957, pp. 6–7.

a Negro girl in the hallway; Brittain expelled him on the spot). Upon hearing that Reverend Turner had been beaten, Brittain closed the school.

Traditionally in Clinton, lines at the polls had dwindled as election day wore on. That day, lines lengthened as indignant citizens registered their protest. The White Citizens Council's candidates for mayor and alderman were overwhelmingly defeated.

In Nashville, the *Tennessean* reacted to the election returns with delight, while in Knoxville, Judge Taylor reacted to the continued segregationist violence in Clinton with angry dispatch. In a response to a plea from Mayor Lewallen and several other citizens of Clinton, the federal district attorney asked Judge Taylor to order the arrest of sixteen persons on charges of contempt of court for allegedly violating the judge's permanent injunction, and the judge promptly so ordered.[24] If white collars were guilty of rousing the rabble, as the *Tennessean* had charged, the rabble thus aroused wore blue. For among the thirteen men, two women, and one teenage boy arrested were two carpenters, two house painters, two grocery clerks, a school bus driver, three employed industrial workers, and three unemployed men (one a laborer, one a used car salesman, and one an itinerant preacher). All sixteen were of course white, and all sixteen surnames were Anglo-Saxon. The sixteen were summoned before Judge Taylor's court in Knoxville to show cause why they should not be punished.

The *Tennessean* was pleased that the sixteen were to be brought to book. But the *Commercial Appeal* was troubled by the scope of the injunction. On December 30, the *Commercial Appeal* editorially catalogued several objections to the degree to which the injunction infringed upon American civil liberties:

This is an injunction against persons never brought into court by indictment or presentment for criminal acts, nor sued under the civil law procedures.

It is a threat of punishment without trial by jury.

It undertakes to punish for a contempt of court out of the presence of the court.

It involves freedom of the people to know through a free press, because a man has been jailed for distribution of a pamphlet.

24. *SSN,* January 1957, p. 4.

The editorial challenged the American Civil Liberties Union to monitor Taylor's procedures and to take a stand consistent with its high principles—a task the ACLU had traditionally assumed with almost masochistic relish. The ACLU, self-appointed watchdog for civil liberties, responded to this challenge with characteristic alacrity by promptly sending observers to Knoxville. In February, representatives of the ACLU issued from Knoxville a statement condemning Taylor's injunction—particularly the part that prohibited picketing or interference "by words or acts or otherwise"—as too broad to be "constitutionally valid." [25] On March 1, the conservative *Commercial Appeal* reported its delight that the liberal ACLU had responded to its suggestion.

Trial of the sixteen, originally scheduled for January 28, was mysteriously postponed indefinitely by Taylor. The judge then issued writs of attachment ordering the arrest of Kasper and one John Gates for violating the injunction. Gates was the owner of a cafe in Clinton where

Public Education in Clinton

Careful—Or We'll Have DISinfegration

Knox in the Banner

Tom Little in the Tennessean

25. *SSN*, March 1957 p. 7.

Kasper's segregationist coterie frequently conferred (but Gates cheated the federal district court out of his trial in bizarre fashion by promptly dying in an insane asylum). Late in May, Taylor set trial of Kasper jointly with the remaining fifteen for July 8 and granted their request for trial by jury.[26]

The trial in Knoxville generated intense interest throughout the country on four counts. First, Judge Taylor's controversial injunctive procedures had attracted attention in regard to their legal merit. Second, the trial began—fortuitously, yet portentously—on the same day (July 8) that debate commenced in the Congress over the highly controversial civil rights bill of 1957. Central to the strategy behind that bill was the contention of its supporters that Southern white juries would fail to convict fellow Southern whites accused of violations of law in connection with desegregation or racial discrimination in voting. Consequently, the trial in Knoxville was seen as a test case. Commenting on the trial, the *News-Sentinel* acknowledged that "East Tennessee is not Deep South." But, the editorial continued, "it is segregation country and the trial here may be viewed as a laboratory test." [27] In Chattanooga, the *News–Free Press* contended that Taylor's court lacked jurisdiction in contempt cases that occurred outside his own courtroom.[28] But all the major dailies in Tennessee awaited the verdict with expressed anticipation.

The trial was of further significance because its *dramatis personae* commanded considerable attention on their own merit. First, the star defendant was the segregationist missionary, John Kasper, who was

26. *SSN,* June 1957, p. 15. The case was designated *McSwain* v. *Board of Education of Anderson County.* Taylor dismissed charges against sixteen-year-old James Dale Patmore, who attended Clinton High School under the alias of Jimmy Pierce. Patmore quit the school in October, returned in November to pick a fight with a white student over an argument "about niggers," slam Brittain's wife against the wall, and threaten to cut the principal's "guts out." As the trial approached, the aggressive youth was serving a term in the state reformatory for burglary.

27. The *News-Sentinel,* 10 July 1957. The editorial denounced Kasper as a "Half-baked fraud" whose "Hitler-like speeches" had purposefully formented the mob's violence.

28. 19 July 1957.

defended by his customary counsel from Washington. But the fifteen Clintonians were outnumbered by a battery of seventeen defense attorneys brought together under the auspices of the Federation; their services had been in part financed by the Federation's much ballyhooed "Freedom for Clinton Fund." [29] The Federation's lawyers made no secret of their displeasure with having their clients stand trial with the discredited Kasper. Furthermore, the jury was composed of twelve Southerners—ten men and two women—and all of them were white. Four Negro veniremen had been challenged off the jury (one, even after he confessed his belief in the wisdom of racial segregation).

Finally, the personality of Judge Taylor was a determining factor of no little importance. The Taylor name was a historic and respected one in East Tennessee. The fifty-seven-year-old judge's father, Alfred, had been a Republican of great power and the judge's uncle and namesake, Robert, had been a Democrat of similar stature. Both brothers had become eminent figures in Tennessee political folklore by opposing one another as candidates for governor in the crucial election of 1886—a campaign that in Tennessee was likened to the War of the Roses. The prestige of Judge Taylor's court was at stake. In his 7,500-word charge to the jury, he firmly instructed the jurors to ignore the question of desegregation and to confine their scrutiny to whether the defendants had violated the terms of the injunction.

At 2:09 p.m. on July 23, the jury's foreman pronounced Kasper and six other defendants guilty. Four were pronounced not guilty; four others had been previously acquitted. The next day, both dailies in Nashville expressed approval. The *Tennessean* did so with considerable enthusiasm, primarily because the verdict seemed to justify the daily's support of Senator Kefauver's so-called "jury trial" amendment to the civil rights bill (see chapter IV). The *Banner* characteristically shifted the focus of the issue from the South to the "South's Enemies," which, it argued approvingly, had been weakened by the jury's decision. Since the *Banner* cherished the notion that its support of racial segregation flowed less from a devotion to biracialism per se—although it did not deny such a preference—than from the high legal principles

29. As reported in the *Times*, 19 July 1957.

that followed from its historic strict construction of the Constitution, it had been embarrassed by Kasper's lawless defense of a system it approved, and it thus denounced him as it had the Klan.[30] Its editorial concluded, again with a characteristic *obiter dictum,* that neither Nashville nor Tennessee nor the South needed Kasper or the Klan; nor, for that matter, did they need the NAACP—"a free-lance trouble-maker," the *Banner* warned darkly, "with designs upon the region."

With the verdict in, law and order were vindicated, and desegregation in Clinton was a *fait accompli.* That case was legally closed. But it was only a small beginning. The residue of latent racial animosity released in 1956 at Clinton was revealed as a potent source of electoral appeal. And if this deep-seated resentment felt by many of Tennessee's whites had not yet attained a position of political dominance across the state as a whole, it was nonetheless an inescapable conclusion that the political wind was blowing strongly from the segregationist quarter. Paradoxically, while pressure was mounting nationally in favor of a bill to guarantee the greater exercise of civil rights on the part of Negroes, in Tennessee the pressures were building up in the opposite direction.

Frank Goad Clement had never been a man to ignore political winds. But because of his ambitions he was caught by early 1957 in conflicting currents. He would not risk excessively offending the legislature. Nor could he well afford, in the light of his ambitions for national office, and quite possibly in the light of his own inner convictions, to join the coterie of Southern governors preaching defiant segregation. But because his office was secure until 1958, he enjoyed more leeway for maneuver than did most Southern governors. Thus, of the two great legislative battles to be fought during 1957, the first to capture the interest of Tennesseans would be their governor's delicate at-

---

30. Kasper's reputation had begun to decline precipitously, even among ardent segregationists, when news was circulated that he had at one time associated most intimately with Negroes. On 10 July 1957, the *News-Sentinel* noted that Kasper had appeared in Clinton, "as a White Citizens Council official, preaching the purity of the white race, free from Negro association. But earlier, in New York, he had preached and practiced the exact opposite—social affairs attended by members of both races."

tempt, during the late winter and early spring, to execute a *pas de deux* at arms' length with the ardent segregationist bloc in his legislature. The task of satisfying his state constituency without offending the national constituency would be a supreme test of his political ingenuity. Then, during the heat of the summer, Tennesseans could watch, through the eyes of their press, the United States Senate struggle with the earnest yet in some ways comic charade of a filibuster against the civil rights bill.

4

Civil Rights and Civil Wrongs

ON 17 May 1957, exactly three years after the Supreme Court decided the Brown case, seventeen-year-old Bobby Cain was handed his diploma in the graduation ceremonies at Clinton High School.[1] He thereby became the first Negro ever to be graduated from an integrated public school in Tennessee. For Southern moderates, Bobby Cain's graduation dramatized the moral that they sanguinely perceived in the Clinton episode: the majority of their fellow Southern whites were basically decent folk who favored segregation but preferred ultimately to abide by the law. In *Neither Black Nor White*, Wilma Dykeman and James Stokely affirmed that the story of Clinton contained "cause for quiet optimism." [2] Harry Ashmore, in predicting *An Epitaph for Dixie*, cited Clinton as exemplary of the determination of the white power structure in the South to prevent disruptive violence no matter what the issue.[3]

But many Tennesseans read in the violence at Clinton a quite different lesson. These Tennesseans, deeply devoted to the biracial system, saw Clinton as a symbol of the doom of the only educational and social system they knew and understood—a system which, they were convinced, had worked best for all concerned. Consequently, for them the story of Clinton contained cause for deep pessimism. They

1. Dykeman and Stokely, *Neither Black nor White*, p. 355.
2. *Ibid.*
3. Ashmore, *Epitaph*, p. 165.

114

knew that the federal courts would not back down. Local officials could never match the awesome power of the federal government. And the Clement administration, by blocking state legislation and by leaving in the hands of local officials decisions concerning desegregation, had effectively removed the power of the state as a buffer between local and federal authorities. Before the Brown decision, Clinton had been a peaceful little town. Now it was a sharply divided community bearing permanent scars. Who would be next? Could nothing be done to defend against this cancer?

Representative of this kind of troubled sentiment was the editorial voice of the *News–Free Press*. As early as 3 September 1956, the *News–Free Press* had forseen that desegregation was eventually inevitable unless drastic positive action were taken to thwart it.

There is no integration-segregation alternative at Clinton High School. The only alternative for those who would maintain segregation is simply to go to school elsewhere where integration has not yet been ordered.

"But," the *News–Free Press* had observed, "that is only a temporary answer, and a local one. The wave of unconstitutional court-ordered integration—improper though it is—is sweeping onward. It will advance across the state." The editorial was entitled "What Kind of Leadership?" and it explicitly excoriated Clement for failing to follow the lead set by several other Southern states in erecting, like Virginia, a legislative "defense in depth" against federal pressures to desegregate.

The violence that accompanied desegregation at Clinton was only the first of a series of events that led the segregationist press to step up its demands that Clement's administration support some sort of segregationist legislation when the General Assembly convened in January of 1957. On October 5, 1956, the supreme court of Tennessee declared unconstitutional the provision in the state's constitution calling for racially segregated schools.[4] Two days later, the *Commercial Appeal* summarily noted a number of occurrences that had convinced its editors that the state needed defensive laws. First, rioting in Tennessee, Ken-

4. *SSN,* November 1956, p. 6. Tennessee's court was the first Southern state supreme court to declare unconstitutional that portion of the state's constitution that required segregation in the schools.

tucky, and Texas had apparently failed to slow the process of desegregation. Second, congressional hearings in Washington—inspired by
powerful Southern congressmen—had "exposed evidence of delinquency,
sex irregularities, increasing discipline problems, and shocking reverses
in academic standards since integration was made the rule within the
District of Columbia." Third, a summary made by the Southern Education Reporting Service of progress made in desegregation had convinced
the *Commercial Appeal* "that there is an infiltration of integration under
way on the public school level in border states." [5] Finally, the supreme
court of Tennessee had declared unconstitutional all laws providing for
segregated schools. The latter decision "leaves Tennessee in an aim-
less, confusing position, one which cannot be endured for long."

'Two Years Ago We Didn't Think' . . .   Acted A Little Hastily, Eh?

Knox in the Banner

Alley in the Commercial Appeal

5. "The Issue Must be Faced," The *Commercial Appeal*, 7 December 1956.
Frank Ahlgren sat on the board of the Southern Education Reporting Service,
as did Coleman Harwell, editor of the *Tennessean,* and his successor, Edward D.
Ball.

What, then, should Tennessee do to defend itself from this new blight of integration? The *Commercial Appeal* noted that action taken by two other Southern states suggested alternatives. First, a new law enacted by the General Assembly of Virginia would deny state funds to integrated schools. This approach had captured the fancy of the *News–Free Press,* but the *Commercial Appeal* entertained doubts as to its constitutionality. More promising to the latter daily was the decision taken by North Carolina to authorize state grants of tuition funds to children who objected to attending integrated schools.[6] The editorial closed with an admonition to Clement to respond with effective leadership to the wishes of that vast majority of Tennesseans who preferred segregation.

Meanwhile, the *Tennessean* was alarmed at the growing tendency on the part of vocal segregationists to equate desegregation with integration. The *Tennessean,* which previously had joined the state's other newspapers in using the two terms more or less interchangeably, now observed that there was in fact a crucial difference between them.[7] On October 8, the *Tennessean* took pains to point out that the Constitution did not require integration per se. Quoted at length in the editorial was a decision written by Judge John J. Parker of Charlotte, North Carolina, senior judge of the Fourth Circuit Court of Appeals:

> It is important that we point out exactly what the Supreme Court has decided and what it has not decided. . . . It has not decided that we must mix persons of different races in the schools. . . . Nothing in the Constitution or in the decision of the Supreme Court takes away from the people freedom to choose the schools they attend. The Constitution, in other words, does not require integration. It does not forbid such segregation as occurs as the result of voluntary action. It merely forbids the use of governmental power to enforce segregation. . . .

The Supreme Court, then, had no complaints against voluntary segregation, continued the *Tennessean:*

6. North Carolina's package of constitutional amendments, known as the "Pearsall Plan," also provided that a majority of residents of a school administrative unit could vote to close their schools to escape "an intolerable situation."

7. The *Tennessean,* 8 October 1956. As early as 9 March 1956, the *Banner* had topped its editorial with this boxed admonition: "Go Slow—Remember: Integration is not compulsory under the law."

At Clinton, nonracial discrimination did mean integration because there was no separate high school for the handful of Negro students there to attend. But in areas which do have dual systems, the abolition of compulsory segregation has frequently produced little integration because of residential segregation and the desire of many Negro students to stay in all-Negro schools.[8]

In January, when another judge on that same court of appeals ordered the schools of Arlington County, Virginia, to desegregate, the *Tennessean* devoted an entire editorial to re-emphasizing that "No Compulsory Integration" was in the offing. The editors of the *Tennessean* felt that no new state laws were needed and so counseled the governor.

8. In Tennessee the task of maintaining segregated school systems had been complicated by the considerable imbalance in the distribution of the state's school population, which in 1956 totaled 595,640 white and 113,794 Negro children. See the *Tennessee Blue Book, 1957–1958,* p. 282. This disparity is illustrated by the following figures which present the total number of white and Negro children of school age residing in 1953 in certain selected counties in East and West Tennessee:

EAST TENNESSEE

Counties	White students	Negro students
Anderson	6,660	116
Bledsoe	1,182	28
Carter	9,064	96
Knox (Knoxville)	34,983	3,566
Sullivan (Kingsport)	19,740	443

WEST TENNESSEE

Counties	White students	Negro students
Haywood	1,834	3,875
Fayette	1,639	4,006
Shelby (Memphis)	43,659	32,841
Crockett	2,966	1,081

Nine counties—all in East Tennessee—had no Negro children in county, city, or special schools, nor any Negro children in the scholastic population between six and eighteen years. There were more than 3,000 white schools and approximately 800 Negro schools; 31 counties were without Negro high schools. See *SSN,* 3 September 1954, 14.

But the segregationist press continued to mount its demands for laws to defend Tennessee's traditional biracial system.

On November 21, the Federation proposed a package of such defensive proposals for the newly elected legislature, and the *Banner* warmly endorsed them.[9] The Federation's proposals, patterned primarily after Virginia's attempt at "massive resistance," included a call for "a strong resolution of interposition." The *Banner*'s editorial broke new ground by condemning the inaction of Clement, whom the daily had always supported. But the *Banner* had no specific recommendations of its own to make to the new legislature. It merely urged on this occasion, and again in early December in response to the new outburst of violence at Clinton, that the legislature get cracking in January on this, "the Number One Item on the 1957 agenda." [10]

Spokesmen for the Clement administration soon began to report that the governor was considering legislation designed to strengthen the hand of local school officials. On December 31, Buford Ellington, Clement's secretary of agriculture and heir apparent, announced that a bill concerning segregation in the schools would be introduced in the General Assembly under Clement's imprimatur.[11]

On January 7, the Eightieth General Assembly convened in Nashville. Two days later, in an extraordinary move, Clement appeared before a joint session of the Senate and the House and in a half-hour speech declared his position on segregation and outlined his proposals. The two galleries in the house chamber were early filled on a nonsegregated basis, and the corridors were jammed with milling people and watchful policemen. The governor began by observing that "no law, no judicial decree can erase 300 years of history.[12] "But," he added, "in our recognition of the existence of different backgrounds, we must

---

9. The *Banner,* 21 November 1956. The federation entitled its proposals in the grand, Victorian manner: "Message to the Members of the General Assembly of the State of Tennessee Containing Proposals for Legislative Action to Preserve the State Educational System and to Safeguard and Maintain the Sovereign Rights of the State of Tennessee and its People."

10. "Clinton Points Up a Case," The *Banner,* 4 December 1956.

11. *SSN,* January 1957, p. 4.

12. Frank G. Clement, quoted in *SSN,* February 1957, p. 10.

not overlook the fact that the Negro is equal to the white in the eyes of the law and in the sight of God." The young governor proceeded to recognize that the Negro rightfully refuses to accept a place in society "if that place is set in shame and degradation."

> When the Negro reads the Declaration of Independence, when he hears our leaders speak of the rights of man, he knows that he is a man, he knows that he is an American, and he will never be content to be treated as anything less.

Clement then outlined his program. It included recommendations for five acts. The first, the so-called Parents' Preference Law, would authorize local school boards to maintain racially separate schools for children whose parents "voluntarily elect" that their children attend school with members of their own race. The second, or Pupil Assignment Law, would authorize school boards to assign pupils on the basis of varied standards ranging from location of residence to "the possibility or threat of friction or disorder among pupils or others." Third, an act would authorize two or more school boards to operate a school or schools jointly. The fourth would merely amend the state statute regulating transportation of pupils on school buses by eliminating therefrom any reference to race. The final bill would so amend the statutes regulating transfer that students could legally be transferred to schools in other systems.

On January 10, Clement had his lieutenants introduce into both houses his package of five bills. They passed both houses with relative ease. Exactly two weeks later, the governor signed all five bills into law. Clement's strategy of pre-empting the field of segregationist legislation with his relatively mild and ambiguous laws had worked admirably. Like Disraeli, he had "dished" his opponents—in this case, the diehard segregationists. He let it be known that any stronger proposals, such as abolishing public schools or abandoning laws compelling attendance, would be vetoed. Finally, his laws possessed the political asset of masterful ambiguity, especially the two central ones providing for the assignment of pupils and voluntarily segregated schools.

On January 10, most of Tennessee's major dailies demonstrated the effectiveness of that ambiguity by joining hands in support of the governor's package. The *Commercial Appeal* thought the package "moderate in tone and realistic"; the laws represented a welcomed "return to the tradition of THOMAS JEFFERSON in which the best government is the government closest to the people." The *Commercial Appeal* was especially pleased because the program "seems to allow a school board with white schools and Negro schools to also have a bi-racial school for parents who are dissatisfied with the one-race schools." Like the *Commercial Appeal,* the *Banner* was pleased by the way in which Clement's program reinforced the hand of local school officials. This feature also appealed to the *Times,* which commended the governor for facing "the most troublesome human, legal, and political problem of a lifetime with realism and forthrightness."

The *Tennessean* also complimented Clement in a rare show of commendation. In an editorial that covered one third of a page, the *Tennessean* complimented the governor more for what he did *not* do than for what he did. He wisely did not contemplate abolishing the system of public schools nor repealing the law compelling attendance. He did not propose to transfer to the state powers that traditionally had belonged to local school officials. Nor did he attempt to force the diverse schools of Tennessee into one procrustean mold. Finally, he did not make his provisions mandatory for local officials. The *Tennessean* was especially pleased that the governor had echoed its theme that only compulsory segregation was unlawful. But it was quick to deflate the chimerical notion that the first of the five bills embodied a magic formula to avoid somehow desegregating the schools. That act, declared the *Tennessean,* was "either unconstitutional or meaningless." Such voluntary segregation would indeed in all probability be a general phenomenon, but "school boards need no special powers to permit it, and they can be cloaked with none."

Four days later, the *Commercial Appeal* conspicuously played down its earlier enthusiasm for the Parents Preference Law, and concentrated its approbation on the law providing for the assignment of pupils. The *Commercial Appeal* saw in this act "the unwritten assumption that some schools will serve white communities, some will serve Negro communities, and . . . some experiments will be made in schools for children whose parents want racial mixing." But the *Tennessean* observed that the act providing for the assignment of pupils only spelled out in detail powers the local school boards were assumed to have possessed without the act. The *Tennessean* reminded its readers that Clement himself had in part justified his veto of the Stainback bill two years ago by pointing out that the assignment of pupils was implicit in the normal powers of school boards. Although the *Tennessean* never endorsed the concept of "tokenism" as such, its editorials seemed to be saying that the only legal alternative to token desegregation was the abandonment of the public schools—a step the powerful daily equated with utter madness.

Of the major dailies, only the *News–Free Press* expressed disapproval of Clement's program as not going far enough. Clement had in fact publicly denied that the bills were designed to circumvent the court rulings. In a letter to the chairman of the school board of Anderson County, Clement had said, in part:

> I am sure you are well aware of the fact that no gubernatorial or legislative action can overturn a decision of the U. S. Supreme Court.
> We have not claimed that under the administration bills a local school system can operate its schools in contravention of the decisions of the Supreme Court of Tennessee and the Supreme Court of the United States. The bills are designed to afford the local school boards the greatest possible latitude of action within the framework of the law.[13]

On February 6, the *News–Free Press* condemned "Gov. Clement's stranglehold on the Legislature which has about killed off efforts to enact effective legislation to maintain segregation in the public schools of Tennessee." The legislature had passed one resolution that pleased the *News–Free Press*. That was the so-called "Tennessee Manifesto"—a resolution deploring and denouncing decisions of the Supreme Court outlawing segregation in the schools. But the resolution, designed primarily for local consumption, required no action by the governor.

A sixth bill, to which Clement did not object, was passed in order to permit local school authorities to segregate students by sex rather than by race. A seventh bill, introduced by the delegation from Hamilton

13. Frank G. Clement, quoted in *SSN,* April 1957, p. 12. Tennessee's laws were by no means unique. In passing a new pupil assignment law, for instance, Tennessee became the seventh Southern state to do so during the state legislative sessions of 1957. The others were Alabama, Arkansas, Florida, Louisiana, North Carolina, and Virginia. See *SSN,* February 1957, *passim.*

County and also passed by the legislature, would permit parents to withdraw their children from public schools if they believed that conditions at the school were "detrimental to the physical, psychological, educational, sociological, moral or spiritual welfare" of their children.[14] Clement vetoed the bill as inconsistent with his position, and the veto stood.

Several other bills and resolutions were introduced and passed by one of the two houses, but were effectively blocked at some state in their development by the administration's forces. Prominent among these abortive maneuvers was an attempt by the delegations from Shelby and Hamilton counties to pass three bills designed to curb operations of the NAACP within the state.[15] The *Times* dismissed these bills as mere "harassment measures" directed against an organization whose tactics the *Times* had "frequently deplored . . . as ill-considered and extreme," but nevertheless an organization that "should not . . . be discriminated against if it merely exercises a legal right in bringing lawsuits."[16]

On March 22, the legislature adjourned *sine die*. The local political spotlight soon therefore shifted to focus on the Congress, where an acrimonious controversy was shaping up over a serious attempt to pass the first law since 1875 designed further to define, protect, and advance the civil rights of Negroes.

Although Congress in 1957 made the first serious attempt since Reconstruction to pass a civil rights bill, the tangled origins of that bill can be traced back to early 1956,[17] for the loose language and broad

14. *SSN*, April 1957, p. 12.
15. *Ibid.* Supporters of the anti–NAACP legislation complained that the NAACP was guilty of barratry—the persistent incitement of litigation.
16. 27 February 1957.
17. J. W. Anderson, editorial writer for the Washington Post, was commissioned by the Inter-University Case Program in the mid-fifties to study the passage of the Civil Rights Act of 1957. Anderson's research convinced him that the passage of the act in 1957 could not be meaningfully understood without a detailed knowledge of the abortive effort to pass a civil rights bill in 1956. Consequently, Anderson's study, *Eisenhower, Brownell, and the Congress*, deals entirely with the legislative effort of 1956. See J. W. Anderson, *Eisenhower, Brownell, and the Congress: The Tangled Origins of the Civil Rights Bill of 1956–57*, Case Study number 80 in the Inter-University Case Program Series (University, Alabama: The University of Alabama Press, 1964).

powers that so disturbed filibustering Southern senators in 1957 were clearly discernible in the bill more than a year previous. The Republicans had hoped that a gesture toward civil rights made under the aegis of the Eisenhower administration might serve to loosen the attachment of the majority of the nation's Negroes for the Democratic coalition. But to this end Eisenhower had approved only two relatively mild bills designed to establish a Civil Rights Commission and an assistant attorney general in charge of a new civil rights division of the Justice Department. Yet spokesmen for the administration presented the Congress with a package of four bills. In addition to the two bills sanctioned by the President, title III (the four suggested bills became separate titles within one omnibus bill) would empower the Justice Department to seek "preventive relief" to protect the general civil rights of all citizens. Finally, title IV would empower the attorney general to enjoin registrars in cases of suspected violations of voting rights. A close study of the history of the civil rights bill has revealed that Attorney General Herbert Brownell—formerly an experienced legislator from New York, chairman of the Republican National Committee and traditionally a staunch supporter of civil rights—had, in an "astonishingly bold" and totally unauthorized maneuver, committed the administration to all four bills.[18] The total package as thus introduced into the Congress in 1956 contained visibly powerful challenges to the jurisdictions so jealously guarded by the traditional Southern defenders of states' rights. Yet, in 1956, little real attention to the illuminating debates over the bill was paid by the House, still less by the Senate, and almost none by the press.[19]

In Tennessee, as elsewhere in the South and indeed throughout the nation, the press had paid scant attention to the civil rights bill of 1956. This was a curious myopia, considering the region's sensitive nerves in this area. Yet several circumstances conspired during the summer of 1956 to conceal the threat from the usually vigilant strict

18. *Ibid.,* pp. 40–43.
19. *Ibid.,* pp. 95–96; 106; 96–98. Title III, which was destined the following year to become the center of controversy, was never even mentioned in the Senate discussions of 1956.

constructionists. First, the bill had not been introduced until mid-April—so late that it had almost no real chance of passing before the session ended on July 31, and busy reporters were prone not to take it seriously. Second, the controversial bill to provide federal aid to schools had a far better chance, and the heated controversy over this bill eclipsed that over the civil rights bill.

The so-called school aid bill was in one sense a companion measure to the civil rights bill in that it also threatened to invade the domain of states' rights. This familiar bill, which had a long history in the Congress, was drawing most of the fire from Southern newspapers of a strict constructionist bent. During the late spring and early summer of 1956, the *Banner* had devoted four editorials to attacking the notion of federal aid to schools; no mention, however, was ever made of the civil rights bill. Even the alert Frank Van der Linden, sympathetic Washington correspondent for the *Banner* and several other prominent Southern newspapers, detected the threat but failed to exploit it with his usual verve.[20] The *Banner* had attacked the school aid bill on June 20 on the constitutional grounds that it violated the sovereignty of the states as guaranteed by the Tenth Amendment. Nowhere in the Constitution, the *Banner* had tirelessly pointed out, were schools explicitly mentioned. How, then, could the federal government justify aiding them? Always implicit in the *Banner*'s arguments against federal largesse was Damon Runyon's practical caveat: whose bread I eat, whose wine I drink, his song I sing. Or, in another metaphor, if Washington paid the piper, local school officials could no longer call their own tune. The *Banner* had also argued that no state legislature had asked for aid and that whatever aid a state might receive must come from the state's taxpayers, anyway—minus a 15 percent handling charge traditionally extracted by bureaucratic Washington.

The *Tennessean*, a strong supporter of federal aid to schools, had countered the latter argument with the pragmatic observation that the thinly populated Southern states stood to receive more aid per capita than they paid out in taxes.[21] But the *Tennessean* had at the same time

20. *Ibid.,* p. 98.
21. 22 June 1956.

strongly opposed Negro Representative Adam Clayton Powell's amendment to the school aid bill, which was designed to deprive segregated
schools of Federal aid. When, in early July, the House had passed the
Powell amendment (many congressmen opposed to the school aid bill
purposefully voted for Powell's amendment only to turn around and
defeat the full measure), the *Tennessean* had mourned and the *Banner* had rejoiced.[22]

A third phenomenon that had contributed to the eclipse of the civil
rights bill was the quickening pace of the presidential campaign. In
Tennessee, political interest had run especially high, for the normally
Democratic state had gone Republican in 1952. Further, the strong
candidacy of Senator Estes Kefauver and the clear ambitions of keynote speaker Frank Clement had sharply divided the state's press and
its Democratic politicians. When Kefauver was nominated to run for
vice president, the *Banner* and the *Tennessean* had characteristically
recorded their respective disgust and delight.

But two important dailies in Tennessee had not been so easily dis-
tracted. In the thick of the campaigning and at the height of the battle
over federal aid to schools, the careful *Times* had paused to produce
a lengthy editorial on *"The Civil Rights Bill."* [23] Like most *Times* editorials, this one was devoted more to patient exposition than to hortatory pleading. The *Times* had first described the progress of the civil
rights bill and explained why its chances for passage in 1956 were
dim. Then the *Times* had focused on the content of the bill:

The Southerners are especially wary of the section of the pending Civil
Rights bill which gives the U.S. attorney general the authority to bring suits
for injunctions for persons whose civil rights are violated or *threatened*. They
claim that to proceed against persons merely suspected of intending to do
something would give the attorney general authoritarian power.

The editorial had noticed disapprovingly that the bill had been introduced in an election year when "both sides play politics with this vital
issue." But because the bill had been introduced so late in the session,
because it would surely prompt a filibuster in the Senate, and because a

22. 6 July 1956.
23. 24 July 1956.

campaigning Congress was eager to adjourn by its deadline of July 31,

the Civil Rights bill will probably go over until another session. Then we shall have a test of the sincerity of members of the Congress. Will they bother with it in an "off-year" session?

In Memphis, the *Commercial Appeal* had published on June 14 an editorial cartoon that exemplified the pattern of *ad hominem* argument that was becoming increasingly dominant in the editorials of that daily, and in those of the *Banner* and the *News–Free Press*. In the car-

Better Check · The Parents, Aunts, Uncles, Etc.

Alley in the Commercial Appeal

toon, Cal Alley pictured the "Civil Rights' Bills" as a blackjack-wield-
ing tough disguised as a foundling abandoned on the South's doorstep.
Hiding behind a nearby fence were its alleged parents: a Sambo-like
Negro labeled "NAACP," an unmistakable likeness of Eleanor Roosevelt labeled "ADA," and a leering white man labeled "Reds."

The *Times* had been safe in its prediction that the civil rights bill
would be heard from again in the not too distant future. When the
Eighty-fifth Congress convened in January of 1957, committee hearings over a civil rights bill were begun in both houses. If the *Banner,*
in its self-appointed role as vigilant defender of states' rights, had
been somewhat remiss in 1956 in covering this section of the water-
front, it was not to be caught napping in 1957. As early as February 6,
the *Banner* began what was to become something of a minor crusade
against what it called a "force bill." For seven months the *Banner*'s
animadversions against the civil rights bill were to strike with the regu-
larity and impact of a jackhammer. Between February 6 and August
30, the *Banner* addressed thirty-one editorials to the iniquities of the
bill; no other newspaper in Tennessee carried even half as many.

On February 6, in an editorial entitled "It's Time To Talk States'
Rights," the *Banner* applauded the performance of an official from
North Carolina who had been subpoenaed to testify before the House
Judiciary Committee. The official commissioner of motor vehicles, Edward Schmidt, who had formerly headed the New York office of the
FBI, had responded to questions put by Representative Kenneth Keat-
ing of New York by propounding the doctrine of states' rights. The
next day, the *Banner* rhetorically asked whether the bill wouldn't "en-
tail a vast new assignment of federal police powers"? Since the bill's
provisions for enforcement would bypass the state courts, they would
presumably also bypass the state police, reasoned the *Banner*. The editorial noted approvingly that the California Peace Officers Association
had expressed alarm at this feature of the bill—thereby recognizing a
truism that the *Banner* so eagerly sought to impress upon the nation:
"that the principle of States Rights is not a matter of concern to the
South alone."

Within a month the *Banner* began to focus on a feature of the proposed bill that was later to generate so much controversy throughout the South and, indeed, the nation: the provision for federal injunctions which involved no trial by jury. Until late in March, the *Banner* held the field alone. But on March 21 the *Commercial Appeal* joined ranks with the *Banner* in insisting categorically that "Jury Trial [was] Imperative," and that such principles were of vital interest not to the South alone.

Throughout the controversy over jury trials, the *Commercial Appeal* revealed a basic ambivalence in its attitudes. Late that summer, while the jury at Knoxville was deciding the fate of Kasper and his cohorts, the *Commercial Appeal* had observed that no Knoxville jury could speak for the Deep South.[24] Yet, when conviction was announced the following day, the *Commercial Appeal* proudly proclaimed that Southern juries *could* fairly convict in cases involving the racial question. And, like the *Banner,* the *Commercial Appeal* took umbrage when Northern liberals insisted that Southern juries could not be trusted to do justice. Yet the *Commercial Appeal* had argued in May that "if there is a probability of juries anywhere refusing to convict, then that fact alone is a strong reason to stay away from proposed changes. Law changes in a democracy follow changes in public opinion." [25] The editorial suggested wryly that it was ironical that this new regional concept of juries was emerging just as differences between the North and the South were being reduced. "Is it . . . standard law," the editorial asked in conclusion, "to force the accused to stand before one judge because he would go free if twelve men heard the case?"

Early in April, the *Banner* indignantly began to attack supporters of the Civil Rights bill. Spokesmen for the liberal Americans for Democratic Action had argued in testimony that Southern juries could not be counted upon to do justice in cases involving Negro voting. To the *Banner,*

they personify the Carpetbag element, brainwashers extraordinary, whose enmity is a compliment to the region they insult. . . . Their audacity is

24. 25 July 1957.
25. 16 May 1957.

boundless. . . . At one time or another, especially campaign seasons, the ADA has lathered itself with hate for almost everybody and region refusing to vote the straight leftwing or egghead ticket.[26]

Late in April, the *Banner* began to employ a tactic that was to become central to efforts of the states' rights press to defeat the bill. It identified the bill, not with the popular President, whom it had warmly supported, but with the unpopular attorney general, Herbert Brownell, whom it profoundly distrusted and frequently chastised.[27] The editorial pointed out that Brownell's "FORCE BILL" would enable the attorney general to seek injunctions in federal courts if *in his opinion* either voting rights in particular or civil rights in general were threatened. Those enjoined for contempt could then be tried in federal courts without a jury.

Earlier in April, the *Banner* had called attention to a critical minority report issued by eight members of the House Judiciary Committee.[28] The report had been especially critical of the absence of guarantees to trial by jury. On May 14, the *Banner* wholeheartedly endorsed a minority report released by Senators Sam Ervin of North Carolina and Olin Johnston of South Carolina—both members of the Senate Judiciary Committee—criticizing the senate version of the civil rights bill (S. 83). The *Banner* was prompted on this occasion, as it so often was, to reprint in its editorial the full text of the Tenth Amendment. One week later, when Senator Ervin offered in the judiciary committee an amendment designed to gut the bill, Senator Kefauver voted against the amendment. The next day, the *Banner* repeated its standard and bitter charge that Kefauver was a traitor of the deepest dye to the South and did not really represent the people of Tennessee. On June 15, the *Banner* denounced both Kefauver and Gore for failing to attend Southern "strategy sessions."

As the controversy was gathering momentum throughout the late winter and spring, the *Tennessean* had remained curiously silent. On June 5, the *Tennessean* broke editorial silence with an editorial entitled

26. "The 'ADA' Doesn't Trust Us," The *Banner,* 2 April 1957, and again on 4 May 1957.
27. "Off Base, Mr. Brownell," The *Banner,* 29 April 1957.
28. 4 April 1957.

"Kefauver Rips 'Rights' Bog As He Backs Jury Trials." The *Tennessean* applauded Kefauver's successful attempt on June 3 to attach an amendment guaranteeing a trial by jury to persons enjoined. His amendment passed in the judiciary committee by a vote of seven to three. The day before, the *Times* had also commended Kefauver for offering his amendment, although the *Times* admitted that "the Administration has a point in claiming that there is no constitutional right to trial by jury in contempt cases." Although both the *Tennessean* and the *Times* supported Kefauver's amendment, both explicitly agreed with Eisenhower's administration that the bill sought only to protect the right to vote, and as such it could not in good conscience be opposed. The *Times* sought to clear up "a great deal of public misinformation as to the nature of the civil rights bill. . . . It is aimed at assuring the vote to all qualified persons. It is not directed at enforcing integration in schools." The *Tennessean* dwelt at length on this point—and in the process not uncharacteristically hurled a thinly veiled barb at its neighbor:

Some reactionary members of the press have overlooked, or pointedly ignored, the fact that the bill considered by the Senate judiciary committee is wholly a product of the Eisenhower administration.

Its main purpose is to guarantee the right of franchise to all citizens, and that is something no good citizen can oppose. If the impression has been created that the four-section bill has anything to do with segregation or integration, which seems to be the case, that is entirely incorrect.

But that impression was *not* entirely incorrect, for under the careful scrutiny of a battery of determined Southern senators, it was revealed that the bill did in fact confer remarkably broad powers upon the Justice Department. Late in June, the *Tennessean* did object that "injunctive powers which would apply not only to those accused of violating civil rights but even to those 'who are about to commit such violations' are sweeping indeed." [29] But the *Tennessean*'s support of the compromise amendment guaranteeing trial by jury applied only to title IV of the bill, which was concerned strictly with the right to vote. Filibustering Southern senators, however, began to focus their fire on the relatively ignored third title of the bill.

29. 20 June 1957.

The broad language of title III had been defended by Brownell as necessary to enable the Justice Department to enjoy a greater use of civil sanctions as opposed to clumsy criminal sanctions.[30] Brownell had argued that a new emphasis on civil sanctions as opposed to punitive criminal ones would produce the doubly salutary effect of speeding up procedures and reducing punitive actions (under a civil injunction, the defendant in a sense possesses the keys to the jail, in that he can free himself simply by desisting from the action for which he was enjoined). But Senator Richard Russell of Georgia, who led the filibustering Southerners,[31] found a joker in title III and exploited his discovery to the full.

On July 2, Russell startled his colleagues and the President by charging that the heart of the bill was not title IV but title III.[32] Talk about voting rights, said Russell, was just a "smoke screen to obscure the uninhibited grant of powers to the Attorney General of the United States to govern by injunction and Federal bayonet." [33] Sections of the bill, Russell said, were grafted craftily onto old laws which would authorize the President to call out troops to enforce integration of Southern schools, hotels, and swimming pools. Title III was legally linked, the Georgia senator explained, to 42 U.S.C. 1985, a law of Reconstruction vintage which enabled the attorney general to assist the aggrieved in civil redress. This statute was in turn linked to 42 U.S.C. 1993, another Reconstruction act which empowered the President to call out troops to enforce the attorney general's efforts. Thus the bill could be construed to authorize the use of federal armies to enforce integration in the schools.

When questioned about Russell's charges at his next press conference, Eisenhower appeared to confirm Russell's view that the President

30. See Douglas Cater, "How the Senate Passed the Civil Rights Bill," *Reporter,* 5 September 1957, pp. 9–13.

31. The filibuster was triggered when Vice President Nixon granted an extraordinary rule which enabled the bill to bypass the Senate Judiciary Committee and be brought directly to the floor. Senator Eastland of Mississippi, chairman of the committee, had hoped to bottle up the bill.

32. *SSN,* August 1957, p. 10.

33. Quoted from C. Vann Woodward, "The Great Civil Rights Debate," *Commentary,* October 1957, p. 286.

did not know what was in his administration's civil rights bill. Eisenhower admitted that there were certain phrases of the bill which he "didn't completely understand," and he insisted that all he wanted to do was to protect the right to vote.[34]

Russell's startling revelation temporarily routed the coalition of loyal Republicans and liberal Democrats, and an embarrassed Senate promptly voted without dissent to repeal the noxious Reconstruction statutes. "Check Up Round One for the South," the *Banner* proudly boasted, "in its battle of Principle vs. Reconstruction." [35] Then, on July 25, the Senate discarded the operative section of title III by a vote of fifty-two to thirty-eight. The *Banner* checked up "Round Two," noting happily that "The Reconstruction Walls Come Tumbling Down."

Attorney General Brownell had never been popular in Tennessee. Even moderate dailies like the *Tennessean,* which supported a bill to protect voting rights, were wary of Brownell's reputation for disingenuous maneuver. By the middle of July, Brownell was thoroughly discredited in the state's press, and even Eisenhower had not come off completely unscathed. As was usually the case, the major dailies in Tennessee differed over the desirability of a civil rights bill, but all joined in rare unison in urging the axe for title III, and in calling for an amendment to title IV that would guarantee trial by jury.

But Round Three—involving the question of attaching a jury-trial amendment to title IV—was considerably more problematical. Most of Tennessee's press, in urging such a compromising amendment, had defended it in categorical terms by simply observing that the right to trial by jury was fundamental to constitutional due process. But the House had earlier rejected just such a categorical amendment by a vote of 199 to 167. Since any bill the Senate might pass would have to be reconciled with HR 6127 in conference, it appeared that differences between the two civil rights bills would have to be resolved by further compromise—that is, an amendment would have to be passed guaranteeing trial by jury in some but not all cases involving injunctive proceedings.

Prominent liberal spokesmen had argued that the jury-trial amend-

34. *SSN,* August 1957, p. 10.
35. 23 July 1957.

ment actually represented not a conservation of due process but a crippling invasion of traditional jurisprudential procedure. Democratic Senator Paul H. Douglas of Illinois denounced the new amendment on the Senate floor. Echoing charges previously advanced by the ADA, the liberal Douglas declared that the amendment was so broad that it would change at least thirty-six statutes, including the Fair Labor Standards Act, the antitrust laws, and laws banning false labeling.[36] In Tennessee, the *Press-Scimitar* observed that an excessive extension of the right to jury trials might seriously hobble normal administrative procedures that had never previously involved cumbersome juries.[37] The *Oak Ridger* pointed out that "injunctions are supposed to be issued only when regular court procedures would in effect defeat the ends of justice." [38] Its editorial observed that "some long drawnout trials amounted to locking the door after the horse was stolen."

Disobedience of an injunction is a recognized form of contempt of court—which in general is conduct bringing the administration of the laws into contempt. When necessary to maintain their authority and when the facts are clear, judges as a rule may sentence for contempt without assent of a jury.

Then the *Oak Ridger* wryly chided both opponents and proponents of the controversial amendment for not always having been entirely consistent with their vaunted high principles:

Most (by no means all) "liberals" support the proposed measure. Yet back in 1932 practically all the liberals supported the Norris–La Guardia Act. This forbade injunctions in labor disputes except under abnormal conditions and ordered jury trials for persons under contempt for violating any injunctions that were issued.

Today practically all Southerners denounce the proposal to allow sentences for contempt without jury trial for violating Civil Rights injunctions. Yet back in 1947 practically all Southern members of Congress voted for the Taft-Hartley Act. This restored the labor injunctions under certain circumstances, and contempt sentences without jury trial for violating it.

For a relatively young newspaper, the *Oak Ridger* had an awkwardly long memory.

36. *SSN*, August 1957, p. 10.
37. 10 August 1957.
38. 20 July 1957.

In late July, the necessary compromise was advanced in the form of an amendment offered by Senators Kefauver, O'Mahoney, and Church. All three senators were Democrats of a progressive persuasion who felt that half a loaf was better than none. Their amendment would allow the attorney general to use injunctions to enforce voting rights, and persons violating the injunction could be charged with civil contempt and tried by a federal judge without a jury. If convicted, they would be confined until they expressed a willingness to comply. But the persons charged with criminal contempt could, if convicted, demand a retrial with a jury. The amendment purposefully stipulated that persons charged with criminal contempt could demand trial by jury in *all* cases, and not just those involving voting rights. By this inclusion the senators were able to attract the support of organized labor, for labor had long been sensitive to the curtailment of its activities by the use of injunctive proceedings. With labor pushing for the amendment, pressure was exerted on Northern liberal senators to support it. Senate Majority Leader Lyndon B. Johnson, a Texas Democrat with clear national ambitions, pressed hard for an acceptable compromise, for he was anxious that his heretofore typically Southern record on civil rights should seem less offensive to Northern Democrats.

On August 2, the so-called jury-trial amendment passed the Senate by a vote of 51 to 42. The *Tennessean* hailed the compromise as a victory for moderates over extremists on both sides and praised the contributions of Kefauver and Gore, O'Mahoney and Church.[39] The *Banner* also hailed the compromise, but its "Honor Roll" included Senators Russell, Byrd, Thurmond, Eastland, Stennis, Talmadge, Ervin, and McClellan.[40] From the *Banner*, Kefauver and Gore received their customary tongue-lashing; they were such opportunistic Johnny-Come-Latelies to the Southern cause that "Tennessee's embarrassment at this conduct turned into nausea." To the *Commercial Appeal*, the vote in the Senate was "An All-American Victory"—not just the South's alone.[41] In support of this statement, the editorial asserted quite without

39. 4 August 1957.
40. 2 August 1957.
41. 3 August 1957.

qualification that "it is an historical fact that under our way of life—under our laws—discretion as to whether or not he will be tried by a jury is left to the defendant rather than to the prosecutor." The concluding twenty-five lines of the *Commercial Appeal's* editorial were devoted to a demand that the original bill's authors be unearthed.

On August 8, S. 83 passed the Senate by a vote of 72 to 18 and was sent to the House. In the House, the unusual coalition of loyal Republicans and liberal Democrats—a coalition of strange political bedfellows that had been shattered by the Southern Democrats in the Senate—remained cohesive enough to amend further the Senate's jury-trial amendment. The House compromise, in its final form, enabled federal judges to convict, on charges of criminal contempt, violators of injunctions without a jury and fine them up to $300 and sentence them to jail for up to 45 days. Fines and sentences for criminal contempt in excess of that, however, would permit retrial by jury on demand.[42] Both the *Banner* and the *Tennessean* expressed alarm at Eisenhower's support of the House compromise and his threat to veto the Senate version. The *Banner* cried, "Let's Be Done With It! Pass The Civil Rights Bill as the Senate Left It." [43] On August 27, the House passed the civil rights bill as amended, although all of Tennessee's representatives except B. Carroll Reece, the Republican whip, voted against the bill. The *Tennessean* saw the "Jury Trial Mangled in Rights Bill Vote." [44]

When the House bill reached the Senate the next day, the Southern senators realized that further filibuster would be likely to invite a tightening of the rules regarding cloture—a precedent they found far more distasteful than the passage of the bill itself. Members of the Southern bloc in the Senate had long been justly proud of their discipline; accordingly, they watched with anger and open dismay as Senator Thurmond of South Carolina broke ranks and melodramatically set a solo

42. According to the *Times,* 27 August 1957, maximum punishment was set at fines of $1,000 and sentences of six months.
43. 22 August 1957.
44. 28 August 1957.

record for the filibuster.[45] Thurmond stood at Armageddon for 24 hours and 18 minutes. When he finally relinquished the floor, hoarse and exhausted, the Senate passed the bill on August 29 by a vote of 60 to 15. Senator Kefauver voted for the bill, and Senator Gore was paired for it. Of the other formerly Confederate states, only Texas provided votes for the civil rights act. The next day, the *Banner* vowed never to forget that Tennessee's "two 'on again off again' Senators, Estes Kefauver and Albert Gore, ended up where they were expected to—on the side of the enemies of the South, namely the NAACP, the ADA, Herbert Brownell, et al."

The press in Tennessee reacted to the passage of the first civil rights act in eight decades with its customary variety. On the day following its enactment, editors of the Clarksville *Leaf-Chronicle* expressed their relief that it was an act the Deep South could live with. "It should do what is obviously right," the *Leaf-Chronicle* said, "and what its proponents sought—to guarantee the right to vote for all citizens regardless of race . . . the compromise bill should go a long way toward enfranchising all minority groups. That is as it should be." The *Times* observed on the following day that the act was in fact a mild one, reasoning that, had it not been so, the Southern bloc would never have abandoned its filibuster. Characteristically, the *Times*—like its cousin in New York—reprinted the text of the act for the record, and wrote a lengthy editorial placing the act within the context of history.

But the majority of the state's newspapers that commented on the act were troubled by it, for it seemed to place the South in the awkward position of appearing to defend the untenable ground of disfranchisement. The general tone of the editorials was defensive, and many were angrily so. The *Tennessean*, which had earlier championed the bill if properly amended, responded to its final passage with a troubled

45. The New York Times aptly observed that Thurmond's talkathon might more precisely be labeled a delaying tactic, for it lacked the organized and collective characteristics essential to a filibuster. *The New York Times,* 30 August 1957. Thurmond broke a record set in 1953 by Senator Wayne Morse, who had vainly delayed the vote placing off-shore deposits of oil under state jurisdiction.

silence. And the *Banner* was joined, predictable, by the *Commercial Appeal* and the *News–Free Press* in expressing acute distress at the act's final form. Among the weeklies prompted by the new act to comment, the Manchester *Times* declared that

the 1957 version of the reconstruction force bill, adopted last week in the Senate by a vote of sixty to fifteen, while watered down from the original NAACP draft, is still an eniquity [sic] and a shameful evasion [sic] of the rights of the states by a federal bureau.[46]

Even the jury-trial amendment, added the weekly *Times*, "was added, over the protest of the President, the NAACP, the lefties and the pinkos." And in Pulaski, another county seat in Middle Tennessee, the weekly *Citizen* complained that "foes of the South have at last succeeded in administering the long sought slap they have hoped to give residents of this area." [47] Now that the Congress had four months until it reconvened in January, "they can spend many hours devising schemes whereby they may again slap the South when they return to Washington for the 1958 session." The *Citizen*'s concluding paragraph struck a note approaching paranoia:

It was far more important to "show the South what the North could do to her" than it was to pass legislation in an effort to avert a depression. "Who cares about inflation or depression? All we want to do is cram segregation [*sic*—the *Times* must have been troubled, indeed, to have made this remarkable error] down the throats of the South, whereby they may have a taste of what we in the North are experiencing. . . . Then, too, there is the Negro vote we want and need. Other than that, we of the North have no particular love for the Negro."

On August 27, the House passed the new civil rights bill in what was to be its final form. That same day, thirteen Negro children registered for the first grade in formerly all-white schools in Nashville, and nine Negroes registered to attend a formerly all-white high school in Little Rock. The school systems in both cities were scheduled to open early in September. Desegregation had not yet been attempted in cities so close to the Southern heartland. The timing of the passage of the civil rights act to coincide with desegregation in Nashville and

46. 30 August 1957.
47. J.H. Smith, "Just Knockin' Around," the Pulaski *Citizen,* 28 August 1957.

Little Rock had of course been inadvertent. But the press in Tennessee had been put on the defensive—and much of it hostilely so—just as desegregation was penetrating the very capitals of two states of the old Confederacy.

At one point during the torid summer of 1957, while the battle over the civil rights bill was raging, the *Times* had paused briefly to assure its readers that, of all the tactical maneuvers available to the federal government in its task of implementing the Brown decision, there was one drastic course of action that could surely be safely ruled out. "It is inconceivable," observed the *Times* quite matter-of-factly on July 14, "that the government would use troops in the South . . . to enforce school integration . . . it is absurd."

5

A Tale of Two Cities

THE battle over the first civil rights bill to be passed by the Congress in more than eighty years dramatically commanded attention throughout the nation, and news of the tanks at Clinton the previous year had circled the globe. But since the delivery of the Brown decision itself no single event in response to that decision so dominated the headlines and editorial pages of the world as did the attempt to desegregate Central High School in Little Rock, Arkansas. Clearly no event since 1954 so fundamentally divided the press in Tennessee.

The dramatic confrontation of the state and federal power at Little Rock was catalytic in the extreme in Tennessee, for the issues involved in that fateful power struggle so intimately impinged upon the very structure and philosophy of federalism that American opinion polarized with compelling alacrity. Like the secession crisis of a century before, the episode at Little Rock so bifurcated public and press opinion that, for many observers, the broad middle ground of the American consensus quickly became untenable. If one was not for Governor Orval Eugene Faubus, one was *ipso facto* against him. The divisions at Little Rock symbolized that deep, historic fault-line that had divided the nation since its birth: strict versus broad construction, Hamilton versus Jefferson, the Tenth versus the Fourteenth Amendment, judicial restraint versus judicial review, *stare decisis* versus "sociological jurisprudence"—and perhaps, ultimately, liberty versus equality.

Although the true motives and justifications behind the maneuverings at Little Rock are still subject to debate, the sequence and substance of those events are not in dispute. In April, 1957, the Eighth Circuit Court of Appeals upheld a decision by the federal district court in Little Rock to permit desegregation of that city's high schools the following September.[1] That spring and summer, Superintendent of Schools Virgil T. Blossom put on an intensive public relations campaign for acceptance of the plan, much as Omer Carmichael had successfully done in Louisville in 1956.[2] Negroes had, in fact, been attending public schools with whites in northwestern Arkansas since 1954. Early in August, a committee of the Negro PTA Councils met with Blossom, Sheriff Tom Culley of Pulaski County, Chief of Police Marvin H. Potts, and Mayor Woodrow Wilson Mann to work out a plan to insure orderly desegregation when school opened early in September. Their intensive efforts at preparing the community for a minimal desegregation of one school seemed to be progressing smoothly.

On August 29, the Mothers' League for Central High School, a recently organized segregationist group, persuaded Chancellor Murray O. Reed to enjoin the school board from desegregating in order to avoid "violence and civil commotion" (Governor Faubus's voluntary testimony strongly supported their contention). The next day, however, Federal District Judge Ronald Davies voided the injunction of the chancery court and enjoined all persons from interfering with desegregation. Central High School was scheduled to be desegregated on Tuesday morning, September 3.

On the evening of September 2, Faubus announced that he feared imminent civil commotion, and he promptly ordered the National Guard to surround Central High School. The next morning, at the

1. The following description of events during the crisis is derived from Corrine Silverman, *The Little Rock Story,* case number 41 of the Inter-University Case Program (University, Alabama: The University of Alabama Press, 1958), and the relevant issues of *SSN.* Professor N. V. Bartley of Georgia Tech has written a recent and fresh appraisal of the Little Rock episode in "Looking Back at Little Rock," *The Arkansas Historical Quarterly,* XXV (Summer 1966), 101–116.

2. *SSN,* September 1956, p. 5. See also Omer Carmichael and Weldon James, *The Louisville Story* (New York: Simon and Schuster, 1957).

suggestion of the school board, the nine enrolled Negroes did not appear. But on the morning of the 4th, the Negroes did appear and were barred from entering the school by the Guard. That evening, Mayor Mann declared that Faubus's grounds for intervening was a trumped up "hoax."

During the following two weeks, while the Guard barred the Negroes, a complex dialogue involving conversations and legal maneuverings developed between Faubus, President Eisenhower, the Justice Department, and Judge Davies. During those two weeks, the press in Tennessee followed the dialogue with close attention. Faubus's bold maneuvers prompted a response in the Tennessee press that revealed more clearly than any previous event the fault-line between the traditionalist and the progressive press. The old progressive coalition—the four major dailies that had informally combined their editorial voices in the late thirties and the forties to combat Boss Crump and the poll tax—reasserted itself and concentrated its fire on the Arkansas governor.

The coalition's most forceful voice—on this occasion, as with the *Press Scimitar* in the war against Crump—was that of the *Tennessean.* On September 4 the *Tennessean,* in a long editorial entitled "Gov. Faubus Rides for Fall in Defiance of High Court," catalogued most of the objections that were to constitute the coalition's case against Faubus. First, the governor had sworn to uphold both the laws and constitution of Arkansas and those of the United States. Of the two sets of laws, the latter was superior. Thus Faubus's aim was clearly to circumvent the law of the land regarding segregation in the schools. He therefore enjoyed the "dubious distinction of being the first Southern governor to 'interpose' the powers of the state against a federal court order calling for orderly desegregation in Little Rock schools." His defiance, which amounted to "open nullification," also violated a federal injunction against interfering with the desegregation process. Furthermore, his justification that he feared violence was a mere "smoke screen" to obscure his real reasons, for local observers had denied that violence was imminent until after the governor's action. In fact, he had by his actions "fed the fires of antagonism"; by so doing he had performed a "major disservice" to a progressive state. His was a "reckless and defeatist course."

Why had Faubus, who previously had been widely regarded as a Southern moderate, and by some as even a liberal, chosen the course of defiance at this time? The *Tennessean* entertained "no doubt as to what his purpose was"; it was to maintain segregation in Pulaski County. But the *Tennessean* was puzzled about the "still unexplained political considerations" that had prompted Faubus to act as he had. His reasons for doing this, the editorial mused, "are as obscure in Arkansas as elsewhere.

For he comes from the hill country where segregation has never been an important issue, and furthermore he defeated a member of the White Citizens Council last summer in the race for governor by a two-to-one vote, opposing extreme views on this question.

The *Tennessean* did not speculate further about Faubus's motives. But other observers have suggested that Faubus, whose support in northwestern Arkansas was assured, was seeking new support in the strongly segregationist southeastern half of his state in order to buck Arkansas' strong tradition of denying third terms to its governors.[3]

Two days later, the *Tennessean* applauded Eisenhower's assertion that he would not tolerate nullification in Arkansas. "Moderation and patience," affirmed the editorial, "have their virtues in dealing with difficult problems involving the relationship between state and federal governments. But there comes a time when silence or evasion are tantamount to defeatism." The *Tennessean* availed itself on this occasion of the opportunity to criticize the popular Republican President, who, "hitherto laggard in defense of the courts on integration questions," had "finally been forced" into their defense. The editorial concluded by calling attention to Mayor Mann's charge that Faubus's

3. Silverman, *op. cit.*, p. 10. Faubus was re-elected in 1958, again in 1960, and yet again—for an unprecedented fifth term—in 1962. In 1964 he successfully turned back a determined and well-financed challenge by Republican Winthrop Rockefeller. In 1966, he retired from politics, undefeated champion of longevity in Arkansas' gubernatorial history. Whatever one's moral convictions about Faubus might be, his political instincts must be judged to have been highly acute. Even Faubus's most persistent critics, publisher Hugh Patterson and editor Harry Ashmore of the highly regarded *Arkansas Gazette*, privately admitted that Faubus was possessed of a keen mind and had been, with the major exception of the aberration of 1957, a generally progressive governor.

predictions of violence had been a "hoax." [4] On September 8 the *Tennessean* branded Faubus a "demagogic governor" who harbored "delusions of grandeur." From September through November, the *Tennessean* carried thirteen editorials specifically criticizing Faubus and a total of twenty commenting on the crisis in general.

Throughout the crisis, the other three members of the old progressive coalition joined the *Tennessean* in criticizing Faubus, and for much the same reasons. The *Times* on October 10 employed its keen sense of history to refute Faubus's claim that more "time for litigation" was needed. The *Times* reported that Faubus, in defending his actions, had urged "time for people to accept peacefully what is being crammed down their throats at bayonet point." But the *Times* observed that, although Faubus's plea "has surface appeal . . . it is not in step with the facts." The *Times* then proceeded in sixty-nine lines to document the extensive three-year debate through which Little Rock had agreed upon a program wherein "a minimum of eleven years would be allowed for working out a total limited, conservative and cautious school integration program for all grades in the city school system." The editorial concluded that

the issue in the Little Rock case is whether or not a governor will uphold the law of the land and a court decision that also approved the plan of responsible citizens of the city itself. And the issue remains.

On September 6, the *News-Sentinel* and the *Press-Scimitar* published identical editorials entitled "Faubus the Bungler." The tone of the editorial was one of ridicule. The "principal disturber of domestic tranquility in Arkansas" was not the Supreme Court, nor the federal district court, nor Negroes, nor racist agitators. It was Faubus himself. He had placed his soldiers "in the ridiculously undignified position

---

4. Mayor Woodrow Wilson Mann had repeatedly condemned Faubus for hypocritically violating Little Rock's autonomy while at the same time invoking states' rights theory in defense of his actions. Mann's needling of the Governor, and possibly the superbly progressive credentials in his historic name, recommended him to the nation's liberal press as a martyred hero. Actually, Mann was a discredited lame-duck mayor whose inadequate political skills had to some degree contributed to a crisis which he blamed entirely on the Governor. See Bartley, *op. cit.,* pp. 105–106.

of brandishing their rifles at a group of colored children, trying to go to school as the school board has told them to do." He then made of himself a "laughing stock by running to President Eisenhower with a plea to call off the courts—a thing the President constitutionally couldn't do even if he wanted to, which he doesn't." The governor "in his delusion" had even "started seeing things [federal agents tapping his telephone] under the bed."

If Governor Faubus can be persuaded, or compelled, to stop his irresponsible blockade of the orderly process of his own local government, this pumped-up tempest should soon blow over.

Although the *Journal*'s editorial stance was customarily one of unapologetic conservatism, it had received the Brown decision more warmly than any other newspaper in the state (excluding, of course, the Negro press), and it resented the way in which the Democratic governor of Arkansas had put President Eisenhower on the spot. Thus the *Journal*, on September 25, joined ranks with the progressive coalition in denouncing Faubus for having "created the situation which he pretended to be concerned about preventing." The *Journal*, whose editorial page frequently exhibited strong Calvinistic convictions, urged that "all men of good will pray that we may find a solution without the bloodshed which the Governor of Arkansas has so rashly invited."

The *Journal* had decisively resolved the dilemma faced by a conservative Southern newspaper when the national administration it supported moved to enforce desegregation. A lesser Republican daily in East Tennessee, the *Kingsport News,* had greater difficulty resolving its ambivalence. On September 5, the *News* asserted that it was as "unfair" to accuse Faubus of "preventing integration as it was to accuse Clement of having enforced it at Clinton in 1956." The *News* defended Faubus on the ground that it was a governor's duty to keep the peace in his state. But the *News* admitted that the order of the federal court still stood. "Sooner or later," the *News* observed, "the school board would have to allow Negro students to enter the white school or stand in contempt of court." But the Negroes were still under directions to attend Little Rock Central by order of the school board. Thus the *News* contradicted its own argument by concluding that "when the board does that, it is reasonable to assume the National Guard will still be charged with keeping the peace. That will not mean that Governor Faubus is 'enforcing' integration."

But the very next day, the *News* admitted that

. . . the result of the governor's order has been the same as if he ordered the troops to stop integration at all costs.

If Governor Faubus should succeed in keeping the Negroes out of Little Rock High School in face of a court order, the entire federal judiciary would be threatened.

For other Southern governors would be tempted to follow suit. The end result might be the end of the federal system.

If the orders of a court cannot be enforced, the courts might as well close down.

Yet on September 13, the *News* insisted that "We must give Governor Faubus credit for sincerity when he says that he sent the National Guard to Little Rock to preserve the peace." On that same day, and frequently thereafter, the *Tennessean* reminded its readers of the fundamental distinction that Clement had ordered the Guard to aid local authorities in enforcing the law, whereas Faubus had ordered his Guard to prevent its enforcement by local authorities.

The Kingsport *Times,* a Democratic daily considerably larger than the *News,* (although both were published by the same firm and jointly published the *News-Times* on Sundays) faced the dilemma with more resolve. During the crisis, the *Times* castigated the Supreme Court for creating new law by interpreting the Fourteenth Amendment "to mean something that could never have been the original intention." [5] Yet the *Times* consistently condemned Faubus for brazenly defying the courts and seeking the limelight and the headlines.[6] On September 8, it reprinted an editorial cartoon by Dowling of the New York *Herald Tribune,* caricaturing Faubus as the antithesis of the little Dutch boy with his finger in the dike. The dike, labeled "Orderly Integration Plans," held back the stormy seas of "trouble." Below, Faubus was cracking the dike with a giant spike and sledge, in order to fill a small bucket labeled "Gov Faubus Political Gains."

5. 20 September 1957.
6. *Ibid.,* 8, 27, and 29 September 1957.

In nearby Bristol, which straddles the border with Virginia, the *Herald-Courier* bemoaned the extremism on both sides that had harried a misunderstood South into violent response.[7] But the *Herald-Courier* also accused Faubus of using "subterfuge to prevent the integration of Little Rock," and concluded that "Little Rock offers no answers for the South." [8] In Maryville, seat of Blount County and site of the giant Alcoa aluminum works, the daily *Maryville–Alcoa Times* on September 25, uncompromisingly accused Faubus of lawless defiance of a process of integration that was as inevitably bound to come in education as it had in business and industry. The following day, the *Times* quoted an opinion by former Chief Justice Charles Evans Hughes, in *Sterling* v. *Constantin*, ruling that the governor of Texas in 1932 had exceeded his authority in calling out state troops in violation of an injunction by a federal court. Hughes had said that the proper use of military power was

to maintain the federal court in the exercise of its jurisdiction and not to attempt to override it; to aid in making its process effective and not to nullify it; to remove, and not to create obstructions to the exercise by the complainants of their rights as judicially declared.

In Oak Ridge, the sameness of editorial logic and exhortation was relieved by an impressionistic essay which surveyed the faces of the *dramatis personae*.[9] The *Oak Ridger* was especially upset by the faces of "the jeering, epithet-calling—yes, even spitting" women in the mobs, who so mocked the image of motherhood. And it was pleased by the "heartening" faces of the judges, which seemed "best to convey understanding and yet firmness for compliance."

Then, there are the faces of the Negroes. Here is where the contrast is most devastatingly against the cause of segregation . . . in the school yard scenes the victory is clear.
We do not pretend that courage in any situation—even a racial one— knows racial barriers. It's mostly a question of the casting of circumstances. However, no one can miss the impact of pictures that show Negro students in restrained attitudes walking bravely through mobs. Surrounding them is much ugliness—such cowardliness—of expression. Superior race?

7. 11 September 1957.
8. 26 September 1957.
9. 13 September 1957.

The *Oak Ridger* concluded by deploring the absence of the face of the moderate—"the great sin of omission in this whole difficult situation."

Of the fifteen dailies in East Tennessee, three of the four major ones and five of the eleven small ones explicitly condemned Faubus's defiance. Of the small dailies which editorialized at all about the crisis, only the Greenville *Sun* avoided criticizing Faubus to some extent. Yet the *Sun*'s support of Faubus was not particularly warm. Of all of the dailies in East Tennessee, only the intrepid *News–Free Press* rallied strongly to Faubus's standard.

In Middle Tennessee, five weeklies joined the *Tennessean* in criticizing Faubus. In Smithville, the farmer who wrote a "A Farmer's Meditations" meditated on September 26, that it would be no more possible for Faubus than it was for Pontius Pilate "to bow out of the picture washing himself of all responsibility." In Dover, editors of the *Houston–Stewart* (County) *Times* on September 10 published a thoroughly researched editorial giving an extensive historical background of the problems of "Enforcing the Court's Orders." They began by surveying Jackson's quarrel with John Marshall, then covered the problems of Reconstruction, and finished with an extensive exegesis of *Sterling* v. *Constantin* that revealed unusual sophistication on the part of a county weekly. The *Times* concluded that Faubus's position was untenable. Nearby, in Waverly, the *News-Democrat* censured Faubus for violating his oath of office.

The Arkansas Governor is in the position of defying the law, yet one in his authority is supposed to uphold the law, even though he might not like it.

We have the strange condition of a Governor of a State using National Guardsmen, paid by the Federal Government, forcibly preventing the enrollment of Negro students in a white school in defiance of a federal court order, and then using some of these same guardsmen to protect him against arrest.[10]

The Gallatin *Examiner* on September 5 called Faubus's order to his Guard ill advised and unjustified by the facts. Faubus, thought the *Examiner*

has been jockeyed into a position that is counter to his original views and

10. 6 September 1957.

has become a tool of the White Citizens Council. By following the advice of extremists he had invited discord and trouble to Arkansas that would not otherwise have happened.

Finally, the Springfield *Herald* self-consciously observed that "The World Is Watching Us." [11] To the Herald, the court's duty was clear: "the Supreme Court's constitutional function is to interpret the Constitution." Also, to the *Herald*, the citizen's duty was equally unequivocal: "the high court's opinion must be obeyed, else anarchy will replace law and order."

In West Tennessee, however, only the voice of the *Press-Scimitar* was heard in criticism of Faubus. The *Commercial Appeal* displayed the same ambivalence that the Kingsport *News* had manifested. On September 5, the *Commercial Appeal* admitted that "successful refusal by anyone to obey the orders of a court would lead to confusion that would eventually amount to chaos." Yet the *Commercial Appeal* revealed the balance of its judgment by concluding that "on the whole, the clash is between an unrealistic law and rulings required by it and the responsibility of a state's chief executive to preserve order."

On September 11, the *Commercial Appeal* published its assessment of how and why the nation found itself impaled on the twin horns of federal and state power at Little Rock.

America had "arrived at this dangerous pass by a compounding of errors." Oldest of the errors, the *Commercial Appeal* admitted, was "our Southern failure to see that all schools for Negroes are the equal of schools for white children." This error was matched by the willingness of Northern politicians to seek Negro votes by using the South as a whipping boy. Associated with this error

has been the assumption of too many Northern suburban dwellers—who thought to leave the Negro difficulties behind in the cities from which they have moved—that Christian brotherly love can be showered on brown-skinned Southerners and can exclude the Southern white Christian.

Most pointed of the errors, however,

11. The Springfield *Herald,* 24 September 1957. The *Herald,* the *Times,* the *News-Democrat,* the *Examiner* and the *Leaf-Chronicle* were published by the same firm in Springfield.

has been the Supreme Court ruling of 1954. The justices wrote a law which it would have been impossible to obtain from the lawmakers—Congress. These justices occupied the highest bench in the land with hardly a smattering of experience in the lower courts.

Associated with that error was the strange coincidence that "the Supreme Court's law came under test in Little Rock before a judge from North Dakota, who has proceeded as though education for Negroes was as casually managed in Little Rock as in Fargo." Judge Davies had in fact been brought to Little Rock on August 26 to fill one of two vacancies in the federal district court of the Arkansas Eastern District (containing Little Rock). That district was part of the Eighth Circuit Court area which included the districts in North and South Dakota, Nebraska, Minnesota, Iowa, Missouri, and Arkansas.

The *Commercial Appeal* thought the crucial borderline position of Little Rock was too little understood. Little Rock, the editorial explained, straddled the geographical border between Arkansas' heavily Negro delta and its hill country, where few Negroes lived and where desegregation had been peacefully accomplished in Fayetteville and Charleston in 1954. This quiet desegregation, moreover, had been accomplished under the administration of one of the hill folk, Orval Faubus (whom the *Tennessean* delighted in unkindly but correctly referring to as "the pride of Greasy Creek"). In many ways, the *Commercial Appeal* observed, the South goes only as far north as the Little Rock region. Thus Faubus had "used the state militia to hold the border on school segregation" in order to slow a process that distressed anxious delta whites. And was his action so patently unconstitutional as many believed?

It seems to shock a great many people to find that their ideas of state Capitols as branches of the Washington Government are disputed by others. Or to learn that it was the state governments that created the Federal structure at the beginning.

In the northeastern corner of West Tennessee, the daily Paris *Post-Intelligencer* supported Faubus's contention that it was better to prevent a riot than to suppress one.[12] When Faubus, on the evening of

12. 6 September 1957.

September 8, defended his actions on television, the *Post-Intelligencer* on the following morning openly sympathized with the governor:

> Last night they saw a man under alien, viscious [sic], unreasonable, hate-engendered fire on television, and they saw that man stand his ground without giving an inch even though he suffered the most uncouth, and most deliberate insult and abuse and tried his dead level best to explain to people everywhere, white and black, that he was not resisting a federal court order to integrate a high school, but that he called out the National Guard to prevent bloodshed.

The *Post-Intelligencer* viewed the crisis in a very personal way. It made much of the fact that Judge Davies's home was Grand Forks, North Dakota, and it insisted that he knew more about Indians than about Negroes. And, to the *Post-Intelligencer*, the Supreme Court quickly became "Earl Warren's court."

In Middle Tennessee, the *Banner* insisted that the issue was "not segregation or desegregation as such." [13]

> The issue is whether Federal authority, judicial or otherwise, can by edict disestablish a Governor's RIGHT and RESPONSIBILITY to employ at his discretion the forces at his command to maintain peace and order as is his sworn duty when in his judgment considerations of public safety so demand.

To the *Banner*, the sovereignty of the states was clear and absolute.

> It is STATE obligation to preserve peace and order in a STATE area of responsibility and jurisdiction by STATE facilities and resources. The National Guard is a STATE militia, subject under the laws of Arkansas to STATE calls.

Thus, the central question was no less vital than whether the federal system was to be fundamentally altered—whether the Republic would survive as the Founders had ordained it.

> If by judicial decree state authority can be set aside, and a governor's sworn duty emasculated by court order, then all basic States Rights will have fallen. Further, it would portend the increasing trend, inevitably, of a strong, dictatorial Federal Government, dominated as already by a usurping Federal judiciary.

In Middle Tennessee, the two weeklies that had been so distressed

13. 21 September 1957.

over the civil rights bill also rallied strongly to Faubus's standard. The Manchester *Times* and the Pulaski *Citizen* praised Faubus for his courageous and heroic stand.[14] The *Citizen* explained that it had regarded decisions of the Supreme Court as the law of the land until "the very heart was removed in the thirties." Then, "during this era of New Dealism, good and true Justices were replaced by men whose viewpoints were curved to fit the ideals of the President."

When the six [*sic*] men who voted in the affirmative for school desegregation and admitted that the decision was their own, rather than a decision based upon the Constitution, that was, in our opinion, the 'straw that broke the camel's back.'

But the *Citizen* feared that Faubus would be compelled to acquiesce, "and by so doing the South takes another stab in the back from the 'dam' Yankees."

And remember, there will be new proposals when the Congress meets next January to punish the South for the action taken by Governor Faubus. Any measure that is considered good punishment for an unruly step-child will be offered, and perhaps passed, with some of our Tennessee lawmakers voting the affirmative.

The *Citizen* concluded by paying Faubus an extraordinary compliment.

Governor Faubus, we, along with millions of others are for your ideals in the present crisis, and we deplore the fact that you are not a duly elected representative of the several Southern states rather than the ruling power of one state. If this were true, this is a possibility through your determination to prevent racial disorder that the South might retrieve a portion of the prestige it has lost during the past few years.[15]

But since Faubus was not a regional representative and was not likely to become one, the *Citizen* called, in another editorial published in the same edition, for the formation of a "Federation of States" to represent the South in Washington. That seemed the "only logical means whereby we may end, or at least minimize the jealousy and hatred that the North, East, and West have for the South."

14. The Manchester *Times,* 20 September 1957, and "Three Cheers for Faubus," The Pulaski *Citizen,* 18 September 1957.
15. "Three Cheers for Faubus," the Pulaski *Citizen,* 18 September 1957.

The South has borne the brunt of ridicule nigh onto one hundred years, and will continue to be a target of hatred until it bands together in sufficient strength to shake its fist into the faces of those who hate it, thereby demanding an armistice from tyranny.

The *Citizen,* a Democratic weekly which had been founded in 1854, could rightfully boast of a fine consistency during those one hundred years.

In East Tennessee, the *News–Free Press* on September 3 expressed pleasant surprise that "a liberal" like Faubus would take such a stand. But the governor of Arkansas had waited too late; Central High School "was doomed." The lesson to be learned from Little Rock, repeated the *News-Free Press,* was that Southern states needed a defense in depth "which provides in the last resort for abandonment of integrated public schools and the substitution of segregated private schools out of reach of the Supreme Court usurpers." The McKinzie *Banner,* a weekly in West Tennessee, also made the point that Faubus was a liberal.

The Battle of Little Rock is the wrong war, fought by the wrong man, at the wrong time. Faubus is a so-called Liberal, has never shown any inclination to States Rights. This invasion is far bigger than Little Rock or Nashville, or even race mixing. This is a battle for States Rights . . . for the freedom of sovereign states to settle their own problems . . . for the right of free choice and voluntary association. This is a fight against a mushrooming federal monster which threatens to destroy individual freedom and liberty in America.[16]

The weekly *Banner* delighted its segregationist readers by reprinting from the *Arkansas Farmer* a parody called "The Second Gettysburg Address" [17]

16. 8 November 1957.

17. "Forescore and seven Mondays ago my Supreme Court brought forth on this continent a new constitution conceived in Washington and dedicated to the proposition that all segregationists are bayonetted equal. Now we are in a second Civil War, testing whether that Black Monday or any other Monday so conceived and so dictated, can long be endured. We are met in a great battlefield of the Little Rock Central High School. Our paratroopers have come to desecrate a portion of that field as a final resisting place for those who there gave their all that States Rights might live. It is altogether fitting and proper that we do this for the sake of our enemies throughout the world, to whom we've given

To the *Hamilton County Herald,* published and edited weekly by two women in Chattanooga, "The time calls for more men such as Orville [sic] Faubus." The angry *Herald* on September 6 changed Herbert Brownell's Christian name to "Simon Legree," and asserted that Eisenhower could take his "gradualism" and "throw it in the deep blue sea off Newport. . . . We don't want it slung around our necks. If the right of the people to govern themselves is to die by strangulation—must it be slow strangulation?" Like the Chattanooga *Times,* the nearby *Herald* had her own acute sense of history.

In 1861 (1954)—because Northern Abolitionists (Integrationists) would not let the South live and work out her destiny under the Constitution and in compatibility with local conditions—the country was thrown into a great Civil War (Civil Rights conflict).[18]

Thus, Little Rock was " 'Appomattox' 1957 Style." [19]

While the crisis over desegregation in Little Rock was festering, another crisis over desegregation was developing in Nashville. As was the case in Little Rock, maneuvers designed to desegregate the schools in Nashville had begun several years earlier. In 1955, parents and relatives of twenty-one Negro and two white children had brought suit against the Nashville Board of Education to desegregate Nash-

---

$60 billion since the second World War to make the world safe for democracy. But in a larger sense, we cannot carry New York, New Jersey, Michigan, nor even the United Nations unless we integrate everything. The brave paratroopers who are living there have restored us into the good graces of Russia, NAACP, Africa, and Mrs. Roosevelt, for above my own poor power to add or substract. The South will little note nor long remember what we say here, but it can never forget what we did here. It is for us, the Modern Republicans, to do this before the Democrats beat us to it. It is rather for us to be here dedicated to the great integration campaigns remaining before us—that from these honored paratroopers we take increasing devotion to that cause for which we gave the last full measure of dictatorship—that we here highly resolve that these States Rights shall not have died in vain—that these States, under Sherman Adams, shall have a new dearth of freedom—and that the government of the Supreme Court, by the paratroopers, and for the minorities, shall not perish at the next election." The McKenzie *Banner,* 8 November 1957.

18. 13 September 1957.
19. 20 September 1957.

ville's school system in the fall of that year.[20] Because the suit involved the question of the constitutionality of Tennessee's law compelling segregation in the schools, the case was scheduled to be heard by a special panel of three federal judges. But because of judicial delays, the case was not heard until the spring of 1956.

The school board of Nashville had defended before the court its failure to plan for desegregation on the grounds that it lacked adequate information; results of a comprehensive census of state schools were not yet in. Attorneys for the school board had asked for a continuance on these grounds, and had also petitioned that the special federal panel be dissolved because the school board admitted the unconstitutionality of the law requiring segregation. As early as March 23, 1956, the *Tennessean* had criticized the board's failure to plan, arguing that by abandoning the moderate "middle ground—staked out by the Supreme Court—between absolute segregation on one side and immediate, complete integration on the other," the board had thereby created a vacuum that would invite extremism on both sides. But on March 28, the court had ruled in favor of both motions by attorneys for the board; it had granted the continuance and then dissolved itself, remanding the case to the federal district court to be heard in the fall. That afternoon, the *Banner* had expressed its pleasure at this granting of additional time.

In November, Federal District Judge William E. Miller held two days of hearings in the case and promised a ruling early in 1957. On January 21, Miller accepted the school board's proposal to desegregate the first grade in the following fall.[21] But Miller ordered the board to return by December 31 of that year with a plan for desegregating the

20. *SSN,* April 1956, 4. The case was *Robert W. Kelley, Etc., et al.* v. *The Board of Education of the City of Nashville, Etc., et al.* See my "Desegregation in Nashville: The Dynamics of Compliance," *Tennessee Historical Quarterly,* XXV, (Summer 1966), 135–154.

21. *SSN,* February 1957, p. 9. Judge Miller, a graduate of the Yale Law School who had been active in Republican politics, was appointed to the bench by President Eisenhower in March 1955. See J. W. Peltason's comparison of desegregation in Nashville and Little Rock in *Fifty-Eight Lonely Men* (New York: Harcourt, Brace & World, 1961), especially pp. 154–178.

remaining grades. Both the *Tennessean* and the *Banner* responded the following day by approving of this moderate plan. To the *Banner*, it was a "considerate" ruling; to the *Tennessean*, a "Victory for Gradualism."

As spring faded into summer and desegregation became more imminent, and as the battle over the civil rights bill further heated the air in Tennessee, the *Banner* began to hedge on its approval of Nashville's plan to desegregate. Early that summer, an *ad hoc* segregationist group organized in Nashville as the Parents School Preference Committee and began to press the school board to abandon its plan to desegregate.[22] On June 24, the *Banner* endorsed the new group's aims. Three weeks later, the *Banner* argued editorially that the board should reconsider its plan because the new state law providing for preferential assignment of pupils had been signed by Governor Clement 44 days *after* Judge Miller's ruling of January 21. Thus, the *Banner* concluded, the board should provide, in accordance with the new law,

separate schools for white and Negro children whose parents, legal custodians or guardians voluntarily elect that such children attend school with members of their own race.

Meanwhile, the Parents' Committee, guided by legal counsel freely offered by the Federation, began to circulate a petition designed to enable parents to "voluntarily elect" to send their children to schools of their own race. The school board responded to the pressure generated by this campaign by rezoning twenty-three of Nashville's thirty-six elementary schools, for the first grade only, in order to minimize the degree of desegregation. But the board did not abandon its plans to achieve some token desegregation. The *Banner* approved of the rezoning, but insisted on August 23 that the 6,000 signatures ultimately to be claimed by the Parents' Committee represented a "reasonable request" to postpone all desegregation and give Tennessee's new laws a chance to work.

The hopes of the *Banner* and the segregationist groups to stem the tide were short lived. On Saturday, September 7, Judge Miller declared

22. *SSN*, August 1957, p. 6.

Tennessee's preference law to be "unconstitutional on its face." [23] The *Tennessean* welcomed the decision with an I-told-you-so, and the *Banner* demanded appeal in apparent unawareness that Judge Miller's retention of jurisdiction made immediate appeal a legal impossibility.

The next day, September 8, Nashville Police Chief Douglas E. Hosse said that he would arrest anyone who attempted to intimidate children or parents at the desegregated schools. On Monday morning, the 9th, 115 policemen were on guard as nineteen Negro first graders entered seven previously all-white schools. During the day, the ubiquitous John Kasper, recently convicted of contempt of court in Knoxville and out on bond pending appeal, appeared with protesting segregationists at several of the schools. There were minor scuffles and the beginnings of a boycott at the desegregated schools, but the city police sternly maintained order. That evening, shortly after midnight, dyamiters blasted one wing of the new Hattie Cotton School, where one six-year-old Negro girl had attended during the day.

As all schools but Hattie Cotton opened later that morning, Nashville police cracked down firmly on the protesting segregationists. Barricades were set up, demonstrating groups were dispersed, and nineteen were arrested. Special target for the policemen's ire was John Kasper. On Wednesday, the 11th, Nashville city police arrested Kasper on four charges—two counts of disorderly conduct, one of vagrancy and one of loitering. Kasper was fingerprinted and booked; he posted a $2,000 bond and left police headquarters to go to his car. There he was rearrested for illegal parking, and posted another $500 as bond on this count. Twelve hours later, Kasper was hauled from his bed at 12:35 a.m. on the 12th and charged by a constable with having incited a riot in a speech made the previous Sunday. The hapless Kasper was held in county jail without bond and was then borrowed by city officials and convicted in city court of all four of the original charges. When he failed to pay his $200 fine, Kasper was committed to the city workhouse. Finally, on Monday the 16th, Judge Miller enjoined Kasper and

---

23. *SSN,* October 1957, p. 6. The details that follow are derived primarily from this source.

nine other segregationists from further interfering with desegregation in Nashville.

Within a week, Hattie Cotton School was back in operation, and the boycott was beginning to crumble. By the end of the month, attendance was reported back to normal throughout the school system, and eleven Negro children were attending previously all-white schools.

During September, editors of the *Tennessean* wrote eight editorials approving of Nashville's gradualistic plan, excoriating Kasper and his supporters, deploring the destruction of Hattie Cotton School, complimenting the firm resolve of Nashville's police, pointing out that the boycott was failing, and proudly noting that the New York *Times* had praised Nashville's official behavior.

The *Banner* also complimented the performance of Nashville's authorities, for it feared that "hoodlums" like Kasper would stain the proud escutcheon of states' rights. But the *Banner* could not merely leave it at that, for it thought the job only half done. "Don't Stop With Kasper," its editors urged.[24] Now that Kasper and his "hooligan oracles" had been purged, it was time to "check and eradicate" the "other side . . . the strife-breeding NAACP, lending a hand to the basic premise of antagonism and dispute." That side—"the missions and the missionaries exciting to this frenzy of collective mischief and assault"— was abetted by the "professional 'liberals,' the sanctimonious, and the do-goodies." The *Banner* did not specify just how the NAACP should be "checked and eradicated."

What was the lesson to be learned from Nashville's experience? In West Tennessee, the Paris *Post-Intelligencer* blamed "the 'law of the land' . . . the present politically appointed and politically minded Supreme Court" for the destruction of Hattie Cotton School.[25] The *Post-Intelligencer* cited the authority of like-minded columnist David Lawrence to bolster its argument. In Middle Tennessee, the Manchester *Times* asserted that, had Nashville followed Faubus's course, it would never have lost a school costing taxpayers a half million dollars.[26] But by far the most interesting causal theory was ad-

24. 11 September 1957.
25. 11 September 1957.
26. 20 September 1957.

vanced by the Spring City *Bulletin,* a small weekly published in East
Tennessee near Chattanooga. On September 12, publisher-editor Jack
Haley paused to reflect on the volatile new racial tensions that had
introduced turmoil into his state.

It was thought to be settled in our state that the white and black race of
people would be going to the same school this year until the day school
started. Thirteen children out of a possible 126 attended a school in Nashville which had traditionally been the property of the other race, and then
the fireworks began. A half million dollar school has been destroyed. Fear
has gripped the, [*sic*] only three out of ten of the students are attending
school at all. Several have been arrested and the situation is all out of
proportion.

How did Tennessee arrive at this miserable state? The *Bulletin,* which
saw in most of the world's tumultous events the dark hand of conspiracy, asked a series of rhetorical questions in an attempt to lay the
blame at the proper doorstep:

What does the Negro want in the United States? Is it he who is responsible
for all this agitation? Is the union using him to further their own interests
in the country? Is this a scheme of the Republican party to crack the
Democratic stronghold in the South? Is it Jewish inspired? Communist controlled? Is there a main issue in this situation or is it the combination of
many interests?

Then the *Bulletin* proceeded systematically to answer its own questions. First, was all this agitation the doing of the Negro? "It cannot
be schooling," the *Bulletin* responded optimistically, "for they are on
an equal basis for both races, the buildings and teachers are equal for
both." Do Negroes desire to "be able to go into public business" and
to be "treated like their white neighbors?" "This may have grounds,"
the *Bulletin* responded candidly, "for the black person is forbidden to
stay at many hotels or eat at a large number of restaurants in our
southland." But the *Bulletin* was confident that this was "not the real
reason for he has sufficient cafes and restaurants of his own. This will
come with his advancement morally and educationally any way rather
than through legislation." What, then, of the often-raised specter of
intermarriage?

Is he anxious to marry into another race? We think not, for a marriage is
happiest where the same interests are involved. Same social standing, same

religion, same background—more than ever people of the same race have a better chance for happiness.

Thus the Negroes could find no real grounds for complaint; "We are acquainted with too many fine people of the Negro race to believe they are causing all this agitation."

Who, then, was responsible? The Communists? "Communists are usually blamed," the *Bulletin* noticed, "but that is such a trite thing." But, having explained that this explanation was trite, the editorial proceeded to explain why it was perhaps not so trite:

It would be serving their interests to have the nation in a civil strife since their plans are to eventually control the world. This could be their method but it is impossible to prove, they seem to be capable of angering us by intergration [*sic*] to the point we cannot fight.

With the question of Communist influence thus left unresolved or unresolvable, the Democratic *Bulletin* posed the unanswered question whether this was not a scheme by the Republicans "to divide and conquer?" And what about labor? "Labor unions have had little success in forming locals in our states, they have an interest in dividing the territory also. Violence and fear seem to promote their objectives. Fear of harm caused some to join a union." So much for Negroes, Communists, Republicans, and labor. But by devoting more of its lines to a consideration of the possibility of a Jewish conspiracy than to any other possible conspirator, the *Bulletin* seemed to assess the balance of the blame against the Children of Israel:

The Jewish race is also capable of planning such a scheme, we look on them as having been the chosen race of the Creator and their history discloses many dealings where they entirely wrecked the people in the land where they lived, one time on leaving, all the money, gold and silver, was borrowed from their host one day and the Israelites left that night.

But what was the operative base of the Jews in Tennessee?

The Chattanooga Times is owned by Jewish interest and for the past two years it has been unusually colored in its news and editorials toward segregation, Al Mynders, editor, is opposed to having a Negro girl at the Cotton Ball but desires to have first graders intergrated [*sic*]. The paper has become a propaganda sheet, reflecting the wishes of its Jewish owners. Whatever their purpose, they could be the agitating force behind this conflict. A long range plan may help them.

But the colorful Spring City *Bulletin* was not particularly representative of the response of weeklies in East Tennessee to the recent racial crisis explosions in Little Rock and Nashville. The Maynardsville *Union County Times* on September 12 expressed its dismay at the recent racial violence and destruction. Its editorial pointed out that such incidents could only "give our communist friends more ammunition in order to help them win their cold war against us." To the weekly *Times,* the issue was clear:

Whether or not we approve or disapprove of integration is not the question, but the question is whether or not we are going to have any respect for the laws of our land. We certainly do not like to pay income taxes, nor have we met anyone who claims to enjoy paying them. Yet we continue to do so. Why? Because it is the law. In the same line of reasoning, it is our duty to obey every law which our government hands down. We have an opportunity through our political leaders to register our protests, but mob violence is not the answer to these problems.

One week later, in Hawkins County, the Rogersville *Review* asked of the North that the South not be judged too harshly. But the *Review* also instructed its readers that

if we do not like to be judged then we must stand up and be counted against hate and violence. The vast majority will have to take a more positive position than it has before. It must make it clear to all that racial problems must be resolved within the national family by good will, reason, and by natural processes.

The Clarksville *Leaf-Chronicle,* a moderate Middle Tennessee daily, seemed to speak for the great majority of the state's newspapers—and certainly of its twenty-eight dailies—in blaming Kasper and his kind. "Their work," the *Leaf-Chronicle* observed on September 10, stood as a symbol of "ignorance, intolerance and wanton, inexcusable violence." Three days later, the Murfreesboro *Daily News Journal,* a segregationist newspaper also published in Middle Tennessee, insisted that such violence only hurt the "white race," not the Negro. And the Kingsport *Times* suggested that "Arkansas could Use the Nashville Plan." [27] But it was the Jewish-owned Chattanooga *Times* which most

27. 27 September 1957. Kingsport, a clean and proudly progressive industrial town in East Tennessee, subsequently adopted the Nashville plan—frequently called the "stairstep" or "grade-a-year" plan—for itself.

pointedly compared desegregation in Nashville to that in Little Rock—and found the latter wanting.[28] To the *Times,* Nashville's success seemed a standing refutation of Faubus's claims. In the light of Nashville's experience, the *Times* reasoned, the chief question now was "whether Gov. Faubus will climb down off the limb or will saw the limb off under himself." But Governor Faubus apparently considered himself too far out on the limb to climb down in humiliating retreat. And since he was too committed and too clever to "saw the limb off under himself," it was left for the government in Washington to do it for him.

In a hearing held in Little Rock on Friday, September 20, Judge Davies granted Attorney General Brownell's petition to enjoin Faubus and the commanders of his National Guard from interfering with the plan to desegregate.[29] That evening, Faubus withdrew the Guard from around Central High School. On Monday, September 23, more than a hundred city and state police were stationed at the high school to keep order while the Negro students attempted once again to attend classes. An expectant crowd estimated at nearly a thousand people gathered about the school. When the schoolbell rang at 8:30, the crowd erupted into violence. While Negro students entered by a side door, Negro newsmen were being chased and beaten. The disappointed crowd grew noisier; some white students walked out of the school in boycott. By the noon break, school and city officials agreed the Negroes should be withdrawn from classes and sent home. At 10:22 a.m. Tuesday, President Eisenhower ordered the Guard into federal service and sent 1,000 paratroopers of the 101st Airborne Division to Little Rock to enforce the order of the court. The paratroopers remained for two months. By November 27, the last of the paratroopers were withdrawn, and patrolling was carried on by soldiers of the federalized Arkansas National Guard until the high school's graduation in May.

The specter of federal troops enforcing integration—an abhorrent image conjured up by filibustering Southern senators during the debate over civil rights to represent the nadir of federal intrusion—had quickly

28. "A Tale of Two Cities," *Times,* 9 September 1957.
29. *SSN,* October 1957, pp. 2–3; and Silverman, *op. cit.,* pp. 12–15.

become a reality. Newspapers of the progressive coalition that had been highly critical of Faubus were embarrassed and defensive. The *Tennessean* agreed with Eisenhower that the basic question involved was "whether law and order under the Constitution are to be respected." [30] "No less important," the *Tennessean* added, "is the right of states to be spared the kind of force now being applied by a President who once said that troops would be used against the South 'over my dead body.' " The *Tennessean* strongly regretted Eisenhower's use of troops from the regular army rather than the Arkansas National Guard, or perhaps federal marshals. The President, who had reacted "more as a military man than as a statesman," was "in sore need of new advisors." His decision to send paratroopers—"a colossal blunder"—

must have been influenced by advisors whose partisan hostility to the South has been apparent from the beginning of the first Eisenhower administration. It can also be seen as an unwelcome result of the G.H.Q. system under which the President has chosen to bridge the gap between the people and himself. It was indeed a far too obvious military decision at a time when wise civilian leadership was needed.

Had the obvious relish enjoyed by a Democratic organ chastizing a Republican administration been a little less readily apparent, the *Tennessean*'s editorial might well have been mistaken for one from the Nashville *Banner*. The *Tennessean* thought correct Eisenhower's charge that Faubus incited the violence that necessitated the intervention. But that conviction did

not excuse his blitz on a Southern city, the flash of bayonets and the wide extension of military authority. This was not enemy country, but rather a prideful community in travail.

The inevitable consequence of such action, coupled with the later order for riot practice in various army camps, has been to demolish confidence in the administration where it still existed, and alert the South to further autocratic incursions.

On Tuesday morning, September 24, before the paratroopers had been dispatched, the Chattanooga *Times* had deplored the "Violent Monday" in Little Rock. But the *Times* repeated its conviction that Federal intervention by force is unthinkable." That afternoon the paratroop-

30. 29 September 1957.

ers surrounded Central High School. In response, the *Times* affirmed the following day that "the president must have the support of every Southerner and every other American who values the foundations of the country in law." But the *Times,* like the *Tennessean,* criticized the President for not having acted earlier with greater firmness, and it especially deplored his choice of enforcement procedures. It was a sad case of too much too late.

It was necessary, but the President's decision to use federal troops was also a tragedy of yet unfathomable proportions. . . . The use of federal troops around Central High School has caused vast and incalculable harm to the whole effort for a peaceful solution. They should be withdrawn as quickly as is humanly possible, commensurate with right and justice. Meanwhile, they are there. But they offer no hope whatever of a solution, of gradual acceptance. Every sector of the land, every highest official must realize that. A climate of amity has been put far into the distance. But law —and reasonable men—must prevail.

The following day in Knoxville, the *Journal* expressed its conviction that since Faubus was "the first governor since the Civil War to personally inspire an insurrection against the federal government," the President was left with "no choice but to take the action which is now history." The *News-Sentinel* accused Faubus on the 27th of trying to "involve the whole people of Arkansas in his shame"

a people with a good name for tolerance and justice, which had integrated universities and many other schools, in a city which was proceeding with orderly token integration until the governor intervened on the side of the rabble.

But the *News-Sentinel* also urged removal of the paratroopers at the earliest possible moment.

In Memphis, the *Press-Scimitar* again published on the same day and by the same title—"Faubus Speaks for Faubus"—an editorial that was for the most part identical with that of the *News-Sentinel* above. The *Press-Scimitar,* in language similar to that employed by the *News-Sentinel,* roundly denounced Faubus for "demagoguery." But the *Press-Scimitar* added a significantly new justification for its displeasure with Faubus.

The *Press-Scimitar* believes that the President, Congress and the Supreme

Court should all take a new look at the whole desegregation question in the light of the reaction to it, not only in the South but elsewhere. We in the South cannot obtain that new look and rehearing if we permit demagogues like Faubus to misrepresent us as they do when they invite violence and talk nonsense, and try to picture Ike as a Hitler, Mussolini or Stalin. Sensible people know it to be nonsense, including sensible Southerners, who are in the majority when they make themselves heard.

Then the *Press-Scimitar* on the same page expanded on this new theme of reappraisal in an editorial entitled "A Calmer Look at Desegregation".

No doubt the intentions of the Supreme Justices in 1954 were good. Many people at the time the decision was handed down thought it would improve America's position in the world. Many of these same people have been compelled by events to change their opinions. The opposition and resentment the decision has aroused in the South has led to incidents which have reversed the trend toward racial good will and these incidents have shocked the world and hurt America's position.

* * *

The question now is whether the pressure for mass school integration should not be relaxed, whether such relaxation would not speed the real progress of the Negro.

The editorial suggested that if separate facilities were made truly equal, and if token desegregation were tolerated, then, with "the stigma of second class citizenship removed, it is more probable that many negroes will prefer to go to all-negro schools."

Of the major traditionalist newspapers, the *Commercial Appeal* was most restrained in its condemnation of the President's "ill-advised" action.[31] Because of it, "we now have an executive order, an official record, of the President of the United States instructing the military as to enrollment and attendance of Little Rock's schools." To the *Commercial Appeal,* the sorry episode at Little Rock proved that the Brown decision has "been a vehicle to push too fast." Racial relations, advised the editorial, "are a matter of personal contact, rather than group policies." The daily's specific recommendation was to adopt a system of "Three-Way Schools"—thereby offering to parents two segregated schools and one integrated one. But the *Commercial Appeal* did not suggest how

31. 25 September 1957.

Negroes could be legally barred from the white school, nor did it guess how large a percentage of white parents might elect to send their children to the integrated school.

In Nashville, the *Banner* had reacted to the violence on Monday by proclaiming that it proved that "Faubus was right."

The disturbance at Little Rock, violent as it was, had no John Kasper or other outside segregation elements stirring it up. It was the spontaneous reaction of local people resisting an interference which they were not prepared to accept, and the outsider was a judge brought in from North Dakota, picked for the job of prescribing integration in the school system of that city.

Integration in Little Rock had in fact been prescribed not by Davies but rather, as the *Tennessean* had observed, by Judge John M. Miller, "whose roots are as deep in Arkansas soil as are Mr. Faubus'." [32] In an editorial inserted on the front page, the *Banner* warned Eisenhower

They Cut Some Corners Getting There

Alley in the Commercial Appeal

The Way To Get Rid of the Troops

Tom Little in the Tennessean

32. 22 September 1957.

on the 24th to beware "the importunings and advice of reckless legal counsel."

Surely the President's memory is not so short as to have forgotten that in the showdown on the miscalled "Civil Rights" bill, authority to send armed forces into the field for that enforcement was expressly forbidden when discovered as a sleeper in that infamous piece of legislation.

The United States had arrived at a showdown—"between state authority and big, overriding, all-powerful central government." The next day, after the paratroopers had arrived in Little Rock, the *Banner* in another front page editorial called "Ike's Airborne Blitz" a "Stupid, Tragic Blunder." Such was the *Banner*'s rage that its editors lapsed easily—as they often did when moved by strong feeling—into the rhetoric of bombast: "History will mark Tuesday, September 24, 1957, as America's day of shame; Double D-Day in Arkansas, inflicted by Operation Dumb-Dumb." The *Banner* then proceeded in 130 lines to elaborate its bitter indictment of Eisenhower, Brownell, Judge Davies, and the "Carpetbag press," and to praise the courage of Orval Faubus. It concluded with a fervent plea: "God Save These United States."

By the end of September, the *Banner* was leading every editorial with a boxed "Daily Memo to Ike: Get Those U. S. Troops Out of Little Rock!" The *Banner*'s traditionally generous use of capital letters and italics for added emphasis was further increased.

THE BANNER agrees, Mr. President, that:
(1) The law alone, "as we found in prohibition," does not cure what it sets out to cure;
(2) To use troops to dictate to local communities is the greatest mistake. To that, a fervent Amen!
(3) The use of troops (A) is not good for the troops. Amen and Amen. (B) Is not good for the locality. Amen, Amen, and Amen. And (C) is not really American when used to uphold the orders of the Federal Court.
To all of that, AMEN, AMEN, AMEN, and AMEN!

And the *Banner* emphasized with italics its charge that desegregation was *"NOT the law, never has been, and cannot be without a specific act of Congress authorized by constitutional amendment."* As time passed and the cost of maintaining the troops in Little Rock mounted, the *Banner* began to estimate what useful articles might instead have been purchased with the taxpayers' money. First it was one new high school, then twelve M-48 tanks, five 280 millimeter atomic cannon, or 400 soldiers for one year.

In Chattanooga, the *News–Free Press* saw "The South as A Conquered Province." [33] The only alternative left to the South, it again repeated, was to abolish the public schools. By far the most strongly negative response, however, was registered on September 27 by the Hamilton County *Herald*. The *Herald*, which customarily covered two thirds of its front page with editorial comment, on this occasion solemnly announced that "The Republic Is Dead." In the *Herald* was to be found the only clear and unapologetic embrace of a racist anthropology that appeared in any newspaper in the state during these ten turbulent years. In a front page reprint of an article from the periodical *South*, published in Birmingham, the genetic indictment finally surfaced.

With his genetic indifference to conventional standards of morals, economics and progress, the continuation of friendly and nondiscriminatory segregation

'I Tried'

Faubused

Tom Little in the Tennessean

Knox in the Banner

33. 25 September 1957.

is the only possible formula not merely to assure amity and social order but to encourage and enable the negro to recognize his responsibility and measure his progress. That is the least service he can render in return for a citizenship so tragically acquired—the broader demands of which in these times are so pathetically beyond his interests, comprehension and aptitudes.

The presence of federal paratroopers in Little Rock pleased no newspaper—again, excluding the Negro press—in Tennessee. But Orval Faubus pleased fewer and smaller newspapers than he displeased. Circulation of the five large dailies who opposed Faubus approached 480,000, whereas that of the three who supported him was closer to 358,000. Only two of Tennessee's eighteen small dailies—the Paris *Post-Intelligencer* in West Tennessee and the Columbia *Daily Herald* in Middle Tennessee—vocally supported Faubus. And their combined daily circulation of 13,500 was dwarfed by the 53,000 circulated daily by the four small dailies which attacked Faubus. The response of the county weeklies was quite the reverse. Only four specifically condemned Faubus, whereas more than twenty were prompted by Eisenhower's dispatch of troops to condemn that action, or to denounce the Supreme Court and especially the Brown decision. Rural and small town Tennessee heard, for the most part, the traditionalist or segregationist, states' rights response. But the combined circulation of these weeklies was relatively small, and even this limited impact was felt, for the most part, but once a week. Still, even at this critical juncture, when negative feelings about desegregation were running higher than at any time since 1954, more Tennesseans were exposed to editorials accepting some degree of desegregation than to editorials defiant of it. Despite a detectable weakening of moderate resolve in racially sensitive West Tennessee, an environment of pluralistic journalism had largely survived the twin crises over desegregation in Nashville and Little Rock.

6

What Is "Deliberate Speed"?

THE message of the popular cliché that "no news is good news" is to be found in its corollary—that newsworthy events are likely to be problematical in their consequences. To be sure, the hot news items for September of 1957 concerned defiance in Little Rock, not compliance in Nashville, and many an American diplomat must have greeted with a shudder the unlikely debut of the capital of Arkansas on international headlines. Nashville managed to attract the attention of the wire services only when Hattie Cotton School was dynamited, thereby bearing further testimony to the ease with which dramatic defiance systematically upstages pedestrian compliance in the marketplace. The first major case study of the Southern response to desegregation similarly reflected the magnetism of untoward events, for it was a chronicle of Virginia's abortive attempt at "Massive Resistance." [1] Yet historical hindsight strongly suggests that, despite all the rhetoric and gestures of defiance, the Brown decision had tolled the knell for *de jure* racial segregation. Would we not, therefore, learn much of abiding importance about Southern society by directing our attentions to the more subtle dynamics of compliance? We are all more or less familiar with the tragically truncated careers of Emmitt Till and Medgar Evers, or with the dramatic and controversial career of James Meredith. But who knows what happened to the daughter of Oliver Brown?— and what books have been written on the desegregation of Topeka, Kansas? Simi-

1. Muse, *Virginia's Massive Resistance.*

larly, we know only too well what happened at Little Rock, but of no less importance was the evolution of successful school desegregation in Nashville.

A. Z. Kelley was a Negro barber in Nashville whose son, like little Linda Brown in Topeka, was greatly inconvenienced by the necessity of taking a bus across town daily to attend a Negro school while a white school stood just a few blocks away. Nashville had only one Negro high school, Pearl, in 1955, and it was located in the northwestern corner of the city near the cluster of Negro colleges that included Fisk University, Tennessee Agricultural and Industrial University, and Meharry Medical School. But young Bobby Kelley lived on the other side of the Cumberland River—only a few blocks from East High School. The Nashville School Board had responded to the Supreme Court's order to desegregate the schools "with all deliberate speed" by emphasizing the adjective rather than the noun; in the summer of 1955 it had assigned its four-man instruction committee to study the problems posed by the task of desegregation, and its spokesmen had affirmed that they intended eventually to comply with the new ruling, but nevertheless the full nine-man board continued to abide by its traditional policy of maintaining a biracial school system.[2] In light of the board's rather dilatory response, A. Z. Kelley had filed, on behalf of his son, an action against the school board in federal district court that September. *Robert W. Kelley* v. *Board of Education of Nashville* was a class action, seeking an injunction to require the admission of children to Nashville's public schools without regard to race or color.[3]

As we have seen, Kelley's litigation had led to the successful if explosive desegregation of the first grade in Nashville in September of

2. *SSN,* September 1955, 13; and *Race Relations Law Reporter* (hereafter cited as RRLR), I, (1956), 1120–1122.

3. *Robert W. Kelley, et al.* v. *Board of Education of Nashvillle,* 139 F. Supp. 578. The Kelley litigation was in large part sponsored by the NAACP. Attorneys representing Kelley were Z. Alexander Looby, dean of Nashville's Negro élite, and Avon Willliams, Looby's aggressive junior law partner. Looby sat with one other Negro, Robert Lillard, on Nashville's City Council. Kelley was joined as plaintiff by 20 other Negro children and by two white children whose parents were teachers at Fisk.

1957. But that initial act of compliance, belated as it was, by no means represented a final resolution of the issue. Rather, it had merely posed the question of means, albeit in a dramatic form. For in ordering desegregation of the first grade for that September, Judge Miller had not officially approved the so-called grade-a-year or "stairstep" plan. Nor had the Nashville Board of Education advanced such a plan. The board had merely suggested that the first grade be desegregated in September of 1957, and Judge Miller had granted his approval of this initial step. But Miller had ordered the board to present no later than the final day of that year a plan for desegregating the remaining eleven grades of the city's schools, and the presumption was strong that the board would propose just such a gradual grade-a-year escalation.

Sharing this presumption and unhappy with its implications of eventual extensive desegregation, the *Banner* emerged from the turmoil of September by once again acting as a public sounding board for the Parents' Committee and its legal advisor, the Federation. On October 9, the *Banner* published a lengthy editorial endorsing a plan that was being urged upon the school board by the Parents' Committee. The plan proposed by the Committee involved three basic points. First, a census of parents was to be taken each year by the board to determine the parents' preference as to which type of school their children should attend. Second, the plan provided for the operation of *three* types of schools; one each for whites and Negroes whose parents preferred that their children attend school with members of their own race, and one for children whose parents preferred racial mixing in the schools. The strong possibility that this sort of option would involve no integration by the whites and therefore no real desegregation was never openly discussed by the *Banner*. Nor did the *Banner* ever reply to the charge, so frequently and impatiently repeated by the *Tennessean,* that the two segregated school systems would still require the very compulsory racial segregation that the Supreme Court had prohibited. The third and final point of the plan provided somewhat cryptically that if parents indicated no preference, "the child shall be assigned by the board under rules in conformity with this plan." [4]

4. *SSN,* January 1958, p. 3.

Although the Parents' Committee urged the board to submit this plan to Judge Miller's federal district court, the *Banner,* in an editorial entitled "Fitted To Need, Justice: A Workable School Plan," seemingly addressed its argument to the nation's highest tribunal. To that end the *Banner* argued that "it will be difficult to find a legal stumbling block in the Parents Voluntary Plan. . . ." Although the *Banner* had frequently in the past expressed its fears of the tyranny of the majority, its displeasure with the Fourteenth Amendment, and its doubts as to that amendment's constitutionality (because of the irregularity of its ratification), its editorial of October 9 took a different tack:

> It is just to school patrons, irrespective of race or color. It does not evade the language of specification in the 14th Amendment; on the contrary, it interprets those provisions literally, as protective of the rights of ALL citizens—the majority as well as the minority.

Reminding readers once again that "the court decree did not provide for compulsory racial integration; it simply forbade mandatory segregation," the *Banner* confidently insisted that

> The proposal now before the Nashville School Board deals with what the court DID do; with what the Constitution provides, including the 14th Amendment, and with the realities of a local situation demanding intelligent treatment if a just and permanent settlement is to be reached.
>
> The three-category school system is not an untried method. It is not one of those as yet under judicial condemnation. It is a plan, the *Banner* understands, under study at Washington as an out—from the twin horns of desperation's dilemma. It certainly partakes of no compulsory integration, pushed both in the absence of law and in reckless misconstruction of degree.

The *Banner* bore down hard on the point that the three-school plan would maximize the degree to which all citizens might enjoy freedom of choice:

> NASHVILLE can provide these three types of school—serving a constituency according to individual preference: (1) Negro schools for Negroes wishing to have their own; (2) White schools for whites who wish to have their own; and (3) mixed schools for those Negroes and whites who wish to go to school together.
>
> Just where would that violate any law, however much it might violate a sociological quirk on the part of any contending for racial mixture by compulsion?

But the *Banner* hastened to add that it had not abandoned its allegiance to the time-honored doctrine of "separate but equal." In fact, it pointed out, such "honored concepts" as those embraced in the historic phrase "separate but equal" were not only imbedded in the Constitution as properly recognized in the Plessy precedent, but were in a real sense *anterior* to the Constitution. They were first enunciated in The Declaration of Independence, which "asserted the right and the propriety to 'assume among the powers of earth the separate and equal station to which the Laws of Nature and of Nature's God entitle them.' "

Three days later, the *Tennessean* remarked that the "New Plan Raises Only False Hope," because it was neither new nor workable and could not be constitutional because individuals would be excluded by law from two of the three schools strictly on account of race.

On December 4, 1957, the Nashville Board of Education adopted, by a voice vote of eight to one,[5] the plan offered by the Parents' Committee. Elmer Lee Petit, chairman pro tem of the board and also chairman of the instruction committee, explained that the board had adopted the Parents' plan in order to have it tested by the courts, much as it had agreed with the Parents' Committee to test the state's new school preference law the previous August.

Ever since last September, these people have been pressuring us to present the court their specific plan. While I don't think there's much difference between their plan and the state law, we decided to go ahead and present it to the court. Once the judge rules on it, the air will be cleared.[6]

The next day, the *Banner* expressed its pleasure at the board's action, and once again approvingly explained how the three-school system would work. The editorial concluded with the rhetorical question; "What could be fairer than that?" On the following day, December 6, the *Tennessean* called the plan "Just Another Delusion." The *Tennessean* repeated its analysis of the plan's "fatal constitutional flaw," and then added the practical observation that Tennessee had strained its relatively meager financial resources enough by maintaining two separate school systems, and that to attempt to add yet another system would create an "economic monstrosity."

5. The lone dissenter was Coyness Ennix, the only Negro on the board.
6. Quoted in *SSN*, January 1958, p. 3.

That same day, the board filed the three-school plan with Judge Miller's court. Seventeen days later, attorneys for the twenty-one Negro plaintiffs to the original suit to desegregate predictably took exception to the plan.[7] They requested that Miller issue a permanent injunction ending racial segregation in *all* grades by the following September. Plaintiffs argued that the three-school plan was substantially identical to the state preference law, which Miller had declared "unconstitutional on its face" three months earlier. Miller set the hearing for January 28, 1958.

When the hearings were held, attorneys for the board defended the three-school plan—or "salt and pepper" plan, as it had come to be called in the press—and in addition asked the court to allow the board to invoke the state's new pupil-assignment law. If this were done, they argued, Miller should declare the case moot because the new law provided "each of the plaintiffs with an adequate administrative remedy" which they must first exhaust before a court could act.[8]

On February 18, Miller ruled the three-school plan unconstitutional for reasons similar to those he had cited in voiding the state's new preference law. Although he did not decide on the constitutionality of the pupil-assignment law, Miller denied the board's petition to invoke it. The reason he gave for doing so was that, since it was clear that the board's "fixed policy was to operate the city's schools on a compulsorily segregated basis," the administrative remedy was inadequate. Miller then ordered the board to propose, by no later than April 7, a "substantial plan and one which contemplates elimination of racial discrimination throughout the school system with all deliberate speed." [9]

The following day, the *Banner* demanded "swift appeal," as it had

7. *Ibid.* Parents of the two white children had subsequently moved from Nashville.

8. *SSN,* March 1958, p. 14.

9. *Ibid.* One month later, the Nashville Jewish Community Center, which had sponsored some racially integrated events, was dynamited. The evening of the explosion, threats were made by phone on Judge Miller's life by self-styled members of the "Confederate underground." The *Banner* promptly offered a

done when Miller had ruled unconstitutional Tennessee's school preference law the previous September. But, as in the earlier case, appeal
remained a legal impossibility because Miller had not yet delivered
a final decision, and consequently he still retained jurisdiction of
the case. Yet, as late as three weeks later, the *Banner* stubbornly
continued to insist that "For School Test: Right of Appeal Is Basic."

The Tennessean expressed no surprise at Miller's ruling on the
following day, February 20. Buts its patience with the "segregationist
element" was being exhausted.

Both the board and the court have been extremely tolerant of the segregationist element represented by the so-called preference committee. Its mis-
leading devices have been thoroughly explored not once but twice and have
been found wanting on both occasions.
Such tolerance, however, has its limits, and they have now been reached.
. . .

The editorial concluded with a plea for no "further side excursions
into dreamland."

On March 31, the board retreated from its recent flirtations with a
three-school plan and voted to adopt a stair-step, or grade-a-year,
plan for a gradual desegregation which would take eleven more years
to complete.[10] The vote was again eight-to-one, with the board's lone
Negro, Coyness Ennix, again dissenting on the grounds that the plan
was too gradual. Ennix pointed out that the second grade would be
desegregated the next September anyway by the advancing Negro
first graders. Thus to him the plan represented essentially no change.
He further reminded the other members of the board that Tennessee's
plan to extend the desegregation of its colleges over a period of five
years had been rejected by the courts as excessively deliberate. Finally,
Ennix observed that a federal district court in neighboring Kentucky
had recently rejected as too gradual a similar grade-a-year plan proposed by the school board of Hopkins County.

$1,000 reward for the culprits, who were never apprehended. See *SSN*, April
1958, p. 10.
   10. *Ibid.*

The board presented its new grade-a-year plan to Miller on April 7, as the judge had ordered, and on April 14 hearings were held for five hours on its merits. Additionally, a plan to desegregate the entire system in two years—one year for elementary schools and the next for high schools—was offered by a Negro educator. Finally, the Negro plaintiffs once again called for desegregation of the entire system the next fall.

On June 19, Judge Miller approved of the school board's plan to complete desegregation by 1968, when the recently integrated first graders would be graduated from high school. It was the longest span of time approved by any federal court for desegregation.[11] The response of the *Tennessean* was, predictably, that Judge Miller's decision represented "Wisdom" and "Moderation." [12] But the *Banner*'s response was somewhat surprising. Executing a realistic about-face, the *Banner* welcomed Miller's ruling as a reasonable one that "accords with the formula of gradualism." [13] For a newspaper that had frequently if inconsistently in the past appeared to be dead-set against any desegregation at all, it was curious that the *Banner* should approve of the decision on the grounds that "it does not satisfy extremists on either side of this controversy—the NAACP element that has insisted on complete and immediate integration, or those dead-set against any desegregation at all."

Three features of the newly approved plan clearly sweetened the *Banner*'s acceptance of it. First, it was by far the most gradual of the three plans before the court. Second, Thurgood Marshall, chief counsel for the NAACP, had offered his services in urging appeal to the Sixth Circuit Court of Appeals in Cincinnati; to the *Banner*, whatever displeased the NAACP could not be totally without merit. Finally and most importantly, the plan as approved incorporated what had been the key to the successful desegregation of the first grade: a liberal and ingenious provision for transfer.

In Nashville, as in most cities, those whites living nearest Negro

11. *SSN*, July 1958, p. 6.
12. 21 June 1958.
13. 20 June 1958.

neighborhoods generally came from the lower educational and economic echelons. Because their jobs were most directly threatened by cheap Negro labor, and because many of them harbored deep psychological insecurities that generated hostility toward the Negro—insecurities that are rather well understood[14]—the notion of introducing Negro children into their previously all-white schools was an explosive one. To these whites, the grim specter of their children enrolled in previously all-Negro schools and instructed by Negro teachers was intolerable. John Kasper had recruited his shock troops from these marginal whites, and the Federation's Jack Kershaw had them in mind when he had bitterly denounced the willingness of Nashville's civic leaders, who lived for the most part in lily-white suburbs, to integrate the poor whites' children.

In pondering how best to modify its segregated school system, the school board in 1957 had faced a dilemma not unfamiliar to other American communities, whether their mode of segregation had been *de jure* or *de facto*. A generally conservative body of community leaders, the board members were interested in minimizing the degree of dislocation that could flow from such a fundamental social change, while not inviting the different but equally severe dislocations that would flow from leading the community in bald defiance. The best way to do this, they were convinced, would be to minimize the degree of desegregation while still appearing to comply with the law. It was in pursuit of some formula whereby, even while complying, such potentially explosive mixing might be minimized that Superintendent of Schools W. A. Bass and Assistant Superintendent William H. Oliver, in lengthy consultations was prestigious Nashville attorneys Edwin Hunt and Reber Boult, devised, in the finest tradition of conservative Southern ingenuity, the following three provisions for transfer: children would be granted a transfer upon receipt of a written application by their parents or guardians (a) when a white student would otherwise be required to attend a school previously serving colored students only; (b) when a colored student

14. See, for instance, Gordon W. Allport, *The Nature of Prejudice* (New York: Doubleday & Co., 1954).

would otherwise be required to attend a school previously serving white students only; and (c) when a student would otherwise be required to attend a school where the *majority* of students in that school or in his or her grade were of a different race.[15]

The effect of such a racially triggered provision for transfer, if accepted by the federal courts, would be clear: no white parent could be compelled to send his child to a school or class where a majority was Negro. Thus, in effect, whatever degree of desegregation that was to occur would take place only in formerly all-white schools. In order further to minimize potential racial mixing, the board had extended equal rights for transfer to Negro parents on the shrewd assumption that relatively few Negro parents in 1957 would want to risk sending their first-grade children to a predominantly white school that previously had been segregated. Finally, the board had so effectively rezoned 23 of the city's 36 elementary school districts that potential racial mixing was even further reduced. In accomplishing this rezoning, the board had expressly denied that it was using race as a criterion. But Negroes with some justice had claimed that the board could and did racially segregate the school districts by employing as zoning criteria certain specific qualities, such as low scores on reading and aptitude tests, which were in effect correlates of race. This stratagem for discrimination was not new, of course; Southern states had historically disfranchised mostly Negroes by excluding from the franchise all illegitimate children, marriage partners in common law, convicted felons, and other categories that tended to include heavily Negro populations.

Given the board's goals and anxieties, its planning had been shrewd.

---

15. *RRLR,* II (1957), 22. This is not to suggest that the Nashville Plan was a totally original product of these men. The wealth of educational and legal experience that they possessed had acquainted them with the previous efforts of officials in border cities, such as Louisville and Evansville, to restrain the pace of social change. The chief importance of the Nashville Plan lies in the fact that, because it passed muster before the federal courts—at least for a time—it became the primary pattern to be emulated by Southern cities in search of a minimal form of compliance.

Not only had Judge Miller accepted its timid first step toward desegregation, but the rezoning and the liberal provisions for transfer had so combined to reduce racial mixing in September of 1957 that the degree of genuine integration was relatively miniscule. Of Nashville's approximately 37,000 public school students, roughly 10,000 were Negro.[16] But only 3,400 students were scheduled to enter the first grade in September of 1957—1,400 of them Negro. After the Board's rezoning, only 115 Negro children had emerged as eligible to attend desegregated first grades in eight of the city's 36 elementary schools. Of these 115 Negro children, parents of 96 had immediately requested and promptly received transfers to all-Negro schools—a fact that had proved particularly galling to the local chapter of the NAACP, which had financed the Kelley litigation. Predictably, parents of all 55 of the white children required by the new zones to attend previously all-Negro schools had requested and were promptly granted transfers.[17] Thus Nashville's desegregation had ultimately involved only 19 six-year-old Negro first graders scattered throughout six elementary schools. Because of this, hindsight reveals that the board had planned well in a dual sense. Not only did their form of compliance avoid extensive desegregation, but the nature of the actual integration was such as to discourage white resistance. The nine Little Rock Negroes, scheduled simultaneously for desegregation in Arkansas, were high school teenagers whose attendance at one centrally located high school would provide a single dramatic focal point for initiating such fundamental social change.

In September of 1958, the second grade of Nashville's city schools was desegregated quietly and routinely. Although 230 Negroes were eligible to attend the desegregated schools, only 34 chose to do so.[18] The other 196 Negroes requested and received transfers to Nashville's 12 all-Negro elementary schools. Only 7 of Nashville's 11 eligible

16. Statistics concerning Nashville's school system are derived from a detailed review of the Kelley case before the Sixth Circuit Court of Appeal, June 17, 1959, Nos. 13,748 and 13,749. *Race Relations Law Reporter* (hereinafter cited as *RRLR*), IV (1959), 584–603.

17. *SSN,* October 1957, p. 6.

18. *SSN.* October 1958, p. 10.

elementary schools were desegregated in this token fashion; the remaining 13 elementary schools contained no Negro children within their districts.

Also during that September, attorneys for both the school board and the plaintiffs—the latter joined by Thurgood Marshall of the NAACP—filed notices of appeal against Miller's decision in the Kelley case to the circuit court of appeals in Cincinnati. Attorneys Looby, Williams, and Marshall declared in appeal for the plaintiffs that Negro pupils who entered school before 1957 had no hope of winning their "constitutional right to attend public schools on a non-discriminatory basis."[19] They also argued that the liberal provisions for transfer permitted transfers solely on the basis of racial discrimination. In cross-appealing, school board attorneys Hunt and Boult insured that the entire record of the case would be reviewed. Further, by objecting to Judge Miller's interlocutory decision that had held both Tennessee's school preference law and the three-school plan to be unconstitutional, they neatly reinforced the appeal of the school board's stairstep plan by sandwiching it between two apparent extremes.

In the light of arguments accepted by the Supreme Court in the Brown decision, it was difficult to deny that Thurgood Marshall's complaints contained real merit. Because of this, and because a stairstep plan had previously been rejected by a federal court in Kentucky, the moderate press—whose gradualist ranks had now been joined on this issue by the *Banner*—followed the appeal with considerable apprehension. In Knoxville, Judge Taylor continued to delay hearings on a suit to desegregate schools there—apparently with an eye to developments in the appeal of the Kelley decision.[20]

19. *RRLR,* IV (1959), 584–602. The highly-regarded Marshall was scheduled to join Looby and Williams in representing plaintiffs before the Sixth Circuit Court of Appeals in Cincinnati, but his airplane was grounded on the east coast due to inclement weather. Marshall was thus unable to argue the appeal and the burden was carried by Looby and Williams, whose appeals to logic and legal precedent were unable to prevail over the defendant school board's substantial accumulation of supportive testimony by an impressive array of Southern educational experts. Attorneys Hunt and Boult, who respected Marshall's legal acumen, privately expressed their delight at his absence.

20. *SSN,* February 1959, p. 6. Negro leaders in Knoxville had repeatedly

While the appeal was pending, the Eighty-first General Assembly convened in Nashville. As had been the case in 1955 and again in 1957, strongly segregationist legislators promised to introduce a host of bills designed to frustrate desegregation. But in 1959 these legislators met at the beginning of the administration of a new governor— one who had professed firm segregationist sentiments while campaigning the summer before. Governor Buford Ellington, formerly Clement's commissioner of agriculture, had enjoyed the administration's strong support in a tight three-way race for the Democratic nomination (see Chapter XI). Ellington was a native of Mississippi, where he had been raised, and his instinctive conservatism had earned him the support of the *Banner* and the *News–Free Press*. Furthermore, the moderating effects of ambitions for national elective office were operative, if at all, to a far lesser degree upon Ellington than they had been upon Clement. With Nashville's stairstep plan in operation, and with the state's school preference law struck down, the oratory of segregationist legislators rang loudly with a now-or-never tone.

In February, 1959, Representative Ralph Kelley, Democrat, of Hamilton County introduced three bills into the House.[21] The first and most important of the so-called Kelley bills would allow the state's law requiring attendance at school to be suspended if parents otherwise would be required to send their children to desegregated schools. The second would provide that state funds for schools be prorated to children whose parents would send them to private schools. The third of Kelley's bills would allow referenda by county on whether

---

but unsuccessfully appealed to an unwilling board of education to desegregate voluntarily the city schools. In January 1957, fourteen frustrated Negroes and their parents petitioned Federal District Judge Robert Taylor in Knoxville to enjoin the board from refusing to admit them and "others similarly situated" to Knoxville's schools. Judge Taylor had twice postponed hearings in their suit, *Goss, et al.* v. *Board of Education of Knoxville,* apparently awaiting legal developments in the appeal of Judge Miller's ruling Kelley case. Once the Nashville Plan had cleared the federal courts, Taylor accepted, on 31 August 1960, a similar plan jointly proposed by both the city and county school systems.

21. *SSN,* March 1959, p. 12.

to abolish the schools, if the referenda were requested by at least 25 percent of the local voters. The *Tennessean* responded to these proposals by promptly labeling them as "Reckless, If Not Useless." [22] The editorial advised that "they deserve defeat," but also noted with dismay that Ellington had said he would probably sign them "unless they would do damage to the school system." Meanwhile, the *Banner* maintained a strict and strange silence regarding the Kelley bills.

No newspaper editorialized about the Kelley bills at as great a length as did the Chattanooga *Times*. The *Times* was embarrassed because it had supported Kelley's candidacy "on the mistaken belief that he would stay on an even keel in Nashville." [23] The *Times* was also embarrassed because "Hamilton County . . . is becoming known as the breeding ground" of segregationist proposals. Kelley's first bill was opposed by the *Times* because it "chills the hearts of true public school partisans."

Mr. Kelley's plan measurably increases the chances that the public schools of this community and other communities will be destroyed. At the very least, it will give opportunists, political troublemakers and the like a field day in hanging the threat of a "school referendum" over the heads of teachers, parents, public officials and civic leaders alike.[24]

The *Times* thought the other two bills were unconstitutional and, in addition to that, they were probably unworkable.

Whether they are constitutional or not, the state education department regards them as unworkable because state funds are based upon average daily attendance in the public schools and, if the Kelley plans were finally carried out, there would be no adequate way to determine this.

22. 12 February 1959.
23. 14 February 1959.
24. 12 February 1959. In Chattanooga, the board of education had voted as early as July of 1955 to begin to plan for desegregation. But a storm of segregationist protest had ensued, and the board had bowed to that pressure nine months later by announcing vaguely that it planned no desegregation for "probably five years or more." Subsequently, as in Memphis, no Negroes brought suit against the board for several years. See "Chattanooga Story—What Happened?", *SSN*, June 1956, p. 6. Much of the protest had stemmed from the ranks of Chattanooga's heavily organized labor. The Central Labor Council, in accordance with the policies of the A.F. of L., had endorsed the plan to desegregate, but seven of the council's locals dissented vigorously.

On March 2, Kelley's first bill passed the House by a vote of 74 to 14.[25] Meanwhile, Ellington had begun to hedge on his conditional approval of Kelley's bills. The governor said his willingness to sign the bills would depend upon his attorney general's opinion of their legal merit. When queried about his opinion, Attorney General George McCanless replied that he considered the bills of "doubtful constitutionality." Ellington then determined to follow Clement's successful precedent and replace Kelley's three bills with one mild and ambiguous one of his own. After he had announced this decision in a press conference, the Senate killed Kelley's initial bill, the legislature hurried all the other miscellaneous segregationist bills to an early burial, and both houses then enacted Ellington's compromise version on March 16.

The new act allowed parents to withdraw their children from school for "any good and substantial reason," provided that: (1) they get the local school board's permission first; and (2) they enroll the child within thirty days either in another public school, designated by the board, or in a private school. On March 20, the legislature adjourned *sine die*. The meaning of the new act was so unclear, and its constitutionality and its effects so dependent upon the future actions of courts and school boards, that none of the state's newspapers ventured to editorialize on it. Its impact—or lack of impact—would be revealed only by distant or unpredictable developments. But desegregation by stairstep was a reality in Nashville, and oral arguments in the appeal of the Kelley decision were a reality before the court of appeals in Cincinnati.[26]

On the 17th of June, 1959, the three-judge Court of Appeals unanimously affirmed all of Judge Miller's decisions.[27] The following morning, the *Tennessean* registered pleasure and relief. Its editorial applauded the Court of Appeals, Judge Miller, the Nashville School

25. *SSN*, April 1959, p. 9.

26. Oral arguments began on April 20. Although Hunt and Boult had cross-appealed Miller's acceptance of the Nashville Plan, they defended its gradual approach before the court of appeals.

27. *SSN*, July 1959, p. 11. Of the three judges, none was a Southerner. Two were from Ohio and one from Michigan.

Board and the city in general, and concluded with a plea that the NAACP not "upset [the program of gradualism] by trying to move too far too fast" in pressing the appeal to the Supreme Court. The *Banner,* consistent with its response to Judge Miller's final ruling—if not with its earlier encouragement of the various schemes of the Federation and the Parents' Committee designed to evade or circumvent desegregation— voiced its approval on the same day. The *Banner* congratulated Nash-ville with the proud if somewhat disingenuous boast that "Nashville did not seek to evade or circumvent that decree." But the *Banner* appended to that unequivocal statement a more characteristic qualifi-cation: "notwithstanding public sentiment in serious question of its constitutional warrant."

Soon after the decision was handed down by the court of appeals, officials on school boards in Atlanta and several other Southern cities requested copies of the Nashville Plan. On July 30, Looby and Williams announced that they would indeed carry their appeal to the Supreme Court.[28] During the following month, the NAACP sponsored in Nashville a series of workshops designed to persuade Negro parents not to transfer their children out of desegregated schools.[29] Nash-ville Superintendent of Schools Oliver vigorously objected to this practice, demanding that the NAACP follow a hands-off policy.[30] In September, 44 Negro children—out of a Negro student population of 12,309—enrolled in 9 elementary schools with white children. Ninety-eight Negroes transferred back to all-Negro schools, and all 74 eli-bible whites—out of a white student population of 18,162—requested and were granted transfers. For the second year in a row there were no untoward incidents. Additionally, Judge Miller ordered sixteen Negro students admitted to the Coleman elementary school, located in adjacent Rutherford County at Smyrna, 20 miles from Nashville. All sixteen were children of Negro airmen serving at nearby Sewart Air Force Base. These children had previously been transported by bus to a Negro school fourteen miles away in Murfreesboro. Ruther-

28. *SSN,* August 1959, p. 10.
29. *SSN,* September 1959, p. 7.
30. *SSN,* October 1959, p. 12. Former Superintendent Bass had retired.

ford County was thus the first rural system to be desegregated and the fourth system to experience this process in Tennessee.

On October 15, the appeal of the Kelley decision was brought before the Supreme Court of the United States. One month later, the court voted six to three to refuse to reconsider the Court of Appeal's affirmative decision.[31] In their dissent, Chief Justice Earl Warren and Associate Justices William O. Douglas and William J. Brennan said said they thought the court ought to make a ruling on the Kelley case on the grounds that the provisions for transfer "explicitly recognize race as an absolute ground for the transfer of students between schools, thereby perpetrating rather than eliminating racial discrimination." [32] But the court's majority of six prevailed.

On the following day, the *Banner* expressed its approval of the decision in a somewhat oblique fashion by emphasizing that the court had written *"finis"* to a five-year-old legal assault by the NAACP. The *Tennessean* proudly boasted on the same day that the moderate and gradualist Nashville Plan had become a "Dixie Guidepost." Its editorial noted that, coincidentally, a federal district judge in Georgia had approved a similar plan for Atlanta. The *Times* was similarly pleased. On the day following the court's critical vote, the *Times* noted that Justice Hugo Black of Alabama, who normally voted in the court's "liberal bloc" with Warren, Douglas, and Brennan, had voted with the majority. Black's vote was crucial, for the court customarily acceded to the wishes of four of its members in requests for judicial review, even though the four did not constitute a major-

31. *SSN,* January 1960, p. 3.
32. *United States Reports,* 14 December 1959, 361 U.S. (U.S. Government Printing Office, 1960). Appealing unsuccessfully for a writ of certiorari on behalf of the plaintiffs were Looby, Marshall, Jack Greenberg, Constance Baker Motley, and James N. Nabrit III. Four years later, in the case of *Henry C. Maxwell* v. *County Board of Education of Davidson County, Tennessee,* the same court unanimously held that the same racially triggered transfer system of which it had approved in the Kelley case "lends itself to the perpetuation of segregation. Indeed," held Justice Clark, "the provisions can only work toward that end." *RRLR,* VIII (1963), 377–379. Perhaps it is more attributable to the wisdom than to the inconsistency of the court that what was approved as a prompt and reasonable start in 1959 was regarded as all *too* deliberate speed in 1963.

ity. The *Times* explained approvingly that "any transfers of students in Nashville would have been voluntary. What the Supreme Court, in its 1954 decision barred was compulsory segregation because of race in the public schools." The *Times* espoused the view, shared by many anxious Southerners, that the federal courts were showing commendable moderation and understanding by approving the gradualist approach. A federal district judge, the *Times* further noted, had successfully granted a two-and-one-half year "breathing spell" from further desegregation in Little Rock. Additionally, the Supreme Court had recently refused to strike down a pupil placement law drawn up by the staunchly segregationist legislature of Alabama (the Alabama law did not mention race, and the court held that no judgement could be made unless and until a detectable pattern of racial discrimination emerged from the act's enforcement). The *Times* gratefully concluded by predicting that "yesterday's decision undoubtedly will further relieve desegregation tensions."

But racial tensions were not destined to stay relieved for long. A new generation of restless young Southern Negroes was rapidly tiring of the slow and limited gains achieved by their elders through tedious and expensive legal maneuvers. Consequently, many of them began the new year, 1960, by taking the matter of desegregation, whether *de jure* or *de facto,* directly into their own hands.

7

From the Courts to the Streets

THE fond hope, expressed by the *Times* and nurtured generally by the press in Tennessee, that the rise of racial antagonism had at least reached a plateau proved to be only a brief and disappointing illusion. During the first half of 1960, the press witnessed with disquietude a succession of events that escalated racial animosity in Tennessee far beyond the peak reached in 1957 over desegregation in Little Rock and Nashville.

When Congress reconvened early in January, a new and more stringent civil rights bill topped the agenda in both houses.[1] Because a new President would be elected in the fall of the new year, leaders of both parties eagerly sought credit for passing a new civil rights bill. It was clear that the rhetoric of civil rights and states' rights would once again dominate the news and elicit heightened emotional responses, as it had done in 1957. Again, as in 1957, forces pressing for a civil rights bill would seek extensive powers of injunction, and resisting Southerners would categorically defend the right of trial by jury. Because confidence in Southern justice was a key to the Southern defense, the press in Tennessee reacted with sharp dismay when, on January 14, a federal grand jury in Biloxi, Mississippi, failed to return

1. In September of 1959, during the last hours of the previous session, Congress had voted to extend the life of the Civil Rights Commission for two years, and had appropriated $500,000 to permit it to continue its work. See *SSN,* January 1960, p. 15.

188

indictments against the alleged lynchers of Mack Charles Parker.[2] Parker, a twenty-three-year old Negro truck driver, had been jailed in Poplarville on charges of raping a pregnant white housewife. On April 25, just two days before he was to stand trial, Parker was kidnapped from his cell and murdered.

In Memphis, the *Commercial Appeal* aired its fear that failure to indict in the Parker case would only add fuel to Senator Jacob Javits's "demagogic" attempts to pass a federal antilynching bill.[3] Besides, argued the *Commercial Appeal,* such failures of justice were an anomaly in the modern South:

> The South abhors lynching. It had proved it by the manner in which, without any outside help or compulsion, it has almost completely rid itself of the heinous crime. Its law agents and courts have in the main been especially vigilant and courageous in preventing its commission and have received public support and applause for their success.
>
> One or two tragic episodes of violence against the process of justice do not mean that the South is going backward instead of forward any more than an unnecessary and unenforceable anti-lynch would change the mores of a section and a people one whit.

The suggestion that an antilynch law would not work anyway because it could not change Southern mores was a curious and probably inadvertent contradiction of the point the *Commercial Appeal* was trying to make.

In Nashville, the *Tennessean* on January 16 echoed the same theme: "Now the South's many critics will be able to ignore the stamping out of lynching before April 25, 1959." But the *Tennessean,* which did not customarily confine its remarks to critics of the South, thoughtfully added: "And her bigots may be encouraged to turn again to the rope

2. *SSN,* February 1960, 7. The grand jury had adjourned in November after refusing to summon witnesses or even to consider evidence against the alleged lynchers compiled by the FBI. For a report of the bitter reaction in the Negro community, see John Howard Griffin, *Black Like Me* (Boston: Houghton Mifflin Co., 1960), p. 63 *passim.*

3. 18 January 1960. Murder was, of course, a crime meriting capital punishment in all Southern states. The goal of the proponents of a federal antilynching bill was to make lynching a federal crime, and thereby circumvent local Southern judicial procedures which had so frequently failed to bring lynchers to justice.

and the hood." The previous morning in Chattanooga, the *Times* bemoaned the fact that "Prejudice and cowardice, cloaked with the power and secrecy of the grand jury system, [had] carried the day."

As was the case in 1957, the new civil rights bill was designed to accelerate the participation of Southern Negroes in the franchise. In 1960, as in 1957, newspapers in Tennessee boasted of the undeniable fact that their state led all others of the old Confederacy in the percentage of Negroes registered and voting. In March of 1960, the *News-Sentinel* proudly published figures compiled by *U.S. News and World Report* which listed Tennessee at the top of all Southern states in granting the franchise to Negroes.[4] By 1958, according to the report, 62.7 per cent of all eligible Negroes were registered to vote in Tennessee. In Texas, the runner-up and a state which retained the poll tax, only 43.6 per cent were registered. Mississippi, predictably, brought up the rear with 5.2 per cent. But the *News-Sentinel* admitted that there were two rather glaring exceptions to this rule: Haywood and Fayette counties in West Tennessee.

Haywood and Fayette were exceptions for two interrelated reasons: whites were in the minority there, and since Tennessee had adopted the white primary in 1901,[5] *no* Negroes were registered in Haywood County, and only 420 of the approximately 10,000 eligible Negroes were registered in Fayette County. Furthermore, both counties had continued to exclude Negroes from participating in their white Democratic primaries, although the white primary had been declared unconstitutional by the Supreme Court in 1944.[6]

Haywood and Fayette were glaring exceptions because the Justice Department had singled out both counties and had initiated legal action against Democratic officials and registrars in an attempt to break down bars to Negro voting. On February 25, Democratic officials of Fayette county filed an answer in federal court in Memphis.[7] They refused to abandon their white primary, claiming that to do so would

4. "Negroes Do Vote Here," The *News-Sentinel,* 26 March 1960.

5. *SSN,* June 1960, 7. Yale historian C. Vann Woodward discusses Tennessee's adoption of the white primary in *The Strange Career of Jim Crow* (New York: Oxford University Press, 1957), p. 68.

6. *Smith* v. *Allwright,* 321 U.S. 649 (1944).

7. *SSN,* March 1960, 6.

abridge the First and Fifteenth amendments by violating the rights of the white minority to peaceful assembly, and would deprive the whites of their liberties without due process of law. The court remained unconvinced by this novel argument.

As newspaper and television reporters and cameramen followed agents of the FBI into the two counties, local Negroes attempted to register in increasing numbers. Fayette county officials responded by filing a consent decree to the federal injunction that they cease barring Negroes from the franchise. But the officials then promptly accepted the resignations of the registrar and the three-man election commission. Subsequently, no official could be found with whom to register. Unofficially, but far more coercively, the white power structure in both counties responded with stringent economic reprisals against the Negroes. Crop loans were suddenly cut off from Negro families attempting to register, as was thirty-day credit and insurance. Many Negro tenants were put off the land. The Negro leaders in both counties, both of whom were grocers, suddenly could find no wholesale dealers willing to sell them groceries. Because of the probing interest of the media, the desperate plight of the Negroes soon commanded nationwide attention.

In neighboring Shelby County, the *Commercial Appeal* on March 6 explained at length and with becoming candor why Southern senators were filibustering against a bill designed to protect the right to vote. It was all very paradoxical, the *Commercial Appeal* explained. The object of the bill purported to guarantee to Negroes the right to vote in the South, but it was actually aimed at securing for its proponents Negro-bloc votes in the North.

To compound the strangeness of the language of Negro rights, the subject is voting in the South, as though Negroes of the South are generally kept away from polling places. The fact is that Negroes of Southern cities vote very much as they do in Northern cities, and that Negroes are fast moving to the cities, both North and South.

The editorial then candidly explained the brute "facts of life" as they appeared to rural whites in such Black Belt counties as neighboring Fayette:

What the talk is about, although it would be hard to tell it from listening, is Southern rural counties, especially in the Southern rural counties of flat lands. There the facts of life show many counties in which the true minority is white, although it has all the responsibility for law, order, taxes, and schools.

Thus we have the hope of votes from Northern city minority Negroes causing a bombardment of methods of politics in Southern rural counties with majority Negroes.

The *Commercial Appeal* admonished Northern liberals to look beyond their own immediate self-interested needs to the hard realities facing the rural Southern whites and to invoke the same sympathy for *him* that they constantly and sometimes piously invoked from others for the Negro.

We doubt very much if some of the white spokesmen for Negro "rights" have ever had the slightest experience with governmental necessities of the Southern counties, which are at the heart of the uproar. They might even ponder the probabilities of white residents of these counties accepting sheriffs elected by Negroes or tax rates set by Negroes.

The Southern politicians currently fighting the bill were well aware of the sentiments that these hard realities inspired in their white constituents.

Beyond a doubt more Southern Negroes are voting now than ten years ago, and it is to be expected that still more of them will be voting ten years from now. But this is a change that comes with more Negroes in Southern cities and thinning of the concentrations of rural Negroes. The pace of the change may be too slow to suit those seeking distant offices, but it is being slowed by politicians who are much closer to the practical needs of the situation.

Once the bill had been sufficiently watered down by Southern objections and amendments, a compromise version was passed by the Senate in April. The new civil rights act empowered the Justice Department to bring suit on behalf of Negroes illegally prevented from registering. It further empowered federal judges to appoint federal registrars to enroll Negroes if an invidious pattern of discrimination was detectable. Southern senators successfully purged their old nemesis, title III (which would empower the Justice Department to initiate legal action to protect the civil rights of all citizens), from the bill.[8]

8. *SSN*, May 1960, 16. Also purged from the bill were sections recognizing

Moderate newspapers in Tennessee generally approved of the "moderate" new bill, and conservative newspapers approvingly emphasized the considerable degree to which its teeth had been extracted. But by April, new and greater worries had beset the state's press.

By 1960, six years after the Brown decision, only 169 of Tennessee's 146,700 Negro children of school age attended desegregated schools. Of the state's school districts, only four were desegregated—and those were integrated in a very token fashion, indeed. To many Negroes in Tennessee, and especially the younger ones, the wheels of court-ordered desegregation seemed to grind far more slowly than surely. Furthermore, the question of voting, especially to urban Negroes in Tennessee, must have seemed somewhat abstract, since, as the *Commercial Appeal* had observed, the great majority of them were not barred from the franchise. What might have seemed abstract to them was the contention that continued voting, lengthy and expensive legal maneuvering, and token desegregation of a few white schools was likely to alter during their lifetime the fixed pattern of segregation in any fundamental way. The biracial system impinged upon their lives less at the polls and even in the schools than it did in the countless details of everyday life. The familiar signs that directed their daily routine were omnipresent reminders of the two races' distinctive paths: "This Portion of the Bus Is Reserved For Colored Persons;" "Colored" water fountains; "Colored" restrooms. But in most of the daily routines, such was the force of custom that signs were not necessary. In Nashville, the old downtown five-and-dime stores relied heavily on Negro trade. Yet not one restaurant existed in the heart of the business district that would serve Negroes.

The story is an old and familiar one, because the conditions of biracial life were old and familiar. What was new, then, was not so much a change in the objective conditions of life. The new and catalytic agent was little more than the explosive power of a new idea. That electric idea was the notion that Negroes need no longer, as Faulkner

decisions of the Supreme Court as the law of the land, granting statutory status to the President's committee on equal employment, and granting special federal incentive funds for schools willing to desegregate.

had so pithily phrased it, simply "endure." Suddenly, "freedom"—a concept of impeccable credentials, of vague and vast dimensions, and one often naively grasped, but nonetheless a concept of enormous power—was attainable. Freedom was not only attainable, freedom was imminent, if only its supreme claims to morality could be dramatically demonstrated.

On the first day of February, 1960, at 4:30 p.m., four freshmen from North Carolina Agricultural and Technical College entered a variety store in Greensboro and sat down at a lunch counter reserved for whites.[9] They were not served. The group sat quietly until the store closed. The next day, 75 Negro students from the college returned to the store, F. W. Woolworth's, and sat pacifically at the counter. Within a week, the new tactic—the "sit-in"—had spread throughout North Carolina. By the end of the month, it had spread through seven other states of the old Confederacy. But nowhere was the nonviolent tactic of sitting in accompanied by such violence as was the case in Tennessee.

On February 13, about 100 Negroes and a few whites left Fisk, Tennessee A & I, and the Baptist Theological Seminary in Nashville and trudged through an unusually heavy snowfall to take seats at lunch counters at Woolworth's, McClellan's, and Kress's. They sat unserved for five hours. Two days later, about 200 returned to these stores, and also to Grants'. By the end of the week, the number of protesters had risen to 350 and Walgreen's was added. As an aggressive group of young whites began, first verbally and then physically, to harass the orderly Negroes, distraught managers summoned police. On February 27, 79 were arrested in Nashville; 74 of them were Negro college students. By the end of the month, an additional 64 arrests had been made.

In Chattanooga, sit-ins prompted the city's first race riot in more than thirty years. There, on February 22, some 200 Negro high school students marched from school to sit in at four downtown five-and-dime

9. The discussion of the sit-ins that follows is derived largely from the March, April, and May editions of *SSN*, 1960. The tactic had first been employed by the Congress of Racial Equality in 1942 to integrate a Chicago restaurant.

stores. Within a few days, mob disorder resulted in the hurling of bottles and bricks, and several Negro students were beaten. Chattanooga firemen resorted to playing water on shivering crowds that swelled to 3,000 and angry police arrested 41.

During March, Negroes began sitting in in Knoxville and Memphis. Sixty-one Negro students were arrested in variety stores, art galleries, and libraries in Memphis, and many were arrested and fined from $25 to $50 in city court. By April, newly militant Negroes—aided by the NAACP—had filed suits for the first time against the boards of education in Memphis and Chattanooga.[10] Also during April, Judge Taylor accepted the plan of the Knoxville school board to implement the Nashville Plan by desegregating the first grade in the following September. Additionally, the school board in Kingsport voluntarily voted to adopt the Nashville Plan. Negroes in Memphis also sued the city to desegregate its municipal auditorium and its recreational facilities.

Up to this point, the press in Tennessee had displayed a considerable range of diversity in regard to racial issues. About the only point of agreement had been that violence was a bad thing. But almost everybody, including the Negroes, deplored violence, especially when they, as was so often the case, were on the receiving end of it. In February of 1960, newspapers throughout Tennessee condemned the new tactic with one voice. The nonviolent Negro demonstrators pleaded that the moral righteousness of their cause was superior to the common law's technical prohibition of trespass—that human rights were anterior to property rights. But in Tennessee their pleas fell on sympathetic ears only among the few small weeklies published by men of their own race.

The *News–Free Press* was first to comment editorially on the sit-ins:

The operator of privately owned facilities has the right to establish his own rules of use and admission, whether they be reasonable or unreasonable. A lunch counter operator has the right to serve only people with red hair,

10. *SSN*, May 1960, p. 5. The new cases were *Northcross et al.* v. *Board of Education of the City of Memphis et al.;* and *Mapp et al.* v. *Board of Education of Chattanooga et al.*

if he wishes, and no one has the right to deprive him of the use of his own facilities by sit-down tactics.[11]

In keeping with the code, the *News–Free Press* deplored the race riots in Chattanooga, but it blamed the "trouble-making Negro demonstrators" more than the "trouble-making young whites."

The other three conservative big dailies echoed the same theme. The *Banner* on February 29 sternly admonished the young Negroes that

the mere disagreement with law does not validate breach of that law, or absolve those striving by coercion to force their way into business premises to the detriment and damage of the firms thus converted into a potential battlefield.

The *Banner* suspected that the "shenanigans" of the "firebrands" were "stage-managed by tacticians afar":

The fact of mimeographed instructions to these demonstrators, and simultaneous outbreaks the nation over indicate an organized effort projected from outside forces. These youngsters are the catspaws of that effort, a fact that cannot escape attention however assiduously sponsors cultivate for them the martyr complex—feeding them the heady stuff of propaganda about thus advancing the crusade of "civil rights."
In actuality, they are retarding that.

In Memphis, the *Commercial Appeal* on the 1st of March confessed to feeling some degree of sympathy with Negro demands that they be allowed to use public libraries and art galleries. But, the *Commercial Appeal* added,

while the library request is a reasonable one because all persons who wish to improve themselves through the medium of books should have the opportunity to do so, any action taken in defiance of law only leads to defiance of other laws.

To the *Commercial Appeal*, the sitins represented an "evil misuse of youth." The editorial included a Menckenesque insult-in-passing, directed at an old and familiar antagonist, the NAACP, and it also included combative recognition of a newly emergent and more militant civil rights group, the Congress of Racial Equality (CORE).

11. 16 February 1960.

The following day in Knoxville, the conservative *Journal*, which had supported efforts made by and on behalf of Negroes to vote and to attend integrated schools, argued that the "young fire-brands" were militating against their own best interests. A "minority of race, creed, or color," the *Journal* reminded the Negroes, "can become so provocative in the effort to achieve relatively small objectives, that it impedes the achievement of far more important ones."

The new flareup of violence in the cities provoked the editorial ire of several county weeklies, the vast majority of which were conservative. In West Tennessee, the Trenton *Herald-Register* scored the Negro students by observing that, "in silliness of conception," sit-ins ranked with goldfish swallowing and telephone booth-stuffing.[12] The *Herald-Register* branded the new tactic as "an organized movement by conscious provocateurs . . . [that] is per se a breach of the peace." If it was not soon halted, voluntarily, it should be stopped by "governmental force."

In Middle Tennessee, the Lawrenceburg *Democrat-Union* admitted that it was the job of the courts, not that of the *Democrat-Union*, to decided "whether or not integration is sound and proper." [13] It was even willing to concede that "in principle, perhaps it is." But the weekly suggested that the verdict should depend upon the six years' accumulation of evidence. "What," it asked rhetorically, "has [integration] accomplished so far?"

It has fomented bitterness and hate; it has resulted in the bombing of schools; it has imposed jail sentences on white and colored; it has encouraged mob violence; it has been the direct result [sic] of the wanton destruction of public property; it has disrupted business; it has caused distrust and envy; it has destroyed personal friendships; it has even broken up family ties; it has flaunted [sic] bitter dissension. It has exploded the peace of communities which residents had enjoyed for generations, with the viscious [sic] employment of racial hatred and sadistic discrimination.

Even in our Congress, it has caused that august body, which is primarily designed to be composed of men of dignity and intelligence, and statesmanship, and Constitutional loyalty, to become a disorganized, shouting, childishly ridiculous scramble of assinity [sic], indulging in antics that would be

12. 25 February 1960.
13. 24 March 1960.

more appropriate to something, first clipped, and then herded into a barbed-wire corral.

The moderate dailies could only agree with their conservative counterparts. Several of them joined the conservative *Commercial Appeal* in openly expressing sympathy for the goals of the frustrated young Negroes. But, like the Memphis daily, none of the moderate dailies could condone the means employed.

In Memphis, the *Press-Scimitar* asserted on the first of March that it could find no evidence to support the charge made by Senator Richard Russell of Georgia, and echoed by the *Commercial Appeal*, that the sit-ins were purposefully "designed by northern groups to 'start a race riot of terrible proportions' in the South to force Senate passage of a civil rights bill." The *Press-Scimitar* carefully emphasized that "the demonstrations seem to have been carefully planned as a passive campaign which the planners and the demonstrators hope would be effective, as a similar one was at Tulsa, Oklahoma, last years." [14] To reinforce this point in defense of the Negro demonstrators, it even reprinted mimeographed instructions which were carried by demonstrators in Nashville:

DO show yourself friendly at the counter at all times.
DO sit straight and always face the counter.
DO refer all information to your leader in a polite manner.
DO remember the teachings of Jesus Christ, Mohandas
    K. Gandhi and Martin Luther King.
DON'T strike back, or curse back, if attacked.
DON'T laugh out.
DON'T hold conversations with floor-walkers.
DON'T leave your seat until your leader has given you permission.
DON'T block entrances to the stores and the aisles.
Remember love and non-violence, may God bless each of you.

But the *Press-Scimitar* also observed that, although the demonstrations

---

14. The Tulsa demonstrators can rightfully claim that they, not the Greensboro group, first resurrected CORE's old wartime tactic. But their passive resistance, though initially more successful than that of the Greensboro Negroes, did not spark a nationwide series of demonstrations as did Greensboro's. Thus their demonstration is less useful to the writer as an introductory device; they will have to settle for a footnote—and for mundane success.

had been peaceful in Oklahoma and had led to voluntary compliance there, in Tennessee they had all sparked racial violence. The editorial concluded that, because of this, all sit-ins should be abandoned. Later that month, when sit-ins occurred for the first time in Memphis, the *Press-Scimitar* urged the "negroes" (it always incorrectly used the lower case) to stick to the courts.[15] The daily feared that, if the Negroes "are going to establish the power of demonstration, even peaceful demonstration, then they are weakening the prestige of law which is now on their side."

In the three other big cities, the *Tennessean,* the *Times,* and the *News-Sentinel* expressed similar disapproval of the sit-ins. From February through April, the *Tennessean* published eight editorials which urged the Negroes to halt the demonstrations. The *Tennessean* also urged a seven-man biracial committee—newly-formed by Mayor Ben West at the request of many local religious and civic groups—to press hard for "community action," for a "solution" of some kind.[16] Like most of the big dailies, the *Tennessean* urged the old, established Negro leaders in the community to curb the zeal of the militant young students.

Ironically, the last week in February had been officially proclaimed to be Brotherhood Week. The *Oak Ridger* on February 26 celebrated Brotherhood Week by observing that "rights can be fought for in the courts and picketed for in the streets. But the courts and the streets can not produce brotherhood." "The goal [of the demonstrators] is an

15. 29 March 1960. Of all the ambitious schemes of Marcus Garvey, black nationalist leader of the twenties, his only ultimately successful endeavor was to convince the publishing world of the propriety of capitalizing the word Negro, as is done with the word "Caucasian." But in the Southern press, "negro" has been so frequently printed interchangeably with "colored," and in opposition to "white," that the lower case "n" still widely and incorrectly prevails.

16. The Nashville Negroes agreed to cease their sit-ins while the new committee deliberated. Three weeks later, the committee submitted a compromise proposal that eating facilities be desegregated on a partial basis over a ninety-day trial period, during which no demonstrations would be held. The *Tennessean* editorially endorsed the proposal, but the Negroes rejected it on the ground that it placed the principle of desegregation on trial. Subsequently, demonstrations were resumed. See *SSN,* May 1960, p. 6.

understandable one," the *Oak Ridger* admitted. But the small daily added the usual admonition that their "method is of questionable ethical as well as practical value:

But how, the impatient ones for progress ask, is anything to be accomplished if not through demonstrations, court orders—forcing the issue? The voluntary moves have been almost nonexistent. This is, indeed, a question with basis in the context of the present. However, it seems at times that those who ask ofttimes tend to be too concerned with truculence and too little active for other more positive ways of advancing their aims.

Although it was a moderate newspaper in matters relating to the racial question, and was to some degree sympathetic to the Negroes' demands, the *Oak Ridger* shared with large dailies and small weeklies a belief in the categorical imperative that the breaking of laws—even if prompted by noble motives—could not be condoned on any grounds.

The young Negroes were admittedly violating the state regulation requiring segregated seating in eating establishments and the state law prohibiting trespass. But they justified the trespass by invoking, as their articulate spokesmen had done a century before, a higher law than the law of man; they appealed to the ultimate law of a just God. Indeed, many of the young Negroes in Nashville were trained in the new technique of nonviolent protest in workshops sponsored by the Nashville Christian Leadership Council (NCLC). The NCLC was a group of Negro ministers affiliated with the Southern Christian Leadership Council (SCLC), which was directed by the Reverend Martin Luther King, Jr. Prominent among the Negro leader of the NCLC was the Reverend James M. Lawson, Jr. Lawson, a native of Pennsylvania, was a student at the Divinity School of Vanderbilt University. The thirty-two-year-old Negro who had served as a missionary in India was an ordained minister in the Methodist church.

On March 3, the executive committee of Vanderbilt's board of trustees voted to dismiss Lawson because of his "strong commitment to a planned campaign of civil disobedience." [17] By expelling Lawson, the board thereby injected into an already stormy dispute over racial discrimination the volatile issues of religious conviction and academic

17. *SSN,* April 1960, p. 5.

freedom. The dean of the divinity school, J. Robert Nelson, together with eleven of his faculty resigned in protest. Additionally, three Negro and sixteen white students at the divinity school announced that they would not return to Vanderbilt, and three white graduates of the school announced that they would return their diplomas.[18] The dean of the Yale Divinity School, Liston Pope, had been invited to dedicate Vanderbilt's handsome new divinity quadrangle. While speaking at the dedication ceremony, Dean Pope displayed his moral commitment, if also perhaps a touch of lese majesty—by praising those who supported Lawson, while strongly criticizing the university's action. Because of the issues involved and because of Vanderbilt's respected reputation, the dramatic case was soon receiving nationwide attention in the media.

Lawson received moral support and offers of scholarships from divinity schools at Yale, Chicago, Denver, and Berkeley. But Lawson received no support from the press in Tennessee. From the conservative press, unanimous approval of Lawson's dismissal came as no surprise. The *Banner* (whose publisher, Stahlman, was also a Vanderbilt trustee) compared Lawson's "shenanigans" with those of "his white counterpart, the outrageous racist, John Kasper, now behind bars in the Davidson County Workhouse. . . ." [19] In characteristic prose, the *Banner* excitedly mixed its metaphors in declaring that Lawson was

so lacking in intelligence that he was innocently absorbed in this monkey-business—or the artless victim of ideological puppy-love; a sort of overgrown juvenile delinquent, finding himself suddenly kneedeep in wild oats which he hadn't realized he was sowing.

The *Banner* helpfully suggested that Lawson go to Harlem, but added that "Rep. Adam Clayton Powell might consider that 'unfair competition.' "

In Memphis, the *Commercial Appeal* on the third of June reported that Lawson had "once served as Southern secretary of the Fellowship

18. *SSN*, July 1960, p. 7. Eventually, ten of the faculty withdrew their resignations at the invitation of Chancellor Branscomb, and the three Negro students reneged on their vow not to return. The embittered Dean Nelson's resignation, however, was accepted.

19. 2 March 1960.

of Reconciliation, a pacifist group." The *Commercial Appeal* also disclosed that Lawson had refused, as a conscientious objector, to report for induction under the Selective Service Act, and had subsequently served eleven months of a three-year sentence before being paroled.

None of the moderate newspapers supported Lawson, either. Nor did they support Dean Nelson. The Springfield *Herald*—a moderate weekly in Middle Tennessee which had criticized Faubus and had frequently observed that the alternative of obeying the law of the land was anarchy—consistently applied that dictum to the Lawson case.[20] The *Tennessean,* while admitting that "the methods and the timing of the dismissal of Mr. Lawson left something to be desired," nevertheless declared on June 9 that Chancellor Harvie Branscomb had little choice but to dismiss him. The *Tennessean* observed that the appeal to Christian principles cuts both ways:

One might assume that, in advocating any principle, a Christian group would aspire, as far as consistent with right, to promotion of harmony rather than disharmony. If the success of an argument becomes more important than its impact for good, nothing is gained. Nothing in this case, except the damage being done to an institution that will, nonetheless, outlast all the parties involved.

But, while failing to support Lawson or Dean Nelson, the moderate dailies did a substantially better job of relating both sides of the dispute. While not supporting Dean Nelson, the *Tennessean* on the first of June admitted that he and his faculty "have an emotional reaction to the sit-in record that they link with a deep moral issue." The *News-Sentinel* on the same day pointed out in Nelson's favor that the divinity school's committee on admissions, which knew Lawson, had recommended that the chancellor re-admit him, and that the trustees, who had overruled the committee on admissions and had sustained the chancellor's action, had never even met Lawson. The *News–Sentinel* approvingly observed that both Dr. Branscomb and Dean Nelson were sincere in their defense of principle. "In either case," the editorial concluded, "it is unfortunate that so sharp a clash within so respected a university had to add another bitter mile along the way to the inevitable legalistic equality of the races."

20. 9 June 1960.

Most exemplary of the troubled ambivalence expressed toward conflicting legal and moral principles was the editorial opinion of the Chattanooga *Times*. Editors of the *Times* asserted with approval on the first of June that "Chancellor Branscomb, pointing out that Vanderbilt was desegregated in phases of its graduate school life, has brilliantly stated the case for obedience to law." Like the Springfield *Herald* the *Times* observed that "those who call for compliance with the law of the land in the school desegregation issue will especially see his point." But the *Times,* unlike the conservative press, did not ignore the merits of the moral issue. With characteristic thoroughness, the *Times* explained that the state law stipulating segregated seating in eating places was not in fact a law as such. It was a regulation of the state's department of conservation, "although it has criminal enforceability and thus the character of law." After conceding "the probable unconstitutionality" of the regulation, the *Times* committed itself on the moral issue with unusual verve:

What is lacking, in the opinion of many who look to a great Southern university for leadership in a time of social travail, is an expression as to the moral honesty of a regulation which denies Negroes eating facilities at stores open to the public even though all the stores' other items are advertised to them.

Tennesseans during the spring of 1960 observed in travail what was probably the state's finest educational institution. During that same spring, they also witnessed one of the state's smallest—and certainly its most unusual and controversial—educational institutions in greater distress. The previous year, the staunchly segregationist attorney general of Arkansas had volunteered his advice that Tennessee's legislature ought to investigate what was going on at the Highlander Folk School. Perched atop Monteagle mountain in the Cumberland range, Highlander was a prolabor and prointegration center for adult education; its workshops reflected the conditions and ideology of its depression-ridden birth in 1932. Since its founding it had conducted racially integrated workshops for adults, whose ideological convictions ranged from the liberal to the radical left, who were interested in learning techniques of organizing labor and of breaking down the South's biracial system.

The *Tennessean* had deplored the proposed "witch hunt" as a revival of McCarthyism and urged Governor Ellington to veto the investigation.[21] Its editorial observed that Highlander did not hide its "ultra-liberal philosophy," but "stands openly on it." Further, the editorial recalled, the House Committee on Un-American Activities had repeatedly investigated Highlander without turning up any red skeletons. The anti-Communist "witch hunt" was, in fact, only a "smoke screen" behind which legislators might "harass and intimidate the institution because of its candid advocacy of integration." But the legislature had approved the investigation for "subversive activities" by a voice vote, and the governor had declined to veto it.

In March of 1959, the joint five-man investigating committee had held hearings in Grundy County at Tracy City, near Highlander.[22] While failing to turn up evidence of subversion, the committee had recommended that the state bring suit to revoke Highlander's charter on legal and financial grounds. Subsequently, Highlander's director, Myles Horton, had invited the committee to attend one of the school's integrated workshops. None had accepted. In August, state and county officials had conducted a raid on Highlander's premises which had interrupted a racially integrated banquet at the school. A few bottles of beer and other alcoholic beverages had been confiscated. A local court subsequently ordered the school's main building padlocked for more than a month as a public nuisance. This had pleased the *Banner,* which referred to Highlander as "a sagging, paint peeled, haunted-looking house known among local folk for strange goings-on, 'integration workshops,' left-wing chin fests and black, and tan hoedowns." [23]

In February of 1960, Circuit Judge Chester Chattin, sitting at little Altamont in mountainous Grundy County, revoked Highlander's charter on the grounds that the integrated classes there violated Tennessee's law prohibiting all inter-racial classrooms.[24] The fifty-

21. "Why Conduct a Witch Hunt for Arkansas?" 29 January 1959.
22. *SSN,* April 1959, 9. No Negroes were permanent residents of Grundy County.
23. 9 September 1959.
24. *SSN,* March 1960, 2.

eight-year-old law had been declared unconstitutional by the state's supreme court in 1956, but Judge Chattin ruled that the law had been declared invalid only in regard to its application to public, not to private, schools. The judge also made reference to the alleged sale of beer at Highlander and to Horton's personal ownership of 70 of the farm's 300 tax-exempt acres as additional grounds for revoking its charter. The attorney for Highlander was Cecil Branstetter, a former member of the legislature who frequently handled litigation for labor unions in Nashville. Branstetter, in immediately filing for a new trial, wryly suggested that Vanderbilt University and the University of the South ought, in the interest of consistency, to have their charters promptly revoked also. The latter university, located at Sewanee, shared Monteagle mountain with Highlander; a highly regarded Episcopal institution, it had admitted Negroes to its school of divinity for several years.

The *News–Free Press* in nearby Chattanooga was ecstatic at news of Highlander's plight.

From its Red-tinged beginnings, HFS near Monteagle, Tennessee, has been a notorious, disgraceful, left-wing, integrationist institution of highly questionable purposes. But it has gone along imperturbably, angeled by a band of nationally-known left-wing quacks.[25]

In reply, Horton, a native Tennessean whose democratic populism was no less native, produced a letter signed by most of his nationally known supporters which declared that they were "profoundly disturbed about the continuing harassment to which Highlander . . . has been subjected." [26] Among the signers were Dr. Reinhold Niebuhr, Dr. Alexander Meicklejohn, Dr. Max Lerner, Dr. Frank Graham, Mrs. Eleanor Roosevelt, Harry Golden, the Reverend Martin Luther King, Jr., Mrs. John Dewey, Harry Ashmore, and Jackie Robinson. Horton thereby countered his critics' charges of guilt-by-association with an appeal to what might be called innocence-by-association.

In South Pittsburg, just a few miles southeast of Monteagle mountain, the weekly *Hustler* suggested a simple solution to the dilemma posed by Highlander:

25. 17 February 1960.
26. Quoted in *SSN*, March 1960, 2.

If the Highlander Folk School is one whose teachings are true to the American way of life, then it should become militant to the extent of self-preservation and self respect by resenting what is being said in the press. If on the other hand its teachings are contrary to Americanism, then it should be picked up by the seat of its pants and pitched off the highest bluff of the Cumberland mountain, westward if you please.[27]

In an editorial curiously inconsistent with its former utterances, the *News-Sentinel* rhetorically asked "if state segregation laws apply to a private institution?" The *News-Sentinel* then answered its own question by responding that "we think they should." [28] The editorial explained that the Knoxville daily had previously tolerated Highlander's existence on the pragmatic grounds that "the school was such a small operation that it had little impact on the people of Tennessee." The *Tennessean* had earlier defended Highlander's right to operate on the principled grounds that, "if the day comes when minority views are not tolerated in this country, no matter how unpopular they may be, then democracy will have lost its meaning." [29] But the *News-Sentinel* in the spring of 1960 was enigmatically suggesting that the school's right to exist should be judged only according to "whether it serves any good purpose."

Deprived of its folk environment in the rustic Cumberland Mountains, Highlander reluctantly retreated to the urban anonymity of Knoxville. It was destined to receive, at the hands of a few incautious and gullible Deep Southerners, even further notoriety—and quite unfairly so—as the allegedly Communist school where Martin Luther King had received his Marxist indoctrination.

Racial relations had deteriorated considerably since the end of the previous year, when the fond hope that a plateau had been reached had brought a too-brief solace to the press in Tennessee. The illusory respite had been abruptly terminated by the failure of the Pearl River Grand Jury to indict the alleged lynchers of Mack Charles Parker, the disfranchisement and the economic reprisals of Haywood and

27. 12 September 1959.
28. 18 February 1960.
29. 29 January 1959.

Fayette counties, the passage of a new and stronger civil rights bill, the sit-ins, the revocation of Highlander's charter, and the turmoil at Vanderbilt. It was in some ways ironical that the moderate newspapers of Tennessee admonished Negroes to abandon their new tactic of nonviolent demonstrations on the practical ground that it was only hindering their efforts to achieve equal rights. The white moderates were saying, in effect, that worthy ends do not justify unworthy means. But the Negroes countered with an argument that was perhaps even more deeply rooted in the heritage of American pragmatism: one cannot argue with success.

In December of 1959, the NCLC had asked several Nashville merchants to desegregate voluntarily their eating facilities. All had refused. On May 10, after the demonstrations, lunch counters in six drug, dime, and department stores in Nashville were quietly desegregated in accordance with the terms of a secret agreement reached between the Negroes and the merchants.[30] On May 13, four lunch counters were successfully desegregated in Knoxville. Even in Memphis, where both dailies had deplored the sit-ins, the moderate *Press-Scimitar* had been prompted by fears of new racial turmoil to endorse desegregation in an unprecedented fashion: "There is no obstacle in the way of the board granting the request of the negro community for equal access to books, and it would be the better part of wisdom for the board to do so." [31]

But the Negroes' limited gains—though impressive in so Southern a context—had been achieved at the price of a marked increase in racial animosity. For the first time, all of the white press in Tennessee had united, at least in opposition to the Negroes' new methods, if not in opposition to their goals. The summer of 1960 was the first of the "long hot summers" of racial unrest that the controversial tactic of civil disobedience, in combination with the depressed soical conditions against which the tactic was designed to protest, had done so much to create.

We know from hindsight that the racial violence occasioned by

30. *SSN,* June 1960, 7.
31. 29 March 1960.

these demonstrations was destined to intensify with the coming of each successive summer throughout the early sixties. The tumultous reception accorded the "Freedom Riders" during the early summer of 1961 was to give way to the riotous greeting of James Meredith at Ole Miss in 1962. Oxford, in turn, was to be tragically upstaged the following year by the agony of Birmingham and the stunning horror of Dallas. Within a year of the young President's assassination, our perspective tells us, the decade of desegregation was to culminate in the historic passage of by far the most comprehensive civil rights act since the Reconstruction, and in a Presidential election that witnessed the nation's most fundamental political and philosphical cleavage of the twentieth century. But our editors, possessed of no crystal ball, perforce responded to this astonishing series of catalytic events in a fashion that was soon to reveal that their own ranks were riven by a political and philosophical cleavage that was well nigh as wide as that dividing the nation as a whole. Although temporarily obscured by the editors' near unanimous condemnation of civil disobedience, this fundamental diversity was to be reflected once again in a vigorous dialogue that bore witness to the essential health of their institution.

8

Those Long Hot Summers

THE scorching heat of summer comes early to the South and lingers late into the fall. Its wilting embrace long ago prompted Southern planters to defend their "peculiar institution" with the rationale—to them, self-evident—that only African Negroes were sufficienctly endowed by Nature's God to work the blistering fields of cotton. But the debilitating heat that drove white men to their shaded verandas— and that drove dogs mad, some said, under the mid-summer reign of Sirius—could also combine with ancient passions and with nascent longings for justice to drive men, white and black alike, out into the sweltering streets in a frenzy of violence. And so it was in Alabama, in the third week of May, 1961. "Freedom Riders," they called them-selves, white and black alike, and they boarded the well-publicized buses for Alabama that May, and later for mississippi, seeking to prove that the court-ordered desegregation of public facilities in interstate commerce was being honored in the breach. "Outside agitators stirring up trouble in the South," Harry Truman called them, and the *Banner* applauded the former President's perception.[1] "Riot Riders," the *Commercial Appeal* labeled them, and many an anxious white in that giant daily's Deep South constituency must have responded with a smile of knowing approval as its editors wryly suggested that the "visitors from the North" be given the "privilege" of a "taste of

1. 3 June 1961.

209

plantation life" by chopping cotton for $3 a day at Mississippi's notorious state penal farm at Parchman.[2]

The riders' bloody reception, first in Aniston, then in Birmingham and, most savagely, in Montgomery—and the conspicuous tardiness and reserve of local police—has been well recorded in the national and indeed the international press.[3] Although the Aniston group originated in Washington, D.C., most of the injured at Birmingham and Montgomery were not freedom-riding "visitors from the North," in fact, but were white newsmen, local Negroes, and Nashville college students of both races. John Seigenthaler, who was within a year to return to Nashville to edit the *Tennessean*, was to have his views on Southern racial relations further sharpened by his unhappy experience in Montgomery. As President Kennedy's special envoy from the Justice Department to Alabama, the 32-year-old Seigenthaler was bludgeoned to the ground while trying to assist an injured white rider, and he lay unconscious in the street for 25 minutes before an ambulance took him away.

The vexatious excursions of the freedom riders differed from the civil disobedience of the dime-store sit-ins in that the law was clearly on the bus-riders' side. There was no law in 1961, whether Southern state or federal, compelling privately owned lunch counters to serve all races—although the legality of using state laws against trespass to enforce such segregation was being challenged in the courts. But the Supreme Court had ruled in 1956, in the case of *Boyton* v. *Virginia*,[4] that a Negro bus passenger in interstate travel had a federal right, under the Interstate Commerce Act, to be served without discrimination—even if the terminal facilities were not owned and operated by the carrier. Thus Tennessee editors, who had condemned the sit-ins

2. 14 June 1961, Mississippi authorities subsequently acceded to the wishes of the *Commercial Appeal,* if not to the wishes of the riders, by transferring a number of them to Parchman from Hinds (Jackson) County Jail. *SSN,* August 1961, p. 15.

3. *SSN,* June 1961, 6–7. Montgomery Police Commissioner L. B. Sullivan was quoted as having said that "we have no intention of standing guard for a bunch of trouble makers coming into our city and making trouble."

4. 364 U.S. 454, 81 Sup. Ct. 182, 5 L. Ed. 2d 206, 1960. See Blaustein and Ferguson, *Desegregation and the Law,* pp. 282–287.

with near unanimity, tended to view the freedom rides with a marked ambivalence. While condemning the familiar specter of outside agitation, and the hypocrisy attendant unto Northern demands that the South atone for the sins of the entire nation, Tennessee editors could not deny that the bus terminals remained illegally segregated, and some of them openly addressed themselves to that awkward and incontrovertible fact. Both the *Tennessean* and the *Commercial Appeal* regretted that the freedom riders were not heeding the call of Attorney General Robert Kennedy for a cooling-off period. But the *Tennessean* admitted that,

as the Freedom Riders demonstrated, and as the [Civil Rights] commission pointed out, "many Negro interstate passengers are subjected to segregation in several forms in substantial part of the United States," even today. . . . Those areas which seek to hold to the old order are again warned by the government that rights of all travelers in interstate commerce will not be denied. It is long past time for these areas to bow to the inevitable.[5]

Even the *Commercial Appeal* did not object to the notion of testing whether the bus terminals were still segregated. What the *Commercial Appeal* did object to was "grandstanding before television and news magazine cameramen in the hope of well-publicized martyrdom. . . . A bona-fide testing could have been done by one person and the court action that followed would have demonstrated segregation or desegregation." [6] The *Commercial Appeal* was even willing to concede that the freedom rides "may have been an honest protest [by "well meaning but misguided Americans"] against a section's mores." [7] But its editors were convinced that the freedom rides had deteriorated to a movement "in which hypocrisy and probably downright subversion had taken over." [8] What most distressed the *Commercial Appeal*, however, was that

it is the South that sincerely and most effectively resists the efforts of communists and fellow travelers in this nation. . . . But it is the South that gets shoved around again, and held up as an object of scorn around the globe.[9]

5. 23 September 1961.
6. 22 May 1961.
7. 14 June 1961.
8. Ibid.
9. 22 May 1961.

While the furor over the freedom rides was commanding the attention of the press, a little-noticed event of great portent occurred in
Jackson, Mississippi. There, on May 31, James Howard Meredith, a
29 year-old married Air Force veteran who was a sophomore at all-
Negro Jackson State College, petitioned Federal District Judge Sidney
C. Mize for an immediate temporary restraining order to enjoin
officials at the University of Mississippi from refusing to allow him to
transfer to the university.[10] Meredith had been attempting to transfer
since January 31, and he had hoped to be admitted to the Ole Miss
summer session. But such are the ways of judicial delay that it was
not until February of 1962 that Judge Mize announced his novel
finding that Ole Miss was "not a racially segregated institution," [11]
and that as a consequence Meredith could not have been racially
discriminated against. Meredith's appeal to the Fifth Circuit Court of
Appeals in New Orleans produced on June 25 a two-to-one reversal
of the district court's decision.[12] This decision was followed by an
intramural squabble among the Southern federal judges of comic-opera
proportions—a jurisdictional donnybrook in which the majesty of the
law took something of a beating. But the upshot of it all was that
Meredith entered Ole Miss on October 1, accompanied by 15,000 in-
fantrymen and 600 United States marshals. The ugly story of Meredith's reception was written in blood at Oxford, and it has been amply
recorded elsewhere in ink.[13] What concerns us here is the extensive

10. *SSN,* July 1961, p. 6. Meredith's suit was financed by the NAACP, and
his chief attorney was Constance Baker Motley. The case was *James H. Meredith*
v. *Charles Dixon Fair* (President of the Board of Trustees of State Institutions
of Higher Learning).

11. *SSN,* February 1962, p. 1. In finding that Meredith's application for transfer
to Ole Miss had been properly rejected as incomplete and inadequate, Judge Mize
observed that Meredith had failed to attach the required six recommendations
from alumni of the university. Meredith replied that since all of the alumni
were white, the requirement was a device designed rather obviously to maintain
a racially segregated student body, and as such was unconstitutional.

12. *SSN,* July 1962, p. 1. Judge John Minor Wisdom's opinion asserted that
"from the moment the defendants discovered that Meredith was a Negro they
engaged in a carefully calculated campaign of delay, harassment and masterly
inactivity."

13. See *SSN,* October 1962, 1, 10; Muse, *Prelude,* Chapter 17; Lewis, *Portrait,*
Chapter 11; Theordore C. Sorensen, *Kennedy* (New York: Harper & Row, 1965).

degree to which the Tennessee press failed to rally around what one editor called "the Bonnie Blue Flag" being waved by Governor Ross Barnett and his beleagured fellow officials in "the sovereign state of Mississippi," as they stood melodramatically if unsuccessfully in the schoolhouse door to bar Meredith's admission, then washed their hands and blamed federal intervention when violence ensued.

That the four progressive dailies of the old anit-Crump coalition should have denounced Barnett as they had denounced Faubus is perhaps no surprise. Nor was it unusual that the rhetorical charge was led by the *Tennessean*, which on eleven separate occasions during that turbulent fall directed its editorial fire at the suicidal "folly" and "infamy" of the defiant Mississippians. (On one of these occasions, however, the *Tennessean* joined the *Commercial Appeal* in reprimanding Meredith for his accurate complaints to the press that Negro soldiers had been carefully culled from the ranks assigned to protect him.) [14] Further, the Scripps-Howard evening dailies in Memphis and Knoxville once again employed nearly identical language as they tongue-lashed the "morally overpowered" governor for the

inflamatory acts and statements [which] have stirred atavistic fears and hatreds of mob material including fanatics and congenital criminals from other states and other Mississippi communities, who have drifted into Oxford. [15]

Finally, rounding out the ranks of the four big moderate dailies was the Chattanooga *Times,* which joined in the excoriation of Barnett. But, in the process of voicing disapproval, the *Times* performed the feat, extraordinarily rare among Southern newspapers, of admitting that there existed in at least one Southern state a climate of opinion so monolithic and overwhelming in its embrace of racial segregation and the states' rights rationale that defended it that the state's defiant leaders *were* in fact democratically responding to the wishes of the

---

pp. 483–488; and Meredith's own account, *Three Years in Mississippi* (Bloomington: University of Indiana Press, 1966).

14. "Mr. Meredith Is in Bad Taste," *Tennessean*, 11 October 1962. The *Commercial Appeal* attacked Meredith on October 11, November 1, and again on the first of February, 1963.

15. The *Press-Scimitar* entitled its editorial "Oxford Incident," whereas the *News-Sentinel* more suggestively entitled its editorial "Oxford Outrage." Both were published on 1 October 1962.

majority of the voters. Southern newspapers had long been in the habit of responding to those occasional and embarrassing acts of demagogery, defiance, or racial violence that have so frequently disturbed Southern tranquility by deploring them—but customarily with the added reassurance that the majority of the good people of "the great state of Alabama," Mississippi, etc., were law-abiding citizens who also deplored such untoward incidents. But the *Times,* on the last day of September, strongly implied that Mississippi had become a totalitarian society:

In Mississippi, Gov. Barnett has majority support. For eight years now, a whole state has been virtually conditioned to such an incredible response. Dissent, which would have warned of the awful consequences now so apparent, has been stifled. Academic faculties have been intimidated. The White Citizens Council has been officially subsidized. Only one lawyer in Mississippi has been willing to take civil rights cases. The illusion was fostered that Mississippi was somehow different from other states, and beyond the law. Almost nothing has been done to head off the inevitability of the most serious federal-state collision since the Civil War.

Not long thereafter, a telling incident occurred which led the *Tennessean* at least inferentially to make the same observation. On November 7, Professor James W. Silver of the department of history at Ole Miss delivered a paper before the Southern Historical Association at Asheville, North Carolina. Silver, who had taught at Ole Miss since 1936, charged in his widely publicized paper that Mississippi had evolved into a "totalitarian society [which] imposes on all its people an obedience to an official orthodoxy almost identical with the proslavery philosophy." [16] The *Tennessean's* editorial of November 13 was written in response to the suggestion of Mississippi Congressman John Bell Williams that "Mississippi ought to fumigate its college staffs" and replace the casualties with "professors who will teach American-

16. "Mississippi: The Closed Society," in George B. Tindal (ed.), *The Pursuit of Southern History: Presidential Addresses of the Southern Historical Association, 1935–1963* (Baton Rouge: Louisiana State University Press, 1964), pp. 462–468. Silver subsequently published his thesis by the same title in book form (New York: Harcourt, Brace and World, Inc., 1964).

ism, not foreign ideologies." [17] The *Tennessean's* editorial reported Silver's charges that Mississippians

are shut off from the mainstream of American thought, and he raked the state's press, pulpit, legislative halls and members of the bar. He contended that every "Mississippi politician not only denies the validity of the 14th amendment but in his heart hungers for the negative days of the Articles of Confederation.

By concluding that "the congressman's outburst serves only to support Dr. Silver's warning about a closed society where no man is free to criticize," the *Tennessean* hinted at the ironical quandry into which Silver had thrown Mississippi officials. For to fire the professor would only serve to validate his charge (and would probably have completed the destruction of a once-great university, for the Southern Association of Colleges and Schools was already threatening to revoke the university's accreditation because of the political interference in its affairs), yet not to fire him would mean continued public subsidy of his outspoken dissent.[18]

Editors of Tennessee's four moderate dailies had never been warm admirers of defiant Southern politicians. But in the fall of 1962, Mississippi officialdom could find precious little support even among Tennessee's traditionalist press. In Knoxville, the *Journal* reminded its readers on October 2 that Barnett had journeyed to Knoxville six years previous as a volunteer lawyer to defend the "racist John Kasper," and concluded that "there is blood on his hands." The following day in Nashville, the *Banner* insisted in a front-page editorial that the "Mississippi Tragedy Could Have Been Averted":

Mississippi could have resolved this issue, as have other states—including Tennessee—no less mindful of states' rights in policy determination, and opposing compulsory integration, but aware of the legal obstacles erected when turned back by every level of the federal judiciary. They bowed to the necessity for observance of the law, however much it incurred individual or mass resentment.

But the strongest language in condemnation of Barnett and his fellow

17. Quoted from *Tennessean*, 13 November 1962.
18. Silver relieved the Mississippi officials of this dilemma first by going on the lecture circuit, and finally by removing his base of operations to Notre Dame.

Mississippi officials came from the traditionalist daily that circulated so widely in Mississippi itself. For out of Memphis on October 2 thundered the *Commercal Appeal's* stern admonition that

disagreement with the court's decisions does not abnegate the Governor's oath. On Sunday, Governor Barnett's statements sounded like hollow disclaimers of responsibility for the rioting which followed. He cannot absolve himself of that burden, and his call for calm and reason after the fact—while certainly needed—is simply too late to clear his record in the case.

The Governor calls this an invasion, although Mississippi National Guardsmen are participating in the Federal action. He has used the Mississippi Highway Patrol to keep Meredith out of Ole Miss, while he could, but has permitted it to step back when civil strife tore his state apart.

While the caravans of agitators poured onto the campus, Mr. Barnett said nothing. Not a Mississippi official rose to reprimand them.

Furthermore, all three traditionalist dailies in Memphis, Nashville, and Knoxville had condemned the widely publicized antics of former Major General Edwin A. Walker, who ironically had commanded the regulars at Little Rock in 1957, and who in 1962 led the Oxford irregulars in an ill-fated advance on the federal bastion at the Lyceum Building on the evening of September 30. Finally, all three newspapers had kind words to say of President Kennedy's televised appeal for law and order on that same turbulent evening.

But Barnett could still count on the sympathetic support of Roy McDonald and the consistent if intractable *News–Free Press*. On the day following the President's broadcast and the simultaneous convergence in Oxford of Meredith, the marshals and the mobs, the *News–Free Press* defended the defiance of Mississippi in vitriolic prose:

With an application of force against Mississippi unequaled by application of force against Communist Cuba, the Warren Supreme Court and President Kennedy have sowed the wind and the nation has reaped the whirlwind, as two lie dead and others bear wounds triggered by dictatorial and illegal actions to which the response was unconscionable violence.

Despite pious protestations to the contrary, the Federal action against Mississippi violated the Constitution in a number of ways and therefore those who dictated it must bear responsibility for the horrible results.

President Kennedy, author of *Profiles in Courage,* had "displayed a profile of cowardice" in employing force against Mississippi instead of against Communist Cuba. He had pleaded for Mississippians to uphold a law that was unconstitutional—first, because "decrees by appointed men are not 'the law' in our Republic," and second, because the "political, sociological and demagogic . . . decrees of appointed men" were based on a Fourteenth Amendment which "was not legally approved and is not legal today." The *News–Free Press*' bitter editorial then digressed into a somewhat lengthy exegesis on strict construction, and concluded by repairing revealingly to three high tenets of the American conservative faith—a pessimistic view of human nature, a devotion to the traditional church, and a vision of America as the New Jerusalem:

And in these troubled times, let us confess the inadequacies of man; let all Americans exercise the freedom that is theirs to bow their heads to God, in subservience to His will and in petition for His guidance, that this may continue to be a Heaven-rescued land of free men seeking liberty and justice for all.

If Mississippi witnessed, during the long hot summer of 1962, a tragic and bloody sequel to Little Rock, Alabama was destined to witness an even bloodier and more tragic sequel the following summer. The plot was much the same: federal supremacy and the Fourteenth Amendment versus states' rights and the Tenth Amendment. Only the names had changed—to identify, in the eyes of most of Tennessee's journalistic leaders, the guilty. The stage had been set long ago in Alabama's flush times, and it had not been greatly altered by a Reconstruction that had largely failed to "take," or by the effulgence of time since the Bourbon redemption. But the *dramatis personnae* were new. Chief among them was former Circuit Judge George C. Wallace, whose victory in the Democratic gubernatorial primary in May of 1962 had prompted the *Tennessean* to observe, with fateful prescience, that the triumph of the "hot-eyed segregationist" surely presaged a "sad day for Alabama, if not for the nation." [19] "Tragic is the possibility," the *Tennessean* had prophesied, "that tears, not stars will fall on Alabama."

The passions of Alabama, destined to explode so destructively

19. 31 May 1962.

during the summer of 1963, began to heat up as early as Eastertide. April witnessed the marshaling of the challenging forces: Negro college students Vivian J. Malone and James A. Hood sued to enter the summer session of the state university at Tuscaloosa;[20] Martin Luther King instructed his disciplined but restive battalions in letters from the Birmingham jail; William L. Moore, a white integrationist from Baltimore, hiked toward the Alabama heartland bearing signs calling for an end to segregation (he fell, just outside of Gadsden, with a bullet in his head). May witnessed, in turn, the counter-maneuvers of the defenders of the status quo. In Montgomery, Governor Wallace affirmed his intentions of honoring an old and unquivocal campaign promise ("I draw the line in the dust and toss the gauntlet before the feet of tyranny. I say . . . segregation now . . . segregation tomorrow . . . segregation forever!") by vowing to "stand in the schoolhouse door." [21] In Birmingham, Police Commissioner Eugene (Bull) Connor and his fellow commissioners steadfastly refused to hand over control of the city to newly elected and more moderately segregationist Mayor Albert Boutwell and his city councilmen—thereby shattering the city's equilibrium as the Negro protest mounted.[22]

Thus, in Alabama that summer, the force that hoped to prove irresistible had purposefully set a collision course for the object that insisted it was immovable. The violence of their impact—first in June, then again in September—led the reluctant President twice to federalize Alabama's National Guard and to set it patrolling streets littered with the debris of bombings and spattered with the blood of Negro Sunday-

20. The University of Alabama was technically desegregated, and had been so since the first of July 1955, when Federal District Judge H. Hobart Grooms, in the case of *Lucy v. Adams,* had issued a permanent injunction desegregating the university. On April 15, Judge Grooms ordered the university to admit the two Negroes to its summer session, which was to begin in Tuscaloosa on June 11, and a third Negro, David M. McGlathery, was ordered admitted to the university's branch at Huntsville on June 13. The case was *Vivian Malone* v. *Hubert Mate.*
    21. SSN, May 1963, p. 2.
    22. The new Mayor-council form of government had been approved by Birmingham voters in the fall of 1962, and Mayor Boutwell and his nine new councilmen were scheduled to take over on April 15. The state supreme court upheld Boutwell on May 23, but Connor remained intractable.

school children. The nation reeled at the mindless carnage, and so, too, did the editors in neighboring Tennessee. They had largely seen it coming and had been at least partially instrumental in staving it off in their own state ("Crosses Burn Southward as Nashville Moves On," [23] the *Tennessean* had pridefully observed). Thus relieved of the onus of hypocrisy, they were quick to point out the wages of sin as the tears fell on Alabama.

Tennessee's press had of course long disagreed over the wisdom of desegregation. But by 1963 they were nearly unanimous in their conviction that prudence, if not conscience, dictated a bowing to the inevitable. How long would it be before the lesson of Little Rock was finally learned? And at what cost? First Faubus, then Barnett, and now Wallace. "The plot is getting old," wearily intoned the *Commercial Appeal*; "the drama has lost its zing because everyone knows how it will come out." [24] Further, such bald defiance was plainly unnecessary because carefully constructed pupil-placement laws, in combination with segregated residential patterns, had thus far proved to be effective and legally acceptable guarantors that school desegregation would remain largely token in character. Even Governor Donald Russell of South Carolina, the *Tennessean* pointed out, had been willing to desegregate Clemson in quiet order.[25] "There has been no comparable trouble in, for instance, the Deep Southern state of South Carolina," echoed both the *Press-Scimitar* and the *News-Sentinel,* "where authorities have held even unpopular law is entitled to respect." [26] And was there not some justice in the Negroes' demands—and therefore not only tragic stupidity but also great injustice in what the *Times* called the "incredible decision to use dogs in the tense Birmingham

---

23. 11 June 1963. Simultaneous with the demonstrations in Birmingham, Nashville's militant Negroes sent their children marching into the streets that summer. But the new Metropolitan government of Mayor Beverly Briley resorted not to mass arrests, fire hoses and dogs, but to a biracial commission and negotiations. As a result, a considerable portion of the downtown business establishments ultimately agreed to desegregate their facilities.

24. 11 September 1963.

25. 28 January 1963.

26. 16 September 1963.

situation which has stirred the revulsion of the civilized world"? [27] The *Tennessean* thought so:

> The world watches in dismay as Birmingham continues to meet its racial problems by filling its jails and turning dogs loose on children and adults who are demonstrating against old grievances.[28]

The *News-Sentinel* expressed sympathy for the Negroes' plight by observing that "Col. Al Lingo and his state police . . . are, for good reason, detested and termed 'head-beaters' by Birmingham Negroes." [29] Even the *Commercial Appeal* was willing to concede that "the fact that mobs are forming and reforming there day after day indicated that there is considerable resentment against the law enforcement

The Ostrich

Tom Little *in the* Tennessean

Four Killed—The Injuries Are Uncounted

Knox *in the* Banı

27. 4 May 1963.
28. 4 May 1963.
29. 19 September 1963.

officials as a result of past injustices." [30] And the *Press-Scimitar* deemed it "a bitter comment on law enforcement" in Birmingham that as of September 16, of the 21 bombings that had rocked that tortured city since the Brown decision, not one had been solved.

The chief failure, then, was one of leadership, and that emanated most pre-eminently from the statehouse in Montgomery. In blunt language, the liberal *Tennessean* deplored the "false hope and prejudice" that had "put into the governor's chair a hate-filled backwoods politician whose only recommendation was that he could render injustice to the Negro with a bloodier hand than any other candidate." [31] Both the *Times* and the *Press-Scimitar* blamed Wallace for encouraging an atmosphere of defiance that had led ineluctably to the Birmingham tragedy—the latter newspaper observing that Wallace had honored his campaign pledge "not to be 'out-segregated' . . . and these murders are a bloody consequence." [32] The *Tennessean* was particularly repelled when Wallace self-righteously labeled the bushwhack-murder of William Moore "a dastardly act" and offered a $1,000 reward for the killer—a reward, the *Tennessean* observed, which "doesn't hide his culpability in encouraging defiance of law." [33] When Medgar Evers, field secretary for the NAACP, was similarly murdered in Jackson, Mississippi, the night of June 12, the *Tennessean* deplored the "belated and dubious cries of shock and self-righteous outrage [that] went up from Mississippi. . . ." [34]

With this cold-blooded murder of an American, these conscience-stricken advocates of reasonable prejudice are demanding capture and punishment of the individual who interpreted his surroundings as an environment for murder.

Sickened by the fruits of their own labors, they now call for the sacrifice of the man whose finger pulled the trigger. . . . But some of those who are so shocked at his depravity should look for blood on the fingers of hate and defiance that pulled the trigger in his twisted mind.

30. 17 September 1963.
31. 17 September 1963.
32. 17 September 1963.
33. 16 September 1963.
34. 25 April 1963.

While the progressive coalition had no use for Wallace's principles or his prejudice, most of the traditionalist dailies were embarrassed by the degree to which Wallace tarnished the principle of states' rights with the stain of racial prejudice and by the Governor's unwillingness to apply to himself the states' rights principle of governmental restraint. In Knoxville, the conservative *Journal* was no more charitable toward Wallace than was the *News-Sentinel*; while the *Journal* held no high opinion of either President Kennedy or Martin Luther King, it saw Governor Wallace as "representing the element which steadfastly refused to recognize the Negro as a human being and a citizen of this country entitled to his constitutional rights." [35] The *Commercial Appeal* denounced the governor's "futile" gestures and "empty" pledges that had fertilized the "seeds of racial unrest." [36] Even the *Banner,* which early in the summer had publicly championed Wallace's expounding of the high principles of states' rights and had consistently deplored the President's federalizing of the National Guard of the "great state of Alabama" as a dangerously unnecessary usurpation of power, had by September come around to the view that

it would be difficult to say which is the more unseemly, a display of jack-assery on the part of a governor—making his I-am-the-law pitch, to divest local school boards and municipal executives of their authority—or an exhibition of Federal trespass on the states by White House and Justice Department command.[37]

But it was only the *Tennessean* that ventured to go a step beyond a condemnation of bad leadership and self-righteous hypocrisy, and to raise, as it and the *Times* had done the summer before in the case of Mississippi, the critical question of the pervasiveness of deep-seated social attitudes. On the morning of June 11, as Wallace was acting out his charade in the schoolhouse door at Tuscaloosa, the *Tennessean* observed that

35. 17 June 1963. The *Commercial Appeal* also denounced "those political and business leaders of Birmingham who have steadfastly refused to provide opportunities for the Negroes and who have insisted upon complete segregation regardless of the needs of the laws." 5 May 1963.
36. 12 June 1963.
37. 13 September 1963.

the real tragedy of Tuscaloosa is the element of truth contained in Governor Wallace's declaration to the people of Alabama: "I am going to stand for you at the university."

Mr. Wallace was elected, as one North Alabama paper declared, because he "shouted 'nigger' the loudest" in a state where a majority of the voters unfortunately have not yet tempered their emotions with feelings of justice, honesty and morality.

Not all of Tennessee's big-league dailies found fault with Wallace, however. The Chattanooga *News–Free Press* found Wallace to be in the great tradition of Faubus and Barnett. On September 16, the day following the fatal Birmingham church bombing, the editors of the *News–Free Press* took the long view that, deplorable as was that "sickening" and "hideous tragedy," it should not obscure the more fundamental lesson of Birmingham. That was that too few Americans seemed to understand the concept of law, which "is written for the protection of all, and is to be binding upon all." Thus the "insane

'I'm Just So Mad At Governor Wallace

Knox in the Banner

'Well, I Told You I Would Stand in the Door for You!'

Tom Little in the Tennessean

criminals" who threw the bomb were of course violators of law, but so were the "Negro agitation leaders [who] have claimed that the law does not bind them, that they consider themselves justified in breaking laws that do not suit their purposes." Worst of all,

not only are the guilty to be found among the agitators on both sides. They are to be found in positions of greatest power. The President has violated the Constitution and the law; whether motivated by politics or conviction or both, his actions have been wrong. The Supreme Court has violated the Constitution and the law; that it considers its sociology superior is no excuse.

The *News–Free Press* concluded with an interesting sentence that was revealing of the logical simplicity and utter impregnability of its strict constructionist, states'-rights defenses, and which pointed to the theme that was destined to dominate so completely the long hot summer of 1964. "The Congress," the editorial concluded, "even now is considering new violations of the Constitution to pass new 'law'; that its members were elected to legislate does not remove the legal bounds placed upon them."

9

Armageddon

CONGRESS was indeed considering new civil rights legislation that fall. The impatient liberals who had rallied with such expectant devotion to the Kennedy standard in 1960 were at long last catching the sweet scent of victory. The Democratic platform in 1960 had carried the most strongly worded civil rights plank in the party's history. Yet the realities of power are harsh to the gullible expectations aroused by campaign oratory. Candidate Kennedy had promised to issue "the long delayed executive order putting an end to racial discrimination in federally assisted housing." [1] But fear that a civil rights controversy would jeopardize enactment of his legislative program had stayed the stroke of President Kennedy's pen for almost two years, until November of 1962. Similarly, candidate Kennedy had asked Senator Joseph Clark of Pennsylvania and Representative Emanuel Celler of New York, both liberal Democrats, to "draw up civil rights legislation embodying our platform commitments for introduction at the beginning of the next session." [2] But when the Clark-Celler bills were dutifully introduced in 1961, the Kennedy administration had publicly disowned them. Kennedy had apparently concluded that, given his perilously thin working majority in the Congress, it would be unwise to alienate

1. *Congress and the Nation, 1945–1964* (Washington, D.C.: Congressional Quarterly Service, 1965), p. 1631. The survey that follows of governmental activities in civil rights is primarily derived from this valuable and comprehensive source, and from Chapter Eighteen of Sorensen, *Kennedy*.
2. *Ibid.*

further Southern Democrats and conservative Republicans by pushing
for new civil rights legislation in the hypersensitive areas of school desegregation, housing, and public accommodations. Consequently, he
confined his efforts in behalf of civil rights largely to a further pursuit
of voting rights—in apparent hopes that this compromise policy would
alienate neither Southern Democrats nor the civil rights forces, yet all
the while would swell the Democratic column with newly enfranchised
Negroes.[3]

The initial Kennedy strategy, then, differed from the Eisenhower
approach to civil rights less in design than in execution. The Justice
Department under the Eisenhower administration had filed only nine
suits charging voting discrimination during the four years following the
enactment of the civil rights act of 1957; [4] during the first ten months
of the Kennedy administration, the Justice Department, headed by the
President's brother, Robert, filed 14 suits. Further, the President's Committee on Equal Employment Opportunity, variously headed by Vice

3. In 1961, Congress extended the life of the Civil Rights Commission for two
years. In 1962, the administration successfully launched a drive to outlaw the
poll tax as a voting requirement in federal elections and primaries by constitutional amendment (this, the Twenty-fourth Amendment, was finally ratified by
the required 38 states in 1964, although its only real effect was in the five states
that still had a poll tax—Alabama, Arkansas, Mississippi, Texas, and Virginia.)
The administration also supported a bill to make any citizen with a sixth-grade
education eligible to pass a literacy test in voting for Federal elections, but the
bill died in a Senate filibuster. But the administration vigorously exerted executive pressure for an end to racial discrimination in employment generated by
federal contracts and far exceeded all previous administrations in the appointment
of Negroes to federal posts.

4. The Eisenhower administration produced another civil rights compromise
in 1960 in the form of a law that authorized judges to appoint referees to help
Negroes register. In a bitter three-way fight that began in 1959, conservatives
had sought to block any new civil rights legislation, and liberals had called for
a new law designed to circumvent the ponderous courts by authorizing the
President to appoint federal registrars to register voters physically in cases where
the Civil Rights Commission certified that discrimination had occurred. As in
1957, Senate Majority Leader Lyndon Johnson forged a compromise acceptable
to Republican senators whose votes he needed to threaten cloture. Again, as in
1957, disappointed liberals charged that Johnson was always willing to compromise too soon, thereby greatly strengthening the resolve of foot-dragging conservatives.

President Johnson, handled several hundred more cases in its first eighteen months than its predecessors had handled in six years. Nevertheless, because the federal quest for voting rights had been channeled through the overburdened and slowly-grinding gears of the federal judiciary, it had generally met with the same fate as had the federal quest for school desegregation: tokenism.[5] But the Negroes who demonstrated in more than 800 cities and towns throughout the nation in 1963 were clearly not in a mood to be propitiated by the seemingly interminable delays and inconsequential results of a few federal suits in voting rights cases in the South, nor by the administration's single legislative accomplishment in civil rights for 1963: a law extending the life of the Civil Rights Commission by one year.

But by June the violence in Birmingham and the murder of Medgar Evers had signaled an alarming deterioration of domestic order. Fully aware of the growing urgency of the situation and of the inadequacy of his former approach, President Kennedy on June 11 delivered a nationally televised plea for an end to racial discrimination in American life, and on June 19 he submitted a civil rights bill to the Congress that, in its final form, represented a fundamentally new departure in federal legislation.[6] The President's omnibus bill called for equal access to public accommodations, federal initiation of suits to desegregate schools, withdrawal of federal assistance from segregated facilities and programs, and the establishment of a Community Relations service to help local communities resolve racial disputes (the bill initially contained no provisions for fair employment practices, but the President's accompanying message expressed support for fair employment bills pending in congress). Administration strategists knew full well that sufficient obstructing maneuvers were available to the adroit conservatives to guarantee that the bill could not possibly be passed before

5. For two revealing examples of the obstacles, both social and judicial, inherent in the judicial approach to voting rights, see Lewis, *Portrait,* pp. 126–28, and 131–35.

6. On February 28, Kennedy had asked the Congress for a relatively slim civil rights package that dealt primarily with further protecting Negro voting rights, plus requests for technical assistance to desegregating schools and a four-year extension of the Civil Rights Commission.

1964. In the House, Judge Howard Smith remained a powerful tactician of delay, although the archconservative Virginia Democrat's omnipotent Rules Committee had been temporarily packed by administration forces in January 1961, and the crucial change had been made permanent the previous January. In the Senate, administration leaders could avoid the Judiciary Committee, that traditional burial ground for civil rights bills that was controlled by Mississippi's intransigent James Eastland. But the expectation of a Senate filibuster dictated that the House pass a civil rights bill first, and so hearings on HR 7152 were held during the summer of 1963 by Emanuel Celler's liberal-leaning House Judiciary Committee.

The provision in the new civil rights bill that was designed to alter most visibly and most radically the routine of Southern life was title II, which would command most Southern businessmen to open their doors to Negroes. Its target area quite obviously was the South, for the racial discrimination that was abundant throughout the rest of the nation was practiced in a more subtle and intractable fashion. Its bullseye, most spectacularly, was that repository of freedom that commanded such veneration in the heritage of Anglo-Saxon jurisprudence: the right of private property. The *Tennessean* sought to defuse this potential bombshell by pointing to the President's observation that property rights were in fact not totally sacrosanct:

The argument that such measures constitute an unconstitutional interference with property rights has consistently been rejected by the courts in upholding laws on zoning, collective bargaining, minimum wages, smoke control and countless other measures designed to make certain that the use of private property is consistent with the public interest.[7]

The *Tennessean* also hailed the President's plea that the problems of civil rights be approached from a moral as well as a legal standpoint, and its editors urged "the entire nation" to "face up to its moral responsibilities" and "resolve the ancient question of human versus property rights in the area of race relations."

But the proposal to open public accommodations by federal ukase cut the conservative sensibilities of Tennessee's traditionalist editors to

7. President John F. Kennedy, as quoted in the *Tennessean*, 1 July 1963.

the quick, and they responded in the high tradition of Paul Revere. Typical of the response of the traditionalist county weeklies was that of the Trenton *Herald Register,* which gloomily celebrated the Fourth of July by observing that the Kennedy Brothers were attempting "to enact into law a lot of recently conceived rights that have never been rights in any country in history." The *Herald Register* concluded with a double-barreled inuendo that cast aspersions on the legitimacy of both the Kennedy fortune and the Fourteenth Amendment:

This country is being troubled by the theories of a lot of impractical youngsters, some of whom got where they are because their ancestors made millions by violating the 18th Amendment, which was without a doubt the law of the land, properly adopted in every particular.

The *Banner* was similarly unimpressed by the practical sagacity of the Kennedys:

Two brothers of great wealth, sheltered in life and politically pampered and tutored—all of which brought them to positions of great power, now seek overnight to change the hearts of men.[8]

With allusions to the "socialistic New Frontier program" and to the failure of the administration to check the Communist advance, Stahlman's *Banner* denounced the civil rights bill as a sellout to lawless minorities that would impose upon the American people "the steel pattern of a police state":

The Kennedys today have passed the point of no return. There is no end in sight to the debate that will determine whether Americans will be deprived of all rights of person and property, whether the citizens will go on with the few privileges left them by the Supreme Court, or whether as homeowners, businessmen and union members, they learn to wait in tension for the tap of the U.S. marshal at the door.

The *Banner* had a good historical case in alluding to the bill as a "Second Reconstruction," and it melodramatically called upon "Southern Congressmen, [who] with the help of conservatives from other areas, have saved the country from dictatorial harassment before," to arise and do it again: *"Gentlemen of the Congress, the hour has come."*

8. "Second Reconstruction, For South—And The North," 20 June 1963.

But no Tennessee newspaper devoted more editorial attention to the civil rights bill in 1963 than did the *Commercial Appeal,* which during June and July published six lengthy editorials in careful analysis of the bill. In voicing its misgivings, the *Commercial Appeal* occasionally lapsed into the hyperbolic style of the aroused *Banner.* On June 5, the *Commercial Appeal* summarized its understanding of the bill being prepared by the administration by tersely observing that, "in other words, the doctrine of private property would go out the window." On June 28, its editors asserted that the President's proposals, if enacted, would "amount to a virtual dictatorship." And on July 3, in an editorial entitled, simply and bluntly, "American Dictatorship," the *Commercial Appeal* quoted at length from an analysis published in the July 8 issue of *U.S. News and World Report*—an analysis written by the news magazine's ultraconservative publisher, David Lawrence, whose alarm drove him to the despairing cry: "O communism, where is thy sting!" The *Commercial Appeal*'s readers were recommended to Lawrence's somber view that the Republic was crumbling:

The competent are to be told to make room for the incompetent. The successful men in business are ordered to obey the Government, which at a moment's notice can destroy their ventures into capitalism. For "private" enterprise has now been superceded by a "public" enterprise system.
. . . .
Is this the road to human happiness? Shall we abandon the Republic and, acceding to the demonstrations and violence in the streets of our cities—North and South, East and West—and become a mobocracy?

But for the most part, the *Commercial Appeal*'s anxious editorializing represented an accurate, thorough, and fair analysis of the bill's many and complex titles. It was a performance, unmatched by the more liberally inclined dailies, that the big traditionalist dailies, barring one glaring exception, were to repeat the following year as the bill's fate was decided in the Senate.

Our gift of hindsight enables us, like the proverbial Monday morning quarterback, to second-guess the past with comfortable certitude. But the very omnisience of our hindsight tempts us too often to view the past as an ineluctable chain of events, leading to foregone conclusions. We speak of the civil rights act of 1964, yet editors of many a traditionalist daily, such as the *Commercial Appeal,* were convinced that the odds were better than even that the reliable tactic of filibuster would prevent passage of the civil rights bill of 1963. Cloture, after all, had *never* been invoked in Senate civil rights debates since Rule 22 had been adopted in 1917. Although eleven attempts to halt anti–civil rights filibusters had been made since 1917, in only four had support-ers of cloture been able to produce even a simple majority in favor of the motion, much less the necessary two-thirds.[9] When, on August 28, an army of 200,000 marchers "For Jobs and Freedom" converged on Washington, Tennessee editors without exception predicted disaster; all were astonished by the triumph of orderliness that ensued. Tennessee editors—and there were quite a few of them—who had grown ac-customed to the habit of villifying the Kennedy name were stunned into silence when the President was murdered by an assassin—or assassins unknown—in Dallas on November 22. On that incredibly cruel occa-sion, they were for the most part content to defer to the genius of television as that medium, so often shoddily irresponsible, arose to the tragic occasion in its finest hour. Tennessee's editors rallied to the new President as did the nation, and they stood by him even when, in his reassuringly familiar drawl, he forthrightly asserted that "no memorial oration or eulogy could more eloquently honor President Kennedy's memory than the earliest possible passage of the civil rights bill for which he fought so long." [10]

But 1964 was a presidential election year. Since President Johnson was assured of the Democratic nomination, and since he was also in a position to hand-pick his running mate, there was every reason to be-lieve that the Democratic state primaries would be relatively tame affairs of largely parochial interest. But Alabama's Governor Wallace

9. *Congress and the Nation,* p. 1637. Cloture required, in 1963, an affirmative vote of two thirds of those senators present and voting. It should be added, of course, that the threat of a successful cloture vote had prompted realistic Southern sena-tors to agree to the mild compromise civil rights acts of 1957 and 1960, and to postpone thereby the dreaded precedent of a successful closing off of an anti-civil rights filibuster.

10. President Lyndon B. Johnson, quoted in *ibid.,* 1635.

willed it to be otherwise. A cunning and embittered politician, the governor was determined to take the offensive by carrying his crusade against federal advancement of civil rights to the national political arena, thereby embarrassing the Johnson administration by revealing the extent to which Northern and Border state whites resented the Negro and opposed the pending civil rights bill.

Accordingly, in March Wallace shrewdly filed to enter the presidential preference primaries in Wisconsin, Indiana and Maryland against "favorite son" Democrats standing in for President Johnson. In each state, Wallace vigorously campaigned not against his local oppo-

This Is Where A Lot Of Voters And Politicians Are Parting Company!

Knox in the Banner

nent but against federal tyranny emanating from the cynical and malevolent power-seekers in Washington. He repeatedly made exaggerated charges that the civil rights bill would enable the "central government" to "take over" homes, schools, businesses and farms, "tell you to whom you may sell or rent a house," "take your job away and give it to somebody else," "destroy union seniority," and force farmers "to fire half their Chinese Lutherans and hire Japanese Methodists." [11] Wallace's adroit fishing in troubled waters paid off handsomely. On April 7 in Wisconsin he polled approximately 34 percent of the vote; in Indiana on May 5, approximately 30 percent; and in Maryland on May 19, a whopping 42 percent.

Tennessee's traditionalist press responded with unconcealed glee. In their eyes, Wallace had not only greatly improved his image as "a calm and articulate spokesman who was a credit to the South." [12] He had, more importantly, "done his country a service" by revealing the extensive opposition to the civil rights bill outside the much maligned South. Stunned by Wallace's strong showing, the progressive dailies sought to reduce the impact of the diminutive Alabamian's reverse carpetbaggery by assessing the three northern forays in the perspective of their political context. In Wisconsin, the *Times* carefully explained, Republicans were free under the state's election regulations to cross over and embarrass the Democrats by voting against Governor John W. Reynolds.[13] Many of them did so because their own candidate, Representative John W. Byrnes, was unopposed. (Byrnes received only 27.7 per cent of the total primary vote, far below the normal Republican vote, while Reynolds received 47.8 per cent.) Further, Wallace had received only one vote in four in the over-all total, and only one in three in his own party balloting—hardly a conservative triumph.

In Indiana, where Republicans were also free to cross over, the *Tennessean* pointed out that Governor Matthew Welsh, the Democratic favorite son, was unpopular because of his tax policies.[14] The *Tennessean*

11. Governor George C. Wallace, quoted in *SSN*, June 1964, p. 5.
12. *Commercial Appeal*, 21 May 1964.
13. 9 April 1964.
14. 21 May 1964.

even expressed some surprise that in Indiana, a state which was generously populated with Southern immigrants and which had been a stronghold of the revived Ku Klux Klan, Wallace had done less well than in liberal Wisconsin.[15] Even in Maryland, the *News-Sentinel* observed, Wallace had, after all, lost once again—and in a border state where the racial disturbance on the Eastern Shore the previous summer had created a residue of resentment. Thus Wallace's candidacy had "allowed a considerable minority of voters the luxury of blowing off steam by voting for a man they knew would never be President." [16]

Still, once the necessary qualifications had been made—qualifications that were conspicuously absent in the traditionalist editorials—Wallace had clearly tapped that sizable and previously latent deposit of resentment against Negroes and their crusade for civil rights that had led political pundits to coin the phrase "white backlash." To Tennessee's traditionalist newspapers, Wallace had taught the nation that the preservation of states' rights was properly a national, not just a sectional concern; to the progressive newspapers, the governor had revealed that the problem of civil rights, as the *News-Sentinel* expressed it, was "not essentially a sectional issue. It is a challenge to the conscience of the whole nation." [17]

The distinct possibility that white backlash might be profitably exploited was to lead Republican Senator Barry Goldwater to advise his party, in a homey metaphor characteristic of the senator's political style, to "go hunting where the ducks are." But Goldwater's views were shared by only a minority, even within his own party—a minority that was strategically located within the party hierarchy, to be sure, but not within the Congress. The Republican majority was represented on Capitol Hill by Representative Charles Halleck of Indiana and Senate Minority Leader Everett McKinley Dirksen of Illinois. The Republican congressional leadership, which possessed great bargaining power because the Democrats were badly split and because cloture could not be invoked in the Senate without Republican consent, was loath to allow Democrats either to claim full credit for passing a civil rights bill in an

15. 7 May 1964.
16. 20 May 1964.
17. 9 April 1964.

election year or to blame the Republicans in the event the bill was blocked. Consequently, late in October of 1963 House Republicans had hammered out in crucial negotiations with administration leaders an omnibus civil rights bill that was acceptable to them.[18] HR 7152 was formally reported on November 20, and was pried out of Judge Smith's Rules Committee on January 30. After nine days of floor debate it was passed, on February 10, by a roll-call vote of 290 to 130.[19] In the argot of the *Tennessean,* House passage of the civil rights bill marked "the end of a skirmish and the beginning of a war." [20]

The Senate on February 26 voted 54 to 37 to place HR 7152 directly on the Senate calendar, rather than refer it to Eastland's Judiciary Committee.[21] On March 9, the Senate began debate on a motion to take up the bill, and on March 26, after 16 days of debate, it voted 67 to 17 to take it up.[22] The Southern filibuster was on.

But there was something different about the filibuster of 1964. To be sure, the eighteen filibustering Southern Democrats (which included, for the first time in the decade, Tennessee's two senators, Albert Gore and the recently appointed Herbert [Hub] Walters),[23] with the support of Texas Republican John Tower, were once again highly disciplined under

18. The bipartisan bill that emerged went beyond the administration's initial request by establishing an Equal Employment Opportunities Commission covering most companies and unions; by authorizing the Justice Department to initiate suits to desegregate public facilities and to enter any civil rights suits pending in federal court; by requiring federal agencies to end discrimination in federal programs; and by providing for federal court intervention in voting rights cases bogged down in state courts.

19. Republicans voted 138 for and 34 against; Democrats voted 152 for and 96 against. Northern Democrats split 141 for and 4 against; Southern Democrats split 11 for and 92 against. See *Congress and the Nation,* p. 1636. The House bill specifically exempted FHA and VA housing from its nondiscrimination clauses, stated that no part of the bill could be construed to correct racial imbalance in the schools, included sex as a category not to legitimatize discrimination, and specifically exempted atheists and Communists from such categories.

20. 12 February 1964.

21. *Congress and the Nation,* p. 1637.

22. Earlier on March 26, the Senate voted 50 to 34 to table a last-ditch Southern motion to refer the bill back to the Judiciary Committee.

23. Walters, a loyal and aged party functionary, had been appointed by Governor Clement to serve out the remaining year of the term of Senator Estes Kefauver, who had died of a heart attack on 10 August 1963.

the expert guidance of Georgia's Richard Russell, dean of the Southern Senate delegation. But the forces pressing for cloture were also highly organized and disciplined. Majority Whip Hubert H. Humphrey of Minnesota and Minority Whip Thomas Kuchel of California had organized 36 Democratic and 16 Republican supporters of cloture into three platoons to insure that the frequent Southern quorum calls would be met in order to forestall time-consuming adjournments. Such organization was an unprecedented phenomenon that greatly disturbed the Southerners.

Another curious and revealing aspect of the filibuster was that the novel title II, which was designed to desegregate public accommodations, was *not* drawing the major fire either of the Southern senators, including the two Tennesseans, or of the state's traditionalist press. This may have been because open opposition to open public accommodations, like open opposition to Negro voting, was difficult to defend on moral grounds. As the *News Sentinel* admitted, "the public accommodation section simply means that Negro citizens cannot, as is the stubborn custom in some sections of the country, be insulted and turned away from public places such as motels and restaurants." [24] Even the *Banner* was willing to concede that it, like Senator Gore, did not

oppose the so-called "rights" bill in details addressed to valid grievances; nor does America at large, conceding adjustments to correct barriers that can in justice be removed. Within the domain of public accommodations, these already are giving way. They are the area, as both Tennessee Senators have recognized, of greatest inconvenience and humiliation as enforced racial boundaries." [25]

But it may also have been because Southern businessmen—who, like their counterparts throughout the nation, were generally quite conservative—were trapped in a dilemma which passage of the civil rights bill would quickly resolve. On the one hand, they deplored the rising tide of civic disturbances that was so disruptive of commerce; on the other, they feared the economic consequences of dropping the old barriers in isolation. "Many Southern businessmen," the *News Sentinel* ob-

24. 21 June 1964.
25. 29 April 1964.

served, "have argued in the past that they would be willing to serve Negroes but could not unless their competitors did." [26] It is certainly arguable that the voluntary desegregation of public accommodations that occurred—to be sure, under the essential pressure of Negro demonstrations—throughout the South before the enactment of the public accommodations law was less a function of moral suasion that of pinched nerves which businessmen could relieve only when acting in concert.[27] Otherwise, how does one explain the paradox that Southern churches and organized labor, whose declared principles might have been expected to place them in the vanguard in pressing for liberal reform, or at least in a willingness to accommodate Negro demands, were outpaced in this regard by conservative Southern businessmen? A more optimistic explanation of why the prospect of open public accommodations did not prompt a torrent of Southern dissent might be that the conscience of the ordinary Southern white citizen was pricked by the Negro tactic of nonviolent demonstration against inherited and humiliating patterns of discrimination. Or, perhaps the white Southerner's capacity for moral outrage was plumbed by scenes of white thugs transforming nonviolence into terror. In view of the surprising felicitude with which the mass of white Southerners greeted the advent of open public accommodations, one might hope that there is some truth in these more sanguine explanations.

Whatever their reasons for avoiding a concerted defense of segregated public accommodations, filibustering Southern senators and conservative Tennessee editors focused their rhetorical fire instead on title VI, which would cut off federal funds to programs practicing discrimination, and title VII, the fair employment practices provision. Their basic complaint, beyond the broad states' rights argument which condemned the entire bill, and beyond their insistence that the contemplated two new federal agencies (the Equal Employment Opportunities Commission and the Community Relations Service) would burgeon according to Parkinson's immutable law of inevitable bureaucratic expan-

---

26. 3 July 1964.

27. Businessmen throughout the nation have been slow to perceive that the same principle might apply in regard to housing.

sion, was that hidden in the 18,000-word bill might be loosely-worded, murky, and ill-defined passages which would confer too much discretionary power on distant Washington bureaucrats. Who was to determine, for instance, what a "substantial connection" with interstate commerce was—and on what grounds? According to what criteria was the Attorney General to have "reasonable cause to believe" that a "practice or pattern" of discrimination existed? Such close, textual criticism was a traditional, honorable, and worthwhile function of political conservatives—a function too often ignored when their ox was not being gored, as in the case of laws designed to combat subversion and "un-Americanism." But in their efforts to discover within the vast and complex bill hidden booby traps, whether planted by sinister design or careless inadvertence, the Southerners found at least a partially sympathetic friend in the marvelously maleable conservatism of Senator Everett Dirksen, and in the border-state sensitivity of Republican Senator Thruston B. Morton of Kentucky.

Administration leaders knew that they had to bargain with the moderate Republican senators in order to close off debate, and the complicated history of these negotiations could detain us almost interminably (more than 70 changes were made in H.R. 7152). Suffice it to say that the thrust of the amendments that Dirksen extracted as the price of his crucial support was to modify the enforcement provisions of the sections relating to public accommodations, fair employment practices, and withdrawal of federal funds so that private parties and local authorities would have the first chance at settling and litigating disputes over discrimination. Federal enforcement, when finally resorted to, would be channeled primarily through the safeguards of the judiciary.[28]

The Morton amendment involved the old dispute over the degree to which jury trials should be allowed in criminal contempt cases. Such cases might involve, for instance, a federal judge punishing a local voter registrar for having failed to obey a decree to register Negroes. The Southerns had a logical case against excluding jury trials in criminal contempt cases, for, as the *Banner* pointed out, even the American Civil

28. See Alexander M. Bickel, "Civil Rights Act of 1964," *Commentary,* XXXVIII (August 1964), 33–39.

Liberties Union had argued (in defending Mississippi's Governor Ross Barnett) that there was "a built-in unfairness in permitting a judge, in order to 'vindicate his authority' and who is the aggrieved party, to act as prosecutor, witness, jury and judge." [29] The historic reluctance of Southern juries to convict in such cases led the Senate to compromise by entitling defendants in criminal contempt cases arising under all sections of the bill *except* title I (voting rights) to a jury trial upon demand. For infractions concerning voting rights, the Morton amendment left intact the jury-trial provisions of the civil rights act of 1957.

Several of Tennessee's traditionalist editors challenged other provisions of the bill on the grounds that they were illogical. Why, for instance, should it be unlawful—and, by presumption, immoral—for a hotel to discriminate against Negroes, but not for "Mrs. Murphy's boarding house" (title II exempted owner-occupied units with five or less rooms)? What superior claim to discriminate had an employer or union with 24 workers over an employer or union with 25 (title VII exempted industries and unions with fewer than 25 workers)? Or, in the case of voting rights, why allow a defendant charged with criminal contempt who is penalized by the judge with a fine of $300 or a prison sentence of 45 days, to demand a jury trial when the defendant fined only $1 less or sentenced to one day less in prison is denied a jury trial? The logic of such complaints was clear enough, yet it was curious for conservatives to appeal to logic when they had historically defended inherited institutions and procedures, not because they were logical or illogical, but simply because they worked. After all, the very requirement that the law be precise in its categories and definitions—a requirement which the conservative senators and editors were quick and correct to demand—automatically necessitated the establishment of somewhat arbitrary and therefore illogical categories, such as setting a magic age to legalize voting, drinking, driving, soldiering, and the like.

One final argument was available to the defenders of the status quo. That was the charge of inconsistency, and it could easily be proved. This charge had long been leveled by conservatives at the Supreme Court, which as an institution had clearly reversed so many of its old

29. Quoted in the *Banner,* 27 April 1964.

precedents. But it could also be leveled at individuals, and the long memory of the *Banner* made made it a foremost practitioner of this art. The *Banner* was fond of quoting from the writings and speeches of the vulnerable Senate Majority Leader of the fifties, Lyndon B. Johnson:

For on the jury trial question, he declared in 1957 (while a Senator, and Majority Leader, writing to Texas constituents) that the amendment in question was vital to the civil rights bill of that year. "Clever lawyers," he said, "have finally devised an adroit method to bypass the jury system. They are attempting to write this method into law under the name of civil rights." But "many of us object to devious schemes to convict men and women under criminal contempt without trial by jury." [30]

And as for fair employment practices laws, the former majority leader had said, according to the *Banner*:

This, to me, is the least meritorious in the whole civil rights program. If the Federal Government can by law tell me whom I shall employ, it can likewise tell my prospective employees for whom they must work. . . . As I see it, such a law would do nothing more than enslave a minority. . . . Such a law would necessitate a system of federal police officers such as we have never seen. . . . I can only hope sincerely that the Senate will never be called upon to entertain any such proposal again." [31]

Not even the late and martyred John F. Kennedy was exempt from the *Banner*'s embarrassing recollections:

On April 19, 1963, the late President John F. Kennedy, speaking before the American Society of Newspaper Editors in convention in Washington, was asked the specific question: "Mr. President, will you attempt to cut off Federal aid to Mississippi as proposed by your Civil Rights Commission?"
He answered, just as specifically:
"I don't have the power to cut off the aid in a general way as was proposed by the Civil Rights Commission, and I think it probably would be unwise to give the President of the United States that kind of power, because if it stopped in one state for one reason or another, it might be moved to another state which was not measuring up as the President would like to see it measure up in one way or another." [32]

Although both the *Banner* and the *Commercial Appeal* devoted more editorial space to a detailed consideration of the bill's eleven complex

30. 10 June 1964.
31. Lyndon B. Johnson, quoted in *ibid.*
32. 12 June 1964.

titles than did any of the four big Tennessee dailies that supported the bill, no newspaper in Tennessee considered the bill more carefully than did the Knoxville *Journal*. The *Journal* shared most of the conservative qualms about the bill. But while editorially airing these concerns, it took the extraordinary step on June 3 of printing the full text of H.R. 7152, and it subsequently published further amendments. The *Journal*'s formidable reproduction covered two solid pages of 8.5 type, and the editors implored the daily's readers in both its printed and its cartoon editorials to "Find Yourself in H.R. 7152."

If the performance of Guy Smith's *Journal* represented the zenith of responsible opposition among Tennessee dailies, the diatribes of Roy McDonald's *News–Free Press* represented the nadir. Perhaps it was to be expected that the *News–Free Press* would summarize its view of the bill with an unmerciful excoriation:

The civil rights bill would impose involuntary servitude, open private property to seizure by outsiders, impose the force of government in dictatorship over virtually every phase of human endeavor.

It is an unenforceable and unworkable proposal that is totalitarian by nature, destructive of good will and inimical to freedom—destroying the rights of all our people.[33]

But when the *News–Free Press* on June 9 attempted to explain the bill to its readers, its editors confined their attentions not to explaining what the various titles were designed to achieve—whether for better or worse—but rather to dispatching summarily each title in succession as a manifest violation of some section of the Constitution. Thus, title I violated Article II, Section I, paragraph 2, guaranteeing state control of elections; title II violated the Fourth Amendment's guarantee of private property and the Thirteenth Amendment's ban on involuntary servitude; title III violated the Tenth Amendment, and so on. The *News–Free Press* did admit that two of the eleven titles were at least not unconstitutional on their face. These were the provisions extending the life of the Civil Rights Commission for four years and establishing the Community Relations Service. But, reasoned the *News–Free Press,* since the Supreme Court in the Civil Rights Cases of 1883

33. 6 June 1964.

had ruled that the interstate commerce clause could not be constitutionally invoked by the Federal Government in its attempt to protect rights guaranteed by the Fourteenth Amendment (which was unconstitutional anyway), then *"the whole mess is unconstitutional!"*

But it was all of no avail. Powerful voices across the land and within Tennessee itself were calling for cloture and passage of the civil rights bill. In Nashville, the *Tennessean* as early as February 14 had begun to call for enactment of the bill as "a first step toward extending full citizenship to all Americans." The *Tennesseean* even countered the argument, most frequently advanced by the *Commercial Appeal,* that sought to discredit the goals of the various civil rights organizations by alleging Communist infiltration, by proclaiming that, whereas (a) the Communist editor of *The Worker* had called for a national work stoppage to force an end to the filibuster; (b) the Communists were sophisticated enough to know that such action would only contribute to the bill's defeat; (c) the Communists had much to lose from the lessening of America's racial tensions; (d) Communists usually meant the opposite of what they said; then therefore, as the editorial's title proclaimed, (e) "Reds See Major Defeat in Rights Bill Victory." [34]

In Chattanooga, the *Times* celebrated the national change of mood, evidenced by the probability of the law's enactment, which had at its heart a "recognition of the basic right of all Americans to share in the privileges and the fruits of our system, and an expanding willingness to safeguard these rights by laws with teeth in them," [35] and it deplored the "Southerners fighting a last-ditch battle against equity of treatment in a multiracial society." [36] In Knoxville, the *News–Sentinel* sympathized with "the nation's Negroes [who] have waited long and patiently to take their place as full and equal partners in American society. They should not have to wait any more." [37] And in Memphis the *Press Scimitar,* which acknowledged that the filibuster had led to some improvement in the bill, felt nevertheless that enough was enough: "for the

34. 2 March 1964.
35. 11 June 1964.
36. 21 June 1964.
37. 3 July 1964.

good of the Senate, whose honor and responsibility is deeply involved, but more especially for the good of the country, we hope the motion to curb the filibuster is passed." [38]

It was passed. On June 10, the Senate voted 71 to 29 to close off a civil rights filibuster for the first time in its history.[39] The vote ended debate 57 days after formal consideration of the bill began, and 74 days after the bill was before the Senate. On June 19 the Senate passed the bill by a vote of 73 to 27. On July 2, the House approved the Senate bill by a vote of 289 to 126, and only a few hours later President Johnson signed it into law in a ceremony broadcast nationwide over television from the White House.

In response to this historic act, the progressive dailies in Tennessee not unexpectedly voiced their relief. But while most of the disappointed conservative newspapers remained silent, a number of the larger dailies—most notably the *Commercial Appeal* and the *Banner*—stuck fast to their principles and insisted that the law was an act of Congress, that a law-abiding nation would have to learn to live with it, and that it ought to be given a fair chance. The *Commercial Appeal* was particularly willing to adjust to the new reality:

> Thoughtful citizens should keep in mind that not all advocates or all opponents of this legislation have been extremists. There have been many who recognize what has thus far been well demonstrated in this area; namely that many Negroes prefer to live and associate mainly with other Negroes but that they want the right to enter public facilities, the right to vote and some of the other things which have been spelled out now in this legislation.
> Let those who wish to test the new law read it carefully first so they will understand it. Then, realizing that this measure now gives them more ready access through the courts, let them follow the new avenues open to them while at the same time ending the struggles in the streets.[40]

But as Southerners were trying to learn to live with the new law, mass Negro rioting in the major Northern cities was simultaneously suggesting that civil rights laws, which had long been on the books in

38. 3 June 1964.
39. It was the twelfth such attempt. Cloture was supported by 44 Democrats and 27 Republicans; it was opposed by 23 Democrats and 6 Republicans.
40. 4 July 1964.

northern states, might not be enough to bring racial peace. That was a
point that Tennessee's traditionalist dailies had repeatedly made throughout the entire controversy. One final and ominous development further
dimmed the prospects of an early end to racial discord. One of the
leading candidates for the Republican presidential nomination, Senator
Barry Goldwater, had let it be known by his vote against the civil rights
bill that, were he to receive the nomination, he would invite millions of
Southern whites to abandon their traditional Democratic affiliation and
rally to him in opposition to federal enforcement of civil rights for
Negroes.

When in the spring of 1964 Governor Wallace had drawn 30 percent
of the Democratic primary votes in Indiana, Republican voters had
simultaneously given Senator Goldwater 260,000 votes to Harold Stas-
sen's 100,000. The scornfully confident reaction of the *Tennessean* to
the Indiana primary had been to conclude that "about the only thing

Cut!

Basset in the News-Sentinel

Glory...Hallelujah

Basset in the News-Sentinel

it proved was that neither Senator Goldwater nor Governor Wallace can be considered as serious contenders for the presidency." [41] While one is tempted to smile in retrospect at this judgmental faux pas, it would be well to recall how few American opinion leaders in the spring of 1964 gave the Arizona senator much chance of being nominated. But nominated he was, and what is pertinent here is not the fantastic history of that remarkable event. Rather it is the corollary that he thereby offered American voters and editors a rare opportunity to express their preferences between such fundamentally contrasting alternatives.

In *The Making of the President 1964,* Theodore White concluded that nothing depressed the Goldwater campaigners more than did the wholesale defection of that normally reliable source of Republican support—the nation's newspapers and magazines.[42] But in the South, Goldwater was hunting where the "ducks" were, and if this open tactic extracted as its price a heavy toll among the defecting Republican newspapers throughout the north and west, could it not be expected in turn to elicit compensating editorial support in the nominally Democratic South? Goldwater strategists in Tennessee hoped to forge a coalition of loyal eastern Republicans, defecting western Dixiecrats, and social and economic conservatives in the bluestocking suburbs that would throw Tennessee into the Republican column for the fourth time in a row.[43] To do this, they needed extensive support from the state's newspapers generally, but especially so from the eight big dailies that dominated the sprawling suburbs.

In Knoxville, the reliable *Journal* stood fast by the Republican standard in support of Goldwater. It frequently joined the like-minded Chattanooga *News–Free Press* in specific denunciations of President

41. 7 May 1964.
42. (New York: Atheneum Press, 1964), p. 351. White observed that "in all the nation, only three major newspapers supported the abandoned Republican: the Los Angeles *Times* . . . the Chicago *Tribune* and the Cincinnati *Enquirer.* Nothing like this had ever happened before in American political history."
43. Norman Parks, *op. cit.* pp. 151–54. Sam Claiborne, Tennessee state representative from La Follette, served as Goldwater's Southern regional campaign director, and for his pains was defeated in his bid for re-election.

Johnson as "surrender prone, fearful, [and] appeasement-minded," [44] and both conservative East Tennessee dailies countered charges of Goldwater extremism by execrating the leftwing radicalism of the Democrats' vice-presidential "Socialist candidate," [45] Hubert Humphrey (the *Journal* delighted in unkindly referring to Humphrey as "Hubird"). The *News–Free Press* countered charges that Goldwater was dangerously irresponsible about nuclear weapons by recalling that Humphrey, as "chairman of the extreme leftwing ADA," had advocated placing American nuclear weapons under international control in the United Nations.[46]

But Goldwater's most forthright editorial advocate in Tennessee published not in the Republican east but in the middle Tennessee heartland of progressive Democratic politics. There Stahlman's Nashville *Banner* boarded the Goldwater bandwagon with an uninhibited zeal that upstaged even the endorsements of both Guy Smith's *Journal* and Roy McDonald's *News–Free Press*. Editors of the *Banner* had amply demonstrated throughout the decade that their pens could be dipped in purple ink when the spirit of the occasion deeply moved them. President Johnson's by no means astonishing announcement, on the evening of August 26 in Atlantic City, that he had selected Senator Humphrey to be his running mate was just such an occasion. To the *Banner,* Johnson's choice of the "pipsqueak" Humphrey was "as nauseating a performance, in point both of dictatorial conceit and product, as history recounts in the annals of Democratic politics."

> Humphrey has made a career of South-baiting; not only the raucous cheer-leader of the leftwing's "Operation Dixie," but the legislative tactitian and field marshal of contemptuous assault. And his election would have the formidable implications of a coup de grace to every principle of constitutional government that has stood thus far in challenge of the erosive spitework he personifies.
>
> The extremists of the Democratic Party finally have captured it in toto.[47]

44. *News-Free Press,* 10 October 1964.
45. *Journal,* 15 October 1964.
46. 8 October 1964.
47. 27 August 1964. Curiously, while pro-Goldwater newspapers hammered away at Humphrey, almost no editorial mention was made of Republican vice-presidential candidate William E. Miller—who also ran.

"Nationally," the *Banner* solemnly intoned, "the party, as America once knew it, is gone."

Perhaps it is in one sense imprecise, although not incorrect, to label the *Banner* a major *advocate* of the Goldwater candidacy, for the *Banner* devoted far more editorial space to lambasting Democrats than to endorsing Republicans. This negative strategy of inverse advocacy was probably dictated by the *Banner*'s awareness that its primary task was to dissuade knee-jerk Southern Democrats from automatically voting for a program that the *Banner* thought to be inimical to their properly conservative interests. Perhaps, also, the sheer intensity of the *Banner*'s bombardment of the Democrats was prompted by its awareness that, in all of Democratic Middle and West Tennessee, it stood starkly alone among major dailies in championing Goldwater. For in Memphis, the largest daily of them all had shattered the traditional unanimity of Tennessee's conservative quartet by defecting to the Democrats. "The reasonable, rational, calm approach of the Johnson Administration," observed the *Commercial Appeal,* "shows how well it can weather changes which could have been traumatic but were not." [48] "The election of LYNDON B. JOHNSON to a continuing four-year term," the *Commercial Appeal* concluded, "becomes imperative."

The *Commercial Appeal*'s imposing voice thereby joined the not-surprising chorus of the state's progressive journalistic quartet in urging the election of Johnson and, more stridently, in attacking the highly vulnerable Goldwater. If the *Banner* waved the Goldwater standard most vigorously, the *Tennessean* sought most asiduously to shoot it full of holes, and in this endeavor Senator Goldwater's disarming (or alarming, depending on one's point of view) candor was his undoing. The *Tennessean*'s carefully documented attack repeatedly turned Goldwater's unguarded—or, from the viewpoint of a serious presidential aspirant, just plain foolish—utterances to good account in advancing the argument that to vote Democratic was both the progressive *and* the conservative thing to do. Goldwater, in this familiar stereotype, was not a true conservative but indeed a reactionary, a radical of the far right

48. 17 October 1964.

who stood not for maintaining the status quo but for repeal of the twentieth century. "In the main," the *Tennessean* complained, "he is 'against' things, and most issues are, for him, uncomplicated." [49] He was repeatedly on record as having spoken against the income tax, social security, medicare, reapportionment, disarmament efforts, and the United Nations. He had refused to vote to censure Senator McCarthy in 1954, and he refused to repudiate the support of such extremist organizations as the John Birch Society and, until late in the campaign, the Ku Klux Klan. He would sell TVA for a dollar. The *Tennessean* did not even hesitate to deplore Goldwater's opposition to the Brown decision and the civil rights bill of 1964. Worst of all was his cavalier attitude toward the use of atomic weapons: "his call Sunday for the use of low-yield atomic bombs to defoliate the forests along South Viet Nam's borders to expose the jungle supply lines of Communist-led rebels, is a new extreme in recklessness even for the Arizona Senator." [50] For all the senator's unchallenged honesty and integrity, the *Tennessean* was able, like Samson, to bludgeon the enemy to death with the jawbone of an ass.

The other four anti-Goldwater newspapers among the state's eight big dailies were perhaps less unkind to the hapless senator from Arizona, but no less opposed. These five large dailies were joined in opposition to Goldwater by the Clarksville *Leaf-Chronicle,* the Maryville *Times,* the Murfreesboro *News-Journal* and the Johnson City *Press–Chronicle* (the latter supporting a Democratic presidential candidate for the first time since 1936) to produce a combined daily circulation of over 682,000. The three large traditionalist dailies which supported Goldwater were joined by the Columbia *Daily-Herald* and by both the commonly-owned morning and evening dailies in Bristol and Kingsport to produce a combined daily circulation of only 288,000. The vast majority of the county weeklies refrained from endorsing either candidate, as was their habit, although many of them carried large Republican-sponsored ads urging readers to "Vote for a Man Friendly to the South," and a few county editors conceded that the election had at

49. 27 July 1964.
50. 26 May 1964.

least breathed needed life into the South's moribund two-party system. Of the less than a dozen county weeklies that did endorse a presidential candidate, the edge went to Goldwater by a slight margin.

By October, a Republican campaign that should have been in climatic full swing was, in the words of Theodore White, staggering on "crushed and punch-drunk." [51] To make things worse for the ruggedly handsome Arizonian, the capriciously malevolent hand of fate intervened to jolt an international equipoise already considerably unsettled by the mere fact of Goldwater's candidacy. In rapid succession, Nikita Khrushchev was dethroned, Communist China exploded an atomic device, and Labour ousted the Conservatives in Britain. By mid-October the Gallup and Harris polls continued to show Johnson's vast lead—a lead so apparently insurmountable and discouraging that Dean Burch, Goldwater's hand-picked chairman of the Republican National Committee, decided to cancel the party's own program of polling reconnaissance which had been conducted by the Opinion Research Corporation.[52]

On election eve, the *Banner* bravely proclaimed in a remarkable front-page editorial that "Tomorrow is a new INDEPENDENCE DAY!" Even more brazen was the *Journal's* unequivocal assertion, whatever the misgivings behind it, that "tomorrow is the day the professional pollsters will be confounded all over the country." But if these embattled editors really believed their own incredible prose, their rose-tinted eyeglasses were rudely shattered. Johnson was elected by a landslide margin of 15,952,085 votes out of 70,305,831 with 43,128,958 against Goldwater's 27,176,873.[53] It was the greatest vote, margin and percentage (60 percent) that any President had ever drawn from the American people. Goldwater's courtship of Dixie netted his party five Southern states (South Carolina, Georgia, Alabama, Mississippi, and Louisiana—the Southern states with the lowest percentage of registered Ne-

---

51. White, *op. cit.,* p. 352.

52. *Ibid.* p. 350 fn.

53. *Congress and the Nation,* p. 59. White gives Johnson a million more votes (*ibid.,* p. 400) than does the *Congressional Quarterly,* but even without these votes, the magnitude of the Johnson victory remains unprecedented.

groes), but Tennessee returned to the Democratic column by a vote of 634,947 to 508,965.[54] Despite the relatively comfortable appearance of that margin, the consensus of political analysts has been that a majority of Tennessee's whites voted for Goldwater; consequently, only the potent bloc of Tennessee's Negroes (69.4 percent or 240,000 of whom were registered to vote in 1964—by far the highest percentage in the South) kept Tennessee from joining its five Southern neighbors and lonely but loyal Arizona in the Republican column.[55] This phenomenon of Democratic bloc-voting by Negroes, which was nationwide, seems on the surface to verify the simplistic notion that Franklin Roosevelt opened the Democratic door to the Negroes, that Truman, Stevenson, Kennedy, and Johnson cordially ushered them in, and that Barry Goldwater obligingly nailed the door shut behind them. Thus, in this view, the Democrats in 1964 were rewarded by a generation of Negroes who had voted smart, voted early and, especially in Chicago, voted often; Republican foolhardiness had sealed the bargain. Even if this picture of the Negro's recent political odyssey were true in broad outline, it erroneously suggests a monolithic and single-minded trek on the part of a Negro community that has always been deeply riven by the contending philosophies and apostles of accommodation and militancy—of Uncle Tom and Nat Turner, of Booker T. Washington versus W. E. B. DuBois, or perhaps even (to demonstrate how far we have traversed along the political spectrum) of Martin Luther King versus Stokely Carmichael. Tennessee's Negroes, unlike Tennessee's whites, voted en masse for Johnson—or more accurately, against Goldwater. But a large and potent bloc of Tennessee's Negroes shared with Tennessee's whites the experience of being exposed to a pluralistic press in which editors of their own race vigorously debated the central question of how Negroes should strive toward equality. The debate of the Negro editors makes for a fascinating case study in American social and intellectual history.

54. *Tennessee Blue Book,* 1965–1966, p. 244.
55. See Dewey W. Grantham, "The South and the Reconstruction of American Politics," *The Journal of American History,* LIII (September 1966), 237. Tennessee joins Virginia, Florida, Arkansas, and probably North Carolina in this category.

10

Who Speaks for the Southern Negro?

PUBLISHING a Negro newspaper in Tennessee has always been a hazardous undertaking.[1] To the difficulties of acquiring sufficient capital to fi-

1. Indeed, Publishing a Negro newspaper anywhere in America after mid-century was becoming an increasingly hazardous proposition. An old and familiar adage among Negroes resentfully explains why the Negro press was born to fill a vacuum: "For the regular [i.e., white] press, Negroes are never born, educated, married and never die." Born in a fitful start as early as 1828, the exclusively Negro press grew slowly to produce, after a century of marginal struggle that paralleled and reflected the struggle of its constitutents, a number of relatively flourishing enterprises in heavily Negro communities. The high degree of insularity of America's Negro communities is suggested the relatively low visibility of the Negro press. Although it is difficult to obtain evidence of white awareness of the Negro press, one might speculate how few white citizens of Pittsburgh in 1949 were aware that their city harbored, in addition to the familiar *Post-Gazette,* the *Sun-Telegraph,* and the *Press,* a Negro weekly called the Pittsburgh *Courier.* Yet the *Courier* was the largest Negro newspaper in the nation, boasting in 1949, its peak year, a weekly circulation of almost 300,000 and printing special weekly editions for Louisiana, Florida, Georgia, New York, Ohio, the District of Columbia, Detroit, Philadelphia, Cleveland, Chicago, and the Far West. The dismal decline of the *Courier* since its heyday in the late forties has been symbolic of the general decline of Negro newspapers (although not of Negro magazines; see Alfred Balk, "Mr. Johnson Finds His Market," *Reporter* (September 1963), p. 204 and *passim*). While metropolitan Pittsburgh grew after 1949, the *Courier's* weekly circulation precipitously declined from that year's high of 296,674 to 126,444 ten years later. By 1963, its circulation had plumeted to 76,969. Although approximately 2,700 Negro newspapers had been founded in the United States by 1964, only 135 survived, and virtually all were in a state of decline. Ironically, their decline has resulted in large part from the relative success of the Negro revolt, which in the very process of capturing the

nance such an expensive undertaking as printing were added the problems inherent in catering to a community that was economically depressed. Yet the profession was sufficiently prestigious and independent, the market so distinctive and concentrated, and the need so compelling, that ambitious and hopeful Negroes frequently had a go at it. Almost as frequently, their ambitions were thwarted and their hopes dashed.

Typical of this pattern have been the repeated, frequently abortive, and always perilous attempts to publish Negroes weeklies in Nashville. The *Globe and Independent,* established in 1906, published in a desultory way until it disappeared in the early fifties. Its successor, the *Commentator,* struggled marginally through the decade. Occasionally, short-lived Negro weeklies would suddenly appear and as quickly disappear, like dim meteors. During the fifties, the Nashville *Star* was hopefully born and quickly faded, only to be succeeded by the *780 Countdown.* Doomed, perhaps, as much by its improbable name as by severe economic realities, the *780 Countdown* folded before the eschatological countdown had reached the halfway mark. Its successor, the *Capital City Defender,* fared little better. During the latter fifties, the suffering but enduring *Commentator* preached to the Negro community in Nashville a message of respectability, self-help, moderation, Godliness, faith in the inherent, if often obscure, goodness of Southern whites and in the inherent evil of Southern Democracy, and profound allegiance to Lincolnian Republicanism.

Only in Memphis was the Negro community large and interested enough to sustain a viable and competing Negro press. The two little Negro weeklies in Memphis are uniquely useful as evidence in a case study, for Memphis at mid-century represented the *only* civic arena in the nation wherein the two American Negro publishers, who as journalistic anchor-men most clearly represented the contending philosophies of accommodation and militancy, could do battle at close quarters for the allegiance of a single Negro community. In Atlanta, appropriately enough, staunchly Republican publisher Cornelius A. Scott of the At-

---

attention of the regular press thereby endowed it with competitive qualities vis-à-vis the Negro press that it had previously lacked. See "A Victim of Negro Progress," *Newsweek* (August 1963), pp. 50–57.

lanta *Daily World* faithfully echoed the philosophy of accommodation and self-help so spectacularly enunciated in that proud Southern city by Booker T. Washington in 1895. In reassuring the receptive Southern whites in his audience that the Negro would be content to remain socially as separate as the fingers, Washington had also pledged that Negroes would remain pleasantly deferential: "you can be sure in the future, as in the past, that you and your families will be surrounded by the most patient, faithful, law-abiding, and unresentful people that the world has seen." [2] Sixty-seven years later, the Mississippi-born Scott declared in the same city that "the Negro has got to quit getting mad and start getting smart. We have everything to lose and nothing to gain. What we want is good will. The less friction we create today, the less we will have to undo tomorrow." [3]

In 1903, the militant W. E. B. Du Bois had declared: "Negroes must insist continually, in season and out of season, that voting is necessary to modern manhood, that color discrimination is barbarism, and that black boys need education as well as white boys." [4] Sixty-one years later, Charles Sumner Stone, Jr., editor-in-chief of the ultra-liberal Chicago *Daily Defender,* was quoted as having bluntly declared: "I'm a nigger, but I'm a proud nigger. If I don't push, nobody will." [5] The *Defender*'s

2. Quoted in Rayford W. Logan, *The Negro in the United States* (Princeton: Van Nostrand, 1957), pp. 128–129 of the Anvil paperback edition.
3. Quoted in *Newsweek, op. cit.*
4. William E. B. Du Bois, "Of Mr. Booker T. Washington and Others," *The Souls of Black Folk: Essays and Sketches* (Chicago: A.C. McClurg & Co., 1903), p. 57. Du Bois's advice to American Negroes regarding Washington was as follows:

The black men of America have a duty to perform, a duty stern and delicate,—a forward movement to oppose a part of the work of their greatest leader. So far as Mr. Washington preaches Thrift, Patience, and Industrial Training for the masses, we must hold up his hands and strive with him, rejoicing in his honors and glorying in the strength of this Joshua called of God and of man to lead the headless host. But so far as Mr. Washington apologizes for injustice, North or South, does not rightly value the privilege and duty of voting, belittles the emasculating effects of caste distinctions, and opposes the higher training and ambition of our brighter minds,—so far as he, the South, or the Nation does this,—we must unceasingly and firmly oppose them.

5. Quoted in *Newsweek, op. cit.* Stone subsequently joined the staff of Congressman Adam Clayton Powell.

militant tone was set by its publisher, John H. Sengstacke, whose higher education in the north had cast the humiliating conditions of his Georgia childhood into a bitter and enduring perspective.

The Atlanta *World* and the Chicago *Defender* were the only Negro daily newspapers in the United States to survive into the nineteen fifties. But at such extremely long range, their respective editorial advocacy of accommodation versus militancy represented less a running dialogue than two distant and discordant monologues. Because no major Negro newspaper in the country was editorially challenged by a viable local competitor, there existed no clearly defined arena in which the contending Washingtonian and Du Boisian persuasions could do battle for the allegiance of a single Negro community. That is, none existed until Sengstacke decided in the early fifties to carry the battle to the Scott syndicate. The battleground chosen was Memphis, Tennessee.

Scott had chosen a difficult year, 1930, to establish the semiweekly Memphis *World*. But his choice of sites was a shrewd one, for Memphis Negroes had long been conditioned to the psychology of quiescent accommodation that rigid patterns of racial segregation demand.[6] By 1952, the last year of Scott's virtual monopoly in Memphis, his immediate urban market of 184,000 Negroes represented 37 percent of a metropolitan population of almost half a million.

A tabloid-sized newspaper, usually of eight pages, the *World* supplemented the local reporting of its small staff by importing boilerplate from the Atlanta *Daily World,* and by subscribing to the National [formerly Negro] Press Association's news service. To make ends meet, it frequently had to submit to the indignity of circulating through the Negro community such advertisements as the one that invited Negro Memphians to watch 745-pound Princess Lola and 72-pound Prince Arthur cha-cha-cha in a honky-tonk down on Beale Street.

Editors of the *World,* like those of its old and proud parent in Atlanta, had drunk deeply at the wells of both Jesus Christ and Booker Washington. The editorials that they wrote, and the ones they frequently

6. Stanley Elkins has argued that the psychological adjustment of American Negro slaves was analagous to the sycophantic behavior of prisoners of war in Nazi Germany. See *Slavery* (Chicago: University of Chicago Press, 1959).

reprinted from the Atlanta *Daily World,* were couched in the measured rhetoric of Christian charity, humility, and beatitude. The *World* called for desegregation, to be sure, but it called more stridently for brotherly love and a spirit of Christian harmony. It was not that the *World* was satisfied with the Negro's lot or that it was incapable of indignation. It had bitterly complained that, as late as 1959, Memphis Negroes were allocated only one day at the public zoo while whites visited on the other six; all three big parks in Memphis were reserved for whites only; the whites had seven golf courses and Negroes had only one; Negroes were still required to sit in the rear of the bus—near the motor—and in the front of the train—near the engine.[7] "It is something for Negroes to think about," the *World* suggested, "at the movies or the wrestling matches at the auditorium as they watch in comfort from their lofty perches up in the buzzard's roost."

But militancy was just not the *World*'s style. It had cordially welcomed the Brown decision in 1954, yet in that welcome it had reaffirmed its abiding conviction that "segregation will eventually fall apart of its own rot."[8] It could see "no reason why legal fiat should have the credit of its destruction when that same grace should be borne by tolerant groups working in Christian harmony to obtain such ends." While fearing that intemperate Southern politicians might "destroy all communications between the races," the *World* nevertheless expressed confidence in the "just administration of law and order in the South."[9]

The Chicago *Daily Defender* had been founded in 1903—the same year, fittingly, in which Du Bois had published his critique of Washington in *The Souls of Black Folk.* Half a century later, Sengstacke was prompted to establish the Memphis *Tri-State Defender* perhaps less by an economic conviction that it could be made to pay its way than by an editorial conviction that the *World* was faulting in its role as spokesman for and mentor to Memphis' large Negro community. Sengstacke

7. "Separate But Equal? There's No Such Animal," Memphis *World,* 1 August 1959.
8. 18 May 1954.
9. 14 September 1957.

ran his Memphis weekly during the fifties, as did Scott, through a series of local editors. In 1959, John Sengstacke dispatched his younger brother, Whittier, to Memphis to direct the fortunes of the *Tri-State Defender.*

The Memphis *World* and *Defender* were similar in size and shared the same constituency; there all similarities ended. The occasional red headlines and the customarily angry editorials of the aggressive *Defender* seethed with moral outrage. Former editor and subsequent columnist Thaddeus Stokes, who like the younger Sengstacke was an articulate northern émigré, unequivocally proclaimed that "we will never compromise on the issue of first-class citizenship. There are no half-citizens in a democracy." [10] To the *Defender,* Governor Faubus's bold démarche at Little Rock was the typical and bitter fruit of appeasement and compromise. Whereas the *World* expressed some disappointment in the relatively mild civil rights act of 1957, but saw it as a good start and a "far climb up the ladder of equality among the citizens of this country" [11] (while carefully pointing out that it was accomplished under a Republican administration), the *Defender* categorically denounced it as an "unholy compromise." [12] In the process of castigating the act as a virtual sellout, the *Defender* struck what historical hindsight reveals to have been perhaps the supreme note of irony of the decade of desegregation:

> The suspicion is unavoidable that Democratic leader Lyndon Johnson (Texas) and Sen. John F. Kennedy (D.-Mass.) will see to it that enough embalming fluid is pumped into the corpse [of the original bill] to make its resurrection [improbable]. Baby-faced Kennedy, who has presidential ambitions, lifted an eloquent voice on behalf of freedom for the Algerians, but the "cat got his tongue" when civil rights proposals were debated. He did not fail to cast his vote with the Southern bloc as the first installment toward Dixiecrat support come 1960.
>
> We have underscored these men's names in our book as arch hypocrites who must be denounced at every "whistle stop." We shall continue to fight the enemies of the Negro people forever and a day until we have won all of our rights under the stars and stripes.[13]

10. 7 September 1957.
11. 14 September 1957.
12. 14 September 1957.
13. 7 September 1957.

While the *World* manfully called attention to the "Cold Facts" that 80 percent of Memphis' 50,000 illiterates were Negroes, that one fourth of Memphis' Negroes could not read or write, and that the majority of illegitimate childbirths were by Negro mothers,[14] the *Defender* animadverted against "week-kneed Negro leadership" and "Twentieth-century Uncle Toms." [15] The *World* preached a gospel of self-help:

> Realizing that it is more popular to point up what others are doing to us "to hold us back," we nonetheless feel that it is high time, actually way past time, to point up some things that we need to do for ourselves!
> For too long we have sought to whitewash our shortcomings by shifting the blame on others while waiting to be miraculously lifted to the status of respect due first-class citizens without any effort on our part.[16]

Its editors concluded: "Equality Cannot Be Granted, It Must Be Earned!" But the *Defender* countered: "We Want The Whole Loaf Now!" [17]

The classically divergent approaches of the *World* and the *Defender* toward the common goal of Negro equality translated easily into political exhortation in Memphis. The city's Negro vote had always figured substantially in the political machinations of "Boss" Crump. But Negroes of the Crump era had performed for the most part as a supine political breed, willing to be "voted" by local Negro ward heelers who were not above supporting an ardent segregationist if the patronage price was right. When Crump died in 1954, his machine began to disintegrate just as the new era was dawning. Within a decade Negro voter registration in Memphis had soared to 95,000—a formidable bloc, freed of the old Crump dominance and highly politicized by the civil rights struggle.[18] Twice during the fifties, the magic name of Eisenhower had swayed both Shelby County (Memphis) and Tennessee from their

14. 30 January 1957.
15. 14 September 1957.
16. 30 January 1957.
17. 19 March 1960.
18. The estimate is that of the Southern Regional Council, which ranks Tennessee first among Southern states in Negro registration, with approximately 70 percent of the eligible 311,000 Negro adults registered. See Norman L. Parks, "Tennessee Politics since Kefauver and Reece," pp. 163–164.

normal Democratic predilection—much to the pleasure of the *World*.[19]
But by 1960, both the political climate and the presidential candidates
were significantly altered.

In pitting a Nixon-Lodge ticket against a Kennedy-Johnson one, the
election of 1960 placed little strain upon the obdurate Republicanism
of the *World*. Its endorsing editorial of November 2 of that year,
entitled "Simple Appreciation and Gratitude Require Us to Support the
Nixon-Lodge Team," revealed as much of the philosophical and psychological underpinnings of its editors as it did of their political loyalty.[20]
The *World* somewhat disingenuously credited school desegregation and
the civil rights acts of 1957 and 1960 exclusively to the Eisenhower-
Nixon administration, and its editors repeatedly cited vice-presidential
candidate Lodge's talk of appointing a Negro to the cabinet as further
evidence of the GOP's abiding devotion to the Lincolnian tradition.

As for the party of Jefferson, the early antipathy developed by the
editors of the *Defender* toward "arch hypocrites" Kennedy and Johnson
had been significantly reduced, if not altogether dispelled, by the strong-
ly-worded civil rights plank adopted by the Democratic National Convention. But the *Defender* was clearly unenthusiastic about either Kennedy or Nixon. It regarded the innovating television debates with cautious cynicism, expressing less interest in what the candidates said or
in the question of who won than in "the refusal of the broadcasting
stations as well as the noncommittal attitude of the contestants on
the question of inclusion of a competent Negro newsman on the
panel. . . ." [21]

<hr/>

19. In 1952, Eisenhower's margin over Stevenson in Shelby County was 6,609,
and his statewide margin was a slim 2,437 out of 892,553 votes cast. In
1956, Eisenhower's edge over Stevenson in Shelby County had been reduced
to 3,639 out of 135,025 votes, and statewide he led Stevenson by 5,781 out of
939,404.

20. The editorial was obviously written in Atlanta. This edition was fattened by
generous pictorial coverage of the Nixon-Lodge campaign and of the Eisenhower-
Nixon administration, plus a column by apostate New Dealer Raymond Moley
in support of the Republican ticket. Both the *World* and the *Defender* frequently
published editorials written in Atlanta and Chicago, respectively.

21. 12 November 1960. The *Defender's* election week edition carried even
more extensive political advertisement for the Democratic ticket than did the
World for the Republican.

Throughout the election the *Defender* generally devoted less editorial space to the campaign than to the dramatic and effective new civil rights tactic of civil disobedience. Commenting on the voluntary desegregation of several dime-store lunch counters in Nashville under the pressure of sit-ins, the *Defender* credited

this change in the social climate of the South . . . to those energetic, farvisioned Negro students who literally took the bull by the horn to achieve their objectives.

Despite arrests, fines and maltreatments, these students continued unabated their demonstrations against hitherto unchallenged social mores. It took courage and a sense of dedication to moral values to carry on such an undertaking in the face of massive resistance and scanty support.[22]

The *Defender* concluded by reflecting its own growing disenchantment—and inferentially that of the impatient younger Negroes—with the seeming inability of judicial decrees and mild compromise civil rights acts to affect fundamentally the Negro's unequal condition. These younger Negroes, the *Defender* observed, "have established a pattern of action that may well prove in the end to be the only rational solvent to America's racial dilemma."

The *Defender*'s editorials before the election were characterized generally by a cool and analytical restraint that revealed its singleminded devotion to a kind of Negro equivalent of organized labor's early Gompers Law: reward your friends regardless of party. Anticivil rights albatrosses, the *Defender* reminded, swing from the neck of both the donkey and the elephant:

Some conservative Republican Senators, particularly from Western states, are lukewarm about civil rights legislation and downright hostile to cloture to prevent filibuster. On the Democrat's side, a band of Dixiecrats played havoc with all liberal measures in which the interest of the Negro people was involved.[23]

"But," continued the *Defender,* since

the Democrats emerged from their National Convention with a stronger pledge to civil rights and the sit-down demonstrations in particular than did the Republicans, and the Great Debates so far have shown no marked changes in the positions of the two parties on the issue of racial equality. . . .

22. 20 August 1960.
23. "The Negro Vote, Which Way?", *Defender,* 22 October 1960. The *Defender* proclaimed itself, "The South's Independent Newspaper" on its masthead.

Then, the editorial concluded with feigned disinterest, "at this juncture it should not be hard to predict the course of the Negro vote." And it was not.[24]

When the Congress, three years after President Kennedy's inauguration, was being pressed to atone in part for his recent martyrdom by passing a strong and comprehensive new civil rights bill, both Memphis Negro weeklies supported the bill in their characteristic fashions. The *Defender*, so circumspect and analytical when editorially reflecting on the role of the Negro vote in elections, fell easily into hyperbolic militancy when confronted with the too-familiar specter of racial injustice. What of the Senate filibuster? "Action Now or Bloodshed!" [25] Were the civil rights bill not promptly passed, the *Defender* threatened, "there will be riots all over this land" and the responsibility will "rest squarely on those unreasonably feeble-minded Southern old men in the U.S. Senate. Their hands will be dripping with blood. Let them bear the consequences." [26] What of the impartiality of Southern juries? "It is indeed pure feeble-mindedness," the *Defender* acridly asserted, "to think that a jury of white men will *ever* [emphasis added] convict a member of their own race for the commission of an act of discrimination against a Negro." [27]

As the Senate filibuster droned on late into June, the *Defender* reiterated its approving prediction that

there'll be demonstrations and riots all over the nation. The Negro people's patience is about exhausted. They are not going to wait another hundred years to be integrated into the American society. There will be civil disobedience on a scale never witnessed before if white folks make the mistake of interfering with Negro demonstrations and protests. Our people are

24. Neither, however, was it difficult to predict the response of many White Protestant–fundamentalist Tennesseans to the grim spector of a Massachusetts Roman Catholic as President. Despite Senator Kennedy's appeal to Negroes, Tennessee's eleven electoral votes went to the Republicans for a third straight time, by a vote of 556,577 to 481,453. Of 176,607 votes cast in Shelby County, the Republican plurality was a fragile 921.

25. 19 April 1964.

26. *Ibid.*

27. 27 June 1964.

in an angry mood. They will fight and die for the cause which they believe to be holy and just.[28]

But the Senate, as we know, did ultimately invoke cloture and pass the bill that was destined on July 2 to become the Civil Rights Act of 1964.

Throughout the long "extended debate" over the controversial bill, the *Defender* had thundered continually against delay. The bill, in the eyes of the *Defender's* editors, accorded no new rights as such for which Negroes need be grateful; it only conferred belated legal recognition on their prior possession of inherent liberties. Thus, to rail at the bill's delay was a proper function of moral indignation. But to show sycophantic appreciation for its enactment would by implication deny the birthright status of the rights in which it dealt. Once passed, then, the law attracted little further editorial notice from the *Defender*.

Conversely, the *World* remained relatively quiescent during the long debate, reserving its editorial purview to reflect, in its characteristic style, on the bill's final enactment. The *World* devoted two editorials to celebrating the Senate passage of the act. The first carefully pointed out, with vindicated partisanship, that the final vote had been

73 to 27, with Republicans representing 80 percent and Democrats 69 percent, which would say in plain language that the wide margin between the percentage of Republicans and Democrats, that the Republicans once again held up the tradition and principles upon which that party was founded and flourished across the century.[29]

The second editorial focused on the problem raised by implementation by calling approving attention to the somewhat cryptic call of Roy Wilkins, executive director of the NAACP, for "true militant responsibility" rather than "reckless adventurism." [30] Warning against further demands for new laws, the *World* urged Negroes not to pick the tough-

---

28. *Ibid.*

29. "Civil Rights Cloture A Historic Act," *World*, 20 June 1964. The *World* apparently meant that 80 percent of the Republican senators voted for the bill (it was closer to 82 percent) as against 69 percent of the Democrats. Twenty-seven of the 33 Senate Republicans voted for the bill, and 46 of the 67 Democrats.

30. "Passage of the Civil Rights Bill Begins New Era in Struggle for Equality in Citizenship," *World*, 27 June 1964.

est places to test the civil rights act's provisions for integrating public accommodations. "It is to our race's interest," the *World* concluded with a fine consistency, "to gain acceptance and compliance with a minimum of opposition and tension between races."

Once the law was passed and Southern communities began to respond to it with surprising accommodation—indeed, almost with a detectable sigh of relief—both Memphis Negro weeklies began to concentrate editorially on the dramatic polarization of the electorate occasioned by the promising drive of Senator Goldwater for the Republican presidential nomination. The *World* had cheered the abortive attempts of Lodge and Rockefeller to block the Goldwater juggernaut in the primaries. But when Goldwater defeated Rockefeller in the critical California primary on June 2, and his nomination seemed thereby assured, the *World* clung tenaciously to its Republican banner. "Republicans are Wise in Not Trying to Unite and Stopping [*sic*] Goldwater," its editorial of June 13 headlined. The editors explained, first, that "we don't believe in ganging up on anyone." Second, they expressed the fond hope that Goldwater would begin moving "back toward the center" to appeal to the "great mass of white voters." Finally, the editors predicted that the delegates at the national convention would embrace a platform similar to that of 1960, "and whoever are their nominees will have to run on that platform." The editorial concluded by adding reassuringly, if somewhat naively, that "the platform is adopted at a convention first and the nominees come second."

But when the Goldwater forces triumphantly swept the Republican convention, and when Goldwater, consistent with his avowed philosophical convictions, cast his Senate vote with the embattled Southerners, the *World* reacted painfully. How, queried the *World,* could the patriotic senator oppose principles of fair employment and equal access to public accommodations "to which no person subscribing to genuine and intense Americanism could object?" [31] As Goldwater's subsequent campaign statements reaffirmed his intention of hunting the segregationist ducks in the South, the *World* lapsed into a troubled editorial silence.

31. 27 June 1964.

If the *World* suffered editorial agony in 1964 through partisan loyalty betrayed, the *Defender*'s editors shouted no hosannas. Their consistent devotion to the proven principle of bloc-voting, balance-of-power politics impaled them, they recognized, on the twin horns of a very different dilemma. Whereas dutiful compliance with Gompers' law had generally paid off handsomely for Negroes from Franklin Roosevelt's New Deal through the election of 1960, it threatened in the fall of 1964 to be self-destructive—or so it seemed to the *Defender*. Its editors had reaffirmed their faith in the efficacy of power-balance politics as late as April of 1964. Then, faced with the surprisingly strong showing made by Governor Wallace of Alabama in the Wisconsin Democratic primary, the *Defender* had observed that any retreat by the Johnson administration from its support of a strong civil rights bill "would be politically inexpedient from the point of view of the Negro vote. And mind you," the *Defender* had added, "that vote today, more than ever, represents the balance of power. No Presidential candidate can have a clear and unquestioned victory without it." [32] But by July, as the politically astute Johnson moved like quicksilver toward the political center to occupy political ground vacated by Goldwater, the *Defender* began editorially to fret over the specter of a recessive suicidal gene surfacing in the Republican party:

A dead GOP would endanger the strategic value of the Negro vote. The lack of effective opposition would cancel out the balance of power of the black electorate. The party in power would have no compelling reason, except perhaps naked humanitarianism, to show concern for the wellbeing of the Negro masses.[33]

Since the *Defender*'s political theory accorded little weight in human affairs to the power of "naked humanitarianism," its editors concluded darkly that "the outlook is dismal." The radicalization of politics in 1964 had, at least temporarily, undermined the operative assumptions upon which both Negro weeklies had based their dissimilar tactics in the quest for Negro equality.

On the eve of the election, the despondent editors of the *World* were

32. "The Wallace Raid," *Defender*, 25 April 1964.
33. "Dismal Outlook," *Defender*, 4 July 1964.

aroused from their political lethargy to reflect on the new stance of their party and its candidate (the *Defender,* when prompted to reflect on Senator Goldwater at all—a manifestly distasteful and infrequent exercise—curtly dismissed him as "malicious" and "ill-smelling"). Once again the *World* reminded its readers that the GOP had historically done more for the Negro than had the Democrats.[34] Its editors implicitly agreed with the editors of the *Defender* that the American two-party system worked best when the parties were in close equilibrium. As a consequence they suggested, without explicitly referring to Goldwater, that Negroes who found the national Republican candidates unattractive could help preserve the balance of the two-party system by voting for Republicans in local elections. As for the presidential nominees themselves, they concluded with unprecedented neutrality, "we make no endorsement or recommendation."

The Negroes of Memphis needed none. On November 3, the vast majority of Memphis' 95,000 Negro voters—and Tennessee's 240,-000—trooped to the polls to vote against Goldwater, and thereby to vindicate the *Defender*'s faith in balance-of-power politics by providing the margin needed not only to return the state to the Democratic column in presidential elections,[35] but also to reject, both in the August Democratic primary and in the general elections, conservative senatorial candidates in favor of the moderate Albert Gore and the liberal Ross Bass—both Democrats. In Memphis, archconservative Congressman Clifford Davis, dean of Tennessee's House delegation, was retired in favor of the progressive George Grider. Finally, in a dramatic gesture, Memphis elected to the state legislature the first Negro—portentously for the Republicans, a Democrat—since the first Reconstruction.[36]

34. "Our Position on the Presidential Election," *World,* 24 October 1964.

35. Parks's sample of nine Negro precincts in Davidson County (Nashville) revealed that 98.2 percent of the vote went to Johnson. See Parks, *op. cit.,* p. 159.

36. The new Negro legislator, A. W. Willis, Jr., was a lawyer for the Memphis chapter of the NAACP. Negroes were further alienated from the Republican party by the total and unprecedented purge of Negro Republican politicians from the Tennessee delegation to the national convention. The purge, engineered by militant Goldwater conservatives, contrasted sharply to the equally unprecedented *de*segregation of Tennessee's Democratic delegation.

But the euphoria of 1964 was short-lived. Its momentum proved sufficient to force the passage of a major voting rights bill in 1965, but the social cancer that surfaced so alarmingly and in such differing ways in Watts and Cicero, by robbing the nation of the self-righteous luxury of baiting the South, invited throughout the north and west the kind of "white backlash" that had thrown the Deep South to Goldwater in 1964. By the summer of 1966, the full-throated cry of "Black Power!" was echoing throughout the Negro ghettoes. The civil rights revolution had found its Robbespierre, and the white middle class majority—what Washington insiders called the "Great White Whale"—quickly called for a thermidor.

In Memphis, the response of the troubled *World* to the emergent refrains of black nationalism was a predictable as the sunrise: the angry chant of "white men must go" that was reverberating in, of all places, neighboring Mississippi, was a deplorable and suicidal form of "racism in reverse." [37] But the ambivalent response of the *Defender* was uniquely revealing of the dilemma of a community of Negroes whose psychological impulses impelled them toward a satisfying embrace of prideful racial identity, yet whose rational faculties quickly computed with depressing arithmetic the cruel odds facing a revolutionary proletariat whose essential racial bond automatically set them at odds with almost 90 percent of the population. The *Defender*'s initial reaction to "the sudden transformation of the Student Nonviolence Coordinating Committee into a black nationalist movement" was to label it "a shocking evolution." [38] The *Defender* reasoned that it was "unthinkable" that liberal, freedom-loving, self-sacrificing white folk should be excluded from a crusade for equality to which many had devoted—and some lost—their lives. "Integration is not irrelevant," insisted the *Defender*, "it is indispensable to social justice."

It is unthinkable that eleven years after this perfidious separate-but-equal concept of equality was dismantled by the high court's 1954 landmark decision on desegregation, we should undertake to revive it as a condition for progressive action.

But the *Defender*'s initial shock at the emergence of Black Power was

37. "This is Wrong and Unwise," *World*, June 25, 1966.
38. "The New SNCC," *Defender*, June 18, 1966.

no match for the bitter frustration accumulated by years of humiliation, and its rational indictment of a self-defeating tactic could not
long suppress the rallying-cry of racial identity and pride. Ironically
indicative of its editors' sensitivity to this latter compulsion was the
editorial that accompanied the *Defender*'s condemnation of "the new
SNCC." Entitled "The Natural Look: A New Mode for Negro Wom-
en?", the editorial celebrated the recent trend, "especially popular among
the younger set, " of rejecting white standards of beauty and embracing
"a new respect and a new self-image of the Negro woman" by wearing
the hair in its natural state.[39] Given the *Defender*'s precarious allegiance to the old liberal orthodoxy, all that was needed to jar its editors
loose from their mooring to passive resistance was an incident that could
symbolize the intolerable price of unprovoked and unresisted white
assault. When a shotgun blast felled James Meredith on a Mississippi
highway early in July, the outraged *Defender* abandoned the preachments of Martin Luther King for the revolutionary rhetoric of Stokely Carmichael.

The voices of those who once preached the use of the other cheek are losing
their sonority. Their logic is one of despair which no longer suits the mood
of the awakening black masses. Power, black power, has become the battle
cry of the Black Revolution.[40]

And again on July 23:

Black Power . . . is a high-water mark in the flux of the Black Revolution.
The young civil rights activists believe that white society has failed them,
that American democracy is a collection of impressive catchwords that
command only lip service from the white man.

Consistent with its radical new creed, the *Defender* trumpeted its
virtues in every subsequent issue throughout the watershed summer of
1966, and its editors hurled their contemptuous abuse, as revolution-
aries are wont to do, at the timid and compromising old-line leaders of
the liberal halfway house: the "bourgeois Urban League" and the

39. The *Defender*'s ambivalence was reflected in its guest columnists, who
ranged the spectrum from Jackie Robinson and Harry Golden to Martin Luther
King and Langston Hughes. It allowed Old Taylor Kentucky straight bourbon to
stimulate Negro pride by sponsoring a series of vignettes in celebration of "Ingenious [Negro] Americans."
40. "We Tried, But the South Wouldn't Let Us," *Defender*, July 9, 1966.

"ultra-conservative NAACP", those "black bourgeois uncletoms who affect the Harvard accent" and whose vanity and ambitions for status lead them to sell out at "frequent pow-wows at the White House." [41]

But the *Defender*, for all its new-found enthusiasm, could not escape the central dilemma that was logically inherent in the Black Power Movement. For implicit in the new doctrine was the principle of racial exclusion: integration, which was the goal of the old coaliton with white liberals, was now regarded as irrelevant, and consequently the coalition and its politics of compromise stood rejected. The *Defender* attempted to escape this dilemma by denying it—by having its cake and eating it too. Thus the Defender sensed no contradiction in calling simultaneously for "racial solidarity" under the banner of Black Power—for a Negro "solid front" to "support his own business institutions," to "create his own financial world, build his own political machine"—while at the same time warning against the "quicksand of racial exclusion" and calling for bringing "into the focus of our endeavors all white people of good will . . . [who] will be helpful links in the chain of power we are trying to forge." [42] In response to the warning that a revolution based on only 10 percent of the population invited disaster, the *Defender* countered that "this view fails to take into consideration the incalculable number of white people of the John Brown devotion to social justice who are willing to shed their blood right now for the cause of Negro freedom as Brown and his two sons did in 1859 at Harper's Ferry." [43] Yet there was reason to speculate that the devotees of Black Power could recruit only a small percentage even of the Negro ten percent. This expectation was supported by no less authority than the Memphis *Defender* itself, which just prior to its recent conversion had confidently predicted that "this type of leadership, which wraps itself in self-sufficiency, will not draw many brethren to its camp. Support for it," the *Defender* had concluded, "will be limited to a corporal's guard." [44]

CORE's former director, James Farmer, once told Robert Penn

---

41. "Struggle for Power," *Defender*, August 20, 1966.
42. "The Need for Power," *Defender*, July 30, 1966.
43. *Defender*, August 20, 1966.
44. *Defender*, July 9, 1966.

Warren that "Malcolm X and I can address a mass rally the same morning, he can get applause talking about separation, I can get applause talking about integration." [45] The historic divisions of American Negro opinion are abundantly manifest in the debates of the Negro editors in Memphis, and the psychological ambivalence, to which Farmer was alluding, that so many of them share is especially apparent in the ambiguous intellectual odyssey of the editors of the *Defender*. Given the hen-and-egg relationship between public opinion and the media, and in light of the limited evidence, we cannot measure the impact of the *World*'s and the *Defender*'s editorial exhortations on Memphis' large Negro community, although it is suggestive to note that the *Defender*'s circulation soon outstripped that of the once unchallenged *World* to such a degree that the formerly semi-weekly *World* was reduced in the early sixties to publishing only one edition per week. But the question of the two weeklies' respective editorial efficacy is less compelling here than that of the manifest degree to which these unique Negro newspapers mirrored the emotional and intellectual strivings of America's increasingly impatient Negro people toward that cruelly elusive goal of equality that the Republic's founding Declaration had proudly promised 191 years before.

45. Robert Penn Warren, *Who Speaks for the Negro?* (New York: Random House, 1965), pp. 191–192.

11

The Politics of Desegregation

WHEN, in May of 1954, the Supreme Court declared racially segregated schools to be unconstitutional, Tennesseans, as we have seen, were represented in the Senate by Estes Kefauver and Albert Gore, and their governor was Frank Clement. Kefauver, who had slain the Crump dragon in 1948, had freely admitted that he was proud to be called a liberal.[1] In the lexicon of state politics, the intensely devoted "Kefauver people" were for the most part unapologetic champions of TVA, organized labor, civil liberties and civil rights, and liberal internationalism. If Senator Gore was less easily identifiable by his friends (a proud, stubbornly independent, and somewhat reserved man, Gore never rallied around himself a comparable band of devoted "Gore people"), his consistent support of consumer interests, conservation, the TVA and public power had earned him the enmity of conservative financiers and big businessmen whose responsive benefactor, the aging Senator K. D. McKellar, he had defeated in 1952. Further, Gore had earned a reputation as a progressive internationalist in the tradition of Cordell Hull (Gore frequently remarked with pride that his father and Hull, both native sons of Carthage, Tennessee, had "run the river together"),[2] and he was regarded as a moderate on the racial issue. Finally, Gover-

1. Quoted in *SSN,* July 1960, p. 7.
2. Quoted in David Halberstam, "The Air Conditioned Crusade Against Albert Gore," *The Reporter,* 4 September 1958, p. 24. Hereafter cited as Halberstam, "Gore".

nor Clement in 1954 was widely regarded as a promising young moderate politician who had worked hard and somewhat successfully to reform Tennessee's archaic constitution.

While much can be made of the proposition that the American—and especially the Southern—liberal is a fairly conservative fellow when viewed against the spectrum of world politics, none of these three politicians had claimed to be or had been publicly classified as a conservative. When the Brown decision ushered in a period of intensifying racial crisis, powerful and well-financed conservative forces in Tennessee saw in the issue of desegregation a means whereby they might once again achieve control of the state that they had enjoyed during the long reign of Boss Crump.

That the pervasive Southern commitment to white supremacy could be used by conservatives as a lever with which to achieve power had been ably demonstrated by the so-called Southern "Redeemers" who had seized power in the Southern states following Reconstruction. That this enduring attitude could also be invoked by Southern conservatives to splinter opposing populistic coalitions of poor Negroes and whites had been demonstrated by so-called Southern "Bourbons" in the 1890s. Since the demise of Populism, however, Southern Negroes for the most part had been successfully intimidated and disfranchised.[3] Even Southern progressives, such as Woodrow Wilson and Josephus Daniels, were content not to disturb the biracial system, and many were in fact willing to reinforce it as the only viable basis for orderly government and racial co-existence.

As the pattern of racial segregation became a Southern norm enforced by the so-called Jim Crow laws, the incidence of lynchings gradually declined and the need to appeal to racial fears was gradually reduced over the years. Old-fashioned Southern demagogues—the Tillmans, Vardamans, and Bilboes—were gradually replaced by Southern politicians whose conservative politics were matched by their more reserved demeanor (witness the considerable difference between the political style of Georgia's Senator Herman Talmadge and that of his red-gal-

3. See generally Woodward, *The Strange Career of Jim Crow.*

lused father, Eugene). As the Southern economy, so savagely decimated by the Great Depression, began to recover under Doctor New Deal and, more spectacularly, under Doctor Win-the-War, the South began to experience the "bulldozer revolution," that dramatic process of urbanization (and suburbanization) whereby the South came increasingly in its physical aspects to resemble the rest of the nation. As a consequence, increasingly numerous, and, doubtlessly, increasingly sophisticated urban voters saw little relevance in the rural orientation and racist demagogic preachments of the Gene Talmadges. As the efficacy of the various devices of disfranchisement was reduced by the courts, sometimes by the voters themselves, and generally by the new affluence and the more moderate and better informed society that accompanied it, many new voters also turned from the more refined Bourbonism of the Herman Talmadges and sent to Washington such men as Frank Graham of North Carolina, Lister Hill and John Sparkman of Alabama, William Fulbright of Arkansas, Russell Long of Louisiana, Ralph Yarborough of Texas, and Estes Kefauver and Albert Gore of Tennessee. Additionally, Southern voters of the postwar era sent to their statehouses such moderate and progressive governors as Luther Hodges and Terry Sanford of North Carolina, LeRoy Collins of Florida, the early Orval Faubus of Arkansas, and Frank Clement of Tennessee.

After May 1954, these latter-day Southern progressives—from moderate to liberal—could expect, as usual, to face more conservative opponents. But after 1954, these new conservative challengers would be men who, traditionally armed with generous financial backing, would additionally be armed with an issue through which to appeal to the newly sensitized but abiding racial attitudes that have always characterized the Southern white masses. Such appeals had historically provided the margin of victory for conservative Southern politicians whose public embrace of racist dogma represented a shrewdly calculated strategem for achieving or perpetuating conservative Bourbon control.

In Southern states surrounding Tennessee, the revitalized formula met with considerable success. Some progressive politicians such as the distinguished Frank Graham, former president of the University of North Carolina, were defeated by segregationists in campaigns characterized by the circulation of scurrilous and often slanderous propaganda aimed at provoking racial animosity.[4] Governor Collins's moderation on the racial question seemingly terminated his career in elective politics in Florida.[5] In Alabama, both Senators Hill and Sparkman were severely threatened by, of all things, strong Republican challengers. Even the colorful "Kissin' Jim" Folsom of Alabama, a populistic politician not above demagoguery but a relative moderate on the racial question, was soundly trounced in a race for an office no loftier than that of Democratic committeeman.

Other moderate politicians met the new challenge, as politicians are frequently wont to do, by publicly adjusting their views to accommodate the new popular demands. Governor Faubus spectacularly and successfully stole the segregationists' clothing in 1957 at Little Rock. Even Senator Fulbright felt compelled to participate, with apparently feigned enthusiasm, in the Southern filibusters against the civil rights bills of 1957, 1960, and 1964. Some moderate politicians were less successful in their readjustments. In race-conscious Mississippi, the relatively moderate Governor James Coleman of the early fifties fervently insisted in the early sixties that he was as staunch a segregationist as any candidate in Mississippi. Still, he was unable to convince white Mississippians, and he was not reelected as their governor.[6]

In Tennessee, both Senators Kefauver and Gore and, to a somewhat lesser extent, Governor Clement were fair game to the revitalized conservative segregationists.[7] No strangers to ambition, all three were known to be casting covetous eyes on the vice-presidential nomination in 1956

4. See Samuel Lubell, "Who Beat Frank Graham?" *The Future of American Politics* (New York: Doubleday and Company, 1952), pp. 106–115.

5. Collins, together with Tennessee's Buford Ellington and North Carolina's Luther Hodges, was appointed by President Johnson in 1964 to guide the new Community Relations Service in persuading fellow Southern governors of the wisdom of moderation and of complying with the civil rights act of that year.

6. Douglas Cater, a Southerner on the staff of *The Reporter,* called Coleman "the least immoderate candidate." See "Beyond Tokenism," *The Reporter,* 10 October 1963, pp. 23–27. White blacklash in Mississippi was necessarily minimal because intractable white racial attitudes had never achieved even a modestly advanced position to lash back *from.*

7. Despite Clement's generally consistent political moderation, he was never as prime a target for conservatives as were Kefauver and Gore. Conservatives

(a prize, albeit one of dubious value, ultimately won by Senator Kefauver). But, in order to be eligible for the lightning to strike, each had first to prove that he could hold Tennessee in a period of heightening racial tension before he could be considered as a Democratic candidate fit to bind up the party's and perhaps the nation's wounds.

Both Clement and Kefauver were up for re-election in November of 1954. Both faced opponents in the Democratic primary, to be held in early August, who could be counted on to play upon the newly sensitized racial nerves of the electorate in eleventh-hour attempts to bolster their faltering campaigns. But the specter of racial desegregation, though recently raised, did not yet seem to be an imminently pressing issue; the court had not even begun hearings on an implementing decree. In the primary, Clement easily dispatched his opponent, former Governor Gordon Browning, by a vote of 481,808 to 195,156, despite the latter's opportunistic appeals to segregationist sentiment.[8] In the senatorial primary, Kefauver defeated Congressman Pat Sutton by a margin of better than two-to-one. The colorless Sutton

were generally comfortable with Clement's administrations, and one student of Tennessee politics has labeled Clement's brand of moderation "neo-Bourbonism" on the grounds that Clement's avoidance of racist appeals and willingness to accept federal grants-in-aid only represented an "apparent moderation" that masked a basically conservative state administration that blocked labor legislation, promoted regressive consumer taxation, and resisted electoral and constitutional reform. See Parks, "Tennessee Politics since Kefauver and Reece," p. 153. It is true that the conservative *Banner* consistently supported Clement and the liberal *Tennessean* as consistently opposed him. Yet even such Clement critics as the *Tennessean*'s John Seigenthaler and state legislator Harold Bradley conceded that Clement's instincts were basically liberal. They argued that the young and inexperienced governor entered office under the tutelage of a cabal of old Bourbons that included "Hub" Walters, Joe Carr (the defendant, as attorney general, in Tennessee's historic reapportionment case, *Baker* v. *Carr*), and Clement's father. Even so, while Ellington supported Lyndon Johnson for the Democratic presidential nomination in 1960, Clement worked for John Kennedy. Further, Clement had fought hard, if unsuccessfully, to abolish capital punishment in Tennessee. He had *never* sent a fellow man to the electric chair during all the ten years of his governorship, and when Ross Bass handed him his first electorial defeat in 1964, he had appeared on television to congratulate his nemesis with becoming graciousness.

8. Returns for the election of 1954 are recorded in the *Tennessee Blue Book*, 1956, pp. 375–376.

had been unable to convince enough voters with his McCarthyistic charge that Kefauver was "soft on communism." [9]

A more meaningful test of the strength of segregationist sentiment in Tennessee came in 1958. In that year—in the ominous shadow of Clinton, Little Rock, the Southern Manifesto, the Civil Rights Act of 1957, and desegregation in Nashville—a new governor was chosen and Senator Gore sought his first re-election. Tennessee's gubernatorial race in 1958 was the state's first truly wide-open race in six years, and probably the most heated one since Gordon Browning had boldly crossed lances with the Crump machine in the late thirties and again in the late forties. Clement, who chose not to challenge the formidable Albert Gore for the Senate seat and who was constitutionally barred from immediate re-election, did tap his commissioner of agriculture, Buford Ellington, to succeed him, and the administration's powerful support gave Ellington an early advantage.

Four other Democratic candidates eagerly joined the fray. Because of heightened public sensitivity to the question of desegregation, all were expected to assume some public posture toward this volatile issue. In Tennessee, as in most Southern one-party states, real issues were normally scarce, and as a consequence most political campaigns centered around personalities and involved the heavy-handed use of the folksy, "friends-and-neighbors" political style. Ellington had been Clement's chief lieutenant in piloting through the legislature in 1957 the package of relatively mild if ambiguous laws designed to forestall the demands of strongly segregationist legislators that Tennessee, like Virginia, erect strong legislative defenses against desegregation. State Senator Stainback, by far the most vocal of the segregationists in the legislature, had complained bitterly about Ellington's successful effort to defeat his prosegregation bills in 1955.

Ellington was early opposed in the race by Andrew T. (Tip) Taylor, circuit court judge of Jackson and an avowed proponent of segregation. Jackson, seat of Madison County, was the municipal center of strongly segregationist West Tennessee, although populous

9. David Halberstam, "The Silent Ones Speak Up in Tennessee," *The Reporter,* 1 September 1960, pp. 28–30. Hereafter cited as Halberstam, "Kefauver".

Memphis dominated the Western Grand Division's politics. Taylor's candidacy was supported in West Tennessee by the powerful Memphis *Commercial Appeal*. Eager to rally to himself segregationist support, Taylor publicized a statement attributed to Stainback that "in my opinion, Ellington was the most active and efficient foe of segregation in 1955 of any man in Tennessee." [10]

Stung by such attacks from the segregationist quarter, the Mississippi-born Ellington on June 14 told an audience at Columbia, near his home town of Lewisburg in Middle Tennessee, that "Yes, I'm a segregationist. I'm an old-fashioned segregationist. And I'm a states'-righter. . . ." Taylor had claimed on June 6 that

I was the first candidate for governor to state that I was unconditionally and irrevocably opposed to the integration of the white and Negro races in our public schools. To prevent such a situation from resulting, I shall exercise all the powers of the office of governor of Tennessee. . . .

I have given this long and thoughtful consideration and I have reached the conclusion that with respect to those city and county schools directly affected by a court decree commanding integration, the General Assembly of the state of Tennessee should vest in such county boards of education and city boards of education, as the case may be, powers to temporarily suspend such schools where, in the judgment of the school board, integration will result in disorder or violence.

In response, Ellington replied in the same speech at Columbia that

I believe in the principle of keeping public school control in local and state hands, responsible to and closest to the people. I helped pilot through the last legislature a set of state laws calculated to keep the responsibility there, letting local preference prevail. If in the future these laws needs strengthening, I favor and will propose legislation to avoid the mixing of races in public schools of our state.

I would not hestitate as governor to close a school in order to prevent violence or bloodshed.

Taylor was generally considered the stronger segregationist, but Ellington was contending sharply for the votes of those numerous anxious white Tennesseans who would vote for a candidate who promised to "do something" to protect the familiar biracial system in Tennessee.

10. The remarks of Stainback and those that follow of the contestants in the election of 1958 are quoted in *SSN*, August 1958, p. 10.

Like Clement before him, Ellington was supported by the Nashville *Banner,* and his loudly trumpeted credentials as a staunch segregationist had additionally earned him the support of the Chattanooga *News–Free Press.*

Three other candidates entered the lists against Ellington and Taylor. All three adopted, in varying degrees, a moderate posture toward the question of desegregation. One was G. Edward Friar, a Knoxville attorney and former secretary of state who had broken with Clement. Friar, on June 21, told an East Tennessee audience that "there must be, and is, a middle ground on which people of good will can meet and find ways of progress out of our present racial discord." But on June 22, Friar, who realized that he was not a major contender, withdrew from the race in favor of Mayor Edmund Orgill of Memphis. A successful businessman, Orgill was the leading contender in support the moderate position that the Supreme Court's ruling should be complied with in a gradual and limited fashion. His candidacy was endorsed by every major daily of the old anit-Crump coaliton: the *Press-Scimitar,* the *Tennessean,* the *Times* and the *News-Sentinel.* But he was a relative newcomer to politics, and his name was not widely known outside of Memphis.

Orgill personified the acute dilemma of the Southern moderate— especially one whose political base was located in West Tennessee with its Deep South orientation—and his plight suggests why the Southern moderate as successful politician has been such a relatively rare phenomonon. Always on the defensive, hypersensitive to innuendoes and direct charges that he was an integrationist, yet compelled by personal conviction to urge compliance with law and with court orders, however distasteful, Orgill began his campaign on a characteristically defensive note:

> I have never advocated integration of our public schools and as governor I shall never do so. This is not only my personal preference but a vast majority of Tennesseans prefer [that] our schools remain as they are.

Customarily, Orgill would then express his confidence in the ability of local school authorities to handle school problems, and link to this appeal to Jeffersonian sentiment a strong if somewhat artfully veiled hint that his administration would not erect the sort of statewide defenses that Virginia had erected:

> Under the law, school boards as representatives of the people in the individual community are given broad authority to handle their own school problems. I shall not interfere at any time or in any way with this lawful right.

In conclusion, Orgill would typically affirm his belief in equal opportunities for all—a belief that could be construed as supporting either the court's new notion of equality or the old separate equality:

> And finally, I believe that all persons, regardless of race, should have equal opportunities, and I will do all I can to see that adequate educational opportunities are provided for all children of Tennessee.

The fifth and final contender was State Senator Clifford Allen of Nashville. Allen was a perennial if somewhat engaging also-ran whose devoted personal following among labor and Negroes had for years guaranteed him a seat in the state senate but little more than that. He frequently angered the state's hopeful moderates and liberals by refusing to withdraw from a race in the face of almost certain defeat, thereby splitting the liberal vote. Allen frequently and categorically declared that local school boards must abide by decisions of the Supreme Court; attempts to circumvent the affects of the decisions through state legislation, he insisted, were meaningless.

As the campaign, approaching the August 7 primary, gained momentum, it settled into what was essentially a tight three-way race between Ellington, Taylor, and Orgill. Orgill complained that "there's been a lot of baloney spread around on segregation," and called Ellington's and Taylor's talk of closing desegregated schools "an invitation to violence." Ellington, recently endorsed by Citizens for Progress, the Memphis remnant of the old Crump machine, frequently reiterated his pledge "not to hesitate as governor to close a school in order to prevent violence or bloodshed." In response, Taylor raised Ellington's bid by asserting that the governor

> should have the power and authority to close a school, in the event federal troops were marched into Tennessee to enforce the integration decree. . . .

Not only should the governor be given the power to close schools; he should be given the power to keep them closed as long as troops remain in the state to enforce such a decree [for integration].

To this the *Tennessean* replied that it was "distressing to hear" that, in the ominous shadow of Sputnik, and in the light of the unfortunate truism that

the schools in our region have for generations lagged behind those in other parts of the country . . . two men aspire to the governorship of Tennessee who come forward in this hour of education's challenge to talk of closing the schools in our state.[11]

The *Tennessean* added that, in addition to the distressing things that Ellington and Taylor had said, they had *not* said simply that they would uphold law and order, whereas the *Tennessean*'s candidate, Orgill, had repeatedly made that vow. Thus, in the *Tennessean*'s view, Ellington and Taylor were in effect issuing an implicit invitation to extreme segregationists to instigate violence at desegregated schools in order to have them closed.

On the morning of August 8, Ellington narrowly won with 213,415 votes. [12] Only 8,786 votes behind was Taylor, and only a scant 247 votes behind Taylor was Orgill. The *News–Free Press* gleefully editorialized that the vote amounted to a two-to-one mandate for segregation.[13] But the verdict of the primary was not that simple. For, in addition to ignoring Allen's 56,854 votes—a relatively unimportant omission, perhaps—the *News–Free Press* editorial had refrained from mentioning that in the senatorial primary of the same day, an election in which the issue of segregation had loomed large, the moderate incumbent, Senator Gore, had soundly defeated a segregationist opponent who had thrice been elected governor of Tennessee.

Prentice Cooper, a former ambassador (by political appointment)

11. 13 July 1958.
12. Returns for the election of 1958 are recorded in the *Tennessee Blue Book*, 1960, p. 175. Mayor Orgill carried neither Memphis nor any country in West Tennessee, although he did relatively well in Middle Tennessee and in the Knoxville area. Taylor carried West Tennessee and the Chattanooga area, the state's most racially sensitive areas, almost solidly.
13. 8 August 1958.

to Peru, had served his three terms as governor of Tennessee during the forties in intimate alliance with Boss Crump. The sixty-two-year-old former governor had been making a poor showing in an attempted comeback in the already crowded gubernatorial primary.[14] On June 5, just four days before the deadline for qualifying for the senatorial primary, Cooper withdrew from the gubernatorial race and challenged Albert Gore for his seat in the Senate.

Cooper had been persuaded to challenge Gore by a small group of wealthy and conservative Tennesseans who had been looking for some time for a man to defeat Gore. They had reportedly approached several state notables, including Governor Clement, with the offer of a well-financed race, plus their own issues. The offer had too many strings attached for most, but both the vision of a seat in the Senate and the prescribed issues appealed to the flagging Cooper. In an article on the election written for *The Reporter* magazine by a political reporter for the *Tennessean*, Cooper's new backers were described as including:

Justin Potter, an immensely wealthy Nashville industrialist, insurance executive, former coal-mine owner, and one of TVA's bitterest enemies; Guy Smith, chairman of the state Republican party and editor of the Republican Knoxville *Journal* which had editorially beckoned Cooper into the race; Roane Waring of Memphis, a lobbyist for the Dixon-Yates contract; A. G. Heinsohn of Knoxville, a wealthy textile man who had been an elector for States'-Rights candidate T. Coleman Andrews in 1956; and Pat French of Nashville, a textile man who two years before had led a Tennessee boycott on Japanese goods and who was still smarting over Gore's lack of co-operation with the textile people.[15]

14. Details of the Gore-Cooper race are derived from Halberstam, "Gore," and the July, August, and September numbers of *SSN*.

15. Halberstam, "Gore." p. 25. A tall, lean New England Jew, Halberstam had been graduated from the editorship of the *Harvard Crimson* in 1956. He subsequently served a challenging if difficult apprenticeship on a small newspaper in Mississippi, then moved to the Nashville *Tennessean,* where he covered the re-election campaigns of both Gore and Kefauver and wrote articles for *The Reporter* about both. Halberstam's acute political observations caught the eye of the New York *Times,* which sent him to cover international crises, first in the Congo, and then in Viet Nam. In 1964, Halberstam was awarded the Pulitzer Prize for international reporting.

Gore complained that Cooper's supporters were trying to reconstruct the same coalition that had carried Tennessee for Eisenhower in 1952 and in 1956 and had been the basis of Crump's statewide power: the alliance between the east-state Republicans and the west-state Dixiecrats. Gore was especially in trouble in West Tennessee over his failure to participate in the Southern filibuster against the civil rights bill of 1957, and his subsequent vote for the bill. Additionally, Gore's campaign was plagued by local recollections of his failure to sign the Southern Manifesto two years earlier. But, in addition to the clear advantage of incumbency, the strikingly handsome senator possessed the advantages of a record which included fourteen years in the House, strong support for TVA, a hand in exposing the Dixon-Yates contract, and sponsorship of the national highway bill.

Against Gore, Cooper mounted a campaign of a type frequently seen in the South and usually very effective: a great deal of indignant talk about states' rights, some fairly earthy discussion of the race problem, the constant background refrains of "Dixie", all well financed by private power and utilities and textile money.[16] Cooper, who called his campaign a "Holy Crusade," concentrated on segregation as a "top issue." He charged in his speeches that Gore "sold us down the river" by failing to sign the Southern Manifesto and vowed that the thing he would do when elected would be to go to Washington and sign it. Vowing "to fight for the Southern way of life," he further accused Gore of voting "to force our children into unwanted social mixing," of "siding with the integrationists," and asserted that "anytime the NAACP orders him [Gore] to vote, he's up there [in Washington]." [17] Cooper also attacked Gore's support of foreign aid as a "do-good

16. Cooper stumped the state in an airconditioned bus. His picture was emblazoned on an estimated 450 billboards, allegedly contributed gratis by outdoor advertisers who were angry at Gore for having tried to regulate billboards along the new interstate highway system. A Nashville advertising firm handled Cooper's campaign and some of his speech-writing, and the total expense was estimated to be as high as $750,000. See Halberstam, "Gore," p. 25.

17. The remarks of Cooper and those that follow of Gore are quoted in *ibid.*

global giveaway" and criticized the Senator for supporting some parts of reciprocal trade.

Gore, campaigning intensively and making up to a dozen speeches daily, retorted that

passage of the civil rights bill as amended into a right-to-vote bill was a victory for the forces of reason and a defeat for the forces of extremism. . . . I genuinely believe in the right to vote, and I thought the enactment of this fair and moderate bill would postpone the enactment of a much more severe bill later.

In cotton-growing West Tennessee, Gore's strategy was simply to hit Cooper as hard as he could on the trade issue and then counteract as much of the civil-rights charges as possible without mentioning the Manifesto.

I drove through this morning and I looked at your cotton crop and it looks good; it looks to be one of the best crops you've ever had. Well, what are you going to do with it? . . . I know what you did last year. You sold sixty percent of it to foreign markets. If you want to stop that and quit those foreign markets, there's a man running for the U.S. Senate who'll accommodate you. But I'm flying back to Washington tonight to vote for extension of the Cordell Hull program. And I'll tell you this: the cotton-mill and textile people would love to have all the cotton they want dirt cheap. Oh yes, you could make a good crop, but they'd pay you what they wanted and you sure couldn't live off that.

As for civil rights:

Now you've heard a lot of propaganda and prejudice on these civil rights bills. This passed three-to-one in the House, a tough anti-South bill, more punitive and severe than its authors realized. I had the chance to stand stubbornly and see the passage of a severe bill or to try—and you notice I said try—to modify the bill into one the South could live with. There were five amendments passed—this wasn't child's play, it took twenty-eight days and I was a leader with the South on those Amendments. And let me tell you that it is a right-to-vote bill, and I believe in the right to vote for every man—white or colored, rich or poor, Jew or Gentile—and I hope you do too. The Southerners got together and decided to let the bill pass. One Southerner jumped the traces, Strom Thurmond, and talked twenty-four hours and all the other Southerners ate his hide off. And one man came up to me and said he couldn't vote for the bill and he couldn't vote for the Ten Commandments if someone called it a civil rights bill. Well, I don't believe in labels and I'll vote my convictions and you wouldn't want it any other way.

When it was all over, Gore had soundly trounced Cooper by a vote of 375,439 to 253,191. He had carried seventy of the state's ninety-five counties. In Middle Tennessee, he carried every county, including Cooper's own, by a margin of two-to-one. Even Memphis turned its back on Cooper and gave Gore a majority of 18,000.

Gore's impressive win, however, had no more signified a clear-cut victory for racial moderation than had Orgill's defeat signified a victory for segregation. For, despite the unchallenged dominance of the inter-related issues of segregation, civil rights and states' rights in Cooper's campaign, the aging challenger—neither colorful, forceful, nor particularly attractive—was ill-matched against the fifty-one year old incumbent, whose youthful face was given dignity by a mop of wavy silver hair.[18] It would have been inaccurate to conclude from the election of 1958 that moderation had bested segregation in an even contest, or that the liberal philosophy had triumphed at the polls over the conservative one. But two years later, just as the sit-ins had begun to rekindle racial fears in a dramatic new way, there occurred an election in Tennessee in which the issues of moderation versus segregation, even of liberalism versus conservatism, were so clearly counterposed that it would be difficult to deny that the voters had made a clear-cut choice.

In the late spring of 1960, as the new sit-ins dominated the headlines in Tennessee, Circuit Judge Andrew Taylor announced his intention to unseat Senator Kefauver in the Democratic primary in August. Taylor's chances of success were considered very good. Despite his narrow defeat in 1958, he had made an impressive showing in the gubernatorial race of that year. Unlike Cooper, he was a forceful, impressive and articulate spokesman of conservative and prosegregationist views, and he enjoyed the same generous financial support that had been afforded Cooper. Unlike the red-baiting Pat Sutton, he was the kind of candidate behind whom responsible conservatives could rally. Furthermore, he avoided the excesses of the Sutton-Kefauver and the

18. When Crump first picked Cooper as his gubernatorial candidate, he was reported to have quipped: "Boys, this time we're goin' fishin' without bait." See Halberstam, "Gore," p. 25.

Cooper-Gore races, and set out to wage a much more subtle campaign against Kefauver.[19]

Taylor's basic approach was a carefully planned appeal to provincialism. While avoiding the time-honored tactic of stirring up fears by means of old-fashioned Southern demagoguery, Taylor nevertheless managed to take advantage subtly of a matrix of fears that already existed just below the surface. To be sure, he made it a point to refer rather frequently to the sit-ins, to the militantly liberal Democratic platform upon which Kefauver had campaigned for the Vice Presidency four years before, to Kefauver's failure to sign the Southern Manifesto, and to his vote for the civil rights bills. But Taylor's primary thrust was a soft sell, the pitch of which was best illustrated by the Taylor slogan, "Our Kind of Folks." Andrew T. Taylor was "Tip" Taylor— a good fellow and a familiar neighbor. He was also Judge "Tip" Taylor—a responsible and respected citizen.

The corollary to Taylor's appeal was that Kefauver was not really "our kind of folks." Taylor tirelessly reminded his listeners that Kefauver had "turned his back" on Tennessee and had aligned himself with "a group of ultra-northern liberals, dogooders and one-worlders" (it is interesting to muse whether, in the eyes of conservative Southerners, it was more odious to be an ultra-northern liberal or an ultra-liberal northerner). He further reminded audiences that outside money was coming into Tennessee. A favorite method by which Taylor depicted this theme was to give a lengthy description of a fund-raising party, given for Kefauver in Washington, in which it was carefully pointed out that the party was held on Sunday, was attended by northern radicals but not by a single Southern congressman, and that the leaders of the party were identified by their easily recognizable Irish-Catholic and Jewish names.

Taylor's folksy appeal, which was visibly paying off throughout the state, was boldly challenging Kefauver on the senator's own ground, for much of Kefauver's political strength was derived from a demeanor of ingenuous rustic folksiness. Alarming reports of Taylor's surging

19. Details of the Taylor-Kefauver race are derived from Halberstam, "Kefauver," and the July, August, and September numbers of *SSN*.

momentum prompted Kefauver to hurry back to Tennessee from Washington; admittedly running scared, he did not even attend the
Democratic National Convention. Like Gore, Kefauver campaigned
with his familiar intensiveness even in West Tennessee, where he
defended his votes for the civil rights acts of 1957 and 1960 in an
aggressive if pre-emptive fashion:

> I thought it was a fair and just bill and I could not clear it with my
> conscience to vote against the right to vote. I don't know how we can hold
> our heads up in the world if we deprive people of this right. I'll tell you
> something else—our friends from the North and West aren't going to help
> us with TVA if they can't reason with us and expect our support on fair
> bills like this. But if there's someone here who's against the right to vote,
> maybe he'll raise his hand and tell us why.

Few hands were ever raised.

Kefauver did enjoy several distinct advantages over his opponent.

'I'm Being Smeared'!   That Line Won't Sell Down Here, Estes.

Knox in the Banner

Knox in the Banner

An incumbent of two terms, he was accumulating valuable seniority— a potent factor in the South. He enjoyed the rather solid backing of labor and Negroes. Further, his record of strong support of TVA contrasted sharply to Taylor's circle of anti–TVA backers.[20] Two additional assets bolstered Kefauver's chances of re-election. First, this enigmatic politician could always count on the support of a large group of admiring volunteers whose devotion to the tall senator was undeniable yet somewhat difficult to explain. He was ostensibly a warm and personal man, yet even those closest to him would confess that he was essentially a loner whom no one really knew well. Nationally famous as he was for his brilliant campaigning, Kefauver generally could neither remember names nor faces nor correlate the two. His schedule was always lined with mixups, and his speeches, frequently painfully delivered, were often cluttered with blunders and faux pas. It was almost as if this very amiable ineptitude prompted his many devotees to work so very hard "to help ol' Estes out." [21] Whatever the reason, probably no Tennessee politician in this century has been able to accumulate such a devoted personal following.

A final important asset for Kefauver was the statewide support of thirty-seven newspapers, including one major daily in each of the four big cities. The same anti-Crump coalition supported Kefauver even more warmly than it had Gore. Taylor was supported by only nineteen newspapers, although he too enjoyed the endorsement of one major daily in each of the four big cities. Taylor's conservative dailies may have oversold the public on their happy expectation that their man was going to unhorse Kefauver. They were especially intrigued by this notion, and Southern moderates and liberals were fearful, because Kefauver was regarded as a sort of buffer for moderate and liberal politicians and newspaper editors in Tennessee and indeed throughout the South who would have been much more vulnerable if he were removed.

20. Stung by Kefauver's reference to his anti-TVA backers, Taylor responded: "I'll fight like a tiger for TVA!" See "Kefauver's Victory", *New Republic,* 15 August 1960, p. 5.
21. Halberstam, "Kefauver," p. 29.

On July 27, just eight days before Tennessee's primary, Arkansas Governor Faubus utterly crushed four challengers in his successful and unprecedented bid for a fourth term in his statehouse. Faubus, carrying all before him, captured all but one of Arkansas' seventy-five counties. Taylor's forces were elated and Kefauver's dismayed. Political observers throughout the nation and even overseas noted Faubus's overwhelming endorsement and focused with great interest on Tennessee's crucial battle of the following week.

On the morning of August 4, Tennessee's newspapers headlined the news of Kefauver's stunning victory. Kefauver had received 450,533 votes to Taylor's 240,609, to win with a margin of 64.6 percent of the vote.[22] He had carried eighty of Tennessee's ninety-five counties and seven of the nine congressional districts. Even in Memphis, where Taylor's spokesmen had predicted majorities of 35,000 to 60,000, Kefauver led by 11,000 votes. The rout was complete, and both candidates expressed genuine surprise.

A pleased editorial in the liberal *New Republic* asserted that "the special sweetness of Estes Kefauver's 210,000-vote victory in the Tennessee Democratic primary lies in the clear liberal-conservative basis on which he fought his campaign against Andrew (Tip) Taylor." [23] From England, an article in the equally pleased *New Statesman* observed that:

Not since the Supreme Court six years ago ratified the surrender at Appomattox has a Southern or border state had as clear a choice as this month's primary election in which Senator Estes Kefauver successfully defended his political life.[24]

Noting that Kefauver was the Senate's "most militantly enlightened Southerner," the *New Statesman* pointed out significantly, if somewhat incorrectly, that Negroes had voted for the first time since Reconstruc-

22. *Tennessee Blue Book,* 1961–1962, pp. 190–191, and *SSN,* September 1960, p. 2. In the general election in November, Kefauver's token Republican opponent received 234,053 votes to the incumbent's 594,460.
23. "Kefauver's Victory," *New Republic, op. cit.*
24. Robert Bendiner, "Twas A Famous Victory," *The New Statesman,* 20 August 1960.

tion in Haywood and Fayette counties[25]—under watchful eyes of the Federal Bureau of Investigation and the Columbia Broadcasting System.

By far the most significant editorial of all, however, appeared in the disappointed *Commercial Appeal*. In a remarkably candid editorial significantly entitled "Ouch," editors of the big Memphis daily publicly confessed on August 8:

> We thought Judge Taylor more closely represented the thinking of the majority of the electorate. We misjudged, quite obviously. . . . Without rancor, and in the best of humor, we will continue to view [Kefauver's] progress with a more thoughtful attitude. In short, Senator Kefauver won, and his victory serves to emphasize the need for some of us to examine more closely the things that brought it about as well as the things he advocates.

Kefauver's triumph in the Democratic primary in 1960 had guaranteed his election in November against only nominal Republican opposition, but the state that sent him to the Senate for the third time in a row simultaneously cast its presidential electoral vote for a Republican— also for the third time in a row. The vital question concerning Tennessee's political future—whether the state would evolve a viable two-party system similar to the national model, with conservative Republicans customarily challenging liberal Democrats—remained unresolved. Nor did the gubernatorial campaign of 1962 greatly contribute to its resolution, for in that election Ellington and Clement re-enacted their familiar Alfonse-and-Gaston routine. The script dictated that the incumbent should marshal the state's powerful governmental apparatus in support of his predecessor. Accordingly, Clement added a third victory to his unblemished record by easily overwhelming two relatively lackluster opponents in the Democratic primary. Clement led Chattanooga's Mayor P. R. (Rudy) Olgiati by 91,000 votes, and Olgiati in turn edged Memphis Public Works Commissioner William W. Farris by 9,000. [26] But if the race failed to further the political polarization of

25. The *New Statesman* was right about Haywood County, but seventeen Negroes had voted in Fayette County since 1952, according to a Justice Department report. See Lewis, *Portrait*, p. 137.
26. *SSN*, July 1962, p. 3.

Tennessee's traditional one-party politics, it did strongly suggest by its thematic content—or more precisely by its lack of content—that one question raised by the elections of 1958 and 1960, the question of whether the voters would turn their back on racist rhetoric, was indeed being resolved in the affirmative. For in the gubernatorial campaign of 1962, all three major contenders openly courted Tennessee's potent and growing Negro vote. All three even made a political pilgrimage to appear before the Tennessee Voters' Council, which claimed to represent 175,000 Negro voters.[27] Both Farris and Olgiati proposed that a committee on human rights be appointed (a suggestion that Clement as governor was subsequently to heed), and Clement strongly hinted that he would appoint a Negro to the State Board of Education. Equally revealing, the old-fashioned appeals of a minor segregationist candidate from Memphis elicited an insignificant response, and in Nashville John Kasper's familiar segregationist refrains lured only 4,807 votes out of 80,119 that were cast for state representative of Davidson County (Kasper ranked 28th in a confusing field of 59, the top 9 of which were declared elected).

Kefauver's untimely death in the summer of 1963 presented Tennesseans with an unusual opportunity in 1964 to vote simultaneously for a president and two senators. Governor Clement had appointed to Kefauver's vacant seat an elderly party functionary, "Hub" Walters, whose sturdy loyalty and precarious health combined effectively to guarantee that as incumbent he would pose no obstacle to Clement's ambitions to win the two unexpired years of Kefauver's term in 1964. Thus, the 44-year-old governor succumbed to the temptation to appeal to Tennessee's voters for a fourth consecutive endorsement just as the Republican party was gambling so spectacularly on the recoil of a white backlash throughout the South. Clement's opponent in the primary was Ross Bass, congressman from middle Tennessee's sixth district, whose ten-year voting record in the House was clearly liberal. As an insecure freshman, Bass had signed the Southern Manifesto of 1956. But he had subsequently apologized for having succumbed to segrega-

27. *SSN,* July 1962, p. 10.

tionist pressure, and in the summer of 1964 he effectively purged himself by courageously voting for the controversial civil rights bill and for Medicare as well.[28] While few of Bass's supporters regarded his intellectual endowment as equal to that of Kefauver or Gore, his liberal credentials earned him the active support of most of the Kefauver people and the strong endorsements of the *Times,* the *Press-Scimitar* and, most importantly if least surprisingly, the powerful *Tennessean,* while Lloye Miller's *News-Sentinel* remained loyal to Clement.

Given Bass's pre-emption of the liberal position, and sensing the potential of the widely-discussed white backlash, Clement moved perceptibly to the right. He began to voice frequent criticism of Bass for having voted for Medicare and the civil rights bill, and he even rejected a "code of fairness" proposed by his own Committee on Human Relations.[29] The *Tennessean* responded by complaining that Clement had "deviated greatly from his former position to follow a line in this campaign which seems to be dictated to the letter by race-bigotry, labor-hating arch conservatives who always fought Senator Kefauver at every turn." [30] Bass in turn attacked Clement's 3 percent tax on electric utilities as an assault upon the sacrosanct TVA. He unapologetically defended his own votes for civil rights and Medicare, and he took credit for helping to push through Congress the federal tax reduction (he sat on the House Ways and Means Committee), while criticizing Clement for amassing a 30 million-dollar tax surplus and for allegedly shaking down the state's 22,000 employees on three separate occasions. The Tennessee Voters' Council turned its back on Clement for the first time and endorsed Bass. Labor, long angry with Clement for having reneged on his pledge of 1952 to repeal Tennessee's "right-to-work" law, supported Bass with alacrity. On election eve, the *Tennessean* dark-

28. Bass was joined by Nashville's liberal Congressman Richard Fulton in voting for the civil rights bill. In the ten other ex-Confederate states, only Florida's Claude Pepper and four of Texas' 23 congressmen voted for the bill when it first passed the House. Atlanta's celebrated young Congressman, Charles Weltner, voted against the original House bill but switched and voted for the Senate version that was assured of approval by the House.
29. *SSN,* September 1964, p. 7.
30. 2 August 1964.

ly, if hyperbolically, warned that "Only Ross Bass Stands Between the People and a Grasping Political Dictatorship."

On August 6, Bass crushed Clement with a vote of 330,213 to 233,245. [31] In Nashville, Bass humiliated the Governor by carrying all but four of the 124 precincts by a vote of 49,552 to 22,703. The Wharton School box, located in a Negro precinct, gave Bass 1,206 votes to Clement's anemic 112. [32] In attempting to explain Bass's "stunning and totally unexpected upset," the *Banner* was quick to de-emphasize the importance of the civil rights issue and to argue instead that the voters had not so much endorsed Bass's liberalism as they had protested Clement's tax program.[33] The *Banner* also observed that the resurgent Republicans, sensing in Goldwater's Southern strategy a golden opportunity to oust Democrats, had become so preoccupied with their own hotly contested primaries that they had failed to take advantage of Tennessee's open-primary law by crossing over to vote for the most conservative Democrat. That the *Banner* was in part correct is suggested by the relative ease with which Clement was able two years later to defeat Bass in the Democratic primary for a full six-year Senate term, only to fall in November before Republican Howard Baker, Jr., Tennessee's first Republican senator since Reconstruction.[34] Bass had

31. A third candidate, Colonel M. M. Bullard, received 86,718 votes. Bullard's limited appeal is difficult to isolate; a consistent supporter of reformers through Kefauver, he had grown wealthy and markedly more conservative with age.

32. See Park's analysis, *op. cit.*, pp. 154–168. In the other senatorial primary, Gore ran virtually unopposed.

33. 7 August 1964. Bass may have been led by his impressive sweep—it was his sixth straight victory—to overestimate his political security. As senator, he generally neglected to keep his fences properly mended at home, and he received wide and damaging criticism just before the election of 1966 when he stormed indignantly out of a meeting of the Women's Press Club in Washington because a satirical skit had referred to him as "Bigmouth Bass".

34. Tennessee Republicans reaped a binger harvest in 1966 as they added one senator and a fourth congressman to their Washington delegation, and their 40-man delegation in the lower house of the state legislature brought them to within ten votes of a majority. The *Tennessean* blamed Clement for having engineered his own and the general Democratic demise by having given the Republicans control of the election commission in the 35 counties that voted for Goldwater in 1964, and by having co-operated with the Republicans in the

beaten Baker in 1964 by 95,000 votes, yet Clement in 1966 lost to Baker by 100,000 votes, even though Baker's total vote in both general elections was roughly the same. Clearly, Tennessee's opportunistic Republicans had learned to vote in the Democratic primary for the most conservative Democrat for governor where their hopes for a November victory were dim, and at the same time to vote for the weakest Democrat for senator, where their chances of winning in November were brightening. This tactic undoubtedly contributed heavily to the election of Ellington over a liberal Democrat, John J. Hooker, in the 1966 primary. Yet even Ellington, the self-proclaimed "old-fashioned segregationist" of 1958, had executed by 1966 a politically realistic about-face. Witness his appeal to Negro voters, as approvingly recorded by the militant Memphis *Tri-State Defender:*

Let's bury the word and practice of segregation. . . . Let's stay in step with the times. Let's march together . . . forgetting old fears . . . and walk together as fellow citizens of the great Volunteer State.[35]

Unencumbered by any ideological rudder, Ellington was free to swim with the tide, and by then the flow of the tide was inexorable. As the chastened ex-segregationist reclaimed the governor's chair, 28.6 percent of Tennessee's Negro children were attending school with whites—an index of compliance surpassed only by Texas (44.9 percent) of all the states of the old Confederacy. The moral of those turbulent years was abundantly clear to State Representative Harold Bradley, Vanderbilt's sagacious practicing political scientist: "Tennessee will never fight the Civil War again." [36]

---

gerrymander of the Memphis congressional district. As a result, 34 of the 35 counties voted for Baker in 1966, and Memphis freshman Democratic congressman, the able and progressive George Grider, was defeated by Dan Kuykendall, a staunchly conservative Republican. See Bill Kovach, "State's Democratic Leaders Gave Victory to the GOP," and Joe Hatcher, "Democrats Need New Leadership," *Tennessean,* 13 November 1966.

35. 23 July 1966.

36. Harold Bradley, personal interview with the author, Memphis, 11 November 1966. The statistical data on school desegregation are derived from the *Statistical Summary,* 1966–1967, published annually by the Southern Education Reporting Service.

12

The Fourth Estate in Tennessee: An Editorial

STUDENTS of the political process have always been plagued by problems of definition and labeling. This difficulty has stemmed primarily from the inherent conflict between the needs of political analysts and the ambitions of political leaders. While the former have sought to devise precise and narrowly defined political categories for the purpose of bringing order to the chaotic mosaic that is the political process, the latter have sought contrarily to identify their aspirations with the broadest possible political base. Throughout history, this conflict has produced abundant confusion. In Hitler's Germany, self-proclaimed National Socialists savagely fought those of their fellow nationals who were genuine socialists. In modern France, in the words of a recent comparative study,

a group unenthusiastic about the Republic was called the Republican Federation. Almost every group which included the world "left" in its title . . . sat in the center or toward the right . . . socialist meant democratic, radical meant center, left meant right, right meant reactionary, and independent might mean fascist.[1]

If ideologically splintered Europe has been the prime example of this semantic conflict, the American child of Europe has necessarily inherited a legacy of political confusion. Although an affluent America, guiltless of the original sin of feudalism, has always enjoyed in her

1. Gwendolen M. Carter, John H. Horz, and John C. Ranney, *Major Foreign Powers: The Governments of Great Britain, France, Germany, and the Soviet Union* (New York: Harcourt Brace, 1957), p. 243.

virginal innocence a truncated political spectrum, it is nevertheless true that politics in America has also been fraught with its familiar and confusing paradoxes. The Republican party—"the party of big business" —has included militant liberals; the Democratic party—"the party of the people"—has embraced deep-dyed conservatives. While Barry Goldwater, a man of the political right, has referred to himself as a conservative, and even on occasion—and quite rightly in the classical sense—as a genuine liberal, liberals have referred to him (more accurately, in the contemporary context) as a reactionary, and socialists have called him (quite incorrectly) a fascist. Still, students of American politics are aware that the paradox is more apparent than real, for in comparison with the protean politics of Europe, the heritage of American political combat takes on a Tweedledum-Tweedledee character that has both confused and bored the sophisticated Europeans.

If the widely heralded American consensus—the "Genius of American Politics," as Daniel Boorstin has called it[2]—has served the relatively young nation well by providing the vital centripetal force necessary to weather recurrent crises of growth, it has also operated to homogenize American politics. The truncated American political spectrum normally so bulges at the center that political labels that imply militance or extremism have generally been opprobrious ones, fit only for the opposition. Thus, while liberals and conservatives of both parties have generally fought over the undecided "swing" vote that customarily has occupied the political center, most have agreed that socialists and Communists, fascists and reactionaries, were bad things—that is, were un-American things. The corollary to this rule has been that certain euphemistic terms have been developed that precisely because they did not automatically align themselves with Democrat or Republican, liberal or conservative, were seen as desirable appelations by almost all factions. Sharing highest honors and esteem in the American political lexicon has been the label "progressive" together with its Southern equivalent "moderate" (who, indeed, among our notable politicians has proudly laid claim to traits of immoderation or tendencies toward retrogression?).

2. Daniel Boorstin, *The Genius of American Politics* (Chicago: University of Chicago Press, 1953).

Frequently, in the preceding pages, Tennessee newspapers have been labeled either conservative, as opposed to progressive, or segregationist, as opposed to moderate. The two implied pairings—conservative with segregationist and progressive with moderate—coincided in most cases if not in all. In response to this convenient labeling, conservative and segregationist editors might with some justification complain that, while they might have been labeled with approximate accuracy, their counterparts were blessed with favorably loaded labels that implied that the conservative segregationist newspapers were somehow necessarily immoderate and retrogressive. Isn't liberalism the ideological counterpart of conservatism (they might ask) and integrationist that of segregationist? Nationally, yes, but in the South, not really.

Consider the case of the Nashville *Tennessean* and the *Banner*. On all issues that did not directly relate to the biracial system, the *Tennessean* rather consistently advocated editorially what might be called the liberal position, and the *Banner* the conservative. Take for instance the question of federal aid to education—a question, infused with great urgency by Sputnik, that was so frequently before the Congress during the decade of desegregation. The *Tennessean* consistently supported the program, arguing that national assistance to the lagging educational efforts of the poor states was an enlightened and far-seeing innovation from which, if the legislation were carefully constructed so as to preclude federal control of instruction, Tennessee could only stand to benefit. The *Banner,* it will be remembered, denounced the proposal on the several grounds that (a) no state legislature had ever asked for it; (b) federal monies would only be extracted from the states, subjected to the traditional bureaucratic handling charge of about 15 percent, and then returned to the states, thereby leaving the states as a collectivity that much poorer; (c) who paid the piper inevitably called his tune; and (d) it was unconstitutional, in that the Tenth Amendment explicitly reserved to the states all jurisdiction over such matters as public education that were not explicitly delegated to the federal government. So far, the liberal-conservative dichotomy remains clear. But when this issue was linked to the sensitive biracial issue—as when Negro Representative Adam Clayton Powell repeatedly appended to federal school aid bills his requirement that segregated school systems be denied such assistance—both dailies would jointly howl their disapproval. (One is tempted to infer that the *Banner,* though vehemently disapproving of Powell and of his pet amendment, was, like many Southern congressmen who gleefully voted *for* the Powell amendment, privately pleased by it because the amendment repeatedly served to seal the doom of federal aid to schools.) In sum, the clear dichotomy between the liberal and the conservative positions breaks down when the biracial issue is injected. When this occurs, the entire Southern political spectrum, which historically has been located several notches to the right of the national political spectrum—although not so far to the right as is commonly assumed—shifts perceptibly even farther to the right.

If we assume that the typically liberal response to the Brown decision was to greet it warmly and to press persistently for its immediate and thorough implementation, then the response of Tennessee's moderate press to the ruling must be regarded as decidedly *not* a typically liberal one. Southern editors and publishers, no matter how liberally inclined, simply could not afford to assume a thoroughgoing liberal posture toward the question of desegregation.

The reason is, of course, not difficult to fathom. Consider the case of Knoxville. With a population not quite 10 percent Negro (a percentage considerably lower than that of many Northern cities), and with an even smaller percentage of Negroes living in the surrounding countryside, Knoxville was clearly the least racially sensitive of Tennessee's four big cities. Because of this, the *News-Sentinel* could call the Brown decision "just and wise," and the conservative Republican *Journal* could endorse it with even greater forthrightness. But both dailies expressed relief when, one year later, the court prescribed implementation at "deliberate speed." The violence at neighboring Clinton the succeeding year further sobered them. Given the inherited convictions of their Knoxville readers, it is not difficult to understand why even Knoxville's moderate editors urged gradualism, and, in effect, tokenism. In 1958, a poll of the attitudes of adult white Knoxvillians concerning desegregation revealed that 90 percent of the sample strongly disapproved of desegregation of the schools (Knoxville's schools had not yet begun desegregation by 1958).[3] Not one of the 167 Knoxvillians who were polled would approve of enrolling one or two white children in a previously all-Negro school, and 71.8 percent objected to enrolling one or two Negroes in a previously all-white school. All preferred that parents be able to transfer their children, regardless of residential requirements. Ninety-four percent opposed any racial integration that included sexually mixed classes also. Eighty-five percent disputed the claim that the Brown decision was legally the law of the land, and 70 percent said they would support a legal battle against desegregation. The pattern was one of clear and overwhelming preference for the traditional biracial system.

Yet strong preference does not necessarily mean intransigence. Twenty-five of the 167 responded favorably toward desegregation of schools (although only fourteen of these were born in Tennessee), and 44 percent acknowledged that, although they objected, they would acquiesce. Only 15.6 percent claimed that they would withdraw their children from the public schools if they were desegregated, and only 6.3 percent were vocally in support of violent resistance. Finally, the majority of Knoxville's community leadership confessed their willingness to go along with desegregation. The key variables, predictably, proved to be Southern birth and proximity of residence to Negro communities. The principal attitude softener, also predictably and perhaps somewhat ironically, was education.[4] Given such a climate of opinion, it is easy to understand why Knoxville temporized for six years following the Brown decision, and then adopted the very gradualistic Nashville plan. Nor is it difficult to surmise why liberal Southern editors, in view of this rather overwhelming white commitment to a maintenance of segregation, would address their appeals, not to humanitarian concern for the depressed separate-and-unequal plight of seg-

3. Douglas R. Jones, "An Abstract of An Opinion Poll On Attitudes of White Adults About Desegregation in the Public Schools of Knoxville, Tennessee," unpublished doctoral dissertation in education, George Peabody College, August 1958.

4. Education, of course, is a correlate of income, occupational status, and other social attributes, and for this reason the direct relationship between education and attitudes should not be overstressed.

regated Negroes, but rather to the civilized requirement that even unpopular laws should be obeyed. Whether this may be judged a moral default, not one white editor in Tennessee during the decade surveyed genuinely attempted to convince his readers that racial segregation was morally reprehensible, although a number of them must surely have believed this to be true. (On the other hand, of all the conservative newspapers, only the tiny Hamilton County *Herald* was honest if cruel enough to give vent to an editorial conviction that Negroes should be segregated because they were genetically inferior.)[5]

Typical of the response of Tennessee's moderate press to the problem of desegregation was that of the *Tennessean.* The *Tennessean,* it will be remembered, greeted the Brown decision with neither praise nor blame, agreed that it was indeed the law of the land, pointed out in its favor that it would at least improve the nation's image abroad, and counseled a prompt and reasonable start toward compliance. Whatever their private opinions, its editors never publicly endorsed the Brown decision, (but then, neither did President Eisenhower, whose tragic failure to enlist his enormous prestige in the cause of desegregation left a vacuum that understandably cautious Southern moderates could never hope to fill). The *Tennessean* tirelessly pointed out to its readers that, in decreeing desegregation, the court had not decreed compulsory integration. It editorially attacked not only Kasper and the Klan, as the conservative press had done, but it also attacked the White Citizens Councils, the Federation and similar segregationist organizations—organizations generally supported by the conservative press—and it defended the right to exist, if not the views, of the Highlander Folk School and the NAACP. In sum, it generally did an effective job of keeping its head, of avoiding self-righteousness, of retaining its objectivity and—not least important—its sense of humor.[6]

5. In *The Children of the South,* Clinton schoolteacher Margaret Anderson argues that the Southern establishment's standard plea for law and order, though obviously necessary as a starting point, nevertheless represented a shibboleth whereby Southerners could postpone a moral decision that was there to be made.

6. When, in May 1959, a children's book named *The Rabbit's Wedding* was

It was another irony of the crisis over desegregation that the Democratic *Tennessean,* which was generally liberal but grew conservative on racial questions, received what was perhaps its highest compliment from the Nashville *Globe and Independent,* a Republican Negro weekly that was generally conservative but grew understandably more liberal on racial questions:

> The law-abiding forces in Nashville undoubtedly had a powerful spokesman in the Nashville *Tennessean* through the period that tried men's souls. Much could be written about this newspaper showing that it is truly dedicated to promoting the best interests of the city. Its readers without regard to race can take pride in the way it has stood by the Constitution in a critical period.[7]

Politically, the powerful *Tennessean* grieved when Mayor Orgill was so narrowly defeated, applauded the solid victories of Gore, and rejoiced at those of Kefauver. But when the state's plan to desegregate its colleges over a period of five years was rejected by the federal courts as too deliberate, the *Tennessean* cried out in alarm against the court's impatience. When the Nashville plan finally cleared the courts, the *Tennessean* expressed both pleasure and relief that the high courts had validated this gradualistic program, which established *de jure* desegregation but which clearly countenanced what amounted to *de facto* segregation. Southern whites, thought the editors of the *Tennessean,* could, should, and would learn to live with a form of token desegregation that would amount in substance to a northernization of the South. And that, in turn, would seem at least to augur a social destiny characterized by a more humane (if perhaps less honest) and

---

banned in Alabama because one of the newlywed rabbits was white and one was black, the *Tennessean* merrily responded:

> Clear the shelves, hide this book,
> And brook no interruption;
> Do not even sneak a look—
> You'll risk your mind's corruption;
> Danger lurks within its covers,
> Evil is the tale
> Of a pair of furry lovers
> Wedded on the bunny trail.

7. The Nashville *Globe and Independent,* 27 September 1957.

more flexible (if also more subtle) form of white-dominated society.

To the degree that Tennessee's moderate publishers, editors, and politicians alike actively promoted a gradualistic and, by implication, tokenistic form of desegregation, they were therefore performing less as liberals than as genuine conservatives. For is not the essence of historical American conservatism a cautious posture toward change— a conviction that, because man is a little (probably a great deal) lower than the angels, because throughout history he has demonstrated not only his rational capabilities but also his dangerous darker tendencies, society had then best proceed cautiously with change? But one cannot proceed cautiously by standing absolutely still. Even Edmund Burke, high priest of British conservatism, admitted that societies without the means of change were without the means of their self-preservation. Thus the Southern moderate editor or politician who, without necessarily endorsing a judicial edict commanding social change, nevertheless urged his fellow Southerners to obey the new ruling whether they approved of it or not, but who *also* stated or strongly implied that he would use his persuasive power or political muscle to insure that the change be *gradual*, was playing a role that has frequently been referred to in our political lexicon as that of an "enlightened conservative." He was acting as a buffer between incipient force and residual intransigence—as an interpreter of the national majority to the South, and of the South to the impatient and sometimes querulous North and West.

If Tennessee's moderate politicians and editors were, on the racial issues, the "enlightened conservatives," who then, by implication, were the "endarkened conservatives"? These were the politicians who campaigned on the impossible promise that they could and would prevent any modification of the biracial system and the publishers and editors who supported them and encouraged them in this illusory belief. These were the strict constructionists of the mid–twentieth century, the latter-day defenders of state sovereignty whose strictures against federal intervention were couched in the rhetoric of Calhoun.

Typical of the states'-rights counterchallenge to desegregation was the indignant protest of the *Banner*. In defense of segregation, the *Banner* advanced every conceivable argument *except* the one that

Negroes were genetically inferior.[8] Fundamental to the *Banner*'s defense
was its devotion to the "bedrock principles," as it called them, of strict
construction of the Constitution: because the "Sovereign" states by
compact had granted limited and specific authority to the federal
government, it followed that states' rights were anterior to federal rights
and could not constitutionally be encroached upon by federal authority.
The *Banner* was fond of quoting the Tenth Amendment, which reserved
for the states and the people all rights not specifically enumerated as
federal rights and powers. Then the *Banner* would rhetorically ask
where in the Constitution one could find reference to the public schools.
Nowhere, it would correctly reply. Thus it followed as the night the day
that federal authorities had absolutely no authority over the states'
public schools. It was that simple.

It was, of course, far too simple. In an analysis of the long tradition
of states' rights in American history, the late historian Arthur M. Schlesinger has concluded that, because the doctrine of states' rights has
historically been invoked primarily as a rationalization for sectional
economic self-interest, there are few states in the untion that have not
at one time or another invoked the doctrine to defend their interests,
only to denounce the same doctrine when it was invoked by other states
in defense of *their* interests.[9] (A corollary of Schlesinger's obervation is
that loose constructionist doctrines have variously been invoked for much
the same reason; self-interested motives neither prove nor disprove the
validity of the principle.) Because the Constitution was essentially a
compromise agreed upon by sagacious men who were desperately
anxious to salvage the union, its language is frequently ambiguous and
even contradictory. This ambiguity, Schlesinger observed, has enabled

8. Although the *Banner's* resentment of court-ordered desegregation was profound, it never counseled outright defiance or advocated such rash policies as the
abandonment of public schools, as did the *News–Free Press*. The *Banner*'s flirta-
tion with the three-school notion may have represented a quixotic aberration into
fairyland, but it consistently sought to avoid the implications of the Brown decision only through legal circumlocution. And when it lost a battle, as in 1964, it
manfully honored the victor. This sensible flexibility was reflected in the *Banner*'s
decision in the mid-sixties to carry the column of the NAACP's Roy Wilkins.

9. Arthur M. Schlesinger, "The States' Rights Fetish," *New Viewpoints in
American History* (New York: Macmillan Co., 1922), pp. 220–243.

both nationalists and states' righters to make a case for their views, but never an impregnable one, without either "ignoring or explaining away phrases and implications which supported the contrary position." Thus the *Banner* frequently recited the Tenth Amendment while virtually ignoring the Fourteenth (except, occasionally, to question the validity of its ratification), which prohibits the states from abridging the rights of citizens, just as the Fifth Amendment prohibits the federal government from abridging the rights of citizens without due process of law.

But the *Banner* and the many Tennessee newspapers that shared its deeply conservative convictions did not rely, in their defense of segregation and state sovereignty, on strict constructionist principles alone. In addition to being unconstitutional, they asserted, desegregation was simply bad social thinking. Many reasons were advanced in support of this position, but they fall primarily into four categories.

First, Southern racial relations were harmonious under a biracial system that was indeed separate-but-equal. Desegregation, however, would destroy that great achievement and replace it with racial strife. Witness the complaint of the weekly South Pittsburg *Hustler*:

"Down there," meaning, if you please, down South in Dixie, where no one disturbs you so long as you don't disturb the peace, the Negro has the best school houses, the best school teachers, the best preachers to be found anywhere and who are going along in the even tenor of their way until those "nine old men" threw the monkey wrench into the cogwheel to start all this strife and turmoil. Mass murder, bombings, burning buildings and other atrocious deeds heretofore unheard of.

Is it, we ask the right-thinking Negro population, worth the price we are now paying and will continue to pay? [10]

And why has segregation worked out so well? Because it is a natural social arrangement, mutually desired by both races. The natural preordination of racial segregation was abundantly clear to the Sparta *Expositor*:

A black minorca rooster is black. A rhode island red is red. And white leghorns are white. Mix them up and you just have chickens, and have lost the best properties of each strain.

It is best to keep them segregated, for the best interests of all concerned.[11]

10. 12 September 1957.
11. 20 May 1954.

The *Banner* further pointed out that, statements of "NAACP fire-brands" notwithstanding,

the "integrate everything right away" drive is drawing protests from respected leaders of the Negro race, who realize that race relations have been strained by the militancy of some groups. And these leaders also fear that distinctive Negro institutions are threatened with extinction.[12]

Second, a corollary of the argument that segregation is the key to racial harmony and progress in the South was the contention that integration was both a farce and a disastrous failure in the North. The chief spokesman of this crusade to unveil Northern hypocrisy was Grover Cleveland Hall, Jr., publisher of the Montgomery (Alabama) *Advertiser*. In the late fifties, Hall published a special series on racial violence in the North, a series that was carried in its entirety in the *Banner*. During 1958 and 1959, the editorial pages of the *Banner* and the *News–Free Press* were rife with allusions to violence in the schools

'My Project Is Mississippi, Terrible Mississippi!'   They Seem To Be Poking The Same Fire!

Knox in the Banner

Knox in the Banner

12. 24 September 1959.

and streets of the District of Columbia, Negro rapists in Brooklyn, the corruption and decay of Harlem, Negro muggings in New York, Chicago, and other Northern cities. Harry Ashmore, who was during the fifties an editor of the progressive Arkansas *Gazette,* critically identified this popular gambit as the "You're Another One school," and accused Hall of "fashioning his editorial page into a sort of moral escape hatch." [13]

There is some merit in his contention, and by pressing it he inferentially makes the point that if his subscribers are guilty of sin, it is not original. This may be soothing but it is irrelevant.

Ashmore's criticism was frequently echoed by the *Tennessean,* which repeatedly pointed out that the North possessed no monopoly on hypocrisy, and that pointing to the mote in thy neighbor's eye did not disguise the beam in thine own.

A third defensive argument was to invoke the Sumnerian dictum that stateways could not change folkways. In this connection, segregationist newspapers made much of the historical parallels between the contemporary attempt to force desegregation on the South and both the abortive experiment with prohibition and the horrors of Black Reconstruction. Emotional appeals to the decidedly distorted Southern image of Reconstruction were repeatedly made, especially when federal bayonets glistened in Little Rock (the *Banner*'s cartoonist, Knox, invariably equipped Senator Kefauver with a carpetbag).

The segregationist press frequently bolstered its case with the use of a fourth defensive weapon: *ad hominem* arguments. Rather than address themselves strictly to the merits of the case at hand, these editorials employed instead the principle of guilt by association. The reasoning behind the Brown decision, the *Banner* and the *News–Free Press* revealed darkly, was derived from the writings of a Swedish socialist, Gunnar Myrdal. A host of segregationist newspapers made frequent reference to the fact that the Communists supported racial integration, and many suggested that sinister Marxist designs were the principal motive behind the whole civil rights movement. The *Commercial Appeal* suspected that Communist money bulged the coffers of the NAACP. Knox pictured in the *Banner* a "Communist liner" and an NAACP "do-gooder" poking together the fire of "race agitation."

13. Ashmore, *Epitaph for Dixie,* p. 165.

The *Banner* was fond of categorizing its long list of Northern bêtes noires—Thurgood Marshall, Walter Reuther, Eleanor Roosevelt, Wayne Morse, and Adlai Stevenson—as simply the "hate brigade." Congressman Adam Clayton Powell was the ideal example of the "liberal's liberal." Senator Paul Douglas was a "pompous Illinois windbag." Desegregation was not the law of the land, it was the "law of Warren." The *Banner* seldom tired of substituting this sort of obloquy for calmer and more rational appeals. Its bombastic editorial prose doubtlessly delighted the true believers, but the *Banner*'s intemperate fusillades probably won over few new converts to the cause.

The essential failing of the archconservative segregationists' defensive crusade was not that they had nothing to contribute to the dialogue, for many of their postures contained important elements of truth. Suspicion of unlimited government is a healthy legacy of the American political tradition. Concern for the possible excesses of judicial review is an equally valid posture. Even the hypersensitivity of the segregationist press to Northern persecution was not entirely a function of paranoia, for there clearly existed in the country at large a predisposition to require the South to expiate sins that were the sins of the whole nation, as the national backlash of the mid-sixties bears witness. The sin of the segregationist press, then, was not so much the sin of postulating self-evidently erroneous assumptions upon which to base logical argument. It was, rather, the sin of dogmatism—the fatal error of believing one's own propaganda. There is, for instance, much wisdom in a posture of wariness toward the notion of quickly changing social customs through legal fiat. But the problem with flatly invoking the Sumnerian dictum that stateways cannot change folkways was that, as a categorical absolute, it simply was not true. For laws, by changing social conditions, *can* over time lead to changes in social customs and mores that were premised upon earlier conditions. If the Eighteenth Amendment did not work, the Thirteenth Amendment did—despite the violence attendant unto both. And if it is argued in response that the Thirteenth Amendment merely ratified legally a solution wrought by war, then who can doubt that the reforms legislated by Progressives and New Dealers did, over the years, profoundly modify the social customs, mores and attitudes of the nation without recourse to violence? The entire tradition of American reform has had its premise in the assumption that stateways, when judiciously applied, can and should change folkways. In 1954, not one lunch counter or restaurant in downtown Nashville would serve a Negro; only a dozen years later, none would think of refusing. This truly revolutionary change in Southern social behavior was produced by a combination of civil disobedience and federal law—all in the face of a profoundly opposed conservative press which, by insisting so frenetically that stateways *could* not change folkways, was in effect acknowledging the vulnerability of the biracial folkways it so strongly preferred.[14]

Knox in the Banner

Knox in the Banner

14. For a penetrating analysis of the degree to which stateways affected Southern folkways in regard to segregation, see Donald R. Mathews and James W. Prothro, "Stateways versus Folkways: Critical Factors in Southern Reactions to *Brown* v. *Board of Education*," in Gottfried Dietze (ed.), *Essays on the American Constitution* (Englewood Cliffs, New Jersey: Prentice-Hall, 1964), pp. 139–156.

Tennessee's states'-rights newspapers had traditionally been proud of their uncompromising support of law and order. But suddenly, after 17 May 1954, they could no longer logically support both law and order, because the new law conflicted with the biracial basis of the old order. Desiring to adhere to both goals as they had traditionally done, yet forced to choose, the states'-rights press chose order in the form of a plea for continuance of the segregated status quo. This led them to attack the new demands of law as unconstitutional usurpations that merited not supine compliance but outraged protests and, for some, bald defiance. Yet, since the ineluctable logic of their attack would compel them to denounce as nonlaw so very much of the giant edifice of statutory law created over the years by the century-and-a-half-old practice of judicial review, they retreated to the mechanical certitude of Jeffersonian liberalism's demand that central power be precisely defined and severly limited—to the dogma that the Founding Fathers in their infinite wisdom had ordained immutable governmental relationships that time could not wither nor custom change. It was an historic and honorable position and, thankfully for so many conservative Tennessee editors, in origin a Democratic one. Yet it was, withal, essentially an eighteenth-century doctrine, geared to the needs of a relatively stable agrarian order.[15] By embracing it so dogmatically, Tennessee's nostalgic states'-rights publishers and editors had responded to the forces of social change by shackling themselves to the archaic platitudes of an era that had passed into history at Appomattox.

15. The *Banner* regarded Tennessee's landmark legislative reapportionment decision with a marked ambivalence. While its editors urged that populous Davidson County be given greater representation, they mourned nostalgically the passing of the old order. In what is perhaps the most remarkably candid editorial of the entire era, the *Banner* on 20 July 1963 unapologetically confessed its profound attachment to measured tenor and easy certitudes of rural and small town American life:

"It is no secret that over the years the rural forces, when they chose to combine and exert their power, have set the over-all course of legislation. In all frankness, the Banner would not have it otherwise, for it respects the consistently sound and fundamental concepts of government that guide lawmakers who come from the farms and public squares of Tennessee's smaller communities."

13

A Concluding Hypothesis

TENNESSEE'S persistent streak of progressivism and her tradition of racial moderation has prompted a great many students of Southern politics to write her off as a border state, more similar to Kentucky than to any of her six neighboring and fellow ex-Confederate states. Yet categorizing a state does not automatically explain the unique dynamics of her society and their expression in the political arena. Although this inquiry into Tennessee's response to desegregation was not designed to stand or fall according to the light that it sheds on the broader question of why Southern whites have historically behaved in such a distinctive fashion, I am hopeful that certain correlates have emerged from it that may help to teach us more about the distinctive dynamics of Southern thought and behavior.

I have traced the response of Tennessee's editors—and correspondingly, if somewhat cursorily, the response of her politicians and voters—to the desegregation crisis. The essential moderation of that response has been consistent with an historic pattern of progressivism and racial moderation that students of Southern politics, whether traditional historians or behavioral scientists, have been anxious to explain. In what is still the most comprehensive analysis of Southern politics, V. O. Key and Alexander Heard traced the tenacity of Tennessee's regional one-party system to voting patterns laid down by the Civil War. But the publication of their monumental *Southern Politics* coincided with the disintegration of Crump's conservative east-west coalition, and Tennes-

see politics in the fifties turned markedly toward moderation and progressivism with the emergence of Kefauver, Gore, and Clement—all of
whom were able in varying degrees to tap an abiding reservoir of
reformist sentiment in Tennessee's electorate. More recent political observers have sought to explain Tennessee's sharp divergence from the
ultraconservative norm that has traditionally characterized her sister ex-
Confederate states by focusing on the complex interaction of geography, demography, and economics. Tennessee has been a poor state (in
1963 Tennessee was ranked forty-fifth among the fifty states in average personal income), and it is no enigma that most proposals, at least
economic ones, that emanate from the liberal end of the political spectrum have traditionally appealed to the poor. Most voters in Tennessee
during the decade surveyed could still remember the Depression, and of
course no state benefited more from TVA—the New Deal's most dramatic monument to liberalism's commitment to social and economic innovation. Yet poverty can explain little in isolation, for many Southern
states are much poorer and yet at the same time much less liberal
than Tennessee. The nation's most conservative state politically is probably Mississippi; at the same time it is the nation's poorest. The cries
of bemused and frustrated economists and sociologists that, of all regions, the South stands to gain the most from liberal programs offering
various forms of federal assistance have either not reached the eyes
and ears of most Southern voters, or have been cast, in the reformer's
view, as pearls before swine. While economic interest is always a powerful determinant of behavior, and economic determism remains a useful
analytical tool (whether credited to Karl Marx or James Madison or
Charles Beard), it often founders on the shoals of human psychology.

Another partial explanation is that Tennessee has fewer Negroes than
Southern states that have defended segregation more tenaciously. Indeed, the most commonly accepted explanation of Southern racial sen-
sitiveness has been that racial moderation varies inversely with the
proportion of Negroes in the population. But in Virginia, Florida, and
Arkansas, moderation and progressivism on the racial issue have been
more often punished than rewarded at the polls. Yet in these states, as
in Tennessee, the number of Negroes in the total population at mid-

century ranged only from 15 to 22 percent. And in North Carolina, where 26 percent were Negro, moderation on the racial question was considerably more in evidence than in the former three states where the Negro percentage was less.

Intimately related to both the economic and racial explanations of Tennessee's distinctive moderation is the geographic one. Tennessee has been, in a sense, three states functioning as one. One might hypothetically argue that, were the state split down the middle, the eastern half ceded to North Carolina and the western half to Arkansas, then Arkansas would become, politically, a Deep Southern and Dixiecrat or conservative Democratic state, and North Carolina would become Republican and racially even more moderate than it traditionally has been. However much this fantasy might appeal to Arkansas Democrats and North Carolina Republicans, Tennesseans have of course remained Tennesseans, and the state's three heterogenous grand divisions have been constrained to function as a unit. The heavy infusion of Negroes in West Tennessee certainly has weighted Tennessee politics heavily in the segregationist direction, but their presence is by no means a prerequisite for segregationist sentiment. Witness the results of the opinion poll that revealed an overwhelming preference for segregated schools on the part of traditionally moderate Knoxville's 90 percent white population. Consider also the supposition that the racially hypersensitive area around Chattanooga is accounted for perhaps less by the presence of a not overwhelming percentage of Negroes (20 percent) than by the strong tradition of racial prejudice among the white hillfolk of that portion of Georgia, Alabama, and Tennessee. Few towns in Tennessee, for instance, evidenced during the racially turbulent decade such animosity toward the Negroes as did Crossville, seat of Cumberland County, which was perched atop crab-orchard stone high on the Cumberland Plateau. Yet precisely *no* Negroes permanently resided in Cumberland County, and none, indeed, were welcome there. It seems that the propinquity of the feared and despised object may be a sufficient but is not a necessary cause for prejudice.

This latter phenomenon, extensively explored by psychologists and sociologists, suggests that the economic, demographic and geographic forces that historians and, to a lesser extent, political scientists have traditionally analyzed can provide only partial explanations for social behavior. We know that men often vote against their own best economic interest and that men can develop hostility toward distinctive groups even when the threatening group remains remote. The more sanguine among us may prefer to believe that such group animosity is only a function of a lack of communication. But psychologists have brutally insisted that men are capable of perceiving only what they *want* to perceive, even in the face of the most overwhelming evidence to the contrary. How else can we explain the conviction, widely entertained by white Southerners following the Brown decision, that the great majority of Southern Negroes were content with the status quo and deeply resented the integrationists for rupturing the South's tradition of interracial good will? Or, more spectacularly, how else can we explain the firm conviction of the Pulaski *Citizen* that northern Negroes maliciously sought to destroy segregation because they were jealous of their Southern brethren and thereby sought revenge? [1] The point of all of this is that the historian interested in understanding Southern racial attitudes would do well to borrow insights from behavioral scientists—from psychologists, social psychologists, and sociologists—who have recently devoted so much attention to understanding how social attitudes are formed and how they change.

The American Southerner has long been notorious for being so aggressively defensive about his regional identification. Unlike most other Americans, who have won their wars, fattened their purses, and have seen their causes triumph, the Southerners have inherited a legacy of tragic failure, and their hypersensitivity is largely a consequence of having uniquely embraced a Lost Cause.[2] But if they have been cruelly

1. The reader may recall that on May 19, 1954, the *Citizen* explained that the Brown decision was the brainchild of Negro "smartalecs who have been denied the many privileges enjoyed by the Southern Negro and have used this method to gain personal revenge."

2. C. Vann Woodward has advanced the provocative argument that although the South's acquaintance with failure contrasts uniquely to the national legacy of success, it is really the latter experience that is unique in human history. Thus the South's tragic encounter with history can be seen as closely resembling

abused by history (begging the question of whether they deserved it) their proud and defiant boast of unreconstructability has earned them a consistently bad press. Whether their latter-day image wears the tattered gray of General Jubilation T. Cornpone, the quaint string-tie of Senator Claghorn, the degenerate leer of Jeeter Lester, or the hooded robe of the Klansmen, their paramount stereotype in the popular folklore has been that of the loud and unsophisticated bigot (it is interesting to ponder why our folklore seemingly assumes that all Southerners are white). To be sure, they allegedly despise Negroes most, but Jews and Catholics in particular and Yankees in general merit their fair share of loathing. Thus, when the recent war against Nazi Germany prompted a rising interest in racial and ethnic prejudice and the authoritarian personality, American psychologists turned as if by reflex to Southerners as the most likely candidates for America's finest home-grown variety of these personality types.

This body of postwar research has clustered around three areas. The first two types of research, measures of anti-Semitism and measures of authoritarianism using the F-scale, sought to test the theory that Southerners typically displayed these prejudicial characteristics as a means of *externalizing* their inner needs. The researchers assumed that the Southern white's prejudice could be explained in terms of frustration-aggression theory, psychoanalysis, authoritarianism, and other forms of externalizing. But what they discovered was to challenge sharply the validity of theories which explained prejudice as a function of externalizing.[3] Actually, *fewer* anti-Semitic rumors had circulated in the South during World War II than in other regions of the United States. Polls conducted by Elmo Roper in 1946 and 1947 revealed that the South, together with the Far West, was the nation's *least* anti-

that of the mass of humanity, and as a consequence the Southerner stands uniquely equipped among Americans to comprehend the common plight of all mankind—even if, by implication, he must remain spiritually at odds with his fellow non-Southern American. See *The Burden of Southern History.*

3. For a brief history of the search for the prejudiced authoritarian personality, see Thomas F. Pettigrew, "Social Psychology and Desegregation," *The American Psychologist,* XVI, (March 1961), 105–112.

Semitic region.[4] Further, Southerners living in communities with relatively small percentages of Negroes were less anti-Negro than those living in communities with relatively large percentages of Negroes, though they were *not* less authoritarian.[5] These data increasingly suggested the importance of cultural pressures, for respondents most likely to be conforming to cultural pressures were more prejudiced against Negroes in the South but *not* in the North, and the percentage of Negroes in the community appeared to be a fairly accurate index of the strength of Southern cultural pressures concerning race.[6] Consequently, these findings prompted researchers largely to abandon the quest for the authoritarian personality and to focus instead on the dynamics of social *conformity* as an explanation of prejudice.

In an address delivered in Atlanta in 1961, Professor Thomas F. Pettigrew, a Harvard social psychologist, concluded from these research trends that

all three types of research agree that conformity to the stern social norms of Southern culture is usually crucial in the South's heightened hostility toward the Negro. Or, in plain language, it is the path of least resistance in most Southern circles to favor white supremacy.[7]

Prejudice, then, was less a function of externalized inner needs than of the need for social adjustment. Convinced of this, Pettigrew postulated three types of conforming Southerners. First, there were the *compliant* Southerners who ostensibly conformed to local cultural norms, but who reacted more warmly to the Negro when his fellow whites weren't looking. Second, some Southerners openly *identified* with the Confederate tradition, not because of any inner hostility toward Negroes, but because such conformity was functional to their desires for upward social mobility, or simply because it enabled them to avoid tension with their associates. Finally, there were those Southerners who so *internalized,*

4. Elmo Roper, "U.S. Anti-Semitism," *Fortune,* XXXIII (February 1946), 258–260, and *ibid.,* XXXVI (October 1947), 5–10.

5. See generally T. W. Adorno, *et al., The Authoritarian Personality* (New York: Harper, 1950).

6. See M. Richard Cramer and Thomas Pettigrew, "The Demography of Desegregation," *The Journal of Social Issues,* XV (1959), 61–72.

7. Pettigrew, *op. cit.,* p. 109.

for whatever psychological reason, the taboos of the culture into which they were born that they openly became confessed and often boastful proponents of white supremacy who supported—and some of them became—white supremacist politicians.

To the latter type, the internalizers, the need to express anti-Negro sentiments had become so strong that there could be little expectation that their attitudes would change, even under altered conditions. But the first two hypothetical types, and especially the compliant Southern- ers, constitute what Pettigrew called the "latent liberal" type; they are neither anti-Semitic nor authoritarian, but their needs to conform to the inherited norms of the Southern culture have led them to manifest the accepted attitudes toward Negroes. Pettigrew's term is in one sense objectionable in that it links, at least by implication, the concept of fairness and tolerance toward Negroes with a particular political faith that can claim no exclusive jurisdiction over what is essentially a hu- manitarian attitude. All that Pettigrew has postulated is that there exist- ed throughout the South a largely untapped reservoir of tolerance toward the Negroes. Indeed, the way in which the South responded to the de- segregation of public accommodations in 1964 with an almost audible sigh of relief strongly suggests the existence of a good deal of latent sympathy that the commanding rhetoric of segregationists has tended to obscure.

If so, why has this reservoir of latent tolerance remained largely un- tapped in so much of the South? Insights derived from the revealing experiments of an experimental psychologist, Solomon E. Asch, sug- gest an answer.[8] Asch hit upon the idea of testing the dynamics of social pressures toward conformity by loading with seven of his confidants an eight-man panel on which the unknowing respondent sat. Asch instruct- ed his seven confidants to respond with the same obviously erroneous answer to prepared questions that were interspersed throughout a series. Thus, when seven panel members confidently described a five-inch line as being only four inches long, the pressure on the unknowing respon-

8. S. E. Asch, "Effects of Group Pressure Upon the Modification and Dis- tortion of Judgments," in H. Guetzkow (ed.), *Groups, Leadership and Men* (Pittsburgh: Carnegie Press, 1951).

dent to conform to what he knew to be in error was so strong that, in an astonishing one-third of such situations, subjects also responded in error. But when only six of the panel's members were instructed to respond erroneously and the respondent was preceded by another panelist who would disturb the unanimity by giving a correct answer, the frequency of the subject's willingness to respond in error dropped sharply to one in ten. Further, the frequency of error continued to plummet dramatically as the erroneous majority was reduced. The key to unlocking latent impulses from the chain of pressures to conform was found, then, to be disturbing the unanimity of the environment. The greater the number of supporting colleagues present, the greater the subject's ability to withstand the pressure of the majority to conform.

Carrying through the analogy to the desegregation crisis in the South, Professor Pettigrew has suggested that, in the South,

obvious five-inch lines are being widely described as four inches. Many Southerners, faced with what appears to be solid unanimity, submit to the distortion. But when even one respected source—a minister, a newspaper editor, even a college professor—conspicuously breaks the unanimity, *perhaps* a dramatic modification is achieved in the private opinions of many conforming Southerners.

Tennessee shares with Mississippi a Confederate past, a common border, the fertile Yazoo Basin and Jackson Plain, and a white population derived almost exclusively from common Anglo-Saxon stock. But Tennessee does not share with Mississippi a social regime that has succeeded in inhibiting dissent from the segregationist norm to such a degree that unorthodox professors could be hounded from their chairs and dissenting editors repeatedly beaten in the streets.[9] There are, to

9. In alluding to the brutal persecution accorded Oliver Emmerich, courageous editor of the McComb (Mississippi) *Enterprise-Journal,* Hodding Carter has modestly sought to deflate the notion that his moderate *Delta Democrat–Times* was primarily responsible for keeping Greenville free of the kind of segregationist tyranny that made McComb the "church-burning and bombing capitol of the world." Instead, Carter, whose consistently humane conservatism has led northern liberals mistakenly to embrace him as one of their own, has insisted that Greenville has remained a racially moderate and fair-minded community because gen-

be sure, important differences in geography, demography, and the nature of their respective encounters with history sufficient to preclude great similarities between these two states, even if all other factors were equal. But all other factors have not been equal.

Illustrative of a crucial difference between these two environments is the attempt that was made in the mid-fifties to establish a moderate daily in Jackson, Mississippi. In the spring of 1955, a well-financed group of stockholders attempted to crack the newspaper monopoly of Jackson's archconservative Hederman family, which published the morning *Clarion-Ledger* and the evening *Daily News,* by founding the *State Times* as Jackson's second evening daily. Norman Bradley, 42-year-old former associate editor of the liberal Chattanooga *Times,* was brought in to edit a brave new daily which would be, according to Bradley, "Democratic by persuasion, independent by nature, middle-of-the-road but slightly more on the liberal side than most Mississippi papers." [10] But by December of that same year, Bradley had conceded defeat and he returned to the Chattanooga *Times* as executive editor. The infant *State Times* within a few years withered quietly away. Mississippi, even urban Mississippi, would not tolerate political heterodoxy on the part of a major newspaper. And if urban Mississippi would brook no heterodoxy, it is small surprise that the citizens of tiny Petal, Mississippi, near Hattiesburg, should have manifested their contempt for P. D. East's impertinent, unorthodox *Petal Paper* by boycotting their own home town's weekly and by systematically persecuting its publisher.[11] Similarly, McComb's Oliver Emmerich has been lavishly hon-

---

erations of "civic leaders who are true conservatives"—the infamous "white-power structure" of civil rights lore—wisely led the community "to seek to adjust amicably to a new order." Carter is probably guilty of excessive self-effacement. But his allusion to the failure of moderate journalism in McComb stands as a welcome admonition to the author and to any of his readers who might be tempted to endow the press excessively with singular powers of persuasion. See Carter's *So The Heffners Left McComb* (New York: Doubleday, 1965).

10. Quoted in *Time,* March 7, 1955, p. 86.

11. P. D. East, *Magnolia Jungle* (New York: Simon and Schuster, 1960). The courageous Hazel Brannon Smith has suffered similarly for her sins of publishing the unorthodox Lexington (Mississippi) *Advertiser.* See Silver, *op. cit.,* pp. 38–40.

ored throughout the land and cursed on his home ground. Even the celebrated Hodding Carter courted violence in Greenville by daring to suggest in his *Delta Democrat–Times* that Negroes might be referred to in his newspaper by the courtesy titles Mr. and Mrs.[12]

Mississippi's Carter, Emmerich, East, and Smith are celebrated because they represent the courage of lonely dissent; their newspapers have been islands of unorthodoxy in a monolithic sea. In Tennessee after 1954, the orthodoxy of segregation did exist, but it was quickly and persistently riven with powerful and multiple voices of dissent. And if this made dissent a less hazardous enterprise, it clearly made it no less vital to creating an atmosphere in which political and social pluralism could survive and prosper. Tennessee's pluralistic press thereby fostered a civic environment better equipped to promote that give and take of ideas so essential to successful adjustment to social change. Of course, this is not to suggest that editorially competitive newspapers by themselves can somehow magically guarantee racial tolerance. But in Mississippi, the state's largely monolithic press acted as a kind of lynchpin, linking that society's varied pressures toward orthodoxy into a reciprocal, self-supportive arrangement that effectively stifled dissent. In Tennessee, on the other hand, where the various economic, racial, geographic, and political factors were more supportive of a pluralistic environment, the state's press, by reinforcing these sources of pluralism, was centrally instrumental in guaranteeing that Tennessee, unlike Mississippi, would remain an open society. By preserving essentially intact an atmosphere of free and open discussion while under the intense conformist pressures generated by the desegregation crisis, Tennessee's newspapers served the interests of all the state's citizens, white and black alike—from segregationist to integrationist, from conservative to liberal—perhaps better than any of them knew.

12. See Hodding Carter, *Where Main Street Meets the River* (New York: Rhinehart, 1953).

Select Bibliography

Primary Sources

The Tennessee newspapers upon which this study is based are listed alphabetically in the appendix, with the daily newspapers listed separately from the weeklies and semiweeklies. The essential facts of publication pertaining to these newspapers are derived from the appropriate annual volumes of the *Director of Newspapers and Periodicals* (Philadelphia: A.W. Ayer & Sons). Statistical data concerning Tennessee are compiled in the relevant editions of the *Statistical Abstract of the United States* and the *City and County Data Book;* both reports are periodically issued by the Bureau of the Census, United States Department of Commerce. Tennessee primary and general election returns are reported in the *Tennessee Blue Book,* published annually by the Tennessee Department of State.

Tennessee

The Tennessee State Historical Commission has published a comprehensive bibliography compiled by William T. Anderson and Robert H. White, *A Guide to the Study and Reading of Tennessee History* (Nashville, 1959). An earlier bibliography of Tennessee county history is Laura S. Luttrell, *Writings on Tennessee Counties* (Tennessee Historical Association, 1944). Tennessee politics before World War II are analyzed in William E. Cole and William H. Combs, *Tennessee: A Political Study* (Knoxville: The University of Tennessee Press, 1940). The classic study of twentieth century Southern politics is V. O. Key, Jr., *Southern Politics in State and Nation* (New York: Alfred A. Knopf, 1950), especially chapter four, "The Civil War and Mr. Crump." This should be supplemented by William Goodman, *Inherited Domain: Political Parties in Tennessee* (Bureau of Public Administration of the University of Tennessee, 1954), and Robert S. Hutchinson, *Economic and Business Statistics of Tennessee* (Bureau of Business and Economic Research, University of Tennessee Record, 1954). The best authority on modern Tennessee government is Robert S. Avery and Lee Seifert Greene, *Government in Tennessee* (Knoxville: The University of Tennessee Press, 1962).

A partisan and colorful account of the reform thrust against Crump is Jennings Perry, *Democracy Begins at Home* (Philadelphia: Lippincott, 1944); Perry was a crusading editor of the anti-Crump Nashville *Tennessean*. Rural journalism in the South is surveyed and analyzed by Thomas D. Clark in *The Rural Press and the New South* (Baton Rouge: Louisiana State University Press, 1948), *The Southern Country Editor* (Indianapolis: Bobbs Merrill, 1948), and for Tennessee in *The Tennessee Country Editor* (East Tennessee Historical Society's *Publications,* 1949).

Tennessee's response to desegregation has been objectively reported by the Southern Educational Reporting Service, which published the monthly *Southern School News* from September 1954 through June 1965; although *SSN* was published in Nashville, its jurisdiction included the District of Columbia and all 17 states that segregated the races in the schools in 1954. The most scholarly analysis of Tennessee politics during this period is Norman L. Parks, "Tennessee Politics since Kefauver and Reece: A 'Generalist' View," *The Journal of Politics,* XXVIII (1966). Partisan accounts of the most important contests by political reporters of the Nashville *Tennessean* include David Halberstam, "The Air-Conditioned Crusade Against Albert Gore," *The Reporter* (September 4, 1958); Halberstam, "The Silent Ones Speak Up in Tennessee," *The Reporter* (September 1, 1960); and Bill Kovach, "The Issue Wasn't Racism in Tennessee," *The Reporter,* (September 24, 1964).

Journalism

The best general history of American journalism is Edwin Emery, *The Press and America* (Englewood Cliffs, N. J.: Prentice Hall, 1962). The role of the media in forming public opinion is discussed in V.O. Key, Jr., *Public Opinion and American Democracy* (New York: Knopf, 1961), especially chapters fourteen and fifteen. Articles by Harold Lasswell, Elmo Roper, George Gallup, and Elihu Katz in the *Public Opinion Quarterly* (Spring, 1957) provide a succinct summary of 20 years of communications research, especially the latter's "The Two-Step Flow of Communications: An Up-to-Date Report on an Hypothesis."

The treatment of racial news in the press has been studied by Roy E. Carter and reported in "Segregation and the News: A Regional Content

Study," *Journalism Quarterly* (Winter, 1957); and "Racial Identification Effects Upon the News Story Writer," *Journalism Quarterly* (Summer, 1959). The Southern Regional Council published two important essays in *Racial Crisis and the Press* (Atlanta, 1960); they are "Racial Stories in the News" by Professor Walter Spearman of the Department of Journalism at the University of North Carolina, and "The Press and the Schools" by Sylvan Meyer, editor of the Gainsville, Georgia, *Daily Times*. For a report on the declining Negro press, see "A Victim of Negro Progress," *Newsweek* (August 26, 1963).

Recent Southern History

By far the most valuable and up-to-date bibliographical aid is Arthur S. Link and Rembert W. Patrick (eds.), *Writing Southern History* (Baton Rouge: Louisiana State University Press, 1965), especially chapter 17, Dewey W. Grantham, "The Twentieth-Century South." A useful supplement is George B. Tindall (ed.), *The Pursuit of Southern History* (Baton Rouge: Louisiana State University Press, 1964), which contains the presidential addresses of the Southern Historical Association since its founding in 1935 through 1963. The most recently published history of the South since the Civil War is Thomas D. Clark and Albert D. Kirwan, *The South Since Appomattox* (Oxford University Press, 1967). The most comprehensive historical survey of the South is Wendell Holmes Stephenson and E. Merton Coulter (eds.), *A History of the South,* a ten volume history published by the Louisiana State University Press. The final volume of this series, *The Present South 1913–1946* by George B. Tindall, was scheduled for publication in the fall of 1967 at the time of this writing.

The Southern Region and Character: Recent Commentaries and Analyses

The evolution of the South's biracial system since the abolition of slavery is traced in C. Vann Woodward's popular if controversial *The Strange Career of Jim Crow* (Oxford, 1955); Woodward addresses himself to the controversy over why Jim Crow's career was so "strange" in his foreword to the Galaxy paperback edition (1957). The collaborative approach to research and publication in Southern studies is reflected in the accelerating emergence of Southern symposia, which in turn reflect the radically increased national interest in the South occasioned by the desegregation crisis. Charles Grier Sellers in *The Southerner as American* (Chapel Hill: University of North Carolina Press, 1960) has collected essays by nine historians whose central concern is that the manifest uniqueness of the Southerner has obscured his fundamental identity as an American; the most relevant of the essays for this bibliography is chapter six, "The Central Theme Revisited" by George B.

Tindall, and the theme being revisited is the contention of Ulrich Bonnell Phillips in "The Central Theme of Southern History," *American Historical Review,* XXXIV (October, 1928) that the unifying principle of Southern history is "a common resolve indomitably maintained" by the white man that the South "shall be and remain a white man's country."

The decennial of *Brown* v. *Board of Education* witnessed a not un-expected effusion of reflections on the South and the decade of desegregation (see Surveys and Analyses of Desegregation, below). The seven essays con-tained in Frank Vandiver (ed.), *The Idea of the South* (Chicago: The Uni-versity of Chicago Press, 1964) generally reflect their authors' collective hope that the old order is passing. Robert B. Highshaw (ed.), *The Deep South in Transition* (Tuscaloosa, 1964) is the report of a symposium spon-sored by the University of Alabama. Avery Leiserson (ed.), *The American South in the 1960s* (New York: Praeger, 1964) contains nine essays on contemporary Southern politics that were originally published in a special issue of *The Journal of Politics* entitled "The American South: 1950–1970," XXVI (February, 1964). The Center for Southern Studies in the Social Sciences and the Humanities, recently founded at Duke University, has produced A. P. Sindler (ed.), *Change in the Contemporary South* (1963) and John C. McKinney and E. T. Thompson (eds.), *The South in Con-tinuity and Change* (1965). Daniel Bradford (ed.), *Black, White and Gray* (New York: Sheed & Ward, 1964) is a pot pourri of opinions that range the spectrum from Martin Luther King, Jr. to George Wallace. Harper & Row has published in book form the eleven essays that constituted the Appomattox centennial edition of *Harper's Magazine* as *The South Today* (1965), edited by Willie Morris. Finally, Dewey Grantham has edited *The South and the Sectional Image* (New York: Harper & Row, 1967), a col-lection of twelve essays on the sectional theme since Reconstruction, several of which appear in the other anthologies.

Several students of the South have written somewhat more subjective reflections on the region's meaning. Harry Ashmore has hopefully penned *An Epitaph for Dixie* (New York: Norton, 1958); Thomas D. Clark has as hopefully painted a portrait of *The Emerging South* (Oxford, 1961); Howard Zinn has debunked *The Southern Mystique* (New York: Knopf, 1964); and Francis Butler Simkins' reflections are contained in *The South in Perspective* (Farmerville, Virginia, 1959) and *The Everlasting South* (Baton Rouge: Louisiana State University Press, 1963). Probably the most provocative reflection on the meaning of Southern history is Woodward's *The Burden of Southern History* (Baton Rouge: Louisiana University Press, 1960), especially chapters one and eight. A similar reflection by an eminent Southern historian is T. Harry Williams, *Romance and Realism in Southern Politics* (Athens: The University of Georgia Press, 1961).

Southern Politics

V. O. Key's monumental *Southern Politics* was complemented by the simultaneous publication of Jasper Shannon, *Toward A New Politics in the South* (Knoxville: The University of Tennessee Press, 1949), and it was further supplemented by the appearance of Alexander Heard, *Two-Party South?* (Chapel Hill: The University of North Carolina Press, 1952), and by Heard and Donald S. Strong, *Southern Primaries and Elections, 1920–1949* (University, Ala.: The University of Alabama Press, 1950).

The political behavior and role of Southern Negroes is analyzed in H. D. Price, *The Negro and Southern Politics* (New York: New York University Press, 1957); Margaret Price, *The Negro Voter in the South* (Southern Regional Council, 1957); and "The Negro Voter in the South," *Journal of Negro Education*, XXVI (Summer, 1957). Recently there has appeared what is clearly the most comprehensive investigation of the role of the Negro in Southern political life: Donald R. Matthews and James W. Prothro, *Negroes and the New Southern Politics* (New York: Harcourt, Brace & World, 1966). These two Chapel Hill political scientists have in recent years dominated the inquiry into the role of race in Southern politics, and together with their UNIVAC they have produced a valuable political analysis. Devotees of the sanguine theory that Negro enfranchisement will automatically solve the Negroes' problems would do well to read the authors' thoughtful conclusions. Useful recent studies of Southern politics that focus less intensively on the Negro are Bernard Cozman, *Five States for Goldwater* (University, Alabama: The University of Alabama Press, 1966); and Dewey Grantham's four interpretive lectures in *The Democratic South* (Athens: The University of Georgia Press, 1963). Alfred O. Hero's encyclopedic *The Southerner in World Affairs* (Baton Rouge: Louisiana State University Press, 1965) promises to join the distinguished ranks of modern classics along with the works of Odum, Cash, and Key.

Behavioral Approaches to Racial Relations

Representative of the views of the contemporarily dominant school of liberal social scientists on the role of race in American society are the writings of anthropologist Franz Boaz, who probably was more than any other individual responsible for overturning the racist consensus that was predominant in popular and even scientific thought before World War I. See especially Boaz's *Race, Language and Culture* (New York: MacMillan, 1940) and *Race and Democratic Society* (Locust Valley, N.Y.; J. J. Augustin, 1945). Boaz's most prominent successor, Ashley Montagu, has carried the attack in *Man's Most Dangerous Myth: The Fallacy of Race* (New York: Columbia University Press, 1942) and *The Idea of Race*

(Lincoln: The University of Nebraska Press, 1965). See also Ruth Benedict, *Race: Science and Politics* (New York: Viking, 1959). The counter-attack of the equalitarian social scientists was crowned by Gunnar Myrdal's *The American Dilemma* (New York: Harpers, 1944), 2 vols., which has been abridged by Arnold Rose as *The Negro in America* (New York: Harpers, 1948).

The war against fascism further sensitized American social scientists to the question of prejudice and the authoritarian personality. For reports of this postwar research, see B. Bettelheim and M. Janowitz, *The Dynamics of Prejudice* (New York: Harpers, 1950); Gordon W. Allport, *The Nature of Prejudice* (Reading, Mass.: Addison-Wesley, 1954); and Thomas F. Pettigrew, "Social Psychology and Desegregation Research," *The American Psychologist*, XVI (March, 1961). Pettigrew's *A Profile of the Negro American* (Princeton, N. J.: Van Nostrand, 1964) is an exhaustive psychological analysis; the bibliography contains 565 citations. For behavorial assessments of the role of race in American life, see Brewton Berry, *Race Relations* (Boston: Houghton Mifflin, 1951); and Oscar Handlin, *Race and Nationality in American Life* (Boston: Little, Brown, 1957). A classic study in Southern sociology is John Dollard, *Caste and Class in A Southern Town* (New Haven: Yale University Press, 1937). Melvin Tumin has published his survey of attitudes of the white residents of Guilford County, North Carolina, toward race in *Desegregation: Resistance and Readiness* (Princeton, N. J.: Princeton University Press, 1958). The role of public opinion in racial relations is assessed in Herbert Hyman and Paul Sheatsley, "Attitudes Toward Desegregation," *Scientific American*, CXCV (1956); and Hazel Gaudet Erskine, "The Polls: Race Relations," *Public Opinion Quarterly*, XVI (Spring, 1962).

Surveys and Analyses of Desegregation

The two Southern-based organizations that have been most actively concerned with desegregation in the South have been the Southern Education Reporting Service, which was designed to function as a neutral observer, and the Southern Regional Council, which was founded in 1946 by liberal Southern whites in Atlanta and has since campaigned aggressively against the invidious consequences of the Southern biracial system. The SRC sponsored the research of Benjamin Muse, a former Virginia state senator turned popular historian whose *Ten Years of Prelude* (New York: Viking, 1964) is probably the best combined survey and analysis of the initial decade of desegregation now extant. SERS has periodically produced analyses of the process of desegregation in book form: Don Shoemaker (ed.), *With All Deliberate Speed* (New York: Harpers, 1958); and Reed Sarratt, *The Or-*

deal of Desegregation (New York: Harper & Row, 1966). SERS also publishes annually a valuable *Statistical Summary* which is cumulative.

Much has been made of the analogy between Reconstruction and the contemporary civil rights movement. In "From the First Reconstruction to the Second," *Harper's* (April, 1965), C. Vann Woodward popularized an analogue that he had earlier suggested in *The Strange Career of Jim Crow* and further developed in several articles published in *Commentary*. The waning pulse of the Second Reconstruction can be taken by reading Woodward's despairing "What Happened to the Civil Rights Movement?" in *Harper's* (January, 1967)—an essay in which the author cautions against too simplistic an embrace of the dual-reconstruction analogy. Other useful book-length commentaries on the civil rights movement and desegregation include Wilma Dykeman and James Stokely, *Neither Black Nor White* (New York: Rinehart, 1957), in which the authors report on their extensive travels throughout the South during the early years of desegregation. Two sober and somewhat pessimistic analyses of the stubborn intractability of America's racial problem are Charles E. Silberman, *Crisis in Black and White* (New York: Random House, 1964); and Samuel Lubell, *White and Black: Test of a Nation* (New York: Harper & Row, 1964). In the same vein, Oscar Handlin has written a briefer alarum in *Fire Bell in the Night: The Crisis in Civil Rights* (Boston: Beacon, 1964). Anthony Lewis has compiled a potboiler of New York *Times* articles on desegregation and civil rights in *Portrait of a Decade: The Second American Revolution* (New York: Random House, 1964); and Harry Golden has written a lively and partisan account of the civil rights movement that is too narrowly entitled *Mr. Kennedy and the Negroes* (Cleveland: World, 1964).

Case Studies of Desegregation

Several state studies have recently emerged, the most useful of them being Benjamin Muse, *Virginia's Massive Resistance* (Bloomington: Indiana University Press, 1961), although James W. Silver, *Mississippi: The Closed Society* (New York: Harcourt, Brace & World, 1963) is the most compelling indictment. In the same vein, Howard Quint's *Profile in Black and White* (Washington, D.C.: Public Affairs Press, 1958), subtitled "A Frank Portrait of South Carolina," is a very dark portrait. Richard Barnett and Joseph Garai, *Where the States Stand on Civil Rights* (New York: Sterling, 1962) is a survey of the 50 states as of 1961; apparently hurriedly produced by civil rights partisans, it is somewhat superficial and of questionable credibility.

Several books and a multitude of articles have been written in response to specific events, and no event has been more heuristically productive than the attempt to desegregate Little Rock's Central High School in 1957. The best of these is Corinne Silverman, *The Little Rock Story* (Inter-University Case Program, No. 41, rev. 1959), and a useful recent reappraisal is N. V. Bartley, "Looking Back at Little Rock," *Arkansas Historical Quarterly,* XXV (Summer, 1966). The recollections of Virgil T. Blossom, Little Rock superintendent of schools, are recorded in *It Has Happened Here* (New York: Harper, 1959); and those of Daisy Bates, president of the Arkansas branch of the NAACP, in *The Long Shadow of Little Rock* (New York: David McKay, 1962). Wilson and Jane Cassels Record, *Little Rock USA* (San Francisco: Chandler, 1960) contains in part I an extensive compilation of documentary evidence concerning the Little Rock episode, and in part II a broad range of opinion on the meaning of Little Rock.

Other useful case studies include that of Omer Carmichael, superintendent of schools in Louisville, Kentucky, during its successful desegregation in 1956: *The Louisville Story* (New York: Simon & Schuster, 1957), with the assistance of Weldon James. Margaret Anderson, who was a schoolteacher in Clinton, Tennessee, during the tumult there in 1956, reveals what happens after a school is desegregated in *The Children of the South* (New York: Farrar, Straus & Giroux, 1966). Russell H. Barrett, *Integration at Ole Miss* (Chicago: Quadrangle, 1965), was written by a faculty member at the University of Mississippi, with a foreword by his former colleague, James Silver.

Desegregation and the Schools

A thorough and recently published bibliography on school desegregation is contained in Elizabeth W. Miller, *The Negro in America* (Cambridge: Harvard University Press, 1966), pp. 115–123. The following are especially useful. The year of the Brown decision witnessed the publication of two studies of the status of the schools and the quality of Negro education under the Plessy doctrine: Harry S. Ashmore, *The Negro and the Schools* (Chapel Hill: The University of North Carolina Press, 1954), which reports the findings of a study sponsored by the Ford Foundation; and Robin M. Williams and Margaret W. Ryan (eds.), *Schools in Transition* (Chapel Hill: The University of North Carolina Press, 1954), subtitled "Community Experiences in Desegregation." See also Truman M. Pierce et al., *White and Negro Schools in the South* (New York: Prentice Hall, 1955). The SERS produced *Southern Schools: Progress and Problems* (Nashville, 1959), edited by Edward D. Ball and Patrick McCauley.

Legal Aspects of Civil Rights

A well-reasoned defense of judicial review and the legitimacy of the

Brown decision is Albert Blaustein and Clarence C. Ferguson, *Desegregation and the Law* (New Brunswick, N.J.: Rutgers University Press, 1957). Carl Brent Swisher, "Dred Scott One Hundred Years After," *Journal of Politics,* XIX (1957) puts the Brown decision in historical perspective. (For attacks on the Warren court, see Defenses of Segregation and States' Rights, below.) The critical role of the federal district courts in defining "all deliberate speed" is discussed in Robert J. Steamer, "The Role of the Federal District Courts in the Segregation Controversy," *Journal of Politics,* XXII (1960). The dilemma of the Southern federal circuit and district judges is surveyed by Jack W. Peltason in *Fifty-Eight Lonely Men: Southern Federal Judges and School Desegregation* (New York: Harcourt, Brace & World, 1961). The legal intricacies of racial relations are explored in *Race Relations Law Reporter,* published quarterly since 1956 by Vanderbilt University Law School and sponsored by SERS through the Ford grant.

The role of the legislative branch in civil rights is nicely covered by the following: Pauli Murray, *State Laws on Race and Color* (Cincinnati: The Methodist Church, 1951); J. W. Anderson, *Eisenhower, Brownell, and the Congress* (University, Alabama: The University of Alabama Press, 1964) examines the tangled origins of the civil rights act of 1957. Daniel Berman, *A Bill Becomes A Law* (New York: Macmillan, 1962) traces the evolution of the civil rights act of 1960. The Bureau of National Affairs has prepared a textual analysis and legislative history of *The Civil Rights Act of 1964* (Washington, D.C., 1964); and the federal role in *The Revolution in Civil Rights* (Washington, D.C., 1965) has been surveyed by the Congressional Quarterly.

The Negro and the Civil Rights Movement

Revealing testimonials of the Negro side of the civil rights struggle in the South are: Martin Luther King, Jr., *Stride Toward Freedom: The Montgomery Story* (New York: Harpers, 1958); James Meredith, *My Three Years in Mississippi* (Bloomington: The University of Indiana Press, 1966); and William Bradford Huie, *Three Lives for Mississippi* (New York: Trident, 1965), which reports on the murder of civil rights workers Schwerner, Chaney, and Goodman. Bernard Taper, *Gomillion Versus Lightfoot* (New York: McGraw-Hill, 1962) reports on the Negro fight against the gerrymander engineered by white officials in Tuskegee, Alabama. John Howard Griffin reports melodramatically on his travels throughout the South while disguised as a Negro in *Black Like Me* (Boston: Houghton Mifflin, 1960).

A good popular history of the contemporary civil rights movement is Louis Lomax, *The Negro Revolt* (New York: Harper & Row, 1962). Representative of the divergent views of the Negro spokesmen of "The Movement" are the following: Martin Luther King, Jr., *Why We Can't Wait* (New York: Harpers, 1964) is the most cogent explication of nonviolent protest and the philosophy of passive resistance. Lerone Bennett has written a popular biography of Dr. King in *What Manner of Man?* (Chicago: Johnson, 1964). James Farmer describes the role of CORE in *Freedom— When?* (New York: Random House, 1966); and Stokely Carmichael reflects the radicalism of SNCC in his discourse on the meaning of "Black Power" in "What We Want," *New York Review of Books* (September 22, 1966). Probably the most incisive of the Negro civil rights leaders is the democratic socialist Bayard Rustin, whose essay "From Protest to Politics," *Commentary* (February, 1965) was widely commented upon and whose " 'Black Power' and Coalition Politics" in *Commentary* (September, 1966) is a thoughtful critique of the proponents of "Black Power."

By far the most nearly comprehensive source of authorities on the American Negro is John P. Davis (ed.), *The American Negro Reference Book* (Englewood Cliffs, N.J.: Prentice Hall, 1966), which is splendidly indexed.

Reflections of Southern Moderates and Liberals

Recent books written in this tradition include James McBride Dabbs, *The Southern Heritage* (New York: Knopf, 1958) and *Who Speaks for the South?* (New York: Funk & Wagnalls, 1964); and Ralph McGill, *The South and the Southerner* (Boston: Little, Brown, 1959). Dabbs is president of the SRC; McGill, publisher of the Atlanta *Constitution* and *Journal*, has been joined by several fellow Southern journalists in calling for an abatement of Southern racism. See Hodding Carter, *Southern Legacy* (Baton Rouge: Louisiana State University Press, 1950), *Where Main Street Meets the River* (New York: Rinehart, 1953), and *So the Heffners Left McComb* (New York: Doubleday, 1965); Harry Golden, *Only in America* (Cleveland: World, 1958); P. D. East, *Magnolia Jungle* (New York: Simon & Schuster, 1960); and Harry Ashmore, *An Epitaph for Dixie* (New York: Norton, 1958).

Reflections of Southern moderate politicians who in various ways have fallen casualty to a resurgent racism include Frank E. Smith, *Congressman from Mississippi* (New York: Pantheon, 1964); Charles Longstreet Weltner, *Southerner* (Philadelphia: Lippincott, 1966); and Brooks Hays, *A Southern Moderate Speaks* (Chapel Hill: The University of North Carolina Press, 1959). Hays is also a spokesman for the moderate wing of the Southern Baptist Church. Robert Penn Warren, *Segregation: The Inner Conflict in the South* (New York: Random House, 1956) is an impressionistic report of the author's travels in Kentucky, Tennessee, Arkansas, Mississippi, and Louisiana that is unusually perceptive in probing the troubled ambivalence of the contemporary Southern mind regarding the region's heritage of biracialism. See also Charles Morgan, *A Time to Speak* (New York: Harpers, 1964); Robert Canzoneri, *"I Do So Politely": A Voice from the South* (Boston: Houghton Mifflin, 1965); and Sarah Patton Boyle, *The Desegregated Heart* (New York: Morrow, 1962).

Defenses of Segregation and States' Rights

The most articulate defenders of the Southern status quo have tended to base their first line of defense on the historic political theory of states' rights and to defend racial segregation in a somewhat more incidental fashion. In the forefront of such aggressive defenders have been Southern journalists; see especially James Jackson Kilpatrick, *The Sovereign States: Notes of a Citizen of Virginia* (Chicago: Regnery, 1957), and *The Southern Case for School Segregation* (New York: Crowell-Collier, 1963); Thomas R. Waring, "The Southern Case Against Desegregation," *Harper's* (January, 1956); and W. D. Workman, *The Case for the South* (New York: Devin-Adair, 1960). Kilpatrick is editor of the Richmond *News-Leader,* Waring is publisher of the Charleston *Courier and News,* and Workman is a conservative Republican columnist.

More strident defenses of segregation include Tom Brady, *Black Monday* (Winona, Mississippi: Association of Citizens Councils, 1954); Herman E. Talmadge, *You and Segregation* (Birmingham: Vulcan, 1955); Charles L. Block, *States Rights: The Law of the Land* (Atlanta: Harrison, 1959); and Ira Calvin, *The Lost White Race* (Countway-White, 1962). Manning Johnson, *Color, Communism and Common Sense* (Alliance, 1958) identifies the civil rights movement with the Communist conspiracy. Earl Lively, *The Invasion of Mississippi* (American Opinion, 1963) reflects the view of the John Birch Society.

The counter-attack of the neo-racists has been led by Carleton Putnam through the National Putnam Letters Committee; see especially his *Race and Reason—A Yankee View* (Washington, D.C.: Public Affairs Press, 1961). Scientific authorities in support of the view that Negroes are genetically inferior to whites include Audrey M. Shuey, *The Testing of Negro Intelligence* (Lynchburg, Virginia, 1958); Nathaniel Weyl, *The Negro in American Civilization* (Washington, D.C.: Public Affairs Press, 1960); Henry E. Garrett's brief pamphlet, *How Classroom Desegregation Will Work* (Patrick Henry Press, no date); Garrett's *Race* (National Putnam Letters Committee, no date); and Wesley C. George, *The Biology of the Race Problem* (Commission of the Governor of Alabama, 1962). An interesting judicial refutation of the Brown decision is the opinion of Sidney C. Mize, United States District Judge, Jackson, Mississippi, in the case of *Evers, et al* v. *Jackson Municipal Separate School District, et al.* For an exemplary attack on liberal equalitarianism, see William A. Massey, "The New Fanatics," *Mankind Quarterly* (December, 1963).

Southern Segregationist Groups

The more ardent segregationists throughout the South have formed such a profusion of groups—myriad councils, klans, ad hoc committees and the like—that there is no really comprehensive authority on them. John Bartlow Martin, *The Deep South Says "Never"* (New York: Ballantine, 1957) reports on the early organizational activities of these groups in response to the threat of desegregation. Hodding Carter, *The South Strikes Back* (New York: Doubleday, 1959) concentrates on the white citizens councils, which have been most respectable in Carter's Mississippi. James Graham Cook, *The Segregationists* (New York: Appleton-Century-Crofts, 1962) employs the interview technique in rendering an impressionistic account of segregationist pressure groups. Three histories of the Ku Klux Klan have recently appeared, and all three concentrate on the first (Reconstruction) and the second (1920s) Klans, but David M. Chalmers, *Hooded Americanism: The First Century of the Ku Klux Klan 1865–1965* (New York: Doubleday, 1965) devotes the final four chapters to the scattering of recent klans.

Appendix

TENNESSEE DAILY NEWSPAPERS

Municipality	*County*	*Title*
Athens	McMinn	*Daily Post Athenian*
Athens	McMinn	Athens *Press*
Bristol	Sullivan	Bristol *Herald-Courier*
Bristol	Sullivan	Bristol *Virginia-Tennessean*
Chattanooga	Hamilton	Chattanooga *Times*
Chattanooga	Hamilton	Chattanooga *News–Free Press*
Clarksville	Montgomery	Clarksville *Leaf–Chronicle*
Cleveland	Bradley	Cleveland *Daily Banner*
Columbia	Maury	Columbia *Daily Herald*
Greeneville	Greene	Greenville *Sun*
Jackson	Madison	Jackson *Sun*
Johnson City	Washington	Johnson City *Press–Chronicle*
Kingsport	Sullivan	Kingsport *News*
Kingsport	Sullivan	Kingsport *Times*
Knoxville	Knox	Knoxville *Journal*
Knoxville	Knox	Knoxville *News–Sentinel*
Maryville	Blount	Maryville–Alcoa *Daily Times*
Memphis	Shelby	Memphis *Commercial Appeal*
Memphis	Shelby	Memphis *Press–Scimitar*
Morristown	Hablen	Morristown *Gazette–Mail*
Murfreesboro	Rutherford	Murfreesboro *Daily News Journal*
Nashville	Davidson	Nashville *Banner*
Nashville	Davidson	Nashville *Tennessean*
Oak Ridge	Anderson	*Oak Ridger*
Paris	Henry	Paris *Post–Intelligencer*
Shelbyville	Bedford	Shelbyville *Times Gazette*
Union City	Obion	Union City *Daily Messenger*

329

TENNESSEE WEEKLY AND SEMI-WEEKLY NEWSPAPERS

Municipality	*County*	*Title*
Alamo	Crockett	*Crockett Times*
Altamont	Grundy	*North Grundy Star*
Ashland City	Cheatham	Ashland City *Times*
Bells	Crockett	Crockett County *Sentinel*
Benton	Polk	*Polk County News*
Bolivar	Hardeman	*Bolivar Bulletin* and *Hardeman County Times*
Brownsville	Haywood	*States Graphic*
Camden	Benton	Camden *Chronicle*
Carthage	Smith	Carthage *Courier*
Centerville	Hickman	*Hickman County Chronicle*
Centerville	Hickman	*Hickman County Times*
Chattanooga	Hamilton	*Hamilton County Herald*
Clinton	Anderson	Clinton *Courier–News*
Collierville	Shelby	Collierville *Herald*
Columbia	Maury	*Maury Democrat*
Cookeville	Putnam	*Citizen*
Cookeville	Putnam	*Putnam County Herald*
Copperhill	Polk	*Copper City Advance*
Covington	Tipton	Covington *Leader*
Crossville	Cumberland	Crossville *Chronicle*
Dandridge	Jefferson	Dandridge *Banner*
Dayton	Rhea	Dayton *Herald*
Decaturville	Decatur	*Decatur County Herald*
Dickson	Dickson	Dickson County Herald
Dover	Stewart	*Stewart–Houston Times*
Dresden	Weakley	Dresden *Enterprise* and Sharon *Tribune*
Dunlap	Sequatchie	Dunlap *Tribune*
Dyer	Gibson	*Tri-City Reporter*
Erwin	Unicoi	Erwin *Record*
Etowah	McMinn	Etowah *Enterprise*
Fayetteville	Lincoln	*Lincoln County News*
Fayetteville	Lincoln	Fayetteville *Observer*
Franklin	Williamson	*Review–Appeal*
Friendship	Crockett	*Tri-County News*
Gainesboro	Jackson	*Jackson County Sentinel*
Gallatin	Sumner	Gallatin *Examiner* and *Sumner County Tennessean*
Gallatin	Sumner	*Sumner County News*
Greenfield	Weakley	Greenfield *Gazette*
Halls	Lauderdale	Halls *Graphic*

Municipality	*County*	*Title*
Harriman	Roane	Harriman *Record*
Hartsville	Trousdale	Hartsville *Vidette*
Hohenwald	Lewis	*Lewis County Herald*
Humboldt	Gibson	*Courier–Chronicle*
Huntingdon	Carroll	*Carroll County Democrat*
Huntingdon	Carroll	*Tennessee Republican*
Jamestown	Fentress	*Upper Cumberland Times*
Jasper	Marion	Jasper *Journal*
Jefferson City	Jefferson	*Jefferson Standard*
Jellico	Campbell	*Advance–Sentinel*
Jonesboro	Washington	*Herald* and *Tribune*
Kingston	Roane	*Roane County News*
Lafayette	Macon	*Macon County Times*
La Follette	Campbell	LaFollette *Press*
Lawrenceburg	Lawrence	*Democrat–Union*
Lebanon	Wilson	Lebanon *Democrat* and *Wilson County News*
Lenoir City	Loudon	Lenoir City *News*
Lewisburg	Marshall	*Marshall Gazette*
Lewisburg	Marshall	Lewisburg *Tribune*
Lexington	Henderson	Lexington *Progress*
Linden	Perry	*Perry Countian*
Livingston	Overton	Livingston *Enterprise*
Loudon	Loudon	*Loudon County Herald*
Lynchburg	Moore	*Moore County News*
McKenzie	Carroll	McKenzie *Banner*
McMinnville	Warren	*Southern Standard*
Madisonville	Monroe	Madisonville *Democrat*
Manchester	Coffee	Manchester *Times*
Martin	Weakley	*Weakley County Press* and *Martin Mail* and *County Times*
Maryville	Blount	Maryville *Enterprise*
Maynardville	Union	*Union County Times*
Memphis	Shelby	*World* (Negro)
Memphis	Shelby	*Tri-State Defender* (Negro)
Milan	Gibson	Milan *Exchange*
Millington	Shelby	Millington *Star*
Morristown	Hamblen	Morristown *Sun*
Mount Pleasant	Maury	Mount Pleasant *Record*
Mountain City	Johnson	*Tomahawk*
Nashville	Davidson	*Commentator* (Negro)
Nashville	Davidson	*Globe and Independent* (Negro)
Nashville	Davidson	Nashville *Record*
Newbern	Dyer	*Newbern Tennessean*

Municipality	County	Title
Newport	Cocke	Newport *Plain Talk and Tribune*
Oneida	Scott	*Scott County News*
Paris	Henry	Parisian
Parsons	Decatur	Parsons *News Leader and Decatur County Herald*
Pikeville	Bledsoe	*Bledsonian–Banner*
Portland	Sumner	*Sumner County Leader*
Pulaski	Giles	Pulaski *Citizen*
Rockwood	Roane	Rockwood *Times*
Rogersville	Hawkins	Rogersville *Review*
Rutledge	Grainger	*Grainger County News*
Savannah	Hardin	Savannah *Courier*
Selmer	McNairy	*McNairy County Independent*
Sevierville	Sevier	*Tri-County News*
Shelbyville	Bedford	*Bedford County Sun*
Smithville	DeKalb	Smithville *Review*
Smyrna	Rutherford	*Rutherford Courier*
Sneedville	Hancock	*Hancock County News*
Somerville	Fayette	*Fayette Falcon*
South Pittsburg	Marion	South Pittsburg *Hustler*
Sparta	White	Sparta *Expositor*
Sparta	White	Sparta *News–Pictoral*
Spring City	Rhea	Spring City *Bulletin*
Springfield	Robertson	Springfield *Herald*
Springfield	Robertson	*Robertson County Times*
Sweetwater	Monroe	*Sweetwater Valley News*
Tazewell	Claiborne	*Claiborne Progress*
Tiptonville	Lake	*Lake County Banner*
Tracy City	Grundy	*Grundy County Herald*
Trenton	Gibson	*Herald–Register*
Trenton	Gibson	Trenton *Weekly Gazette*
Tullahoma	Coffee	Tullahoma *News and Guardian*
Waverly	Humphreys	*News–Democrat*
Waynesboro	Wayne	*Wayne County News*
Whitehaven	Shelby	Whitehaven *Press*
Winchester	Franklin	Winchester *Herald-Times*
Woodbury	Cannon	*Cannon Courier*

Index

Because so much of the text concerns the editorial response of Tennessee's eight major dailies (the Knoxville *Journal* and *News Sentinel,* the Chattanooga *News–Free Press* and *Times,* the Nashville *Banner* and *Tennessean,* and the Memphis *Commercial Appeal* and *Press-Scimitar*) to specific events, readers interested in the response of any of these eight dailies to any given event should look up the event (e.g., Clinton, Civil Rights Bill of 1964, etc.), rather than the newspaper. All other newspapers are listed according to their full title, e.g., Clarksville *Leaf-Chronicle.*

333